Praise for *The Bible: A Biography*:

"Of all the 'Books that Changed the World' surely the Bible is among the most important. And of all contemporary popularizers of religious history, surely Armstrong is among the best-selling. Who better, then, to recount the history of the Bible in eight short chapters than this former nun and literature professor who relishes huge topics and panoramic descriptions? Armstrong not only describes how, when, and by whom the Bible was written, she also examines some two thousand years of biblical interpretation." —*Publishers Weekly*

"Dispels any notion of religion as a rigidly fixed reading of sacred texts. Spanning millennia, from the scripture's origins in oral stories to the conflicting beliefs, ancient and modern, over its message, her book will discomfort fundamentalists who believe that the Bible means what it says and says what it means." —*The Boston Globe*

"A whirlwind tour through biblical studies . . . Armstrong's analysis of the freedom previous generations (however far removed) felt with adapting, editing, redacting and rewriting the texts to suit contemporary purposes will undoubtedly remind savvy readers of all the current uses to which these same texts are being put." —*Sacramento News & Review*

"[Armstrong] shows how the highly disparate writings that now compose the Jewish and Christian scriptures came together and examines the very different methods of interpretation used over the centuries. Her book's great strength is the way she unfolds the Jewish and Christian histories of formation and interpretation in parallel with one another." —*The Guardian*

"A handy, erudite primer on the Holy Books." —*The Jerusalem Report*

"Armstrong's book points . . . to the modern origin of literalist interpretations of Scripture, and then revisits the preceding centuries of Biblical scholarship to bring its considerable diversity to the notice of modern readers."

—*Literary Review*

"[Armstrong] has never written on such a broad scale, or with as much passion. . . . [Her] concern that religion should no longer be used to promote violence animates her measured, lucid prose and vivifies her summary of the development of the Bible and its interpretation."

—*New York Sun*

"Karen Armstrong preaches the gospel truth in *The Bible*, explaining how the spiritual guide for one out of three people on the planet came into being and evolved over the centuries"

—*Vanity Fair*

"While there are countless guides to reading the Bible, noted academic Karen Armstrong looks at the history of the book with a keen historian's eye. . . . Armstrong condenses into a manageable volume the many ideas and traditions that influenced the creation of the Good Book."

—*Kirkus Reviews*

"Armstrong judiciously summarizes centuries of history and writes with remarkable insight."

—*Christian Science Sentinel*

"Armstrong is at her best when explaining how today's focus on the Bible as a literal, static text runs counter to a longstanding interpretative tradition that viewed study of the Good Book as 'an activity for attaining transcendence.' "

—*Shambhala Sun*

"A fascinating investigation."

—*Christian Advance*

The Bible
A Biography

Current and forthcoming titles in the Books
That Changed the World Series:

The Bible
A Biography

KAREN ARMSTRONG

Grove Press

NEW YORK

First published in Great Britian in 2007 by Atlantic Books, an imprint of Grove Atlantic Ltd.

Printed in the United States of America

ISBN-10: 0-8021-4384-9
ISBN-13: 978-0-8021-4384-6

Designed by Richard Marston

Grove Press
an imprint of Grove/Atlantic, Inc.
841 Broadway
New York, NY 10003

Distributed by Group West

www.groveatlantic.com

12   10 9 8 7

In Memory of Eileen Hastings Armstrong
(1921–2006)

CONTENTS

INTRODUCTION

Human beings are meaning-seeking creatures. Unless we find some pattern or significance in our lives, we fall very easily into despair. Language plays an important part in our quest. It is not only a vital means of communication, but it helps us to articulate and clarify the incoherent turbulence of our inner world. We use words when we want to make something happen outside ourselves: we give an order or make a request and, one way or the other, everything around us changes, however infinitesimally. But when we speak we also get something back: simply putting an idea into words can give it a lustre and appeal that it did not have before. Language is mysterious. When a word is spoken, the ethereal is made flesh; speech requires incarnation – respiration, muscle control, tongue and teeth. Language is a complex code, ruled by deep laws that combine to form a coherent system that is imperceptible to the speaker, unless he or she is a trained linguist. But language has an inherent inadequacy. There is always something left unsaid; something that remains inexpressible. Our speech makes us conscious of the transcendence that characterizes human experience.

All this has affected the way we read the Bible, which for both Jews and Christians is the Word of God. Scripture has been an important element in the religious enterprise. In nearly all the major faiths, people have regarded certain texts as sacred and ontologically different from other documents. They have invested these writings with the weight of their highest aspirations, most extravagant hopes and deepest fears, and mysteriously the texts have given them something in return. Readers have encountered what seems like a presence in these writings, which thus introduce them to a transcendent dimension. They have based their lives on scripture – practically, spiritually and morally. When their sacred texts tell stories, people have generally believed them to be true, but until recently literal or historical accuracy has never been the point. The truth of scripture cannot be assessed unless it is – ritually or ethically – put into practice. The Buddhist scriptures, for example, give readers some information about the life of the Buddha, but have included only those incidents that show Buddhists what they must do to achieve their own enlightenment.

Today scripture has a bad name. Terrorists use the Qur'an to justify atrocities, and some argue that the violence of their scripture makes Muslims chronically aggressive. Christians campaign against the teaching of evolutionary theory because it contradicts the biblical creation story. Jews argue that because God promised Canaan (modern Israel) to the descendants of Abraham, oppressive policies against the Palestinians are legitimate. There has been a scriptural revival that has intruded into public life. Secularist opponents of religion claim that scripture breeds violence, sectarianism and intolerance; that it prevents people from thinking for themselves, and encourages delusion. If religion preaches compassion, why is there so much hatred in sacred texts? Is it possible to be a 'believer' today when science has undermined so many biblical teachings?

Because scripture has become such an explosive issue, it is important to be clear what it is and what it is not. This biography of the Bible provides some insight into this religious phenomenon. It is, for example, crucial to note that an exclusively literal interpretation of the Bible is a recent development. Until the nineteenth century, very few people imagined that the first chapter of Genesis was a factual account of the origins of life. For centuries, Jews and Christians relished highly allegorical and inventive exegesis, insisting that a wholly literal reading of the Bible was neither possible nor desirable. They have rewritten biblical history, replaced Bible stories with new myths, and interpreted the first chapter of Genesis in surprisingly different ways.

The Jewish scriptures and the New Testament both began as oral proclamations and even after they were committed to writing, there often remained a bias towards the spoken word that is also present in other traditions. From the very beginning, people feared that a written scripture encouraged inflexibility and unrealistic, strident certainty. Religious knowledge cannot be imparted like other information, simply by scanning the sacred page. Documents became 'scripture' not, initially, because they were thought to be divinely inspired but because people started to treat them differently. This was certainly true of the early texts of the Bible, which became holy only when approached in a ritual context that set them apart from ordinary life and secular modes of thought.

Jews and Christians treat their scriptures with ceremonial reverence. The Torah scroll is the most sacred object in the synagogue; encased in a precious covering, housed in an 'ark', it is revealed at the climax of the liturgy when the scroll is conveyed formally around the congregation, who touch it with the tassels of their prayer shawls. Some Jews even dance with the scroll, embracing it like a beloved object. Catholics also carry the Bible in procession, douse it with incense, and stand up when it is recited, making the sign of the cross on forehead, lips and heart. In Protestant communities, the Bible reading is the high point of the service. But even more important were the spiritual disciplines that involved diet, posture and exercises in concentration, which, from a very early date, helped Jews and Christians to peruse the Bible in a different frame of mind. They were thus able to read between the lines and find something new, because the Bible always meant more than it said.

From the very beginning, the Bible had no single message. When the editors fixed the canons of both the Jewish and Christian testaments, they included competing visions and placed them, without comment, side by side. From the first, biblical authors felt free to revise the texts they had inherited and give them entirely different meaning. Later exegetes held up the Bible as a template for the problems of their time. Sometimes they allowed it to shape their world-view but they also felt free to change it and make it speak to contemporary conditions. They were not usually interested in discovering the original meaning of a biblical passage. The Bible 'proved' that it was holy because people continually discovered fresh ways to interpret it and found that this difficult, ancient set of documents cast light on situations that their authors could never have imagined. Revelation was an ongoing process; it had not been confined to a distant theophany on Mount Sinai; exegetes continued to make the Word of God audible in each generation.

Some of the most important biblical authorities insisted that charity must be the guiding principle of exegesis: any interpretation that spread hatred or disdain was illegitimate. All the world faiths claim that compassion is not only the prime virtue and the test of true religiosity but that it actually introduces us to Nirvana, God or the Dao. But sadly the biography of the Bible represents the failures as well as the triumphs of the religious quest. The biblical authors and their interpreters have all too often succumbed to the violence, unkindness and exclusivity that is rife in their societies.

Human beings seek *ekstasis*, a 'stepping outside' of their normal, mundane experience. If they no longer find ecstasy in a synagogue, church or mosque, they look for it in dance, music, sport, sex or drugs. When people read the Bible receptively and intuitively, they found that it gave them intimations of transcendence. A major characteristic of a peak religious insight is a sense of completeness and oneness. It has been called *coincidentia oppositorum:* in this ecstatic condition, things that seemed separate and even opposed coincide and reveal an unexpected unity. The biblical story of the Garden of Eden depicts this experience of primal wholeness: God and humanity were not divided but lived in the same place; men and women were unaware of gender difference; they lived in harmony with animals and the natural world; and there was no distinction between good and evil. In such a state, divisions are transcended in an *ekstasis* that is separate from the conflicted fragmentary nature of ordinary life. People have tried to recreate this Edenic experience in their religious rituals.

As we shall see, Jews and Christians developed a method of Bible study that linked together texts that had no intrinsic connection. By constantly breaking down barriers of textual difference, they achieved an ecstatic *coincidentia oppositorum,* which is also present in other scriptural traditions. It is, for example, essential to the proper interpretation of the Qur'an. From a very early period, the Aryans of India learned to apprehend the Brahman, the mysterious potency that held the diverse elements of the world together, when they listened to the paradoxes and riddles of the Rig Veda hymns, which fused apparently unrelated things. When Jews and Christians tried to find a unity in their paradoxical and multifarious scriptures, they also had intuitions of divine oneness. Exegesis was always a spiritual discipline rather than an academic pursuit.

Originally, the people of Israel had achieved this *ekstasis* in the Jerusalem temple, which had been designed as a symbolic replica of the Garden of Eden.[1] There they experienced *shalom*, a word that is usually translated 'peace' but is better rendered as 'wholeness, completeness'. When their temple was destroyed, they had to find a new way of finding *shalom* in a tragic, violent world. Twice their temple was burned to the ground; each time its destruction led to an intense period of scriptural activity, as they sought healing and harmony in the documents that would become the Bible.

CHAPTER 1

Torah

In 597 BCE, the tiny state of Judah in the highlands of Canaan broke its vassalage treaty with Nebuchadnezzar, ruler of the powerful Babylonian empire. It was a catastrophic mistake. Three months later, the Babylonian army besieged Jerusalem, Judah's capital. The young king surrendered immediately and was deported to Babylonia, together with some ten thousand of the citizens who made the state viable: priests, military leaders, craftsmen and metal workers. As they left Jerusalem, the exiles would have taken one last look at the temple built on Mount Zion by King Solomon (c.970–930 BCE), the centre of their national and spiritual life, sadly aware that in all likelihood they would never see it again. Their fears were realized: in 586, after yet another rebellion in Judah, Nebuchadnezzar destroyed Jerusalem and burned Solomon's temple to the ground.

The exiles were not ill-treated in Babylon. The king was comfortably housed with his entourage in the southern citadel, and the rest lived together in new settlements by the canals and were allowed to manage their domestic affairs. But they had lost their country, their political independence, and their religion. They belonged to the people of Israel and believed that their god Yahweh had promised that if they worshipped him exclusively, they would live in their land forever. The Jerusalem temple, where Yahweh had dwelt among his people, was essential to his cult. Yet here they were in an alien land, cast out of Yahweh's presence. This must be a divine punishment. Time and again, the Israelites had failed to keep their covenant agreement with Yahweh and had succumbed to the lure of other deities. Some of the exiles assumed that, as the leaders of Israel, it was up to them to rectify the situation, but how could they serve Yahweh without the temple that was their only means of making contact with their god?

Five years after his arrival in Babylon, standing beside the Chebar canal, a young priest called Ezekiel had a terrifying vision. It was impossible to see anything clearly because nothing in this stormy maelstrom of fire and tumultuous sound conformed to ordinary human categories, but Ezekiel knew that he was in the presence of the *kavod*, the 'glory' of Yahweh, which was usually enthroned in the inner sanctum of the temple.[1] God had left Jerusalem and, riding on what seemed to be a massive war chariot, had come to live with the exiles in Babylon. A hand stretched towards Ezekiel holding a scroll, which was inscribed with 'lamentations, wailing, and moanings'. 'Eat this scroll,' a divine voice commanded him, 'feed and be satisfied by the scroll I am giving you.' When he forced it down, accepting the pain and misery of his exile, Ezekiel found that 'it tasted sweet as honey'.[2]

It was a prophetic moment. The exiles would continue to long for their lost temple, because in the Middle East at this period, it was impossible to imagine religion without one.[3] But the time would come when Israelites would make contact with their God in sacred writings, rather than a shrine. Their holy book would not be easy to understand. Like Ezekiel's scroll, its message often seemed distressing and incoherent. Yet when they made the effort to absorb this confusing text, making it a part of their inmost being, they would feel that they had come into the presence of God – just as they did when they had visited his shrine in Jerusalem.

But it would be many years before Yahwism became a religion of the book. The exiles had brought a number of scrolls from the royal archive in Jerusalem with them to Babylon, and there they studied and edited these documents. If they were allowed to return home, these records of the history and cult of their people could play an important role in the restoration of national life. But the scribes did not regard these writings as sacrosanct and felt free to add new passages, altering them to fit their changed circumstances. They had as yet no notion of a sacred text. True, there were many stories in the Middle East about heavenly tablets that had descended miraculously to earth and imparted secret, divine knowledge. There were tales in Israel about the engraved stones that Yahweh had given to his prophet Moses, who had spoken with him face to face.[4] But the scrolls in the Judaean archive were not in this league, and did not play any part in the cult of Israel.

The Israelites, like most peoples in the ancient world, had always handed on their traditions by word of mouth. In the early days of their nation, in about 1200 BCE, they had lived in twelve tribal units in the Canaanite highlands but believed that they had a common ancestry and a shared history, which they celebrated in shrines associated with one of their patriarchs or an important event. Bards recited the epic stories of the sacred past and the people formally renewed the covenant agreement that bound them together as the *am Yahweh*, 'the family of Yahweh'. Already, at this very early stage, Israel had a distinctive religious vision. Most peoples in the region developed a mythology and liturgy that centred on the world of the gods in primordial time, but Israelites focused on their life with Yahweh in *this* world. From the very beginning, they thought historically, in terms of cause and effect.

From early fragments embedded in the later biblical narratives, we can infer that the Israelites believed their ancestors to have been nomads. Yahweh had led them to Canaan, and promised that one day their descendants would own the land. For many years they had lived as slaves under Egyptian rule, but Yahweh had liberated them with great signs and marvels, led them back to the Promised Land under the leadership of Moses, and helped them to conquer the highlands from the indigenous inhabitants.[5] But there was as yet no master-narrative: each tribe had its own version of the story, each region its local heroes. The priests of Dan, in the extreme north, for example, believed that they were descended from Moses; Abraham, the father of the whole nation, had lived in Hebron and was especially popular in the south. At Gilgal, the local tribes celebrated Israel's miraculous entry into the Promised Land, when the waters of the river Jordan had miraculously parted to let them through. The people of Shechem annually renewed the covenant that Joshua had made with Yahweh after his conquest of Canaan.[6]

By about 1000 BCE, however, the tribal system was no longer adequate, so the Israelites formed two monarchies in the Canaanite highlands: the kingdom of Judah in the south, and the larger, more prosperous kingdom of Israel in the north. The old covenant festivals were phased out in favour of royal rituals at the national shrines that centred on the person of the king. On his coronation day, the king was adopted by Yahweh, became a 'son of God', and a member of Yahweh's Divine Assembly of heavenly beings. We know almost nothing about the cult of the northern kingdom, because the biblical historians had a bias towards Judah, but many of the psalms later included in the Bible were used in the Jerusalem liturgy[7] and show that the Judahites had been influenced by the cult of Baal in neighbouring Syria, which had a similar royal mythology.[8] Yahweh had made an unconditional covenant with King David, the founder of the Judaean dynasty, and had promised that his descendants would rule in Jerusalem forever.

Now that the old tales had been liberated from the cult, they acquired an independent, literary life. During the eighth century, there was a literacy revolution throughout the Middle East and the eastern Mediterranean.[9] Kings commissioned documents that glorified their regime and housed these texts in libraries. In Greece, the epics of Homer were committed to writing at this time, and in Israel and Judah historians began to combine the old stories to create national sagas, which have been preserved in the earliest strata of the Pentateuch, the first five books of the Bible.[10]

From the multifarious traditions of Israel and Judah, the eighth-century historians built a coherent narrative. Scholars usually call the southern epic of Judah 'J' because the authors always called their God 'Yahweh', while the northern saga is known as 'E' because these historians preferred the more formal title 'Elohim'. Later these two separate accounts were combined by an editor to form a single story that formed the backbone of the Hebrew Bible. During the eighteenth century BCE, Yahweh had commanded Abraham to leave his home town of Ur in Mesopotamia and settle in the Canaanite highlands, where he made a covenant with him, promising that his descendants would inherit the whole country. Abraham lived in Hebron; his son Isaac in Beersheba, and his grandson, Jacob (also called 'Israel'), eventually settled in the countryside around Shechem.

During a famine, Jacob and his sons, the founders of the twelve Israelite tribes, migrated to Egypt, where they flourished initially but, when they became too numerous, were enslaved and oppressed. Finally, in about 1250 BCE, Yahweh liberated them under the leadership of Moses. As they fled, Yahweh parted the waters of the Sea of Reeds, so that the Israelites passed over in safety, but Pharaoh and his army were drowned. For forty years the Israelites wandered in the wilderness of Sinai, south of Canaan. On Mount Sinai, Yahweh had made a solemn covenant with Israel and gave them the law, which included the Ten Commandments inscribed on stone tablets in Yahweh's own hand. Finally, Moses's successor Joshua led the tribes across the Jordan river into Canaan; they destroyed all the Canaanite cities and villages, killed the native population and made the land their own.

However, Israeli archaeologists, who have been excavating the region since 1967, have found no evidence to corroborate this story: there is no sign of foreign invasion or mass destruction, and nothing to indicate a large-scale change of population. The scholarly consensus is that the story of the Exodus is not historical. There are many theories. Egypt had ruled the Canaanite city states since the nineteenth century BCE, and had withdrawn at the end of the thirteenth century, shortly before the first settlements appeared in the formerly uninhabitable highlands. We first hear about a people called 'Israel' in this region in about 1200 BCE. Some scholars argue that the Israelites were refugees from the failing city-states on the coastal plains. They may have been joined there by other tribes from the south, who brought with them their god Yahweh, who seems to have originated in the southern regions around Sinai.[11] Those who had lived under Egyptian rule in the Canaanite cities may have felt that they had indeed been liberated from Egypt – but in their own country.[12]

J and E were not modern historical accounts. Like Homer

and Herodotus, the authors included legends about divine figures and mythological elements that try to explain the meaning of what had happened. Their narratives are *more* than history. From the very beginning, there was no single, authoritative message in what would become the Bible. The J and E authors interpreted the saga of Israel very differently, and later editors made no attempt to iron out these inconsistencies and contradictions. Subsequently historians would feel at liberty to add to the JE narrative and make radical alterations.

In both J and E, for example, very different views of God were expressed. J used anthropomorphic imagery that would embarrass later exegetes. Yahweh strolls in the Garden of Eden like a Middle Eastern potentate, shuts the door of Noah's ark, gets angry and changes his mind. But in E there was a more transcendent view of Elohim, who scarcely even 'speaks' but prefers to send an angel as his messenger. Later Israelite religion would become passionately monotheist, convinced that Yahweh was the *only* God. But neither the J or E authors believed this. Originally Yahweh had been a member of the Divine Assembly of 'holy ones', over which El, the high god of Canaan, had presided with his consort Asherah. Each nation of the region had its own patronal deity, and Yahweh was the 'holy one of Israel'.[13] By the eighth century, Yahweh had ousted El in the Divine Assembly,[14] and ruled alone over a host of 'holy ones', who were warriors in his heavenly army.[15] None of the other gods could measure up to Yahweh in his fidelity to his people. Here he had no peers, no rivals.[16] But the Bible shows that right up to the destruction of the temple by Nebuchadnezzar in 586, Israelites also worshipped a host of other deities.[17]

Abraham, a man of the south, not Moses, was the hero of J's history. His career and the covenant God made with him looked forward to King David.[18] But E was more interested in Jacob, a northern character, and his son Joseph, who was buried in Shechem. E did not include any of the primeval history – the creation of the world, Cain and Abel, the Flood and the rebellion at the Tower of Babel – that was so important to J. E's hero was Moses, who was more widely revered in the north than the south.[19] But neither J nor E mentioned the law that Yahweh gave to Moses on Sinai, which would become so crucial later. There was as yet no reference to the Ten Commandments. Almost certainly, as in other Near Eastern legend, the heavenly tablets given to Moses originally contained some esoteric cultic lore.[20] For J and E, Sinai was important because Moses and the Elders had a vision of Yahweh on the mountaintop.[21]

By the eighth century, a small group of prophets wanted to make the people worship Yahweh exclusively. But this was not a popular move. As a warrior, Yahweh was unsurpassed, but he had no expertise in agriculture, so when they wanted a good harvest, it was natural for the people of Israel and Judah to have recourse to the cult of the local fertility god Baal and his sister-spouse Anat, practising the usual ritual sex to make the fields fertile. In the early eighth century, Hosea, a prophet in the northern kingdom, inveighed against this practice. His wife Gomer had served as a sacred prostitute of Baal and the pain he felt at her infidelity was, he imagined, similar to what Yahweh experienced when his people went whoring after other gods. Israelites must return to Yahweh, who could supply all their needs. It was no use hoping to appease him by temple ritual: Yahweh wanted cultic loyalty (*hesed*) not animal sacrifice.[22] If they continued to be unfaithful to Yahweh, the kingdom of Israel would be destroyed by the mighty Assyrian empire, their towns laid waste, and their children exterminated.[23]

Assyria had established unprecedented power in the Middle East; it regularly devastated the territories of recalcitrant vassals and deported the population. The prophet Amos, who preached in Israel in the mid-eighth century, argued that Yahweh was leading a holy war against Israel to punish its systemic injustice.[24] As Hosea condemned the widely respected cult of Baal, Amos turned the traditional cult of Yahweh the warrior on its head: he no longer reflexively took Israel's side. Amos also poured scorn on the temple rituals of the northern kingdom. Yahweh was sick of noisy chanting and devout strumming of harps. Instead he wanted justice to 'flow like water, and integrity like an unfailing stream'.[25] From this early date, the biblical writings were subversive and iconoclastic, challenging prevailing orthodoxy.

Isaiah of Jerusalem was more conventional; his oracles conformed entirely to the royal ideology of the House of David. He had received his prophetic commission in about 740 in the temple, where he saw Yahweh, surrounded by his Divine Assembly of celestial beings, and heard the cherubim crying 'holy [*qaddosh*] holy, holy!'[26] Yahweh was 'separate', 'other' and radically transcendent. Yahweh gave Isaiah a grim message: the countryside would be devastated and the inhabitants put to flight.[27] But Isaiah had no fear of Assyria. He had seen that Yahweh's 'glory' filled the earth;[28] as long as he was enthroned in his temple on Mount Zion, Judah was safe, because Yahweh, the divine warrior, was once again on the march, fighting for his people.[29]

But the northern kingdom enjoyed no such immunity. When the king of Israel joined a local confederacy to block Assyria's western advance in 732, the Assyrian king Tigleth-Pileser III descended and seized most of Israel's territory. Ten years later, in 722, after another rebellion, the Assyrian armies destroyed Samaria, Israel's beautiful capital, and deported the ruling class. The kingdom of Judah, which had become an Assyrian vassal, remained secure, and refugees fled to Jerusalem from the north, probably bringing with them the E saga and the recorded oracles of Hosea and Amos, who had foreseen the tragedy. These were included in Judah's royal archive where, at some later date, scribes combined the 'Elohist' tradition with J's southern epic.[30]

During these dark years, Isaiah was comforted by the imminent birth of a royal baby, a sign that God was still with the House of David: 'A young woman [*almah*] is with child and will soon give birth to a son whom she will call *Immanu-El* [God-with-us].'[31] His birth would even be a beacon of hope, 'a great light', to the traumatized people of the north, who 'walked in darkness' and 'deep shadow'.[32] When the baby was born, he was in fact named Hezekiah, and Isaiah imagined the entire Divine Assembly celebrating the royal child, who, like all the Davidic kings, would become a divine figure and a member of their heavenly council: on his coronation day he would be called 'Wonder-Counsellor, Mighty-God, Eternal-Father, Prince-of-Peace'.[33]

Although the biblical historians revere Hezekiah as a devout king who tried to outlaw the worship of foreign gods, his foreign policy was a disaster. After an ill-advised rebellion against Assyria in 701, Jerusalem was almost destroyed, the countryside brutally laid waste and Judah reduced to a tiny rump state. But under King Manasseh (687–42 BCE), who became a vassal of Assyria, Judah's fortunes improved. In an attempt to integrate with the empire, he reversed his father's religious jurisdiction, setting up altars to Baal, erecting an effigy of Asherah and statues of the divine horses of the sun in the Jerusalem temple, and instituting child sacrifice outside the city.[34] The biblical historian was horrified by these developments, but few of Manasseh's subjects would have been surprised, since most of them had similar icons in their own homes.[35] Despite Judah's prosperity, there was widespread unrest in the rural districts that had borne the brunt of the Assyrian invasion, and after Manasseh's death the smouldering discontent erupted in a palace coup, which deposed Manasseh's son Amon and put his eight-year-old son Josiah on the throne.

By this time, Assyria was in decline and Egypt in the ascendancy. In 656 the Pharoah forced Assyrian troops to withdraw from the Levant and the Judahites watched with astonishment, as the Assyrians vacated the territories of the former kingdom of Israel. While the great powers fought for supremacy, Judah was left to its own devices. There was a surge of national feeling and in 622 Josiah began to repair Solomon's temple, the symbolic memorial of Judah's golden age. During the construction, the high priest Hilkiah made a momentous discovery and hurried with the news to Shaphan, the royal scribe. He had found the 'scroll of the law' (*sefer torah*), which Yahweh had given to Moses on Mount Sinai.[36]

In the older stories, there was no mention of Yahweh's teaching (*torah*) being committed to writing. In the JE accounts, Moses had passed on Yahweh's directions by word of mouth and the people had responded orally.[37] The seventh-century reformers, however, added verses to the JE saga which explained that Moses 'put all the commands of Yahweh into writing' and read the *sefer torah* to the people.[38] Hilkiah and Shaphan claimed that this scroll had been lost and its teachings never implemented, but its providential discovery meant that Judah could make a new start. Hilkiah's document probably contained an early version of the book of Deuteronomy, which described Moses delivering a 'second law' (Greek: *deuteronomion*) shortly before his death. But instead of being an ancient work, Deuteronomy was an entirely new scripture. It was not unusual for reformers to attribute new ideas to a great figure of the past. The Deuteronomists believed that they were speaking for Moses at this time of transition. In other words, this was what Moses would say to Josiah if he were delivering a 'second law' today.

Instead of simply recording the status quo, for the first time an Israelite text was calling for radical change. After the scroll had been read aloud to him, Josiah tore his garments in distress and immediately inaugurated a programme that followed Yahweh's new *torah* to the letter. He burned down Manasseh's abominations in the temple and, because the Judahites had always regarded the royal shrines of the northern kingdom as illegitimate, demolished the temples of Bethel and Samaria, killed the priests in the rural sanctuaries and contaminated their altars.[39]

It is instructive that the Deuteronomists, who pioneered the idea of scriptural orthodoxy, introduced startlingly new legislation, which – had it been implemented – would have transformed the ancient faith of Israel.[40] To ensure purity of worship, they tried to centralize the cult,[41] create a secular judiciary independent of the temple, and strip the king of his sacral powers, making him subject to the *torah* like everybody else. The Deuteronomists actually changed the wording of earlier law codes, sagas and liturgical texts to make them endorse their proposals. In some ways, Deuteronomy, with its secular sphere, centralized state and constitutional monarchy, reads like a modern document. It was even more passionate about social justice than Amos and its theology more rational than the old cultic mythology of Judah:[42] you could not *see* God and he did not live in a humanly constructed building.[43] Israelites did not own their land because Yahweh dwelt on Zion, but because the people observed his commandments.

The reformers did not use their scripture to conserve tradition, as is often done today, but to introduce radical change. They also rewrote the history of Israel, adding fresh material that adapted the JE epic to the seventh century, paying special attention to Moses, who had liberated the Israelites from Egypt, at a time when Josiah hoped to become independent of Pharaoh. The climax of the Exodus story was no longer a theophany on Sinai, but the gift of the *sefer torah* and the tablets that Yahweh gave to Moses were now inscribed with the Ten Commandments. The Deuteronomists extended the Exodus story to include Joshua's conquest of the northern highlands – a blueprint for Josiah's reconquering of the northern territories.[44] They also wrote a history of the two kingdoms of Israel and Judah in the books of Samuel and Kings, arguing that the Davidic monarchs were the only legitimate rulers of the whole of Israel. Their story culminated in the reign of Josiah, a new Moses and a greater king than David.[45]

Not everybody was enamoured of the new *torah*. The prophet Jeremiah, who began his ministry at about this time, admired Josiah and agreed with many of the reformers' aims, but had reservations about a written scripture: the 'lying pen of the scribes' could subvert tradition by a mere sleight of the pen and a written text could encourage a superficial mode of thought that concentrated on information rather than wisdom.[46] In a study of modern Jewish movements, the

eminent scholar Haym Soloveitchik argues that the transition
from an oral tradition to written texts can lead to religious
stridency by giving the reader an unrealistic certainty about
essentially ineffable matters.[47] Deuteronomist religion was
certainly strident. The reformers depicted Moses preaching a
policy of violent suppression of the native Canaanites: 'You
must destroy completely all the places where the nations you
dispossess have served their gods ... you must tear down
their altars, smash their pillars, cut down their sacred poles,
set fire to the carved images of their gods and wipe out their
name from that place.'[48] They described with approval Joshua
massacring the people of Ai as though he were an Assyrian
general:

> When Israel had finished killing all the inhabitants of Ai in
> the open ground and where they followed them into the
> wilderness, and when all to a man had fallen by the edge of
> the sword, all Israel returned to Ai and slaughtered all its
> people. The number of those who fell that day, men and
> women together, was twelve thousand, all people of Ai.[49]

The Deuteronomists had absorbed the violent ethos of a
region that had experienced nearly two hundred years of
Assyrian brutality. It was an early indication that scripture
reflects the failures as well as the high points of the religious
quest.

Although these texts were revered, they had not yet
become 'scripture'. People felt free to alter older writings and

there was no canon of prescribed sacred books. But they were beginning to express the community's highest aspirations. The Deuteronomists who celebrated Josiah's reform were convinced that Israel was on the brink of a glorious new era but in 622 he was killed in a skirmish with the Egyptian army. Within a few years, the Babylonians had conquered Nineveh, the Assyrian capital, and became the major power in the region. Judah's brief independence was over. For a few decades the kings veered in their allegiance between Egypt and Babylon. Many still believed that Judah would be safe as long as Yahweh dwelt in his temple, even though Jeremiah warned them that to defy Babylon was suicidal. Finally, after two futile rebellions, Jerusalem and its temple were destroyed by Nebuchadnezzar in 586.

In exile, the scribes pored over the scrolls in the royal archive. The Deuteronomists added passages to their history to account for the disaster, which they attributed to Manasseh's religious policies.[50] But some of the priests, who in losing their temple had lost their whole world, looked back to the past and found a reason for hope. Scholars call this priestly layer of the Penateuch 'P', though we do not know whether P was an individual or, as seems more likely, an entire school. P revised the JE narrative and added the books of Numbers and Leviticus, drawing upon older documents – genealogies, laws and ritual texts – some written down, others orally transmitted.[51] The most important of his sources was the 'Holiness Code'[52] (a collection of seventh-century laws) and the Tabernacle Document, a description of

Yahweh's tent shrine during the Israelites' years in the Sinai wilderness, which was central to P's vision.[53] Some of P's material was very old indeed, but he created an entirely new vision for his demoralized people.

P understood the Exodus story very differently from the Deuteronomists. The climax was not the *sefer torah* but the promise of God's continual presence during their desert years. God had brought Israel out of Egypt simply in order 'to live [*skn*] among them'.[54] The verb *shakan* meant: 'to lead the life of a nomadic tent dweller'. Instead of residing in a permanent building, God preferred to 'tent' with his wandering people; he was not tied to one place, but could accompany them wherever they went.[55] After P's revision, the book of Exodus ended with the completion of the tabernacle: the 'glory' of Yahweh filled the tent and the cloud of his presence covered it.[56] God, P implied, was still with his people in their latest 'wandering' in Babylonia. Instead of ending his saga with Joshua's conquest, P left the Israelites on the border of the Promised Land.[57] Israel was not a people because it dwelt in a particular country, but because it lived in the presence of its God.

In P's revised history, the exile was the latest in a sequence of migrations: Adam and Eve had been expelled from Eden; Cain condemned to a life of homeless vagrancy after murdering Abel; the human race had been scattered at the Tower of Babel; Abraham had left Ur; the tribes had emigrated to Egypt, and eventually lived as nomads in the desert. In their latest dispersal, the exiles must build a community to which the presence could return. In a startling innovation, P suggested that the entire people observe the purity laws of the temple personnel.[58] Everybody must live as though he were serving the divine presence. Israel must be 'holy' (*qaddosh*) and 'separate' like Yahweh,[59] so P crafted a way of life based on the principle of separation. The exiles must live apart from their Babylonian neighbours, observing distinctive rules of diet and cleanliness. Then – and only then – Yahweh would live among them: 'I will place my tabernacle in your midst,' God told them, 'and I will walk about among you.'[60] Babylonia could become another Eden, where God had walked with Adam in the cool of the evening.

Holiness also had a strong ethical component. Israelites must respect the sacred 'otherness' of every single creature. Nothing could be enslaved or possessed, therefore, not even the land.[61] Israelites must not despise the foreigner: 'If a stranger lives with you in your land, do not molest him. You must count him as one of your own countrymen and love him as yourself – for you were once strangers in Egypt.'[62] Unlike the Deuteronomists, P's vision was inclusive. His narrative of alienation and exile constantly stressed the importance of reconciliation with former enemies. Nowhere was this more apparent than in his most famous work, the first chapter of Genesis, in which P describes Elohim creating heaven and earth in six days.

This was not a literal, historically accurate account of creation. When the final editors put the extant biblical text together, they placed P's story next to J's creation narrative, which is quite different.⁶³ In the ancient world, cosmogony was a therapeutic rather than a factual genre. People recited creation myths at a sickbed, at the start of a new project, or at the beginning of a new year – whenever they felt the need for an infusion of the divine potency that had, somehow, brought all things into being. P's story would have been consoling to the exiles who felt that Yahweh had been ignominiously defeated by Marduk, god of Babylon. Unlike Marduk, whose creation of the world had to be repeated annually at New Year in spectacular rites in the ziggurat of Esagila, Yahweh was not obliged to fight other gods to create an ordered cosmos; the ocean was not a frightening sea-goddess like Tiamat, who fought Marduk to her bitter end, but simply the raw material of the universe; the sun, moon and stars were not deities but mere creatures and functionaries. Yahweh's victory did not have to be renewed: he finished his work in six days and rested on the seventh.⁶⁴

This was no bombastic polemic, however; there was no taunting, no aggression. In the ancient Near East, gods usually created the cosmos after a series of violent, terrifying battles; indeed, the Israelites told stories of Yahweh slaying divine sea-monsters at the beginning of time.⁶⁵ But P's creation myth was non-violent. God simply spoke a word of command and one by one the components of our world came into being. After each day, God saw that all he had made was *tov*, 'good'. On the last day, Yahweh confirmed that everything was 'very good' and blessed his entire creation,⁶⁶ including, presumably, the Babylonians. Everybody should behave like Yahweh, resting calmly on the Sabbath, serving God's world and blessing every single one of his creatures.

But another prophet, who preached in Babylonia during the second half of the sixth century, espoused a more aggressive theology and could not wait to see the *goyim*, the foreign nations, marching behind Israel in chains. We do not know his name, but because his oracles were preserved in the same scroll as Isaiah's, he is usually known as the Second Isaiah. The exile was drawing to a close. In 539, Cyrus, king of Persia, defeated the Babylonians and became the master of the largest empire the world had yet seen. Because he promised to repatriate all deportees, Second Isaiah called him Yahweh's *meshiah*, his 'anointed' king.[67] For Israel's sake, Yahweh had summoned Cyrus as his instrument and caused a revolution of power in the region. Could any other god compete with him? No, Yahweh declared scornfully to the gods of the *goyim*, 'you are nothing and your works are nothingness.'[68] He had become the *only* God. 'I am Yahweh, unrivalled,' he announced proudly. 'There is no other god besides me.'[69] This is the first unequivocally monotheistic statement in what was becoming the Hebrew Bible. But its triumphalism reflected the more belligerent characteristics of religion. Second Isaiah relied upon a mythical tradition that had little connection with the rest of the Pentateuch. He revived the ancient tales of Yahweh slaying sea dragons to order primordial chaos, declaring that Yahweh was about to repeat this cosmic triumph by defeating the historical enemies of Israel.[70] He did not, however, reflect the views of the whole exiled community. Four 'Servant Songs' punctuated Second Isaiah's exuberant prophecies.[71] In these, a mysterious figure, who called himself Yahweh's servant, was entrusted with the task of establishing justice throughout the world – but in a non-violent campaign. He was despised and rejected, but his suffering would redeem his people. The servant had no desire to subjugate the *goyim*, but would become 'the light of the nations', and enable God's salvation to reach to the ends of the earth.[72]

Cyrus fulfilled his promise. Towards the end of 539, a few months after his coronation, a small party of exiles set out for Jerusalem. Most of the Israelites chose to stay in Babylon, where they would make an important contribution to the Hebrew scriptures. The returning exiles brought home nine scrolls that traced the history of their people from the creation until their deportation: Genesis, Exodus, Leviticus, Numbers, Deuteronomy, Joshua, Judges, Samuel and Kings; they also brought anthologies of the oracles of the prophets (*neviim*) and a hymn book, which included new psalms composed in Babylon. It was still not complete, but the exiles had in their possession the bare bones of the Hebrew Bible.

The Golah, the community of returning exiles, were convinced that their revised religion was the only authentic version of Yahwism. But the Israelites who had not been deported to Babylonia, most of whom lived in the territories of the former northern kingdom, could not share this vision and would resent this exclusive attitude. The new temple, a rather modest shrine, finally completed in 520 BCE, made

Yahwism a temple faith once again. But another spirituality began, very gradually, to develop alongside it. With the help of those Israelites who had remained in Babylonia, the Golah were about to transform their medley of texts into scripture.

CHAPTER 2

Scripture

Once the Judahites had completed their second temple on Mount Zion, they imagined that life would continue as before. But they were overcome by spiritual malaise. Many were disappointed with the new temple, which could not compete with the legendary splendour of Solomon's shrine; the Golah had encountered stiff opposition from foreigners who had settled in Judah during the exiles' absence in Babylonia; and they had received a less than cordial welcome from those Israelites who had not been deported by the Babylonians. The priests had become lazy and apathetic and provided no moral leadership.[1] But at the beginning of the fourth century, in about 398 BCE, the Persian king dispatched Ezra, his minister for Jewish affairs, to Jerusalem with a mandate to enforce the *torah* of Moses as the law of the land.[2] Ezra would make this set of hitherto miscellaneous teachings an absolute value, so that it became *the* Torah.

The Persians were reviewing the legal systems of all their subjects to make sure that they were compatible with the security of the empire. An expert in Torah, Ezra had probably worked out a satisfactory modus vivendi between Mosaic law and Persian jurisprudence. When he arrived in Jerusalem, he was appalled by what he found. The people were not maintaining the holy separation from the *goyim* that P had prescribed: some had even taken foreign wives. For a whole day, the inhabitants of Jerusalem were dismayed to see the king's envoy tear his garments and sit in the public street in the posture of deep mourning. Then Ezra summoned the entire Golah to a meeting. Anybody who refused to attend would be cast out of the community and have his property confiscated.

On New Year's Day, Ezra brought the Torah to the square in front of the Water Gate. Standing on a raised wooden dais, he read the text aloud, 'translating and giving the sense, so that the people understood what was read', while Levites[3] versed in the Torah circulated among the crowds, supplementing this instruction.[4] We are not sure which laws were proclaimed on this occasion, but, whatever they were, the people had clearly never heard them before. They burst into tears, frightened by these unfamiliar demands. 'Do not weep!' Ezra insisted. They now 'understood the meaning of what had been proclaimed to them'. This was the season of Sukkoth, a festive time, and Ezra explained the law that commanded the Israelites to spend this sacred month in special 'booths' (*sukkoth*), in memory of their ancestors' forty years in the wilderness.[5] At once, the people rushed into the hills to pick branches of olive, myrtle, pine and palm, and leafy shelters appeared all over the city. There was a carnival atmosphere, as the people assembled each evening to listen to Ezra's exposition.

Ezra had begun to craft a spiritual discipline based on a sacred text. The Torah had now been elevated above the other writings and, for the first time, was called 'the law of Moses'. But, if it was simply read like any other text, the Torah could seem demanding and disconcerting. It must be heard in the contexts of rituals that separated it from ordinary life and put the audience in a different frame of mind. Because the people had begun to treat it differently, the Torah was becoming 'sacred scripture'.

Perhaps the most important element of this Torah spirituality was Ezra himself.[6] He was a priest, 'a diligent scribe in the Torah of Moses', and a guardian of tradition.[7] But he was also a new type of religious official: a scholar who 'set his heart to investigate (*li-drosh*) the Torah of Yahweh and to do and teach law and ordinance in Israel'.[8] He was offering something different from the usual priestly instruction about ceremonial lore. The biblical author makes a point of telling us that 'the hand of Yahweh rested upon him' – a phrase traditionally used to describe the weight of inspiration that had descended on the prophets.[9] Before the exile, priests had been wont to 'consult' (*li-drosh*) Yahweh, by casting lots with the sacred objects known as Urim and Thummim.[10] The new seer was not a fortune teller but a scholar who could interpret the scriptures. The practice of *midrash* (exegesis) would always retain this sense of expectant inquiry.[11] Torah study was not an academic exercise but a spiritual quest.

Yet Ezra's reading had been prefaced by the threat of expulsion and seizure of property. It was followed by a more sombre assembly in the square in front of the temple, during which the people stood shivering as the torrential winter rains deluged the city and heard Ezra command them to send away their foreign wives.[12] Membership of Israel was now confined to the Golah and those who submitted to the Torah, the official law code of Judah. There was always the danger that enthusiasm for scripture could foster an exclusive, divisive and potentially cruel orthodoxy.

Ezra's reading marks the beginning of classical Judaism, a religion concerned not merely with the reception and preservation of revelation but with its constant reinterpretation.[13] The law that Ezra read was clearly unknown to the people, who wept in fear when they heard it for the first time. When he expounded the text, the exegete did not reproduce the original *torah* imparted in the distant past to Moses but created something new and unexpected. The biblical writers had worked in the same way, radically revising the texts they had inherited. Revelation had not happened once and for all time; it was an ongoing process that could never end, because there were always fresh teachings to be discovered.

By this time, there were two established categories of scripture: the Torah and the Prophets (*Neviim*). But after the exile, another set of texts were produced that would become known as the *Kethuvim*, the 'Writings', which sometimes simply reinterpreted the older books. Thus Chronicles, a historical narrative written by priestly authors, was essentially a commentary on the Deuteronomic history of Samuel and Kings. When these two books were translated into Greek, they were called *paralipomena*: 'the things omitted'.[14] The authors were writing between the lines to make good what they regarded as deficiencies in the earlier accounts. They shared P's ideal of reconciliation and wanted to build bridges with the Israelites who had not gone into exile and were now resident in the north. They therefore omitted the Deutero-nomists' harsh polemic against the northern kingdom.

A significant number of the Writings belonged to a school that was distinct from either the Law or the Prophets. In the ancient Near East, sages attached to the court as teachers or advisers tended to see the whole of reality as shaped by a vast, underlying principle of divine origin. The Hebrew sages called it *Hokhmah*, 'Wisdom'. Everything – the laws of nature, society, and events in the lives of individuals – conformed to this celestial blueprint, which no human being could ever grasp in its entirety. But the sages who devoted their lives to the contemplation of Wisdom believed that they occasionally had glimpses of it. Some expressed their insight in such pithy maxims as: 'A king gives a country stability by justice, an extortioner brings it to ruin', or 'The man who flatters his neighbour spreads a net for his feet'.[15] The Wisdom tradition had originally little connection with Moses and Sinai but was associated with King Solomon, who had a reputation for this type of acumen[16] and three of the *Kethuvim* were attributed to him: Proverbs, Ecclesiastes and the Song of Songs. Proverbs was a collection of common-sense aphorisms, similar to the two quoted above. Ecclesiastes, a flagrantly cynical medita-tion, saw all things as 'vanity', and appeared to undermine the entire Torah tradition, while the Song of Songs was an erotic poem with no apparent spiritual content.

Other Wisdom writings explored the insoluble problem of the suffering of innocent people in a world ruled by a just God. The book of Job was based on an ancient folktale. God gave Satan, the legal prosecutor of the Divine Assembly, permission to test Job's virtue by afflicting him with a series of wholly undeserved calamities. Job eloquently railed against his punishment and refused to accept any of the conventional explanations of the friends who tried to console him. Eventually Yahweh answered Job, not by referring to the events of the Exodus, but by forcing him to contemplate the underlying masterplan that governed creation. Could Job visit the place where snow was kept, fasten the harness of the Pleiades, or explain why a wild ox was willing to serve human beings? Job was forced to admit that he could not comprehend this divine Wisdom: 'I have been holding forth on matters I cannot understand, on marvels beyond me and my knowledge.'[17] The sage acquired Wisdom by meditating on the marvels of the physical world, not by studying Torah.

But by the second century BCE, some Wisdom writers were beginning to come closer to the Torah. Ben Sirah, a devout sage living in Jerusalem, no longer regarded Wisdom as an abstract principle but imagined her as a female figure and a member of the Divine Assembly.[18] He depicted her giving an account of herself before the other Counsellors. She was the Word by which God had called all things into being. She was the divine Spirit (*ruach*), which had hovered over the primal

ocean at the beginning of the creative process. As God's Word
and masterplan, she was divine and yet separate from her
Maker, present everywhere on earth. But God had commanded her to pitch her tent with the people of Israel and she
had accompanied them throughout their history. She had
been in the pillar of cloud that had guided them in the wilderness and in the rituals of the temple, another symbolic expression of divine order. But above all, Wisdom was identical
with the *sefer torah*, 'the law that Moses enjoined upon us'.[19]
The Torah was no longer simply a legal code; it had become
an expression of the highest wisdom and most transcendent
goodness.

Another author, writing at about the same time, per-
sonified Wisdom in a similar way, as divine and yet separate
from God's essence. 'Yahweh created me when his purpose
first unfolded,' Wisdom explained, 'before the oldest of his
works.' She was at his side – 'a master craftsman' – as he
established the cosmos, 'delighting him day after day, ever at
play in his presence, at play everywhere in the world, delighting to be with the sons of men'.[20] A new lightness and grace
had entered Yahwism. The study of the Torah was beginning
to arouse emotion and yearning that were almost erotic. Ben
Sirah depicted Wisdom calling out to the sages like a lover:
'Approach me, you desire me, and take your fill of my fruits.
For memories of me are sweeter than honey, inheriting me is
sweeter than the honeycomb.'[21] There was no end to the quest
for Wisdom: 'They who eat me will hunger for more, they
who drink me will thirst for more.'[22] The tone and imagery of

Ben Sirah's hymn were very similar to the Song of Songs, which may explain why this love poem was eventually included in the Writings. It seemed to express the lyrically passionate experience of the *sefer* scholar when he studied the Torah and encountered a presence 'wider than the sea', whose designs were 'more profound than the abyss'.[23]

Ben Sirah described the *sefer* scholar delving into all categories of scripture: Torah, Prophets and Writings. He was not shut away from the world in an ivory tower but engaged in state affairs. His exegesis was wholly informed by prayer: 'At dawn and with all his heart he resorts to the Lord who made him', and, as a result, he received an influx of wisdom and understanding[24] that transformed him and made him a force for good in the world.[25] In a most important phrase, Ben Sirah claimed that the teachings of the sage were 'like prophecy, a legacy to all future generations'.[26] The scholar was not simply learning about the prophets; his exegesis had made him a prophet himself.

This becomes clear in the book of Daniel, which was written in Palestine during the second century BCE at a time of political crisis.[27] By this time, Judah had become a province of the Greek empires founded by the successors of Alexander the Great, who had conquered the Persian empire in 333 BCE. The Greeks introduced a diluted version of Athenian classical culture, known as Hellenism, into the Near East. Some Jews were enthalled by the Greek ideal but opposition to Hellenism became entrenched among the more conservative Jews after 167 BCE, when Antiochus Epiphanes, ruler of the

Seleucid empire in Mesopotamia and Palestine, violated the Jerusalem temple and introduced a Hellenistic cult there: Jews who opposed his regime were persecuted. Judas Maccabeus and his family led the Jewish resistance; in 164 they were able to oust the Greeks from the temple mount, but the war continued until 143, when the Maccabees were able to shake off Seleucid rule and establish Judah as an independent state, which was ruled by their Hasmonean dynasty until 63 BCE.

The book of Daniel was composed during the Maccabean war. It took the form of an historical novel, set in Babylon during the exile. In real life, Daniel had been one of the more virtuous exiles,[28] but in this fictional work he was an official prophet in the courts of Nebuchadnezzar and Cyrus. In the early chapters, written before Antiochus's sacrilege, Daniel was presented as a typical Middle Eastern court sage[29] with a special talent for 'interpreting every kind of vision and dream'.[30] But in the later chapters, composed after Antiochus's desecration of the temple but before the Maccabees' final victory, Daniel becomes an inspired exegete, whose study of scriptures endows him with prophetic insight.

Daniel experienced a series of perplexing visions. He saw a succession of four fearful empires (represented by fabulous beasts), each more terrible than the last. The fourth, a clear reference to the Seleucids, was of an entirely different order of wickedness, however. Its ruler would 'speak words against the Most High, and harass the saints of the Most High'.[31] Daniel foresaw 'the disastrous abomination' of Antiochus's

Hellenistic cult in the temple.[32] But there was a glimmer of hope. Daniel also saw 'coming on the clouds of heaven, one like a son of man', a figure representing the Maccabees, who was mysteriously human and yet more than human. The saviour entered the presence of God, who conferred upon him 'sovereignty, glory and kingship'.[33] These prophecies would later become very important, as we shall see in the following chapter. But what concerns us now is Daniel's inspired exegesis.

Daniel had another series of visions, which he was unable to understand. He sought enlightenment in scripture and was particularly preoccupied by Jeremiah's prediction of the number of years that must pass 'before the successive devastations of Jerusalem would come to an end, namely seventy years'.[34] The second-century author was clearly not interested in the original meaning of the text: Jeremiah had obviously prophesied, in a round figure, the length of the Babylonian exile. He wanted to find an entirely new significance in the ancient oracle that would bring comfort to the Jews who were anxiously awaiting the outcome of the Maccabean wars. This would become typical of Jewish exegesis. Instead of looking back to uncover its historical meaning, the interpreter would make the text speak to the present and the future. In order to seek out the hidden message in Jeremiah, Daniel put himself through a rigorous ascetic programme: 'I turned my face to the Lord God begging for time to pray and to plead with fasting, sackcloth and ashes.'[35] On another occasion, he said, 'I ate no rich food, touched no meat or wine, and did not anoint myself, until these three weeks were over'.[36] As a result of these spiritual disciplines, he became the recipient of a divine inspiration: Gabriel, the angel of revelation, flew towards him and enabled him to discover a new meaning in the problematic passage.

Torah study was becoming a prophetic discipline. The exegete now prepared himself to approach these ancient documents by purifying rituals, as if he were about to enter a holy place, putting himself into an alternative mental state that gave him fresh insight. The second-century author deliberately described Daniel's enlightenment in a way that recalled the visionary experiences of Isaiah and Ezekiel.[37] But where Isaiah had received his prophetic initiation in the temple, Daniel found his in the sacred text. He did not have to eat the scroll like Ezekiel; instead he lived with the words of scripture constantly in his mind, interiorizing them, and found himself transformed – 'purged, purified and made white'.[38] Finally the second-century author made Daniel predict the successful outcome of the Maccabean war by finding an entirely novel message in Jeremiah's words. In riddling, enigmatic verse, Gabriel indicated that whether it took 'seventy weeks' or 'seventy years', the Maccabees would win through! The text had proved its holiness and divine origin by speaking directly to circumstances that the original author could not have foreseen.[39]

Sadly, the Hasmonean dynasty founded by the Maccabees was a huge disappointment. The kings were cruel and corrupt; they were not descendants of David; and, to the horror of the more pious Jews, they violated the sanctity of the temple by assuming the office of High Priest, even though they were not of priestly descent. Outraged by this sacrilege, the historical imagination of the Jewish people projected itself into the future. At the end of the second century there was an explosion of apocalyptic piety. In new texts, Jews described eschatological visions in which God intervened powerfully in human affairs, smashed the present corrupt order and inaugurated an age of justice and purity. As they struggled to find a solution, the people of Judah split into myriad sects, each insisting that it alone was the true Israel.[40] This was, however, an extraordinarily creative period. The canon of the Bible had not yet been finalized. There was still no authoritative scripture and no orthodoxy and few of the sects felt bound to conform to traditional readings of the Law and the Prophets. Some even felt at liberty to write entirely new scriptures. The diversity of the Late Second Temple period was revealed when the library of the Qumran community was discovered in 1942.

Qumran manifested the iconoclastic spirit of this era. The sectarians had withdrawn from Jerusalem to the shore of the Dead Sea, where they lived in monastic seclusion. They revered the Law and the Prophets, but believed that they alone understood them.[41] Their leader, the Teacher of Righteousness, had received a revelation which convinced him that there were 'hidden things' in the scriptures that could only be uncovered by a special *pesher* (deciphering) exegesis. Every single word in the Law and the Prophets looked forward to their own community in these last days.[42] Qumran was the culmination of Jewish history, the true Israel. Soon God would usher in a new world order; and after the final victory of the children of light, a massive temple, not made with human hands, would be constructed and the Mosaic covenant would be rewritten. In the meantime, the Qumran community was a pure, symbolic temple that replaced the desecrated shrine in Jerusalem. Its members observed the priestly laws, purified their garments, and walked into the dining room as into the temple precincts.

Qumran was an extreme wing of the Essene movement, which had about four thousand members by the first century BCE.[43] Most Essenes also lived in tight-knit communities, but in towns and villages rather than the desert; they married and had children but conducted their lives as though the end time had already begun, observing the purity laws, eschewing private property, holding all things in common, and forbidding divorce.[44] They held communal meals, in which they looked forward to the coming kingdom, but though they anticipated the destruction of the temple, they continued to worship there.

The Pharisees, another sect which comprised about 1.2 per cent of the population,[45] were highly respected. Even though their approach to the Law and the Prophets was more conventional, they were open to such novel ideas as the general resurrection, when the righteous dead would rise from their tombs to share God's final triumph. Many of them were laymen, who made a dedicated effort to live like priests, observing the purity laws in their own homes as though they dwelt in the temple. They were opposed by the more conservative Saducees, who interpreted the written texts more stringently and did not accept the newfangled ideas about personal immortality.

People focused on the temple because it provided them with access to God; if it failed, religion lost its point. There was a desperate search for a new way of entering the divine presence, for new scriptures and new ways of being Jewish.[46] Some sects completely rewrote the older texts. The author of the First Book of Enoch imagined God rending the earth and the Mosaic revelation asunder on Mount Sinai to begin again with a clean slate. The author of Jubilees, which was widely read well into the second century CE, was distressed by the cruelty of some of the earlier writings and entirely revised the JEP narrative. Had God really tried to exterminate the human race in the Flood, commanded Abraham to kill his own son, and drowned the Egyptian army in the Sea of Reeds? He decided that God did not intervene directly in human affairs and that the suffering we see all around us was the work of Satan and his demons.

Before the first century CE, there was no widespread expectation that a messiah, an 'anointed one', would arrive to put the world to rights.[47] Despite occasional references to such a figure, this was still a peripheral, undeveloped idea. The apocalyptic scenarios of the Late Second Temple period usually imagined God establishing the new order, without human assistance. There were a few sporadic references to concepts that would later become crucial. There was mention of a Davidic king who would inaugurate the 'kingdom of God' and 'sit forever over the goyim in judgment'.[48] Another text spoke of a ruler who would 'be called son of God and . . . son of the most high and bring peace to the world'[49] – clearly a nostalgic harking back to Isaiah's prophecy of Immanu-El. But these isolated notions did not yet form a coherent vision.

This changed after Palestine was conquered by the Roman general Pompey in 63 BCE and became a province of the Roman empire. In some ways, Roman rule was beneficial. King Herod, the protégé of Rome who reigned in Jerusalem from 37 to 4 BCE, rebuilt the temple on a magnificent scale and pilgrims flocked there to celebrate the festivals. But the Romans were unpopular and some of the prefects, notably Pontius Pilate (26–36 CE), went out of their way to insult Jewish sensibilities. A number of prophets tried to mobilize the population to revolt.[50] A certain Theudas led four hundred men into the desert, promising that God would liberate them there. A prophet known as the 'Egyptian' persuaded thousands of people to congregate on the Mount of Olives in order to storm the Roman fortress that was positioned provocatively beside the temple. Most of these uprisings were savagely suppressed and on one occasion the Romans crucified as many as two thousand rebels outside Jerusalem. During the 20s CE, John the Baptizer, an ascetic prophet who may have belonged to the Essene movement, drew large crowds to the Judaean desert where he preached that the 'kingdom of heaven' was at hand.[51] There would be a great judgement for which Jews must prepare by confessing their sins, immersing themselves in the river Jordan, and vowing to live a blameless, honest life.[52] Even though John does not seem to have preached against Roman rule, he was executed by the authorities.

John seems to have been related in some way to Jesus of Nazareth, a Galilean healer and exorcist, who announced the imminent arrival of the kingdom of God at about the same time.[53] Anti-Roman feeling was especially rife during the great national festivals, and Jesus was executed by Pontius Pilate in about 30 CE when he went to Jerusalem to celebrate Passover there. But that did not end the Jesus movement. Some of his disciples were convinced that he had risen from the tomb; they claimed that they had seen him in visions and that his personal resurrection heralded the last days, when the righteous dead would rise from their graves. Jesus would soon return in glory to inaugurate the kingdom. Their leader in Jerusalem was Jesus's brother James, who was known as the *Tzaddik*, the 'Righteous One' and had good relations with both the Pharisees and the Essenes. But the movement also attracted Greek-speaking Jews in the diaspora and, most surprisingly, a significant number of 'God-fearers', non-Jews who were honorary members of the synagogues.

The Jesus movement was unusual in Palestine, where many of the sects were hostile to gentiles, but in the diaspora Jewish spirituality tended to be less exclusive and more open to Hellenistic ideas. There was a large Jewish community in

Alexandria in Upper Egypt, a city created by Alexander the Great, which had become a major centre of learning. Alexandrian Jews studied in the gynmnasium, spoke Greek and would achieve an interesting fusion of Greek and Jewish culture. But because few of them could read classical Hebrew, they could not understand the Torah. Indeed, even in Palestine, most Jews conversed in Aramaic rather than Hebrew, and needed a translation (*targum*) when the Law and the Prophets were read aloud in the synagogue.

Jews had started to translate their scriptures into Greek during the third century BCE on the island of Pharos, just off the coast of Alexandria.[54] This project was probably initiated by the Alexandrian Jews themselves but over the years it acquired a mythical aura. It was said that Ptolemy Philadelpus, the Greek king of Egypt, was so impressed by the Jewish scriptures that he wanted a translation for his library. So he asked the High Priest in Jerusalem to send six elders from each of the twelve tribes to Pharos. They all worked on the text together and produced a translation that was so perfect that everybody agreed that it must be preserved forever 'imperishable and unchanged'.[55] In honour of its seventy-plus translators, it was known as the Septuagint. Another legend seemed to have absorbed elements of the new Torah spirituality. The seventy translators proved to be 'prophets and priests of the mysteries': 'Sitting . . . in seclusion . . . they became as it were possessed, and under inspiration, wrote, not each several scribe something different, but the same word for word.'[56] Like the exegete, the translators were inspired and uttered the word of God in the same way as the biblical authors themselves.

This last story was told by the famous Alexandrian exegete Philo (70 BCE to 45CE), who came from a wealthy Jewish family in Alexandria.[57] Although Philo was a contemporary of John the Baptizer, Jesus and Hillel (one of the most distinguished of the early Pharisees), he inhabited a very different intellectual world. A Platonist, Philo produced a large number of commentaries on Genesis and Exodus, which transformed them into allegories of divine *logos* (reason). This was another species of *translatio*. Philo was trying to 'transfer' or 'carry over' the essence of the Semitic tales into another cultural idiom and place them in an alien conceptual framework.

Philo did not invent the allegorical method. The *grammatikoi* of Alexandria were already 'translating' Homer's epics into philosophical terms, so that Greeks who were trained in the rationalism of Plato and Aristotle could use the *Iliad* and *Odyssey* as part of their quest for wisdom. They based their *allegoria* on numerology and etymology. Besides its everyday connotation, every name had a deeper, symbolic meaning that expressed its eternal, Platonic form. By means of reflection and study, a critic could discover this deeper significance and thus transform the Homeric stories into allegories of moral philosophy. Jewish exegetes had already started to apply this method to the Bible, which seemed barbarous and incomprehensible to their Greek trained minds. They consulted manuals that gave Greek translations of Hebrew names. Adam, for example, became *nous* (natural reason); Israel, *psyche* (soul); and Moses, *sophia* (wisdom). This method threw an entirely new light on the biblical narratives. Did the characters live up to their names? What did a particular story reveal about the human dilemma? How could a reader apply it to his own search for insight?

In applying this method to the biblical narratives, Philo did not think he was distorting the original. He took the literal meaning of these stories very seriously,[58] but like Daniel he was looking for something fresh. There was more to a story than its literal meaning. As a Platonist, Philo believed that the timeless dimension of reality was more 'real' than its physical or historical dimension. So while the Jerusalem temple was undoubtedly an actual building, its architecture symbolized the cosmos; the temple was, therefore, also an eternal manifestation of the God who was Truth. Philo wanted to show that the biblical tales were what the Greeks called *mythos*. These events had happened in the real world at a particular moment, but they also had a dimension that transcended time. Unless they were liberated from their historical context and became a spiritual reality in the lives of the faithful, they could have no religious function. The process of *allegoria* 'translated' the deeper meaning of these stories into the inner life of the reader.

Allegoria was a term used by rhetoricians to describe a discourse that meant something different from its surface meaning. Philo preferred to call his method *hyponoia*, 'higher/deeper thought', because he was trying to reach a more fundamental level of truth. He also liked to speak of his exegesis as a 'conversion' of both the text and the interpreter. The text had to be 'turned around' (*trepain*).[59] When the interpreter was struggling with an obscure piece of writing, he had, as it were, to twist it this way and that, bringing it closer to the light to see it more clearly. Sometimes he had to change his own position in order to stand in a correct relation to the text and 'change his mind'.

Trepain revealed many different levels of a story, but Philo insisted that the exegete must find a central thread which ran through all his readings. He wrote four theses on the story of Cain and Abel in an attempt to discover its underlying philosophical significance. Eventually, he decided that its main theme was the battle between love of self and love of God. 'Cain' meant 'possession'. Cain wanted to keep everything for himself, and his chief aim was to serve his own interests. 'Abel' meant 'One who refers everything to God'. These qualities were present in every single individual and were constantly at war within him.[60] In another 'conversion', the story illustrated the conflict between true and false eloquence: Abel could not reply to Cain's specious arguments, but remained tongue-tied and helpless until his brother murdered him. This, Philo explained, was what happened when egotism got out of hand and destroyed the love of God within us. As mediated by Philo, Genesis gave to the Greek educated Jews of Alexandria a structure and symbolism that enabled them to contemplate difficult but basic truths about the spiritual life.

Philo also refined the biblical conception of God, which could seem hopelessly anthropomorphic to a Platonist. 'The apprehension of me is something more than human nature, yea, more even than the whole heaven and universe, will be able to contain,' he made God tell Moses.[61] Philo made the enormously important distinction between God's *ousia*, his essence, which was entirely incomprehensible to human beings, and his activities (*energeiaei*) and powers (*dynameis*) that we *can* apprehend in the world. There was nothing about God's *ousia* in the scripture; we only read about his powers, one of which was the Word or Logos of God, the rational design that structures the universe.[62] Like Ben Sirah, Philo believed that when we caught a glimpse of the Logos in creation and the Torah, we were taken beyond the reach of discursive reason to a rapturous recognition that God was 'higher than a way of thinking, more precious than anything that is merely thought'.[63]

It was, Philo argued, foolish to read the first chapter of Genesis literally and to imagine that the world had been created in six days. The number 'six' was a symbol of perfection. He noticed that there were two quite different creation stories in Genesis, and decided that P's account in Chapter One described the creation of the Logos, the masterplan of the universe that was God's 'first born',[64] and that J's more earthy account in Chapter Two symbolized the fashioning of the material universe by the *demiourgos*, the divine 'craftsman' in Plato's *Timaeus*, who had arranged the raw materials of the universe to establish an ordered cosmos.

Philo's exegesis was not simply a clever manipulation of names and numbers but a spiritual practice. Like any

Platonist, he experienced knowledge as remembrance, as known to him already at some profound level of his being. As he delved beneath the literal meaning of a biblical narrative and uncovered its deep philosophical principle, he experienced a shock of recognition. The story became suddenly fused with a truth that was a part of himself. Sometimes he struggled grimly with his books and seemed to make no progress, but then, almost without warning, he experienced rapture, like a priest in one of the ecstatic mystery cults:

> I . . . have suddenly become full, the ideas descending like snow, so that under the impact of divine possession, I have been filled with Corybantic frenzy and become ignorant of everything, place, people, past, present, myself, what was said and what was written. For I acquired expression, ideas, an enjoyment of life, sharp-sighted vision, exceedingly distinct clarity of objects such as might occur through the eyes as a result of clearest display.[65]

In the year of Philo's death, there were pogroms against the Jewish community in Alexandria. Throughout the Roman empire, there was widespread fear of Jewish insurgency, and in 66 CE a group of Jewish zealots orchestrated a rebellion in Palestine that, incredibly, managed to hold the Roman armies at bay for four years. Fearing that the rebellion would spread among the Jewish communities of the diaspora, the authorities were determined to crush it ruthlessly. In 70 the emperor Vespasian finally conquered Jerusalem. When the Roman soldiers broke into the temple's inner courts, they found six thousand Jewish zealots there, ready to fight to the death. When they saw the temple catch fire, a terrible cry arose. Some flung themselves on to the Romans' swords; others hurled themselves into the flames. Once the temple had gone, the Jews gave up and showed no interest in defending the rest of the city but watched helplessly as Titus's officers efficiently demolished what was left of the city.[66] For centuries, the temple had stood at the heart of the Jewish world and was central to Jewish religion. Once again it had been destroyed, but this time it would not be rebuilt. Only two of the Jewish sects that had proliferated during the Late Second Temple period were able to find a way forward. The first to do so was the Jesus movement, which was inspired by the disaster to write a wholly new set of scriptures.

CHAPTER 3

Gospel

We have no idea what Christianity would have been like if the
Romans had not destroyed the temple. Its loss reverberates
throughout the scriptures that comprise the New Testament,
many of which were written in response to this tragedy.[1]
During the Late Second Temple period, the Jesus movement
had been just one of a multitude of fiercely competing sects. It
had some unusual features, but, like several of the other
groups, the first Christians regarded themselves as the true
Israel, and had no intention of breaking away from Judaism.
Even though we have little first-hand knowledge, we can
make an educated guess about the history of the group
during the forty years that had elapsed since Jesus was executed by Pontius Pilate.

Jesus himself remains an enigma. There have been interesting attempts to uncover the figure of the 'historical' Jesus, a
project that has become something of a scholarly industry.
But the fact remains that the only Jesus we really know is the
Jesus described in the New Testament, which was not interested in scientifically objective history. There are no other
contemporary accounts of his mission and death. We cannot

even be certain why he was crucified. The gospel accounts indicate that he was thought to be the king of the Jews. He was said to have predicted the imminent arrival of the kingdom of heaven, but also made it clear that it was not of this world. In the literature of the Late Second Temple period, there had been hints that a few people were expecting a righteous king of the House of David to establish an eternal kingdom, and this idea seems to have become more popular during the tense years leading up to the war. Josephus, Tacitus and Suetonius all note the importance of revolutionary religiosity, both before and after the rebellion.[2] There was now keen expectation in some circles of a *meshiah* (in Greek, *christos*), an 'anointed' king of the House of David, who would redeem Israel. We do not know whether Jesus claimed to be this messiah – the gospels are ambiguous on this point.[3] Other people rather than Jesus himself may have made this claim on his behalf.[4] But after his death some of his followers had seen him in visions that convinced them that he had been raised from the tomb – an event that heralded the general resurrection of all the righteous when God would inaugurate his rule on earth.[5]

Jesus and his disciples came from Galilee in northern Palestine. After his death they moved to Jerusalem, probably to be on hand when the kingdom arrived, since all the prophecies declared that the temple would be the pivot of the new world order.[6] The leaders of their movement were known as 'the Twelve': in the kingdom, they would rule the twelve tribes of the reconstituted Israel.[7] The members of the

Jesus movement worshipped together every day in the temple,[8] but they also met for communal meals, in which they affirmed their faith in the kingdom's imminent arrival.[9] They continued to live as devout, orthodox Jews. Like the Essenes, they had no private property, shared their goods equally, and dedicated their lives to the last days.[10] It seems that Jesus had recommended voluntary poverty and special care for the poor; that loyalty to the group was to be valued more than family ties; and that evil should be met with non-violence and love.[11] Christians should pay their taxes, respect the Roman authorities, and must not even contemplate armed struggle.[12] Jesus's followers continued to revere the Torah,[13] keep the Sabbath,[14] and the observance of the dietary laws was a matter of extreme importance to them.[15] Like the great Pharisee Hillel, Jesus's older contemporary, they taught a version of the Golden Rule, which they believed to be the bedrock of the Jewish faith: 'So always treat others as you would like them to treat you; that is the message of the Law and the Prophets.'[16]

Like the Essenes, the members of the Jesus group seem to have had an ambiguous relationship with the temple. Jesus was said to have predicted that Herod's magnificent shrine would soon be laid waste. 'You see these great buildings?' he asked his disciples. 'Not a single stone will be left on another; everything will be destroyed.'[17] At his trial, it was claimed that he had vowed to destroy the temple and rebuild it in three days. But like the Essenes, Jesus's followers continued to pray in the temple and in this respect were in tune with other strands of Late Second Temple piety.

In other ways, however, Christianity was highly eccentric and controversial. There was no general expectation that the messiah would die and rise again. Indeed, the manner of Jesus's death was a source of embarrassment. How could a man who had died like a common criminal have been God's Anointed? Many regarded the messianic claims for Jesus as scandalous.[18] The movement also lacked the moral rigour of some of the other sects: it claimed that sinners, prostitutes and those who collected the Roman taxes would enter the kingdom ahead of the priests.[19] Christian missionaries preached the gospel or 'good news' of Jesus's imminent return in marginal and religiously dubious regions of Palestine, such as Samaria and Gaza. They also established congregations in the diaspora – in Damascus, Phoenicia, Cilicia and Antioch[20] – where they made an important breakthrough.

Even though the missionaries preached in the first instance to their fellow Jews, they found that they were also attracting gentiles, especially among the God-fearers.[21] In the diaspora, Jews welcomed these pagan sympathizers, and the huge outer court of Herod's new temple had been deliberately designed to accommodate crowds of gentiles who liked to participate in the Jewish festivals. The pagan worshippers had not become monotheists. They continued to worship other gods and participate in the local cults, and most Jews did not object to this, since God had only demanded exclusive worship of Israel. But if a gentile converted to Judaism, he had to be circumcised, observe the whole Torah and eschew idol worship. So the arrival of significant numbers of gentile converts in their congregations put the leaders of the Jesus sect in a quandary. Nobody seems to have felt that gentiles should be excluded, but there was considerable disagreement about the terms on which they could be admitted. Some believed that gentile Christians should convert to Judaism, take on the Torah and face the dangerous ordeal of circumcision, but others felt that, since the present world order was passing away, conversion was unnecessary. The debate became heated but eventually it was agreed that those gentiles who accepted Jesus as messiah need not convert to Judaism. They must simply shun idolatry and follow a modified version of the dietary rules.[22]

But instead of seeing these gentile converts as problematic, some enthusiasts were actually seeking them out and undertaking ambitious missions to the gentile world. Peter, one of the Twelve, had made converts in the Roman garrison town of Caesarea; Barnabas, a Greek-speaking Jew from Cyprus, had many gentiles in his *ekklesia* (church) in Antioch,[23] the city where those who believed that Jesus was the *christos* were first given the name of 'Christians'.[24] Somebody – we have no idea who – had even founded a church in Rome. Some of the Jerusalem congregation of Christians, especially Jesus's brother, James, found this disconcerting. These gentiles were showing a truly impressive commitment. Many Jews regarded pagans as chronically addicted to vicious habits:[25] the fact that so many of them were able to observe the high moral standards of their Jewish sect suggested that God must be at work among them. Why was he doing this? The gentile converts were prepared to cut themselves off entirely from the cults that were basic to social life in a pagan city and found themselves in an unenviable limbo; they could eat no meat that had been sacrificed to false gods, so socializing with neighbours and relatives had become well-nigh impossible.[26] They had lost their old world and did not feel wholly welcome in the new. And yet gentile converts kept arriving. What did this mean?

The Jewish Christians searched the scriptures for an answer. Like the Qumran community, they developed their own *pesher* exegesis, scouring the Torah and the prophets for prophetic references to Jesus and gentiles in the end time. They found that while some of the prophets had predicted that *goyim* would be forced against their will to worship the God of Israel, others believed that they would share in Israel's triumph and voluntarily throw away their idols.[27] So, some of the Christians decided, the presence of gentiles proved that these were indeed the last days. The process foretold by the prophets had begun; Jesus was truly the messiah and the kingdom was really at hand.

One of the most forceful champions of this new eschatology was Paul, a Greek-speaking Jew from Tarsus in Cilicia, who had joined the Christian movement some three years after Jesus's death. He had never known Jesus personally, and had initially been hostile to the sect, but had been converted by a revelation, which convinced him the *christos* had appointed him to be the apostle to the gentiles.[28] Paul travelled widely in the diaspora and founded congregations in

Syria, Asia Minor and Greece, determined to spread the gospel to the ends of the earth before Jesus returned. He wrote letters to his converts, answering their questions, exhorting them and explaining the faith. Paul did not think for a moment that he was writing 'scripture'; because he was convinced that Jesus would return in his own lifetime, he never imagined that future generations would pore over his epistles. He was regarded as a premier teacher, but was well aware that his explosive temperament meant that he was not universally popular. Nevertheless his letters to the churches in Rome, Corinth, Galatia, Philippi and Thessalonica[29] were preserved, and after his death in the early 60s, Christian writers who revered Paul wrote in his name and developed his ideas in letters to the churches in Ephesus and Colossae, and wrote supposedly posthumous letters addressed to Paul's associates, Timothy and Titus.

Paul insisted that his gentile converts renounce all pagan cults and worship only the God of Israel.[30] But he did not believe that they should convert to Judaism, because Jesus had already made them 'sons of God', without circumcision and the Torah. They must live as if the kingdom had already arrived: taking care of the poor and behaving with charity, sobriety, chastity and modesty. The fact that gentile Christians prophesied, performed miracles and, in the grip of ecstasy, spoke in strange tongues – all hallmarks of the messianic age[31] – proved that the spirit of God was alive in them and that the kingdom would arrive in the very near future.[32]

But Paul never suggested that Jews should cease to observe the Torah, because this would have put him outside the covenant. Israel had received the precious gift of the revelation of Sinai, the temple cult, and the privilege of being God's 'sons', enjoying a special intimacy with him, and Paul valued all this.[33] When he inveighed bitterly against 'Judaizers', he was not condemning either Jews or Judaism per se but those Jewish Christians who wanted the gentiles to be circumcised and observe the entire Torah. Like other sectarians in the Late Second Temple period, Paul was convinced that he alone was in possession of the truth.[34] In the messianic age, his mixed congregations of Jews and gentiles were the true Israel.

Paul also searched the scriptures, whose meaning, he believed, had changed since the coming of the *christos*. A psalm, which had seemed to refer to David, had actually been speaking of Jesus.[35] 'Indeed, everything that was written so long ago in the scriptures was meant to teach *us* something.'[36] The true significance of the Law and the prophets had only just come to light, so those Jews who refused to accept Jesus as the messiah no longer understood them. Sinai was no longer crucial. Hitherto, the people of Israel had not realized that the Mosaic covenant was only a temporary, interim measure, so their minds had been 'veiled' and they could not see what the scriptures had been about. The veil was still over their minds today, when they listened to the Torah in the synagogues. The Jews needed to be 'converted', turned around so that they saw correctly. Then they too would be transformed, their 'unveiled faces reflecting like mirrors the brightness of the Lord'.[37]

There was nothing heretical about this. Jews had been finding new meaning in older writings for a long time and the Qumran sect practised the same kind of *pesher*, finding a secret message in the scriptures that referrred to their own community. When Paul quoted biblical stories to instruct his converts, he interpreted them in a wholly novel way. Adam now prefigured Christ, but where Adam brought sin into the world, Jesus had put humanity into a correct relationship with God.[38] Abraham had now become not merely the father of the Jewish people but the ancestor of all the faithful. His 'faith' (Greek: *pistis,* a word which, it is important to note, should be translated as 'trust' rather than 'belief') had made him a model Christian, centuries before the coming of the messiah. When scripture praised Abraham's faith,[39] it was referring 'to *us* as well':[40] 'Scripture foresaw that God was going to use faith to justify the pagans, and proclaimed the Good News long ago, when Abraham was told: *In you all the pagans will be blessed.*'[41] When God commanded Abraham to abandon his concubine Hagar and their son Ishmael in the wilderness, this had been an *allegoria*: Hagar represented the Sinai covenant, which had enslaved Jews to the Law, while Sarah, Abraham's free-born wife, corresponded to the new covenant, which had liberated gentiles from Torah obligations.[42]

The author of the epistle to the Hebrews, who was probably writing at about the same time, was even more radical. He was trying to console a community of Jewish Christians who were beginning to lose heart by arguing forcefully that Christ had superseded the Torah, was more exalted than Moses [43] and that the sacrificial cult had simply foreshadowed Jesus's priestly act in giving his life for humanity.[44] In an extraordinary passage, the author saw the entire history of Israel as exemplifying the virtue of *pistis*, trust in 'realities that at present remain unseen'.[45] Abel, Enoch, Noah, Abraham, Moses, Gideon, Barak, Samson, Jephthah, David, Samuel and the prophets had all exhibited this 'faith': that had been their greatest, indeed their sole achievement.[46] But, the author concluded, 'they did not receive what was promised, since God made provision *for us* to have something better, and they were not to reach perfection except *with us*.'[47]

In this exegetical tour de force, the whole of Israelite history had been redefined, but in the process the old stories, which had been about far more than *pistis*, lost much of their rich complexity. Torah, temple and cult simply pointed to a future reality because God had always had something better in mind. Paul and the author of Hebrews showed future generations of Christians how to interpret the Hebrew Bible and make it their own. The other New Testament writers would develop this *pesher* and make it very difficult for Christians to see Jewish scripture as anything more than a prelude to Christianity.

The Jesus movement was becoming controversial even before the disaster of 70.[48] Christians, like all the other Jewish groups, were shocked to the core when they saw Herod's magnificent shrine reduced to a pile of burnt, stinking masonry. They may have dreamed of replacing Herod's temple but nobody had envisaged life without a temple at all. But the Christians also saw its destruction as an *apokalypsis,* a 'revelation' or 'unveiling' of a reality that had been there all along but had not been seen clearly before – namely that Judaism was finished. The temple ruins symbolized its tragic demise and were a sign that the end was approaching. God would now pull down the rest of the defunct world order and establish the kingdom.

The destruction of the first temple in 586 BCE had inspired an astonishing burst of creativity among the exiles in Babylon. The destruction of the second temple spurred a similar literary effort among the Christians. By the middle of the second century, nearly all the twenty-seven books of the New Testament had been completed. Communities were already quoting Paul's letters as though they were scripture,[49] and readings from one of the biographies of Jesus that were in circulation had become customary during Sunday worship. The gospels attributed to Matthew, Mark, Luke and John would eventually be selected for the canon, but there were many others. The Gospel of Thomas (*c.*150) was a collection of secret sayings of Jesus that imparted a redemptive 'knowledge' (*gnosis*). There were gospels, now lost, of the Ebionites, Nazarenes and Hebrews, that catered to Jewish-Christian congregations. There were many 'gnostic' gospels representing a form of Christianity that emphasized *gnosis* and distinguished a wholly spiritual God (who had sent Jesus as his envoy) from the *demiourgos,* who had created the corrupt material world.[50] Other writings did not survive: a gospel known to scholars as Q, because it was a source (German: *quelle*) for Matthew and Luke; various anthologies of Jesus's teachings; and an account of his trial, torture and death.

In the second century there was, however, no canon of prescribed texts because there was, as yet, no standard form of Christianity. Marcion (*c.*100–165), who held many gnostic ideas, wanted to sever the link between Christianity and the Hebrew scriptures, since he believed that Christianity was an entirely new religion. Marcion wrote his own gospel, based on the epistles of Paul and an expurgated reading of Luke. This made many Christians deeply uneasy about their relationship with Judaism. Irenaeus, bishop of Lyons (*c.*140–200) was appalled by both Marcion and the Gnostics and insisted on the link between the old scriptures and the new. He compiled a list of approved texts in which we see the future New Testament in embryo. It began with the gospels of Matthew, Mark, Luke and John – in that order – continued with the Acts of the Apostles (a history of the early church), included epistles by Paul, James, Peter and John, and concluded with two prophetic descriptions of the end: Revelation and the Shepherd of Hermas. But the canon was not fixed until well into the fourth century. Some of Irenaeus's chosen books, such as the Shepherd of Hermas, would be rejected and others, such as Hebrews and the epistle of Jude, would be added to Irenaeus's list.

The Christian scriptures were written at different times, in different regions and for very different audiences, but they shared a common language and set of symbols, derived from the Law and the Prophets as well as the Late Second Temple texts. They brought together ideas that originally had no connection with one another – son of God, son of man, messiah and kingdom – into a new synthesis.[51] The authors did not argue this logically but simply juxtaposed these images so repeatedly that they merged together in the reader's mind.[52] There was no uniform view of Jesus. Paul had called him the 'son of God', but had used the title in its traditional Jewish sense: Jesus was a human being who had a special relationship to God, like the ancient kings of Israel, and had been raised by him to uniquely high status.[53] Paul never claimed that Jesus *was* God. Matthew, Mark and Luke, who are known as the 'synoptics' because they 'see things together', also used the title 'son of God' in this way, but they also implied that Jesus was Daniel's 'son of man', which gave him an eschatological dimension.[54] John, who represented a different Christian tradition, saw Jesus as the incarnation of the Word and Wisdom of God which had existed before the creation of the world.[55] When the final editors of the New Testament put these texts together, they were not disturbed by these discrepancies. Jesus had become too immense a phenomenon in the minds of Christians to be tied to a single definition.

The title of 'messiah' was crucial. Once Jesus had been identified as God's 'anointed' (*christos*), the Christian writers gave the term a radically new meaning. They read the Hebrew scriptures in Greek and whenever they found a reference to a *christos* – be it a king, prophet or priest – they immediately interpreted it as a coded reference to Jesus. They were also attracted to the mysterious figure of the servant in Second Isaiah, whose suffering had redeemed the world. The servant had not been a messianic figure, but by constantly comparing the servant with Jesus *christos*, using the same 'blurring' technique, they established for the first time the idea of a suffering messiah. Thus three separate figures – servant, messiah and Jesus – became inseparable in the Christian imagination.[56]

So thorough was the Christians' *pesher* exegesis that there is scarcely a verse in the New Testament that did not refer to the older scriptures. The four evangelists seemed to use the Septuagint as another source for the biography of Jesus. As a result it is difficult to disentangle fact from exegesis. Did his executioners really give Jesus vinegar to drink and cast lots for his garments or was this incident suggested by certain verses from the Psalms?[57] Did Matthew tell the story of the virgin birth of Jesus simply because Isaiah had prophesied that a 'virgin' would conceive and bear a son called Immanu-El (the Septuagint translated the Hebrew *almah*, 'young woman' as *parthenos*, 'virgin')?[58] Some scholars have gone so far as to suggest that it would be possible to construct an entire gospel from the Jewish scriptures, without quoting a single word by Jesus himself.[59]

We do not know who wrote the gospels. When they first appeared, they circulated anonymously and were only later attributed to important figures in the early church.[60] The authors were Jewish Christians,[61] who wrote in Greek and lived in the Hellenistic cities of the Roman empire. They were not only creative writers – each with his own particular bias – but also skilled redactors who edited earlier material. Mark wrote in about 70; Matthew and Luke in the late 80s, and John in the late 90s. All four gospels reflect the terror and anxiety of this traumatic period. The Jewish people were in turmoil. The war with Rome had divided families and communities and all the different sects had to rethink their relationship with the temple tradition. But the *apokalypsis* of the ruined shrine seemed so compelling to the Christians that they felt inspired to proclaim the messiahship of Jesus, whose mission, they believed, had been bound up with the temple.

Mark, who was writing immediately after the war, was especially preoccupied by this theme. His community was in deep trouble. Christians had been accused of rejoicing at the temple's destruction, and Mark shows that members of his *ekklesia* were being beaten in the synagogues, dragged before the Jewish elders and universally vilified. Many had lost faith.[62] Jesus's teachings seemed to fall on stony ground and Christian leaders seemed as obtuse as the Twelve, who, in Mark's gospel, rarely understood Jesus.[63] There was a grim sense of painful rupture with mainstream Judaism. You could not patch an old garment with new cloth, Jesus warned: 'the patch pulls away from it, the new from the old, and the tear gets worse. And nobody puts new wine into old wineskins; if he does, the wine will burst the skins, and the wine is lost and the skins too!'[64] Discipleship meant suffering and an endless struggle with demonic forces. Christians must stay awake; they must be perpetually vigilant![65]

Paul, who wrote while the temple was still standing, had scarcely mentioned it; but the temple was central to Mark's vision of Jesus.[66] Its destruction was only the first stage in the imminent apocalypse.[67] Daniel had already foreseen this 'desolating sacrilege' long ago so the temple had been doomed.[68] Jesus was not a renegade, as his enemies claimed, but deeply in tune with the great figures of the past. He quoted Jeremiah and Isaiah to show that the temple had been intended for all the nations as well as for the Jews.[69] Mark's *ekklesia*, which admitted gentiles, had fulfilled these ancient prophecies but the temple had not conformed to God's plan. No wonder it had been destroyed.

Jesus's death was not a scandal, but had been foretold in the Law and the prophets:[70] it had been foreseen that he would be betrayed by one of his own followers[71] and deserted by his disciples.[72] Yet the gospel ended on a note of terror. When the women went to anoint the body, they found that the tomb was empty. Even though an angel told them that Jesus had risen, 'the women came out and ran away from the tomb because they were frightened out of their wits; and they said nothing to a soul, for they were afraid'.[73] Mark's story ended here, epitomizing the sense of fearful suspension that Christians experienced at this time. Yet Mark's terse, brutal tale was 'Good News', because the kingdom had 'already arrived'.[74]

But by the time Matthew was writing in the late 80s, these hopes were beginning to fade. Nothing had changed: how could the kingdom have come? Matthew replied that it was coming unobtrusively, and was working silently in the world like yeast in a batch of dough.[75] His community was frightened and angry. They were accused by their fellow Jews of abandoning the Torah and the prophets;[76] they had been flogged in the synagogues, dragged before tribunals of elders,[77] and expected to be tortured and killed before the End.[78] Matthew was, therefore, especially anxious to show that Christianity was not only in harmony with Jewish tradition but was its culmination. Almost every single event in Jesus's life had happened 'to fulfil the scriptures'. Like Ishmael, Samson and Isaac, his birth was announced by an angel.[79] His forty days of temptation in the desert paralleled the Israelites' forty years in the wilderness; Isaiah had foretold his miracles.[80] And – most importantly – Jesus was a great Torah teacher. He proclaimed the new law of the messianic age from a mountaintop[81] – like Moses – and insisted that he had come not to abolish but to complete the Law and the prophets.[82] Jews must now observe the Torah more stringently than ever before. It was no longer sufficient for Jews to refrain from murder; they must not even get angry. Not only was adultery forbidden; a man could not even look at a woman lustfully.[83] The old law of retaliation – eye for eye, tooth for tooth – was superseded: Jews must now turn the other cheek and love their enemies.[84] Like Hosea, Jesus argued that compassion was more important than ritual observance.[85] Like Hillel, he preached the Golden Rule.[86] Jesus was greater than Solomon, Jonah and the temple.[87] The Pharisees of

Matthew's day claimed that Torah study would introduce Jews to the divine presence (*Shekhinah*) that they had formerly encountered in the temple: 'If two sit together and words of Torah are between them, the Shekhinah rests between them.'[88] But Jesus promised: 'where two or three meet in my name, I shall be there with them.'[89] Christians would encounter the Shekhinah through Jesus who had now replaced the temple and the Torah.

Luke was the author of some portions of the Acts of the Apostles as well as the gospel. He too was anxious to show that Jesus and his followers were devout Jews but he also emphasized that the gospel was for everybody: Jews and gentiles; women as well as men; the poor; tax collectors; the good Samaritan and the prodigal son. Luke gives us a precious glimpse of the spiritual experience that their *pesher* exegesis gave to early Christians. He told an emblematic story of two of Jesus's disciples, who were walking from Jerusalem to Emmaus three days after the crucifixion.[90] Like many of the Christians in Luke's own time they were distraught and despondent, but on the road they fell in with a stranger, who asked them why they were so troubled. They explained that they were followers of Jesus and had been certain that he was the messiah. But he had been crucified and, to make matters worse, the women in their company were spreading wild tales of an empty tomb and a vision of angels. The stranger gently rebuked them: had they not realized that the messiah must suffer before entering his glory? Starting with Moses, he began to expound 'the full message' of the prophets. When the disciples arrived at their destination that evening, they begged the stranger to lodge with them, and when he broke bread at dinner they suddenly realized that all along they had been in the presence of Jesus, but their 'eyes had been held' from recognizing him. As he vanished from their sight, they recalled how their hearts had 'burned' within them when he had 'opened the scriptures'.

Christian *pesher* was a spiritual discipline, rooted in grief and bewilderment, which spoke directly to the heart and set it alight. Christians would gather 'in twos and threes' and discuss the relationship of the Law and the prophets to Jesus. As they conversed together, the texts 'opened' and yielded a momentary illumination. This would pass, just as Jesus vanished as soon as he had been recognized, but afterwards apparent contradictions locked together in a numinous intimation of wholeness. The stranger played a crucial role. When they confided in somebody they had never seen before, the disciples made an act of trust *(pistis)*. In Luke's *ekklesia*, Jews and gentiles found that by reaching out to the 'other', they experienced the Shekhinah, which, increasingly, they identified with their *christos*.

A number of churches in Asia Minor were developing a different understanding of Jesus, represented by the gospel and three epistles attributed to John and the eschatological book of Revelation. All these 'Joannine' texts saw Jesus as the incarnate Logos who had descended to earth as God's ultimate revelation.[91] Jesus was the Lamb of God, a sacrificial victim who took away the sins of the world, like the lambs ritually slaughtered in the temple at Passover.[92] They believed that their most important duty was to love one another,[93] but they did not reach out to the stranger. This community felt beleaguered and clung together in opposition to 'the world'.[94] The whole of existence seemed polarized into conflicting opposites: light against darkness, world against spirit, life against death, and good against evil. The churches had recently suffered a painful schism: some of their members had found their teachings 'intolerable' and 'stopped going with Jesus'.[95] The faithful saw these apostates as 'antichrists', filled with murderous hatred of the messiah.[96]

The members of this Christian sect were convinced that they alone were right and that the whole world was against them.[97] John's gospel in particular was addressing an 'in group', which had a private symbolism that was incomprehensible to outsiders. Constantly Jesus had to tell 'the Jews' that they would look for him and fail to find him: 'where I am you cannot come'.[98] His audience was continually baffled but because Jesus was God's ultimate revelation to the world, this lack of acceptance was a judgement: those who rejected him were the children of the devil and would remain in darkness.

For John, Judaism was well and truly over. He systematically depicted Jesus replacing every single one of God's major revelations to Israel. Henceforth the risen Logos would be the place where Jews would encounter the divine presence: Jesus the Logos would take over the function of the ruined temple, and become the place where Jews would encounter the divine presence.[99] When he walked out of the temple, the Shekhinah withdrew with him.[100] When he celebrated the festival of Sukkoth, during which water was ceremonially poured over the altar and the giant torches of the temple were set alight, Jesus – like Wisdom – cried aloud that *he* was the living water and the light of the world.[101] On the feast of Unleavened Bread, he claimed that *he* was the 'bread of life'. Not only was he greater than Moses[102] and Abraham, but he embodied the divine presence: he had the temerity to pronounce the forbidden name of God: 'before Abraham ever was, I Am [*Ani Waho*]'.[103] Unlike the synoptics, John never showed Jesus attracting non-Jewish converts. His *ekklesia* was probably entirely Jewish at the beginning and the apostates were probably Jewish Christians, who found the community's controversial and potentially blasphemous Christology 'intolerable'.[104]

The book of Revelation reveals the bitterness of Joannine Christianity. Here the dualism that was a recurrent motif in John's gospels became a cosmic battle against good and evil forces. Satan and his cohorts assailed Michael and his angelic army in heaven, while the wicked attacked the good on earth. It seemed to the troubled *ekklesia* that evil must prevail, but John of Patmos, the author of Revelation, insisted that God would intervene at the critical moment and vanquish their enemies. He had received a special 'revelation' (*apokalypsis*), which would 'unveil' the true state of affairs, so that the faithful would know how to conduct themselves during the last days. The apocalypse is informed, through and through, by fear: the church was terrified of the Roman empire, the local Jewish communities and rival Christian groups. But, the author assured them, eventually Satan would give his authority to a Beast, who would rise from the depths of the sea and demand universal obeisance. Then the Lamb would come to the rescue. Even though the Whore of Babylon arrived drunk with the blood of the Christian martyrs, angels would pour seven hideous plagues over the earth and the Word would ride into battle on a white horse, to fight the Beast and fling him into a pit of fire. For a thousand years, Jesus would rule the earth with his saints, but then God would release Satan from prison. There would be more destruction, more battles until peace was restored and the New Jerusalem descended from heaven like a bride to meet the Lamb.

Like all the Joannine writings, Revelation is deliberately obscure, its symbols unintelligible to outsiders. It is a toxic book and, as we shall see, would appeal to people who, like the Joannine churches, felt alienated and resentful. It was also controversial and some Christians were reluctant to include it in the canon. But when the final editors decided to place it at the end of the New Testament, it became the triumphant finale of their *pesher* exegesis of the Hebrew Scriptures. It transformed the historical story of the rise of Christianity into a future-oriented apocalypse. The New Jerusalem would replace the old: 'I saw no temple in the city, for its temple was the sovereign Lord God and the Lamb.' Judaism and its most sacred symbols had been replaced by a victorious, militant Christianity.[105]

A thread of hatred runs through the New Testament. It is inaccurate to call the Christian scriptures anti-Semitic, as the authors were themselves Jewish, but many of them had become disenchanted with Jewish religion. Paul did not share this hostility towards Judaism, but much of the New Testament reflected the widespread suspicion, anxiety and turbulence of the period immediately after the destruction of the temple, when the Jews were so bitterly divided. In their anxiety to reach out to the gentile world, the synoptics were too eager to absolve the Romans of their responsibility for Jesus's execution and claimed, with increasing stridency, that the Jews must shoulder the blame. Even Luke, who had the most positive view of Judaism, made it clear that there was a good Israel (represented by Jesus's followers) and a 'bad Israel', epitomized by the self-righteous Pharisee.[106] In the gospels of Matthew and John, this bias had become more entrenched. Matthew made the Jewish crowd cry aloud for Jesus's death: 'His blood be upon us and upon our children',[107] words that for centuries inspired the pogroms that made anti-Semitism an incurable disease in Europe.

Matthew was particularly incensed by the Pharisees: they were self-important hypocrites, obsessed with the letter of the law to the utter neglect of its spirit; they were 'blind guides', a 'brood of vipers', fanatically intent on the destruction of the Christian churches.[108] John too denounced the Pharisees as malicious, oppressive and chronically addicted to evil; it was the Pharisees who gathered information against Jesus and engineered his death.[109] Why this vitriolic hatred of Pharisees? After the destruction of the temple, the Christians had been the first to make a concerted effort to become the authentic Jewish voice and initially they seemed to have had no significant rivals. But by the 80s and 90s, Christians were becoming uncomfortably aware that something extraordinary was happening: the Pharisees were initiating an astonishing revival.

CHAPTER 4

Midrash

During the last days of the siege of Jerusalem, it was said that in order to get past the Jewish zealots who were guarding the gates, Rabbi Johanan ben Zakkai, leader of the Pharisees, was smuggled out of the city in a coffin. Throughout the war, he had repeatedly argued that rebellion against Rome was not only futile but self-destructive, and that the preservation of religion was more important than political independence. Once outside the city, he made his way to the Roman camp and asked Vespasian to spare the coastal city of Yavneh, south-west of Jerusalem, as a safe haven for Jewish scholars. After the destruction of Jerusalem and its temple, Pharisees, scribes and priests began to congregate at Yavneh, which for over sixty years became the centre of a remarkable religious synthesis. The story of Johanan's dramatic escape has obvious apocryphal elements, but the powerful image of the rabbi rising from the coffin outside the doomed city was prophetic, since Yavneh ensured the resurrection of a new version of temple Judaism from the ruins of the old.

We do not know very much about the Yavneh period, however.[1] The coalition of scholars was led by the Pharisees, initially by R. Johanan and his two gifted pupils, R. Eliezer and R. Joshua, and later by R. Akiba. Long before the tragedy of 70, the Pharisees had encouraged the laity to live as though they were serving in the temple, so that each hearth became an altar, each householder a priest. Yet the Pharisees had continued to worship in the real temple as well and never imagined that Jews would one day have to manage without it. Even during their years at Yavneh, they seem to have believed that Jews would be able to build a new temple, but their ideology was well suited to the post–70 world because they had, as it were, constructed their daily lives around a virtual temple which became the focus of their spirituality. Now R. Johanan and his successors would begin to build this imaginary shrine in more detail.

The first task of the rabbis at Yavneh was to collect and preserve all the available memories, practices and rituals of traditional religion, so that when the temple was rebuilt the cult could be resumed. Other Jews might plan new rebellions against the Roman empire; Christians could insist that Jesus had replaced the temple; but together with the scribes and priests who had joined them at Yavneh, the Pharisees would make a heroic effort to keep every single detail of the lost shrine in their minds, at the same time as they revised the Torah to meet the needs of their drastically altered world. It would take the Pharisees many years to become the undisputed leaders of the new Judaism. But by the late 80s and 90s, as we have seen, some of the Christians had begun to feel seriously threatened by Yavneh, whose vision seemed more compelling and authentic to many Jews than the gospel. Yet in fact the Pharisaic enterprise had much in common with early Christian churches. The Pharisees would also search the scriptures, invent another form of exegesis, and compose new sacred texts – even though they would never claim that these formed a 'New Testament'.

When two or three of the Pharisees studied the Torah together, they found – like the Christians – that the Shekhinah was in their midst. At Yavneh, the Pharisees pioneered a spirituality in which Torah study replaced the temple as the chief means of encountering the divine presence. But, unlike modern biblical scholars, they were not interested in recovering the original significance of a given scriptural passage. Like Daniel, they were looking for fresh meaning. In their view, there was no single authoritative reading of scripture. As events unfolded on earth, even God had to keep studying his own Torah in order to discover its full significance.[2] The rabbis called their exegesis *midrash*, which, as we saw in Chapter 2, derived from the verb *darash*: to investigate; to seek. The meaning of a text was not self-evident. The exegete had to go in search of it, because every time a Jew confronted the Word of God in scripture, it signified something different. Scripture was inexhaustible. The rabbis liked to point out that King Solomon used three thousand parables to illustrate every single verse of the Torah, and could give a thousand and five interpretations of each parable – which meant that there were three million, fifteen thousand possible expositions of each unit of scripture.[3]

Indeed, a text that could not be radically reinterpreted to meet the needs of the day was dead; the written words of scripture had to be revitalized by constant exegesis. Only then could they reveal the divine presence latent within God's Torah. Midrash was not a purely intellectual pursuit and study was never an end in itself: it had to inspire practical action in the world. The exegete had a duty to apply the Torah to his particular situation and make it speak to the condition of every single member of his community. The goal was never simply to clarify an obscure passage but to address the burning issues of the day. You did not understand a text until you had found a way of putting it into practice.[4] The rabbis called scripture *miqra*: a 'summons' that called the Jewish people to action.

Above all, midrash must be guided by the principle of compassion. In the early years of the first century, the great Pharisaic sage Hillel had come from Babylonia to Jerusalem, where he had preached alongside his rival Shammai, whose version of Pharisaism was more stringent. It was said that one day a pagan had approached Hillel and promised to convert to Judaism if he could summarize the entire Torah while he stood on one leg. Standing on one leg, Hillel replied: 'What is hateful to yourself, do not to your fellow man. That is the whole of the Torah and the remainder is but commentary. Go study it.'[5] This was an astonishing and deliberately controversial piece of midrash. The essence of Torah was the disciplined refusal to inflict pain on another human being. Everything else in the scriptures was merely 'commentary', a gloss on the Golden Rule. At the end of his exegesis, Hillel uttered a *miqra,* a call to action: 'Go study!' When they studied the Torah, rabbis should attempt to reveal the core of compassion that lay at the heart of all the legislation and narratives in the scriptures – even if this meant twisting the original meaning of the text. The rabbis of Yavneh were followers of Hillel. R. Akiba, the leading sage of the later Yavneh period, declared that the greatest principle of Torah was the commandment in Leviticus: 'Thou shalt love thy neighbour as thyself.'⁶ Only one of the rabbis contested this, arguing that the simple words 'This is the roll of Adam's descendants' were more important because they revealed the unity of the entire human race.⁷

R. Johanan had been taught by the pupils of Hillel, and immediately after the catastrophe of 70 he applied this insight to the grim realities of the post-temple world. One day, he had walked past the burnt ruins of the temple with R. Joshua, who had cried out in distress: how could Jews atone for their sins now that they could no longer perform the sacrificial rituals there? R. Johanan consoled him by quoting words that God had spoken to Hosea: 'Grieve not, we have atonement equal to the temple, the doing of loving deeds, as it is said: "*I desire love* (hesed) *and not sacrifice*".'⁸ The practice of compassion was a priestly act that would atone for sins more effectively than the old expiatory rites, and it could be performed by ordinary lay folk, instead of being the preserve of an exclusive priestly caste. But R. Johanan's exegesis would probably have surprised Hosea. If he had looked closely at the original context, the rabbi would have realized that God had not been speaking to Hosea of charitable deeds. *Hesed* should properly be translated as 'loyalty' rather than 'love'. God had not been concerned with the kindness that human beings should show to one another, but with the cultic fealty that Israel owed to *him*.

But this would not have disturbed R. Joshua, who was not attempting a historical exposition of the text, but seeking to console his traumatized community. There was no need to mourn the temple too extravagantly: practical charity could replace the old ceremonial ritual. He was building a *horoz*, a 'chain' that linked together quotations that originally had no connection to each other but which, once 'enchained', revealed their integral unity.[9] He began by citing a well-known maxim of Simeon the Just, a revered high priest of the third century BCE:[10] 'Upon three things the world is based: upon the Torah, upon the temple service, and upon the doing of loving deeds.'[11] Like the quotation from Hosea, this proved that practical compassion was as important as the Torah and temple worship. Loving kindness was, as it were, an essential leg of the tripod that supported the entire world, and now that the temple had gone, Torah and charity were more important than ever before. To back up this insight, R. Johanan quoted – or slightly misquoted – the psalmist: 'The world is built by love.'[12] In juxtaposing these three unrelated texts, R. Johanan had shown that, as Hillel claimed, charity was indeed central to scripture: it was the exegete's job to elucidate this hidden principle and bring it to light.

The *horoz* was essential to rabbinic midrash. It gave the

exegete an intuition of wholeness and completeness that was similar to the *shalom* that Jews had found in the temple and the *coincidenia oppositorum* that Christians experienced in their *pesher* exegesis. Like the Christians, the rabbis were reading the Law and the prophets differently, giving them a meaning that often bore little relationship to the original authors' intention. R. Akiba perfected this innovative midrash. His pupils liked to tell a story about him. The fame of R. Akiba's genius reached Moses in heaven, and one day he decided to come down to earth to attend one of his classes. He sat in the eighth row behind the other students, and to his dismay found that R. Akiba's exposition was incomprehensible to him, even though it was said to have been part of the revelation he had received on Mount Sinai. 'My sons have surpassed me,' Moses mused ruefully but proudly as he made his way back to heaven. But why, he asked, had God entrusted the Torah to him, when he could have chosen a man of Akiba's intellectual stature?[13] Another rabbi put it more succinctly: 'Matters that had not been disclosed to Moses were disclosed to R. Akiba and his colleagues.'[14] Revelation had not happened once and for all on Mount Sinai; it was an ongoing process and would continue for as long as skilled exegetes sought out the inexhaustible wisdom hidden in the text. Scripture contained the sum of human knowledge in embryonic form: it was possible to find 'everything in it.'[15] Sinai had just been the beginning. Indeed, when God had given the Torah to Moses, he knew that future generations would have to complete it. The written Torah was not a finished object; human beings were supposed to use their ingenuity to bring it to perfection, just as they extracted flour from wheat and weaved a garment from flax.[16]

Some of the rabbis thought that R. Akiba went too far. His colleague R. Ishmael accused him of imposing his own meaning on scripture: 'Indeed, you say to the text "Be silent until I interpret".'[17] A good midrash kept as close to the original meaning as possible and R. Ishmael contended that it should only be changed when absolutely necessary.[18] R. Ishmael's method was respected, but R. Akiba's carried the day because it kept scripture open. To a modern scholar, this method seems transgressive; midrash regularly goes too far, seems to violate the integrity of the text, and seeks meaning at the expense of the original.[19] But the rabbis believed that because scripture was the word of God, it was infinite. Any meaning that they discovered in a text had been intended by God if it yielded fresh insight and benefited the community.

When they expounded Torah, the rabbis regularly amended the words, telling their students, 'don't read this . . . but that.'[20] By altering the text in this way, they sometimes introduced into scripture a note of compassion that had been absent from the original. This happened when R. Meir, one of R. Akiba's most distinguished pupils, discussed a ruling in Deuteronomy:

> If a man guilty of a capital offence is put to death and you hang him on a tree, his body must not remain on the tree overnight; you must bury him the same day, for one who

has been hanged is accursed of God, [*qilelat Elohim*] and you
must not defile the land that Yahweh your God has given
you for your inheritance.[21]

There was self-interest in this legislation, because if the
Israelites polluted the land they would lose it. But R. Meir
suggested a new reading, based on a pun: 'Do not read *qilelat
Elohim*,' he said, 'but *qallat Elohim* ("the pain of God")'. R. Meir
explained that the new text revealed the pathos of God, who
suffered with his creatures: 'When a person is in grave
trouble, what does the Shekhinah say? It says, as it were: "My
head is in pain, my arm is in pain".'[22] It was possible to find
love and the Golden Rule in the most unlikely parts of the
Torah. As a modern scholar remarks: 'the midrashic shuttle
weaves a texture of compassion around a stern legal rule';
because the rabbi invited his pupils to change the text, they
too became involved in the active process of endless reinterpretation.[23] The same applied to R. Judah's exposition of
God's words to Zechariah: 'Whoever hurts you [i.e. Israel] is
like one who hurts his own (*eyno*) eye.' 'Do not read *eyno*
("his"), but *eyni* ("my") eye,' R. Judah instructed his colleagues; the text now claimed that a loving God shared the
pain of his own people: 'Whoever hurts Israel is like one who
hurts My [*eyni*] eye.'[24]

There could be no definitive interpretation of scripture.
This point was made in the very early days at Yavneh, when
R. Eliezer was engaged in an intractable argument with his
colleagues about a legal ruling (*halakha*) in the Torah. When

they refused to accept his opinion, R. Eliezer asked God to back him up with some miracles, and – *mirabile dictu* – a carob tree moved four hundred cubits of its own accord; water in a conduit flowed uphill; and the walls of the house of studies shook so violently that the building seemed about to collapse. But the other rabbis were not impressed by this show of supernatural force. In desperation, R. Eliezer asked for a *bat qol* ('voice from heaven') to adjudicate and the divine voice obligingly declared: 'What have you against R. Eliezer? The Halakah is always as he says.' But Rabbi Joshua quoted a verse from Deuteronomy: 'It is not in heaven'.[25] The Torah was no longer confined to the celestial world; once it had been promulgated on Mount Sinai, it no longer belonged to God but was the inalienable possession of every single Jew. So, commented a later rabbi, 'We pay no attention to a heavenly voice.' And furthermore, it had been decreed at Sinai: 'By a majority you are to decide',[26] so R. Eliezer, a minority of one, could not override the popular vote. When God heard that his opinion had been overruled, he laughed and said: 'My children have conquered me.'[27]

Any limitations in a midrash were due to the weakness of the exegete, who lacked the ability to make sense of a text in a given situation or to find fresh meaning.[28] The Golden Rule also meant any midrash that spread hatred was illegitimate. A mean-spirited interpretation that poured scorn on other sages and sought to discredit them must be avoided.[29] The purpose of midrash was to serve the community, not to inflate the ego of the exegete, who should, R. Meir explained, study the Torah for 'its own sake', not for his own benefit. A good midrash, the rabbi continued, sowed affection rather than discord, because anyone who studied scripture properly was full of love and brought joy to others: he 'loves the Divine Presence and all creatures, makes the Divine Presence glad and makes glad all creatures'. Torah study transformed the exegete, robing him with humility and fear, making him upright, pious, righteous and faithful, so that everybody around him benefited. 'The mysteries of the Torah are revealed to him,' R. Meir concluded, 'he becomes like an over-flowing fountain and ceaseless torrent . . . And it makes him great and lifts him above the entire creation.'[30]

'Does not my word burn like fire?' Yahweh had asked Jeremiah.[31] Midrash released the divine spark that lay dormant in the written words of the Torah. One day, R. Akiba heard that his pupil Ben Azzai was caught in a nimbus of flame that flashed around him while he was expounding the Torah. He hurried off to investigate and Ben Azzai told him that he had simply been practising *horoz*:

I was only linking up the words of the Torah with one another and then with the words of the Prophets, and the Prophets with the Writings, and the words rejoiced, as when they were delivered at Sinai, and they were sweet, as at their original utterance.[32]

The Sinai revelation was renewed every time a Jew confronted the text, opened himself to it, and applied it to his own situation. Like Ezekiel, the midrashist found that when he had absorbed it and made it uniquely his own, the Word of God tasted sweet as honey and set the world aflame.

Like several of the early rabbis, Ben Azzai was a mystic. They liked to contemplate Ezekiel's account of his vision of God's 'glory' (*kavod*) while performing exercises – fasting, putting their heads between their knees, and whispering God's praises – that put them into an altered mental state. Then it seemed as though they flew through the seven heavens until they beheld the 'glory' on its heavenly throne. But this mystical journey was fraught with danger. A very early story tells how four of the sages tried to 'enter the *pardes*', a symbolic 'orchard' that recalled the paradisal garden of Eden. Ben Azzai managed to arrive at this spiritual state before his death, but two of the other mystics were spiritually and mentally damaged by the experience. Only R. Akiba had the maturity to emerge unscathed and live long enough to tell the tale.[33] R. Akiba himself found the Song of Songs especially conducive to this *ekstasis*; it not only signified but actually made the love that God felt for his people a burning reality in the heart of the mystic. 'The whole of time is not worth the day on which the Song of Songs was given to Israel,' R. Akiba declared. 'All the Writings (*Kethuvim*) are holy. The Song of Songs is the Holy of Holies.'[34] In R. Akiba's interior world, the Song had replaced the inner sanctum of the temple, where the divine presence had rested on its ancient throne.

Other rabbis experienced the Spirit of Yahweh as an

electrifying divine presence within and around them. On one occasion, when R. Johanan had discussed Ezekiel's vision with his pupils, a fire descended from heaven and a *bat qol* declared that he had a special mission from God.[35] But the Holy Spirit in the form of fire also descended upon R. Johanan and R. Eliezer – just as it descended upon Jesus's disciples at Pentecost – while they were engaged in *horoz,* linking the scriptural verses together.[36]

At this stage, the rabbis had not yet committed their insights to writing. It seems that they learned the traditions they were accummulating by heart and transmitted them orally, although R. Akiba and R. Meir arranged the material in blocks that made them easier to memorize.[37] It seemed risky to write down this precious lore. A book could be burned like the temple or fall into the hands of the Christians, and would be safer in the minds and hearts of the sages. But the rabbis also valued the spoken word for its own sake. Graduates of Yavneh, who had managed to learn these oral texts by rote, were called *tannaim,* 'repeaters'. They spoke the Torah aloud and developed their midrash in conversation. The House of Studies was noisy with lively discussion and clamorous debate.

But by 135 the rabbis felt the need for a more permanent written record. In an attempt to drag the Jews into the modern Graeco-Roman world, the emperor Hadrian announced that he intended to plough the ruins of Jerusalem into the ground and build a modern city on the sacred site. Circumcision, the training of rabbis and the teaching of Torah were all forbidden by law. The hard-headed Jewish soldier Simeon bar Koseba led a revolt against Rome and when he managed to oust the Tenth Legion from Jerusalem, R. Akiba hailed him as the messiah. R. Akiba himself refused to stop teaching and, it is said, was executed by the Roman authorities. Eventually Bar Koseba's rebellion was brutally quashed by Hadrian in 135.[38] Thousands of Jews had died; the new city was built, though the temple ruins remained; Jews were forbidden to reside in Judah and were confined to the north of Palestine. The academy at Yavneh was disbanded and the rabbinic cadre dispersed. But the situation improved under the emperor Antoninus Pius (158–161), who relaxed the anti-Jewish legislation, and the rabbis regrouped at Usha in Lower Galilee.

The disastrous outcome of the Bar Koseba rebellion had horrified the rabbis. A few radicals, such as the mystic R. Simeon ben Yohai, continued to campaign against Rome, but most withdrew from politics. The rabbis were now wary of messianism and discouraged the practice of mysticism, preferring a disciplined life of study to dangerous flights of the spirit. At Usha they settled the canon of the Hebrew Bible, by making a final selection of the Writings (*Kethuvim*) of the Second Temple period.[39] They chose the more sober historical works and rejected apocalyptic fantasies, selecting Chronicles, Esther, Ezra and Nehemiah; and from the Wisdom genre: Proverbs, Ecclesiastes, the Song of Songs and Job, but not Ben Sirah. The Bible, which now consisted of the *Torah*, *Neviim* ('Prophets') and *Kethuvim*, became known as the TaNaKh.

Between 135 and 160 the rabbis also started to create an entirely new scripture, which they called the Mishnah, an anthology of the traditions that the rabbis had collected at Yavneh, arranged according to the scheme of R. Akiba and R. Meir, which they now committed to writing.[40] The rabbis had finally admitted to themselves that the temple would never be rebuilt, so they added a mass of fresh material, most of which was concerned with the cult and festivals. The Hebrew term *mishnah* meant 'learning by repetition': even though it took written form, the new scripture was still conceived as an oral work and students continued to learn it by heart. The Mishnah was completed by R. Judah the Patriarch in about 200 and became the rabbis' New Testament. Like the Christian scriptures, it regarded the Tanakh as belonging to a phase of history that had gone forever but which could be used to legitimize post-temple Judaism. But there the resemblance ended. There was no history, no narrative and no theology. The Mishnah was simply a formidable collection of legal rulings, arranged in six *Sederim* ('Orders'.): *Zeraim* ('Seeds'), *Moed* ('Festivals'), *Nashim* ('Women'), *Niziqin* ('Damages'), *Qodeshim* ('Holy Things') and *Tohoroth* ('Purity Rules'). These were then subdivided into sixty-three tractates.

Unlike the New Testament, which never missed an opportunity to cite the Hebrew scriptures, the Mishnah held proudly aloof from the Tanakh, rarely quoting from the Bible or appealing to its teaching. The Mishnah did not claim to derive its authority from Moses, never discussed its origins or authenticity, but loftily assumed that its competence was beyond question.[41] The rabbis, who were living, breathing incarnations of Torah, were supremely capable of interpreting the will of God and did not need support from the Bible.[42] The Mishnah was not concerned with what Jews believed but with how they behaved. The temple had gone but the Shekhinah was still in the midst of Israel. The rabbis' task was to help Jews to live in holiness, as though the temple was still standing.

The six Orders were constructed like a temple.[43] The first and last Orders – *Zeraim* and *Tohoroth* – dealt respectively with the holiness of the land and the holiness of the people. The two innermost Orders – *Nashim* and *Niziqin* – legislated for the private, domestic lives of Jews and their business relationships. But the subject of the second and the fifth Orders – *Moed* ('Festivals') and *Qodeshim* ('Holy Things') was the temple. These two *Sederim*, which were compiled almost entirely at Usha,[44] were like two equidistant, load-bearing pillars on which the whole edifice depended. They lovingly recalled the homely details of life in the lost temple: what each room was used for and where the high priest kept his wine. How did the night-watch comport themselves? What happened if a priest fell asleep on duty? In this way, the temple would live on in the minds of Jews and would remain the centre of Jewish life. Studying the obsolete temple laws set forth in the Mishnah was equivalent to actually performing the rites.[45]

It had been one thing for the early Pharisees to live as priests while the temple was still standing, but quite another when all that remained were a few charred ruins. The new spirituality demanded a heroic exegetical denial. But the Mishnah did not simply look back to the past. Thousands of entirely novel rulings worked out the implications of the temple's virtual presence. If Jews were to live like priests, how should they deal with gentiles? What was the role of women, who now had the priestly task of supervising the purity rules in the house? The rabbis would never have been able to persuade the people to observe this formidable body of law if it had not given them a satisfying spiritual experience.

About fifty years after the Mishnah had been completed, a new text provided this oral tradition with a spiritual pedigree that went back to Mount Sinai.[46] The author of *Pirke Avoth* ('Chapters of the Fathers') traced the line of transmission from the rabbis of Usha and Yavneh, back to R. Johanan ben Zakkai, who had learned the Torah from Hillel and Shammai. He then showed how the teaching had passed through generations of distinguished sages of the Second Temple period, ending with the men of 'the Great Assembly',[47] who had received the Torah from the prophets; the prophets had been instructed by the 'elders' who had conquered the Promised Land,[48] the elders by Joshua, Joshua by Moses, and Moses, the source of the tradition, had received the Torah from God himself.

The genealogy was not intended to be factual; like all *mythos,* it was concerned with meaning rather than historically accurate information and described a religious experience. When Jews studied the Torah according to the Mishnah, they felt as though they were participating in an ongoing conversation with all the great sages of the past and with God himself. This would become the charter myth of rabbinic Judaism. There was not one Torah but two – written and oral. Both had been given to Moses on Sinai. The Torah could not be confined to a text; it had to be revivified by the living voices of the sages in each generation. When they studied the Torah, the rabbis felt as though they were standing beside Moses on Sinai. Revelation continued to unfold and the insights of all Jews past, present and to come derived from God as surely as the written Torah given to Moses.[49]

The position of Jews in the Roman empire deteriorated after the conversion of the emperor Constantine to Christianity in 312. After the Bar Koseba revolt, when the *christos* had so signally failed to return, Jewish Christianity had dwindled and the churches were now predominantly gentile. When Theodosius II (401–50) made Christianity the official faith of the empire, Jews were forbidden to hold civil or military posts, Hebrew was prohibited in the synagogues, and if Passover fell before Easter, Jews were not allowed to observe it on the correct date. The rabbis responded by obeying the instructions of the sages in *Pirke Avoth*, who had urged their disciples to 'build a fence for Torah'.[50] They produced more scriptures, which encircled the living Torah with learned, devoted commentary, shielding it from a hostile world as the temple courts had once protected the Holy of Holies.

The Tosefta, a 'supplement' to the Mishnah, was composed in Palestine between 250 and 350: it was a commentary on the Mishnah, gloss upon gloss. Sifra, also written in Palestine at about the same time, tried to reverse the trend that seemed to be taking Jews away from the Tanakh, and attempted, respectfully, to subordinate the Oral to the written Torah. But the two Talmuds made it clear that the Jewish people did not feel inclined to take this path. The Jerusalem Talmud, known as the *Yerushalmi,* was completed in the early fifth century in Palestine, at a very bad time for the Jewish community. *Talmud* means study; but the Yerushalmi studied the Mishnah not the Bible, though it mitigated the Mishnah's proud independence of the Tanakh.[51] The Yerushalmi quoted from the Bible more frequently, and often demanded scriptural proof for its legal rulings – though it never allowed the Bible to be the sole arbiter of legislation. Legal cases involve matters of fact as well as principle, and the Tanakh could not provide this necessary information. But one sixth of the Yerushalmi consisted of scriptural exegesis and anecdotes about the great rabbis, which helped to humanize the formidable legal corpus.

Poor conditions in Palestine may have prevented the completion of the Yerushalmi, which should, perhaps, be regarded as work in progress. But during the sixth century, the Jews of Babylonia produced a more satisfying and polished Talmud.[52] There had been constant interchange between the rabbis of Palestine and Babylonia. The Iranian rulers were more liberal than the Christian emperors, so the Jews of Babylonia had the freedom to manage their own affairs under an officially appointed exilarch. As Palestinian Jewry declined, Babylonia became the intellectual centre of the Jewish world and the Babylonian Talmud, known as the *Bavli*, has a quiet confidence that reflected these more favourable circumstances. It would become the key text of rabbinic Judaism. Like the Yerushalmi, it was a commentary (*gemara*) on the Mishnah, but did not ignore the Tanakh, which was used to support the Oral Torah. In some ways, the Bavli was similar to the New Testament in that its author-editors regarded it as the completion of the Hebrew Bible – a new revelation for a changed world.[53] Like the New Testament, the Bavli was highly selective in its treatment of the older scripture, choosing only those portions of the Tanakh that it found useful and ignoring the rest.

The commentary of the Bavli went systematically through the Mishnah, portion by portion. The gemara referred not only to the Bible but also to the opinions of the rabbis, legends, history, theological reflections and legal lore. This method compelled the student to integrate the written and oral traditions, so that they merged together in his mind. The Bavli included a good deal of material that was older than the Mishnah but much of its content was new, so the student gained a fresh perspective that changed his view of both the Mishnah and the Bible. The Bavli revered the older texts but saw neither as sacrosanct. In their commentary, the author-editors would sometimes reverse the legislation of the Mishnah, play off one rabbi against another, and point out serious gaps in the Mishnah's arguments. They did exactly the same with the Bible, noting lacunae in the biblical texts,[54] suggesting what the inspired authors *should* have said,[55] and even changing a biblical law to more congenial rulings of their own.[56] When read in conjunction with the Bavli, the Bible was transformed, in the same way as the New Testament altered the Christians' reading of the 'Old Testament'. If biblical texts were included in the gemara, they were never discussed on their own terms and in a biblical context, but were always read from the point of view of the Mishnah. As R. Abdini of Haifa explained, the rabbis were the new prophets: 'Since the day the temple was destroyed, prophecy has been taken from the prophets and given to the sages.'[57] The Torah was thus a transcendent reality embodied in two earthly forms: a written scripture and an oral tradition.[58] Both came from God; both were necessary, but the rabbis privileged the Oral Torah because a written text could encourage inflexibility and a backward-looking orientation, whereas the spoken word and the ever-shifting currents of human thought made the Word more sensitive to changing conditions.[59]

We hear many voices in the Bavli: Abraham, Moses, the prophets, the Pharisees and the rabbis. They were not confined to their historical period but brought together on the same page, so that they seemed to be debating with each other across the centuries – often disagreeing quite vehemently. The Bavli gave no definitive answers. If an argument ended in impasse, the students had to sort it out to their own satisfaction with their teachers. The Bavli has been described as the first interactive text.[60] Its method replicated the process of study used by the rabbis themselves and thus compelled the students to engage in the same discussion and make their own contribution. The layout of each page was crucial: the portion of the Mishnah under discussion was placed in the centre, and surrounded by the gemara of sages from the distant and more recent past. The prophets and patriarchs of the Bible were not regarded as superior to the rabbis because they had participated in the original revelation. As R. Ishmael had already explained: 'There is no anteriority or posteriority in scripture.'[61] On each page there was also space for the student to add his own commentary. When studying the Bible through the Bavli, the student learned that nobody had the last word, that truth was constantly changing, and that while tradition was numinous and valuable, it must not constrict his own powers of judgement. The student must add his own *gemara* to the sacred page, because without it the line of tradition would come to an end. 'What is Torah?' asked the Bavli, 'It is: the interpretation of Torah.'[62]

Torah study was not a solitary pursuit. R. Berachiah, a seventh-century Palestinian sage, compared rabbinic discussion to a shuttlecock: 'words fly back and forth when the wise come into a house of study and discuss Torah, one stating his view, still another stating another view, and another stating a different view'. Yet there was a fundamental unity, because the sages were not merely voicing their own opinions: 'The words of these and of the other sages all of them were given by Moses the Shepherd from what he received from the Unique One of the Universe.'[63] Even while he was embroiled in a heated debate, the truly engaged student was aware that both he and his opponent were in some way participating in a conversation that stretched back to Moses and would continue into the future and that what they both said had already been foreseen and blessed by God.

Even though they were now regarded as the enemies of Judaism, Christians were developing a similar spirituality.

CHAPTER 5

Charity

Before the conversion of Constantine in 312, it seemed unlikely that Christianity would survive, as Christians were subjected to sporadic but intense persecution by the Roman authorities. Once they had made it clear that they were no longer members of the synagogue, the Romans regarded the church as a *superstitio* of fanatics, who had committed the cardinal sin of impiety by breaking with the parent faith. Romans were highly suspicious of mass movements that threw off the restraints of tradition. Christians were also accused of atheism because they refused to honour the patronal gods of Rome and thus endangered the empire. The persecutions were designed to stamp out the faith and could easily have done so. As late as 303, the emperor Diocletian began a war of annihilation against the Christians. This time of terror and anxiety left its mark. The martyr, who was ready to follow Jesus to the death, became the Christian hero par excellence.

Some Christians tried to persuade their pagan neighbours that Christianity was not a destructive break with past piety by writing *apologiae*, 'rational explanations', of their faith. One of their chief arguments was that Jesus's life and death had been predicted by the Hebrew prophets, an argument that the Romans, with their respect for augury and oracles, took very seriously. The evangelists had relished their *pesher* exegesis, but the apologists found it more difficult. Once Marcion had urged Christians to jettison the Hebrew scriptures, gentile converts felt increasingly uneasy about their Jewish heritage.[1] They no longer worshipped in the synagogues, so what had they to do with the Jewish god? Had God changed his mind about the old covenant? How could the sacred history of Israel be Christian history? What had the prophets really known about Jesus and how had they known it? Why had Isaiah and Zechariah been preoccupied by Jesus, the founder of a gentile religion?

One of the earliest of these apologists was Justin (100–160), a pagan convert from Samaria in the Holy Land who eventually died as a martyr. He had studied various Greek philosophies, but found what he was looking for in Christianity. The *logos* in the prologue to John's gospel reminded Justin of the fiery, divine breath that the Stoics believed organized the whole of reality and called *Logos* ('Reason'), *Pneuma* ('Spirit') or God. Evidently Christians and pagans had a set of common symbols. In his two *Apologiae*, Justin argued that Jesus was the incarnation of the Logos, which had been active in the world throughout history, inspiring Greeks and Hebrews alike. It had spoken through the prophets, who had thus been able to foretell the coming of the messiah. The Logos had taken many forms before its definitive revelation in Jesus. It had spoken through Plato and

Socrates. When Moses thought he heard God speaking from the burning bush, he had really been listening to the Logos. The oracles of the prophets had not been uttered 'by the inspired [prophets] themselves, but by the divine Word who moved them'.[2] Sometimes the Logos had foretold the future; at other times, it spoke in the name of God. But the Jews had imagined that God was talking to them directly and had not realized that it had been God's 'first-begotten Logos'.[3] In the Jewish scriptures, God had sent a coded message to humanity that the Christians alone had managed to decipher.

Justin's notion of the Logos became central to the exegesis of the theologians who are known as the 'fathers' of the church, because they created the seminal ideas of Christianity and adapted this Jewish faith to the Graeco-Roman world. From an early date, the fathers regarded the Tanakh as an elaborate sign system. As Irenaeus explained, the writings of Moses were really the words of Christ, the eternal Logos, who had been speaking through him.[4] The fathers did not see the 'Old Testament' as an anthology of writings but as a single book with a unified message, which Irenaeus called its *hypothesis*, the argument 'beneath' (*hypo*) the surface. The Hebrew scriptures did not mention Jesus directly but his life and death formed the coded subtext of the Bible and also revealed the secret of the cosmos.[5] Material objects, invisible realities, historical events and natural laws – indeed, everything that existed – formed part of a divinely organized system, which Irenaeus called the 'economy'. Everything had its proper place in the economy and connected with everything else to form a harmonious whole. Jesus was the incarnation of this divine economy. As Paul had explained, his coming had finally revealed God's plan: 'that the universe, everything in heaven and earth, might be brought into a unity [*anakephalaiosis*] in Christ'.[6] Jesus was the reason, purpose and culmination of God's grand design.

Because Christ lay at the heart of the Hebrew scriptures, they also expressed the divine economy, but this subtext only became apparent if the Bible was interpreted correctly. Like the cosmos itself, scripture was a text (*textus*), a tissue made up of an infinite number of interconnecting entities that were 'woven together' to form an inextricable whole.[7] Contemplating the encoded *textus* of scripture helped people to understand that it was Jesus who held everything together and explained the deeper significance of the entire economy. The task of the exegete was to demonstrate this, fitting all the clues together like the interlocking pieces of a vast puzzle. Irenaeus compared the scriptures to a mosaic, composed of innumerable tiny stones which, once they had been placed together correctly, formed the image of a handsome king.[8]

The interpretation of scripture had to conform to the teaching of Jesus's apostles, which Irenaeus called the 'rule of faith', namely that the Logos, which had become incarnate in Jesus, had been implicit in the structure of creation from the very beginning:[9]

Anyone who reads the scriptures with attention will find in them a discourse about Christ, and a prefiguration of a new calling. For Christ is *the treasure hidden in the field*, that is, in this world, *for the field is the world*,[10] but he was also hidden in the scriptures, since he was signified by types and parables which could not be understood, humanly speaking, before the consummation of those things that were prophesied as coming, that is, the advent of Christ.[11]

But the fact that Christ was 'hidden' in scripture meant that Christians had to make a strenuous exegetical effort if they wanted to find him.

Christians could only make sense of the Tanakh by transforming it into an *allegoria*, in which all the events and characters of the 'Old Testament' became types of Christ in the New. The evangelists had already found 'types and parables' of Jesus in the Hebrew scriptures, but the fathers were more ambitious. '*Every* prophet, *every* ancient writer, *every* revolution of the state, *every* law, *every* ceremony of the old covenant points *only* to Christ, announces *only* him, represents *only* him,' insisted Eusebius, bishop of Caesarea (260–340).[12] Christ the Logos had been present in Adam, the progenitor of the race; in Abel the martyr; in Isaac the willing sacrificial victim; and in the afflicted Job.[13] Christians were developing their own distinctive *horoz*, 'linking' people, events and images that had hitherto been separate, in order to reveal what they believed to be the central reality of scripture. Like the rabbis, they were not interested in discovering the intention of the biblical author and seeing a text in its historical context. A good interpretation gave new insight into the divine economy.

Not everybody shared this enthusiasm for allegory. In Antioch, exegetes concentrated on the literal sense of scripture. Their aim was to find out what the prophets themselves had intended to teach – not what could be read into their words with the benefit of hindsight. The prophets often used metaphors and similes, but this figural language was part of the literal sense – essential to what the prophets and psalmists had meant to say. The Antiochenes saw no need for allegory. The late fourth-century preacher John Chrysostom showed that it was possible to derive sound moral lessons from the plain sense of the Bible. The Antiochenes could not discard all typological exegesis, because it had been used so copiously by the evangelists, but they urged scholars to stick to the allegories in the New Testament and not to go in search of new ones. Theodore, bishop of Mopsuestia from 392 to 428, could see no value in the Song of Songs, for example; it was just a love poem and could only be read as a sacred text if entirely alien meanings were superimposed upon it.

But in Alexandria, the Song was popular precisely because it offered such rich opportunities for *allegoria*. Versed in the same hermeneutic tradition as Philo, the Christians of Alexandria had developed an art of reading that they called spiritual interpretation – an attempt to reproduce the experience of the disciples on the road to Emmaus. Like the rabbis, they saw the Bible as an inexhaustible text, capable of yielding endlessly new meanings. They did not think that they were reading into scripture things that were not there but would have agreed with the rabbis that 'everything is in it'. The most brilliant Alexandrian exegete was Origen (185–254), the most influential and prolific author of the day.[14] Besides his biblical commentaries, he produced the *Hexapla* (an edition of the Bible that placed the Hebrew text beside five different Greek translations), and two monumental works: *Against Celsus*, an apologia to refute a pagan philosopher's critique of Christianity, and *On First Principles*, a comprehensive account of Christian doctrine.

For Origen, Jesus was the beginning and end of all exegesis:

> Jesus reveals the law to us when he reveals to us the secrets
> of the Law. For we who are of the catholic Church, we do not
> spurn the law of Moses but accept it, so long as it is Jesus
> who reads it to us. Indeed, we can only possess a correct
> understanding of the Law when he reads it to us, and we are
> able to receive his sense and understanding.[15]

For Origen, the Jewish scriptures were a midrash on the New Testament, which had itself been a commentary on the Tanakh. Without allegory, the Bible made no sense at all. How could you explain literally Christ's command: 'If your right eye should cause you to sin, tear it out and throw it away'?[16] How could a Christian accept the savage command that uncircumcised boys be killed?[17] What possible relevance to Christians were the lengthy instructions for the building of the tabernacle?[18] Did the biblical writer really mean that God 'walked' in the Garden of Eden?[19] Or insist that Christ's disciples should never wear shoes?[20] If you interpreted it literally it was 'a very difficult, not to say impossible task' to revere the Bible as a holy book.[21] Reading scripture was far from easy – a fact that Origen emphasized again and again. All too often heretics twisted the text for their own purposes or gave a facile interpretation of a highly complex passage. It was hard to find inspiration and sound teaching in some of the more problematic or unedifying biblical stories, but because the Logos spoke in scripture, 'We ought to believe that it is possible, even if we do not recognize the profit.'[22] So when Origen discussed Abraham's dubious behaviour in selling his wife to the Pharaoh, pretending that she was his sister,[23] he argued that Sarah was a symbol of virtue and that Abraham wanted to share this rather than keep it to himself.

A modern reader is likely to feel that Origen was as guilty of distorting the scriptures as the heretics he castigated. Like rabbinic midrash, his exegesis seems deliberately transgressive, a quest for meaning at the expense of the author's intention. Origen would have encountered Jewish midrash in Alexandria and later in Caesarea, where he set up his own academy. His methods were similar. In his commentary on Exodus, for example, Origen was not content with the big picture – seeing the Israelites' liberation from slavery as a type of the salvation brought by Christ – but was determined to find a reference to Christ in apparently insignificant details. All Christians had to leave the darkness of 'Egypt' behind, giving up their worldly ways to follow Jesus. On the first leg of their journey out of Egypt, scripture tells us that the

Israelites 'left Rameses for Succoth'.[24] Like Philo, Origen always researched the etymology of proper names, and discovered that *Rameses* meant 'the commotion of a moth'. He then found a 'chain' of scriptural quotations, which gave this seemingly inconsequential sentence entirely new meaning. The word 'moth' reminded him of Jesus's warning against attachment to earthly possessions that were vulnerable to moths and woodworm.[25] So every Christian had to 'depart from Rameses,'

> if you wish to come to the place where the Lord may be our leader and precede you *in the column of the cloud*[26] and the *rock* may follow you,[27] which offers you *spiritual food* and *spiritual drink,* no less.[28] Nor should you store treasure *there where the moth destroys or thieves dig through and steal.*[29] This is what the Lord says clearly in the Gospels: *If you wish to be perfect, sell all your possessions and give to the poor, and you will have treasure in heaven.*[30] This, therefore, is to depart from Rameses and follow Christ.[31]

Thus the Israelites' sojourn in Rameses looked forward to Christ's demand for total commitment. For Origen, scripture was a *textus*, a densely woven fabric of words, every one of which was spoken by Christ the Logos and summoned the reader to follow him. Origen did not believe that his exegesis was arbitrary, because God had planted the clues; his task was to solve them and make the divine voice audible in a way that had not been possible before the coming of Jesus.

Exegesis brought the interpreter and his students a moment of *ekstasis*, a 'stepping outside' of the mundane. Modern biblical scholarship seeks to place a text in the worldly economy of academe, treating it like any other ancient document.[32] Origen's goal was different. Central to early Christian spirituality was what has been called the 'perennial philosophy', because it has been found in almost every pre-modern culture. According to this mythical speculation, every earthly reality has its counterpart in the divine sphere.[33] It was an attempt to articulate the inchoate sense that our lives are somehow incomplete and fragmentary, separate from the more satisfying version that we can imagine so clearly. Because heaven and earth were linked together in the great chain of being, a symbol was inseparable from its unseen referent. The word 'symbol' comes from the Greek *symballein*, 'to throw together'. The archetype and its earthly replica were inextricably combined, like gin and tonic in a cocktail. To taste one, you must also taste the other. This was the basis of Christian ritual: when Christians drank wine and ate bread during the Eucharist, they encountered the Christ these objects represented. In the same way, when they struggled with the time-bound words of scripture, they encountered the Logos, the prototype of all human utterance. This was central to Origen's hermeneutics. 'The contents of scripture are outward forms of certain mysteries and the images of divine things,' he explained.[34] When he perused the New Testament, he was constantly 'amazed by the deep obscurity of the unspeakable mysteries contained therein'; at every turn, he came upon 'thousands of passages that provide, as if through a window, a narrow opening leading to multitudes of deepest thoughts'.[35]

But Origen did not neglect the literal sense of the Bible. His painstaking work on the *Hexapla* showed his determination to establish a dependable text. He learned Hebrew, consulted rabbis and was also fascinated by the geography, flora and fauna of the Holy Land. But the unsatisfactory surface meaning of so many of the teachings and narratives of the Bible compelled him to look beyond it. Scripture had a body and a soul. Our bodies shape our minds and thoughts. They caused us pain and constantly reminded us of our mortality. Our physical lives, therefore, provided us with a built-in ascetic, which, if we responded properly, led us to cultivate our spiritual, immortal nature.[36] In the same way, the glaring limitations in the body – the literal meaning – of scripture forced us to seek its soul, and God had planted these anomalies on purpose:

> Divine wisdom has arranged for certain stumbling blocks
> and interruptions of the historical sense . . . by inserting in
> the midst a number of impossibilities and incongruities, in
> order that the narrative might, as it were, present a barrier to
> the reader and lead him to refuse to proceed along the
> pathway of the ordinary meaning.[37]

These difficult pasages 'bring us, though the entrance of a narrow footpath, to a higher and loftier road precisely by "shutting us out and debarring us" from an acceptance of their plain sense'.[38] By means of the 'impossibility of the literal sense', God led us 'to an examination of the inner meaning'.[39]

Spiritual exegesis was hard work: we had to transform the scriptures in the same way as we transformed our recalcitrant selves. Biblical interpretation required 'the utmost purity and sobriety and ... nights of watching'; it was impossible without a life of prayer and virtue.[40] It was not like solving a mathematical problem, because it involved a more intuitive mode of thought. But if the scholar persevered, pondering the scriptures 'with all the attention and reverence they deserve, it is certain that, in the very act of reading and diligently studying them, his mind and feelings will be touched by a divine breath and he will recognize that the words he is reading are not the utterances of a man but the language of God'.[41]

This apprehension of the divine was acquired gradually, step by step. In the prologue to his commentary on the Song of Songs, Origen pointed out that the three books attributed to Solomon – Proverbs, Ecclesiastes and the Song of Songs – represented the stages of this journey. Scripture had a body, a psyche and a spirit that went beyond our mortal nature; these corresponded to the three different senses in which scripture could be understood. Proverbs was a book of the body. It could be comprehended without allegory, so it represented the *literal* sense of scripture, which the exegete had to master before he could progress to anything higher. Ecclesiastes worked at the level of the psyche, the natural powers of mind and heart. By pointing out that earthly things were vain and empty, Ecclesiastes revealed the futility of placing all our hope in the material world; it therefore exemplified the *moral* sense of scripture, because it showed us how to behave, using arguments that required no supernatural insight. In their reading of the Bible, most Christians rarely progressed beyond the literal and moral senses.

Only an exegete who had been properly initiated into the higher mysteries of scripture could tackle the Song of Songs, which was providentially placed after Proverbs and Ecclesiastes and represented the *spiritual*, allegorical sense. For those Christians who read the Bible in a purely literal way, the Song was just a love poem. But an allegorical interpretation revealed its deeper meaning: 'The love of the Bride for the celestial Bridegroom – that is, of the perfect soul for the Word of God.'[42]

Earthly love, which seems to promise so much, nearly always disappoints; it can be fulfilled solely by its archetype, the God who *is* love.[43] The Song depicted the drama of this ascent to the divine. Throughout, Origen interpreted the Song on three levels. When he expounded the opening verse, 'Let him kiss me with the kisses of his mouth,' he began with the *literal*, historical sense. This was the beginning of an epithalamium: the bride was waiting for her groom; he had sent her dowry but had not yet joined her, and she longed for his presence. *Allegorically*, however, the image of bride and groom referred to the relationship between Christ and the Church, as Paul had explained[44] and the verse symbolized the period before the coming of Christ. Israel had received the Law and the prophets as a dowry but was still waiting for the incarnate Logos, who would complete them. Finally, the text must be applied to the individual soul, whose 'only desire is to be united to the Word of God'.[45] The soul was already in possession of her dowry of natural law, reason and free will, but they could not satisfy her. So she prayed the opening words of the Song, in the hope that her purified 'pure and virginal soul may be enlightened by the illumination and the visitation of the Word of God himself'.[46] The *moral* sense of this verse showed that the bride was a model for all Christians, who must train themselves to yearn without ceasing to transcend their nature and achieve union with God.

Exegesis must always lead to action. For Origen this meant contemplation (*theoria*). Readers must meditate on the verse until they were 'capable of receiving the principles of truth'.[47] They would thus acquire a new orientation towards God. Origen's commentaries often seem to lack a firm conclusion, because his readers had to take the last and final step for themselves. Origen's commentary could only place them in the correct spiritual posture; he could not do the meditation for them. Without prolonged *theoria*, it was not possible to understand his exegesis fully.

Origen had longed to be a martyr as a young man. But after the conversion of Constantine, when Christianity became a legitimate religion in the Roman empire, there was no further opportunity for martyrdom and the monk became the chief Christian exemplar. During the early fourth century, ascetics started to retire to the deserts of Egypt and Syria to engage in a life of solitary prayer. One of the greatest of these monks was Antony of Egypt (250–356), who had felt unable to reconcile his wealth with the gospels. One day, he had heard read aloud in church the story of the rich young man who refused Jesus's invitation: 'go and sell what you own and give the money to the poor . . . then come, follow me'.[48] Like the rabbis, Antony experienced this scripture as a *miqra*, a 'summons'. That very afternoon, he gave all his possessions away and set off for the desert. Monks were revered as doers of the Word.[49] In their desert caves, the monks recited the scriptures, learned texts by heart and meditated on them. As these biblical passages became part of a monk's interior world, their original meaning became less important than this personal significance. Monks believed that Jesus showed them how to read the Bible: in the Sermon on the Mount, he had given scripture new meaning, emphasizing some portions of the Bible more than others. He also stressed the importance of charity. Monks were pioneers of a new Christian lifestyle, which required a different reading of the gospel. They had to allow the texts they had learned to reverberate in their minds, until they achieved the self-forgetfulness of *apatheia*, a lack of concern about their personal well-being that gave them the freedom to love. As a modern scholar explains:

> They could be ignored enough, invited outside themselves
> enough, to love and be loved in a way that met the deepest

social needs of the tension-filled world of late antiquity.
Loving God, loving other people, loving the created world in
which they were placed – this was the great and hoped-for
conclusion of *apatheia* – the sublime indifference that ended
in love.[50]

Origen had concentrated on the love of God in his commentary on the Song; the monks stressed love of neighbour.
Living together in community, they had to dethrone themselves from the centre of their lives and put others there.
Monks did not turn their backs on the world: literally thousands of Christians descended upon them from nearby towns
and villages to seek their counsel. Living in silence had taught
monks how to listen.

One of Antony's most ardent admirers was Athanasius of
Alexandria (296–373), a central figure in the tumultuous
fourth-century debate about the divinity of Christ. Now that
Christianity was a gentile faith, people found it difficult to
understand Jewish terms, such as 'Son of God' or 'Spirit'. Was
Jesus divine in the same way as his Father? And was the Holy
Spirit another God? The debate focused on a discussion of
Wisdom's song in Proverbs which began:[51]'Yahweh created
me when his purpose first unfolded, before the oldest of his
works.' Did this mean that Christ was a mere creature, and, if
so, how could he be divine? In a letter to Athanasius, Arius, a
charismatic presbyter in Alexandria, insisted that Jesus was a
human being who had been promoted by God to divine
status. He was able to produce an armoury of scriptural texts

to support his view. Arius argued that the very fact that Jesus had called God his 'Father' implied a distinction between them, since paternity involves prior existence; he also quoted gospel passages that stressed the humanity and vulnerability of Christ.[52] Athanasius took the opposite view: Jesus was divine in the same way as God the Father, an equally controversial idea at this time, which Athanasius backed up with his own proof texts.

At the beginning of the controversy, there was no orthodox teaching on the nature of Christ and nobody knew whether Athanasius or Arius was right. Discussion raged for over two hundred years. It was impossible to prove anything from scripture, since texts could be found to support either side. But the Greek fathers of the Church did not allow scripture to dominate their theology. In the creed he formulated after the Council of Nicaea, Athanasius used an entirely unscriptural term to describe Jesus's relationship with God: he was *homoousion*, 'of one substance' with the Father. Other fathers based their theology on religious experience rather than a detailed reading of the Bible, which could not tell us everything about a God who transcended all human words and concepts.

Basil of Caesarea in Cappadocia (329–79) argued that there were two kinds of religious teaching, both of which derived from Jesus: *kerygma* was the public teaching of the Church, based on the Bible, while *dogma* expressed everything that could *not* be said; it could be suggested only in the symbolic gestures of the liturgy or experienced in silent meditation.[53] Like Philo, Basil distinguished between God's essence (*ousia*), which lay beyond our understanding, and his operations (*energeiai*) in the world that are described in scripture. God's *ousia* was not even mentioned in the Bible.[54] This was central to the doctrine of the Trinity, which Basil formulated together with his brother Gregory of Nyssa (335–95) and their friend Gregory of Nazianzus (329–91). God had a single essence (*ousia*) which would always remain incomprehensible to us. But in scripture, God had made himself known to us in three *hypostases*, 'manifestations' (Father, Logos and Spirit), divine *energeiaei* that adapted the ineffable mystery of God to our limited intelligence.

The Cappadocian fathers were contemplatives; their daily *theoria* on scripture had introduced them to a transcendence that was beyond even the inspired language of the Bible. The same was true of the Greek father who wrote under the pseudonym Denys the Areopagite[55], whose work is almost as authoritative as scripture in the Greek Orthodox world. He promoted an apophatic theology of 'silence'. God had revealed some of his names to us in scripture, which tells us that God is 'good', 'compassionate', and 'just', but these attributes were 'sacred veils' that hid the divine mystery which lies beyond such words. When Christians listen to scripture, they must continually remind themselves that these human terms were too limited to apply to God. So God was 'good' and 'not-good'; 'just' and 'not-just'. This paradoxical reading would bring them 'into that darkness which is beyond intellect'[56] and into the presence of the indescribable

God. Denys liked the story of the cloud descending on Mount Sinai: on the summit, Moses was enveloped in a thick cloud of unknowing. He could see nothing but he was in the place where God was.

Scripture had not been able to settle the issue of Jesus's divinity, but the Byzantine theologian Maximus the Confessor (c.580–662) arrived at an explanation that became standard among Greek-speaking Christians, because it reflected their interior experience of Christ. Maximus did not believe that the Logos became human to make reparation for the sin of Adam; the incarnation would have occurred even if Adam had not sinned. Jesus was the first fully deified human being and we could all be like him – even in this life. The Word was made flesh in order that 'the whole human being would become God, deified by the grace of God become man – whole man, soul and body, by nature, and becoming whole God, soul and body, by grace'.[57]

The Latin-speaking fathers of Western Europe and North Africa were more down to earth. It is significant that in the West, *theoria* came to mean a rational construct and *dogma* expressed everything that *could* be said about religion. This was a frightening time in the West, where the Roman empire was falling to the barbarian tribes from Germany and Eastern Europe. One of the most influential Western exegetes was Jerome (342–420), who was born in Dalmatia, studied litera-ture and rhetoric in Rome and, fleeing the invading tribes, travelled in Antioch and Egypt before settling in Bethlehem where he founded a monastery. Jerome had initially been attracted to the allegorical hermeneutics of Alexandria, but as a gifted linguist, unique in his day for his mastery of both Greek and Hebrew, his chief contribution was his translation of the entire Bible into Latin. This was called the Vulgate ('vernacular') and it remained the standard text in Europe until the sixteenth century. At first Jerome, who had a great respect for what he called *Hebraica veritas* ('the truth in Hebrew'), wanted to exclude the Apocrypha, books which had been excluded from the Canon by the rabbis, but at the request of his colleague Augustine he agreed to translate them. As a result of his work on the text, Jerome tended increasingly to concentrate in his commentaries on the Bible's literal, historical sense.

His friend Augustine, bishop of Hippo in North Africa (354–430), had studied rhetoric and was at first disappointed in the Bible, which seemed inferior to the great Latin poets and orators. Yet the Bible played a crucial role in his conversion to Christianity after a long, painful struggle. At a moment of spiritual crisis, he had heard a child in the next garden singing a refrain: *'tolle, lege'* ('Pick it up and read it') and he remembered that Antony had decided to embrace the monastic life after a reading from the gospel. In great excitement, he snatched up a copy of Paul's epistles and read the first words that caught his eye: 'no drunken orgies, no promiscuity or licentiousness, and no wrangling or jealousy. Let your armour be the Lord Jesus Christ; forget about satisfying your bodies with all their cravings.'[58] In one of the first recorded 'born-again' conversions that would become a feature of Western Christianity, Augustine felt all his doubts fall away: 'It was as if the light of steadfast trust poured into my heart, and all the shadows of hesitation fled away.'[59]

Augustine later realized that his earlier difficulties with the Bible were due to pride: scripture was only accessible to those who had emptied themselves of conceit and self-importance.[60] The Logos had descended from heaven in order to share our human frailty; and in the same way, when God revealed his Word in scripture, he had to come down to our level and use time-bound images that we could understand.[61] We could never know the whole truth in this life; even Moses could not gaze upon the divine essence directly.[62] Language was inherently defective: we rarely convey our thoughts adequately to others and this makes our relationships with other people problematic. So our struggle with scripture should remind us of the impossibility of expressing the divine mystery in human speech. Bitter, angry disputes about the meaning of scripture were, therefore, ridiculous. The Bible expressed a truth that was infinite and beyond the comprehension of every single person, so nobody could have the last word. Even if Moses appeared in person to explain what he had written, some people would be unable to accept his interpretation of the Pentateuch, because each of us could hold only a tiny facet of the entire revelation in our minds.[63] Instead of engaging in uncharitable controversies, in which everybody insisted that he alone was right, a humble acknowledgement of our lack of insight should draw us together.

The Bible was about love; everything that Moses had

written 'was for the sake of love', so to quarrel about scripture was perverse: 'There are so many meanings to be extracted from these words; so how foolish it is, then, to be in a hurry to assert which of them Moses really meant, and with destructive controversies to offend against the spirit of love – when it was for the sake of love that Moses said all the things that we are trying to elucidate.'[64] Augustine had arrived at the same concluson as Hillel and the rabbis. Charity was the central principle of Torah and everything else was commentary. Whatever else Moses had written, his chief purpose was to preach the dual commandment: love of God and love of neighbour. This had also been the central message of Jesus.[65] So if we insult others in the name of the Bible, 'we *make the Lord a liar*'.[66] People who quarrelled about scripture were full of pride; they 'know not Moses' meaning, but love their own, not because it is true but because it is theirs'.[67] So 'let no one be filled with pride against his brother over what is written,' Augustine begged his congregation, 'But let us love the Lord our God with all our heart, with all our soul, and with all our mind, and our neighbours as ourselves.'[68]

As a Platonist, it was natural for Augustine to elevate the spiritual above the literal meaning. But he had a strong sense of history, which enabled him to steer a middle course. Instead of rushing to give a figurative interpretation of an unedifying story, Augustine was more inclined to point out that moral standards were culturally conditioned. Polygamy, for example, was common and permissible among primitive peoples. Even the best of us fall into sin, so there was no need to allegorize the story of David's adultery, which had been included in the Bible as a warning to us all.[69] Righteous condemnation is not only unkind but smacks of the self-satisfaction and self-congratulation that is a major impediment to our understanding of scripture. So 'we must meditate on what we read, until an interpretation be found that tends to establish the reign of charity,' Augustine urged. 'Scripture teaches nothing but charity, nor condemns anything except cupidity, and in this way shapes the minds of men.'[70]

Irenaeus had insisted that exegesis must conform to the 'rule of faith'. For Augustine, the 'rule of faith' was not a doctrine but the spirit of love. Whatever the author had originally intended, a biblical passage that was not conducive to love must be interpreted figuratively, because charity was the beginning and end of the Bible:

> Whoever, therefore, thinks that he understands the divine scriptures or any part of them so that it does not build the double love of God and of our neighbour does not understand it at all. Whoever finds a lesson there useful to the building of charity, even though he has not said what the author may be shown to have intended in that place, has not been deceived.[71]

Exegesis was a discipline that trained us in the difficult art of charity. By habitually seeking a charitable explanation of disturbing texts, we could learn to do the same in our daily lives. Like the other Christian exegetes, Augustine believed that

Jesus was central to the Bible: 'Our whole purpose when we hear the Psalms, the Prophets and the Law,' he explained in a sermon, 'is to see Christ there, to understand Christ there.'[72] But the Christ he found in scripture was never simply the historical Jesus, but the whole Christ, who, as St Paul had taught, was inseparable from humanity.[73] After finding Christ in scripture, the Christian must return to the world and learn to seek him in loving service to the community.

Augustine was not a linguist. He knew no Hebrew and could not have encountered Jewish midrash, but he had come to the same conclusion as Hillel and Akiba. Any interpretation of scripture that spread hatred and dissension was illegitimate; all exegesis must be guided by the principle of charity.

CHAPTER 6

Lectio Divina

In 430, the last year of his life, Augustine had watched the
Vandals besieging the city of Hippo, as the western pro-
vinces of the Roman empire fell helplessly before the invading barbarian tribes. A deep sadness pervades Augustine's
work during these final years, and is especially evident in his
interpretation of the fall of Adam and Eve. The tragedy of
Rome's collapse had convinced Augustine that this original
sin had sentenced the human race to eternal damnation.
Even after our redemption by Christ, our humanity was
impaired by concupiscence, the irrational desire to take
pleasure in creatures rather than in God. The guilt of original
sin was transmitted to Adam's descendants through the
sexual act: when our reasoning powers were swamped by
passion, God was forgotten, and men and women revelled
shamelessly in one another. The image of rationality dragged
down by a chaos of sensation reflected the plight of Rome,
source of order in the West, brought low by the barbarians.
This interpretation of the third chapter of Genesis is unique
to Western Christianity; neither the Jews nor the Greek
Orthodox, who did not experience the fall of Rome, have

subscribed to this tragic vision. The collapse of the empire plunged Western Europe into centuries of political, economic and social stagnation and the trauma convinced the more educated Christians that men and women were indeed permanently damaged by Adam's sin. They could no longer hear what God said to them, and this made it well-nigh impossible to understand the scriptures.

Europe had become a pagan wilderness. From the fifth to the ninth centuries, the Christian tradition was confined to the monasteries, the only places that could provide the stability and quiet necessary for the study of the Bible. The monastic ideal had been brought to the West by John Cassian (360–435). He had also introduced Western Christians to Origen's threefold interpretation of scripture according to the literal, moral and allegorical senses, but added a fourth: the *anagogical* or mystical sense, which revealed a text's eschatological significance. When, for example, the prophets had described the future glories of Jerusalem, this referred anagogically to the heavenly Jerusalem in Revelation. Cassian taught his monks that the study of scripture was a lifelong task. In order to appreciate the ineffable realities that lay hidden behind the veil of human words, they must rectify their fallen nature – training their powers of concentration, disciplining their bodies in fasts and vigils, and cultivating a habit of inwardness.[1]

Lectio divina ('sacred study') was also central to the Rule of St Benedict of Nursia (AD 480–543). Benedictine monks spent at least two hours every day studying the scriptures and the writings of the fathers. Scripture, however, was not experienced as a book: many of the monks would never have seen the Bible as a single volume but read it in separate manuscripts; much of their biblical knowledge came to them at second hand in the liturgy or the works of the fathers. The Bible was read aloud during meals and the Psalter chanted at regular intervals throughout the day in the Divine Office. The rhythms, imagery and teaching of the Bible became the substratum of their spirituality, built up incrementally and undramatically day by day, year by year, in silent, regular meditation.

There was nothing formal or systematic about *lectio divina*. Monks were not obliged to cover a given number of chapters per session. *Lectio* was a peaceful, leisurely perusal of the text in which the monk learned to find a quiet place in his mind that enabled him to hear the Word. The biblical story was not studied as a historical event but experienced as a contemporary reality. Monks were encouraged to enter the action imaginatively – visualizing themselves beside Moses on Sinai, in the audience when Jesus delivered the Sermon on the Mount, or at the foot of the cross. They were supposed to consider the scene according to each of the four senses in turn, moving from literal to spiritual in a process that marked an ascent to mystical union with God.[2]

A formative influence in the West was Gregory the Great (540–604), a Benedictine monk who was elected Pope. Gregory was steeped in the discipline of *lectio divina* but his biblical theology revealed the shadow that haunted the

Western spirit in the aftermath of Rome's fall. He had fully absorbed the doctrine of original sin, and saw the human mind as irreparably damaged and twisted. God was now difficult to access. We could know nothing about him. It took a massive mental effort to experience a momentary joy in contemplation before falling back into the darkness that was our natural element.[3] In the Bible, God had condescended to our sinfulness, and come down to the level of our puny minds, but human language had splintered under the divine impact. That was why the grammar and vocabulary of Jerome's Vulgate departed from classical Latin usage and why, on first reading, it was hard to find any religious value in some of the biblical stories. Unlike Origen, Jerome and Augustine, Gregory wasted no time on the literal meaning. Studying the plain sense of scripture was like looking at somebody's face without seeing what was in his heart.[4] The literal text was like a flat expanse of land surrounded by mountains that represented the 'spiritual senses that would take us beyond the broken human words'.[5]

By the eleventh century, Europe had started to emerge from the Dark Ages. The Benedictines of Cluny, near Paris, initiated a reform to educate the laity, whose knowledge of Christianity was woefully inadequate. Uneducated layfolk could not read the Bible, of course, but were taught to experience the Mass as a complex allegory that symbolically re-enacted Jesus's life: the readings from scripture in the first part of the liturgy recalled his ministry; during the offering of the bread and wine, they meditated on his sacrificial death, and the communion represented his resurrection in the lives of the faithful. The fact that lay people could no longer follow the Latin added to the mystique: much of the Mass was recited by the priest in an undertone, and the silence and the sacred language transported the ritual into a separate space apart, introducing the congregation to the gospel as a *mysterium*, a power-filled act. By enabling them to enter imaginatively into the gospel story, Mass was the laity's *lectio divina*.[6] The Cluniacs also encouraged lay people to make pilgrimages to places associated with Jesus and the saints. Not many could make the long trip to the Holy Land, but, it was said, some of the apostles had travelled to Europe and were buried there: Peter in Rome; Joseph of Arimathea in Glastonbury, and James at Compostela in Spain. During the journey, pilgrims learned Christian values, living for a while like monks: they left secular life behind, were celibate during the journey, lived in community with other pilgrims, and were forbidden to fight or bear arms.

But Europe was still a dangerous, desolate place. People were barely able to farm the land, there was famine and sickness and constant warfare, as the nobility engaged in ceaseless battles with one another, devastating the countryside and wrecking entire villages. The Cluniacs tried to impose a periodic truce and some tried to reform the barons and kings. But the knights were soldiers and wanted an aggressive religion. The first communal, cooperative act of the new Europe, as she crawled out of the Dark Ages, was the First Crusade (1095–99). Some of the Crusaders began their journey to the

Holy Land by attacking the Jewish communities in the Rhine Valley; at its conclusion, the Crusaders massacred some thirty thousand Jews and Muslims in Jerusalem.The crusading ethos was based on a literal interpretation of Christ's warning in the gospel: 'Anyone who does not carry his cross and come after me cannot be my disciple.'[7] Crusaders sewed crosses on their clothes and followed in Jesus's footsteps to the land where he had lived and died. With tragic irony, crusading was preached as an act of love.[8] Christ was the Crusaders' feudal lord, and as loyal vassals they were duty-bound to recover his patrimony. In the Crusades, Christianity absorbed and baptized the feudal violence of Europe.

While some Europeans were fighting Muslims in the Near East, others were studying with Muslim scholars in Spain, who helped them to recover much of the culture they had lost during the Dark Ages. In the Muslim kingdom of al-Andalus, Western scholars discovered the medicine, mathematics and science of classical Greece that had been preserved and developed in the Islamic world. They read Aristotle for the first time in Arabic, and translated his work into Latin. Europe embarked on an intellectual renaissance. Aristotle's rational philosophy, which was more down to earth than the Platonism that they had imbibed from the fathers of the Church, filled many Western scholars with excitement and encouraged them to use their own reasoning powers.

This inevitably affected the study of the Bible. As Europe became more organized and the rational ideal took hold, scholars and monks tried to impose some kind of system on the somewhat chaotic traditions they had inherited. The text of the Vulgate had been corrupted by the compounded errors of generations of monk-copyists.[9] The copyists had usually prefaced each book of the Bible with a commentary by Jerome or one of the other fathers. By the eleventh century, the most popular books were accompanied by several prefaces, which often contradicted each other. So a group of French scholars put together a standard commentary, known as the *Glossa Ordinaria*. Anselm of Laon (d. 1117), who began this work, wanted to provide teachers with a clear explanation of each verse of the Bible. If the reader encountered a problem, he could look at the notes written in the margins or between the lines of the manuscript, which provided him with explanations by Jerome, Augustine or Gregory. The *Glossa* was little more than a crib: the notes were necessarily brief and basic and there was no space for an elaborate exploration of the finer points. But it provided scholars with a rudimentary knowledge on which they could build. Anselm completed the commentary on the most popular books: Psalms, Paul's letters and John's gospel. He also collected *Sententiae*, anthologies of the fathers' 'opinions', arranged according to topic. Anselm's brother Ralph tackled Matthew's gospel, while his students, Gilbert of Poitiers and Peter Lombard, completed the project.

In the classroom, the master would read the glossed text to his students, who would then have the opportunity to ask questions and engage in further discussion: later, as the number of queries accumulated, a separate session was devoted to *quaestiones*. Discussion became more intense, as students began to experiment with Aristotelian logic and dialectic. Others applied the new science of grammar to the biblical text: why did the Latin of the Vulgate break basic rules of classical Latin? Gradually a rift developed between the monasteries and the cathedral schools. In the monasteries, masters concentrated on *lectio divina*: they wanted their novices to read the Bible meditatively and develop their spirituality. But in the cathedral schools, masters were more interested in the new learning and objective biblical criticism.

There was also a dawning interest in the literal sense of the Bible, which had been initiated by the rabbis of northern France. Rabbi Shlomo Yitzhak, known as RaSHI (1040–1105), had no interest in Aristotle. His passion was for philology, and he was concerned above all with the plain meaning of scripture.[10] He wrote a running commentary on the text of the Hebrew Bible, concentrating on individual words in a way that threw new light on the text. He noticed, for example, that *bereshit*, the first word of the first chapter of Genesis, could mean 'In the beginning *of*', so the sentence should read: 'In the beginning of God's creation of heaven and earth, the earth was a formless void (*tohu bohu*).' This implied that the raw materials of the earth were already in existence when God started his creative work, and that he simply brought order to *tohu bohu*. Rashi also noted that in one midrashic interpretation, *bereshit* was understood to mean: 'because of the beginning' and that the Bible called both Israel and the Torah 'the beginning'. Did this mean that God had created the world in order to give Israel the Torah? Rashi's method forced the reader to look at the text closely before he imposed his own midrash upon it: his commentary would become one of the most important and influential guides to the Pentateuch.

Rashi saw his literal exegesis as complementary to traditional midrash but his successors were more radical. Joseph Kara (d. 1130) argued that anybody who did not concentrate on the plain sense was like a drowning man clutching at a straw. Rashi's grandson, R. Shemuel ben Meir, known as the RaSHBaM (d. 1174), was more tolerant of midrash, but still favoured a more rational explanation. Rashi's method of literal exposition was proceeding at a feverish place in his circle, he said, 'new examples come up every day'.[11] Joseph Bekhor Shor, a pupil of the Rashbam, always tried to find a natural explanation for the more fantastic biblical stories.[12] There was no mystery about the death of Lot's wife, for example; she had simply been enveloped by the volcanic lava that destroyed Sodom and Gomorrah. Joseph had dreamed of future greatness simply because he was an ambitious young man, and had needed no help from God when he interpreted Pharaoh's dreams: anybody with a modicum of intelligence could have done the same.

Despite the Crusades, relations between Jews and Christians in France were still reasonably good, and scholars from the Abbey of St Victor on the left bank of the Seine, who were also becoming interested in the literal sense, began to consult the local rabbis and learn Hebrew. The Victorines tried to combine traditional *lectio divina* with the more academic scholarship of the cathedral schools. Hugh of St Victor, who taught at the abbey until his death in 1141, was a committed contemplative but did not find that this conflicted with his rational powers. Aristotelian grammar, logic, dialectic and natural science could help students to understand the Bible. Hugh was convinced that the study of history was the foundation of what he called 'the house of exposition'. Moses and the evangelists had all been historians, and students should start their study of the Bible with the historical books. Without a correct literal understanding of the Bible, allegory was doomed to failure. Students must not run before they could walk. They must begin by examining the Vulgate's syntax and vocabulary in order to discover what the biblical author had intended to say. 'We must not read our own meaning (*sententia*) into scripture, but must make the sentence of scripture ours.'[13]

Andrew of St Victor (1110–75), Hugh's gifted pupil, was the first Christian scholar to attempt a wholly literal interpretation of the Hebrew Bible.[14] He had nothing against allegory, but it did not interest him. He learned a great deal from the rabbis and found that scripture read 'more clearly in the Hebrew'.[15] His academic commitment to the literal never failed, even when the rabbis discounted interpretations that were essential to the Christian understanding of the Old Testament. After discovering that the Hebrew text did not support the traditional Christian interpretation, which saw the verse as a prophecy of Jesus's virgin birth, Andrew accepted Rashi's exegesis of Isaiah's oracle: 'Behold a young woman (*almah*) shall conceive and bear a child.' (Rashi thought that Isaiah had referred to his own wife.) In his exposition of the Servant Songs, Andrew did not even bother to mention Christ, but accepted the Jewish view that the servant symbolized the people of Israel. Instead of seeing the figure in Ezekiel's vision that was 'like a son of man' as a prediction of Jesus, Andrew simply wanted to know what this imagery had meant to Ezekiel and the exiles. He decided that because the 'son of man' was the only human element in a very weird and frightening theophany, the exiles would have been reassured that God was interested in their own predicament.

Andrew and his Jewish friends had taken a first step towards modern historical criticism of the Bible, but Andrew, a morose, uncharismatic man, had few followers in his own day. During the twelfth century, the men of the hour were the philosophers, who were beginning to develop a new kind of rationalistic theology in which they used reason to sustain their faith and clarify what had hitherto been deemed ineffable. Anselm of Bec (1033–1109), who would become Archbishop of Canterbury in 1189, thought that it was possible to prove anything.[16] As a monk, *lectio divina* was essential to his spiritual life but he wrote no commentaries on scripture and seldom quoted the Bible in his theological writing. But religion, like poetry or art, requires an intuitive rather than a purely rational approach and Anselm's theology shows its limitations. In his treatise *Cur Deus Homo,* for example, he attempted a logical account of the Incarnation that bore no relation at all to scripture: any biblical quotations simply carried the argument along. The Greek Orthodox had also produced a theology that was independent of scripture, but Anselm's forensic explanation of the incarnation lacks the spiritual insight of Maximus. He argued that the sin of Adam required atonement; because God was just, a human being must atone; but because the fault was so serious, only God could make reparation. Therefore God had to become man.[17] Anselm makes God weigh the matter up as if he were a mere human being. It is not surprising that at this time the Greek Orthodox feared that Latin theology was too anthropomorphic. Anselm's theory of the atonement, however, became normative in the West, while the Greek Orthodox continued to prefer Maximus's interpretation.

The French philosopher Peter Abelard (1079–1142) developed a different account of the redemption, which again owed little to scripture but came closer to the spirit of the fathers.[18] Like some of the rabbis, he believed that God suffered with his creatures and argued that the crucifixion showed us one moment in the eternal pathos of God. When we contemplate the flayed figure of Jesus we are moved to pity, and it is the act of compassion that saves us – not Jesus's sacrificial death. Abelard was the intellectual star of his generation; students flocked to his lectures from all over Europe. Like Anselm, he rarely quoted scripture and raised questions without appearing to offer solutions. In fact, Abelard was more interested in philosophy and his theology was rather conservative. But his iconoclastic, aggressive manner made it sound as though he was arrogantly pitting his human reason

against the mystery of God and this brought him into head-
long collision with one of the most powerful churchmen of
the day.

Bernard (1090–1153), abbot of the Cistercian monastery of
Clairvaux in Burgundy (1090–1153), dominated Pope Eugene
II and King Louis VII of France and was as charismatic in
his own way as Abelard. Scores of young men had followed
him into the new Cistercian Order, a reformed branch of
Benedictine monasticism. He accused Abelard of 'attempting
to bring the Christian faith to naught because he supposes
that human reason can comprehend all that is God'.[19] Quoting
Paul's hymn to charity, he claimed that Abelard 'sees nothing
as an enigma, nothing as in a mirror, but looks on everything
face to face'.[20] In 1141, Bernard summoned Abelard, who by
this time was suffering from Parkinson's disease, to the
Council of Sens, and attacked him so ferociously that he
collapsed and died the following year.

Even though Bernard could not be described as a charitable man, his exegesis and spirituality were based on the love
of God. His most famous work was his exposition of the Song
of Songs, eighty-six sermons delivered to the monks of
Clairvaux between 1135 and 1153, which mark the apogee
of *lectio divina*.[21] 'It is desire that drives me,' he insisted, 'not
reason.'[22] In the incarnation of the Logos, God had descended
to our level so that we could ascend to the divine. In the Song,
God shows us that we make this ascent in three stages. When
the bride cried: 'The king has brought me into his chambers',
this referred allegorically to the senses of scripture. There

were three 'chambers': the garden, the storeroom and the bedchamber. 'Let the garden ... represent the plain, unadorned sense of scripture,' Bernard suggested, 'the storeroom its moral sense, and the bedroom the mystery of divine contemplation.'[23] We began by reading the Bible as a simple story of creation and redemption but we must then progress to the storerooms, the moral sense which teaches us to modify our behaviour. In the 'storerooms', the soul was refined by the practice of charity. She became 'pleasant and temperate' to others; 'an earnest zeal for the works of love' leads her 'to forgetfulness of self and indifference of self-interest'.[24] When the bride looked for her groom 'by night' in her bedchamber, she showed us the importance of modesty. It was better to avoid ostentatious piety and pray in the privacy of one's cell because 'if we pray when others are present, their approbation may rob our prayer of ... its effect'.[25] There would be no sudden illumination; by dint of regular *lectio divina* and the practice of charity, monks would make steady, unobtrusive and incremental progress.

Eventually, the soul might be permitted to enter the groom's 'bedchamber' and attain the vision of God, though Bernard admitted that he had only had momentary intimations of this final state. The Song could not be understood rationally. Its meaning was a 'mystery' that was 'hidden' in the text[26] – an overwhelming transcendence that would always elude our conceptual grasp.[27] Unlike the rationalists, Bernard constantly quoted scripture: his commentary on the Song has 5,526 quotations ranging from Genesis to Revelation.[28] And instead of seeing the Bible as an objective academic challenge, Bible study was a personal, spiritual discipline. 'Today the text we are to study is the book of our experience,' he told his monks, 'you must therefore turn your affections inwards, each one must take note of his own particular awareness of things.'[29]

During the thirteenth century, the new Order of Preachers, founded by the Spaniard Dominic Guzman (1170–1221), managed to marry the old *lectio divina* with the rationalism of the schools. The Dominicans were the intellectual heirs of both the philosophers and the scholars of St Victor.[30] They did not abandon spiritual exegesis, but gave more serious attention to the literal sense and they were systematic academics, whose aim was to adapt Aristotelian philosophy to Christianity. The fathers had compared allegory to the 'soul' or 'spirit' of scripture, but for Aristotle the soul was inseparable from the body; it defined and shaped our physical development and relied on the evidence of the senses. So for the Dominicans, the 'spirit' of scripture was not hidden beneath the text but found within the literal and historical meaning.

In his *Summa Theologica*, Thomas Aquinas (1225–74) reconciled the older spiritual method with the new philosophy. According to Aristotle, God was the 'First Mover' who had set the cosmos in motion; Thomas extended this idea, pointing out that God was also the 'First Author' of the Bible. The human authors who made the divine Word an earthly reality, were God's instruments. He had set them in motion too, but they were solely responsible for the style and literary form of the text. Instead of disregarding the plain sense, the exegete could discover a great deal about the divine message by studying the work of these writers in a methodical and scientific way. Like the twelfth-century rationalists, the scholastics, as these schoolmen were called, felt sufficiently confident of their reasoning powers to liberate their theological speculation from exegesis. But Aquinas himself took a more conservative position. God was not like a human author, who could merely convey his message in words. God also had the power to orchestrate historical events in order to reveal the truths of salvation. The literal sense of the 'Old Testament' could be found in the words used by the human authors, but its spiritual meaning could be discerned in the events of the Exodus and the institution of the Paschal Lamb, which God had used to prefigure the redemptive work of Christ.

Meanwhile, Jews who lived in the Islamic world had also tried to apply the rationalism of classical Greek culture to the Bible and found it difficult to square the revealed God of scripture with the deity described by Aristotle and Plato, which was timeless and impassable, took no notice of mundane events, had not created the cosmos – which, like God itself, was eternal, – and would not judge it at the end of time. Jewish philosophers insisted that the most anthropomorphic passages of the Bible must be interpreted allegorically. They could not accept a God who walked and talked, sat on a throne, was jealous, became angry and changed his mind.

They were particularly worried by the idea that God had created the world *ex nihilo*, 'out of nothing'. Saadia ibn Joseph (882–942) insisted that because God lay beyond all speech and concepts, one could only say that he existed.[31] Saadia felt obliged to accept creation *ex nihilo* because it was now deeply rooted in Jewish tradition, but argued that if you accepted a divine Creator, you could logically make other statements about him. Because the world he made was intelligently planned and had life and energy, it followed that the Creator must have the attributes of Wisdom, Life and Power. In an attempt to explain rationally how the material world had derived from a wholly spiritual God, other Jewish philosophers imagined creation as an evolutionary process of ten emanations from God that became progressively more material. Each emanation had generated one of the spheres of Ptolemy's universe: the fixed stars, then Saturn, Jupiter, Mars, Sun, Venus, Mercury and finally the Moon. Our sublunary world, however, had developed in the opposite direction: it had begun as inanimate matter, and progressed through plants and animals to humans, whose souls participated in the divine reason, but whose bodies derived from the earth.

Maimonides (1135–1204) tried to reassure Jews who were perturbed by the conflict between Aristotle and the Bible.[32] In *The Guide of the Perplexed*, he argued that since truth was one, scripture must be in harmony with reason. He had no problem with creation *ex nihilo*, because he did not find Aristotle's argument for the eternity of matter convincing. Maimonides agreed that anthropomorphic descriptions of

God in the Bible must not be interpreted literally, and tried to find rational reasons for some of the more irrational biblical laws. But he knew that religious experience transcended reason. The intuitive knowledge of the prophets, which was accompanied by tremulous awe, was of a higher order than the knowledge we acquire by our rational powers.

Abraham ibn Ezra (1089–1164), one of the great poets and philosophers of Spain, was another medieval forerunner of modern historical criticism.[33] Exegesis must give priority to the literal sense; while legend (*aggadah*) had spiritual value, it must not be confused with fact. He found discrepancies in the biblical text: Isaiah of Jerusalem could not have composed the second half of the book attributed to him because it referred to events that occurred long after his death. He also cautiously and elliptically hinted that Moses was not the author of the entire Pentateuch: he could not, for example, have described his own death and since Moses never entered the Promised Land, how could he have written the opening verses of Deuteronomy, which positioned the site of his final address *'on the other side* of the Jordan river'.[34] This must have been written by somebody who lived in the land of Israel after its conquest by Joshua.

Philosophical rationalism inspired a mystical backlash in Spain and Provence. Nahmanides (1194–1270), an outstanding Talmudist and an influential member of the Jewish community in Castile, believed that Maimonides's rationalistic exegesis did not do justice to the Torah.[35] He wrote an influential commentary on the Pentateuch, which rigorously elucidated its plain meaning, but in the course of his study he had encountered a numinous significance that entirely transcended the literal sense. In the late thirteenth century, a small group of mystics in Castile took this further. Their study of scripture had not merely introduced them to a deeper level of the text but to the inner life of God. They called their esoteric discipline *kaballah* ('inherited tradition'), because it had passed from teacher to pupil. Unlike Nahmanides, these kabbalists – Abraham Abulafia, Moses de Leon, Isaac de Latif and Joseph Gikatilla – had no expertise in Talmud but they had all been interested in philosophy before deciding that its attenuated God was empty of religious content.[36] Instead, they explored a hermeneutic method, which they may have learned from their Christian neighbours.

Their mystical midrash was based on the Talmudic story of the four sages who entered the 'orchard' (*pardes*).[37] Because R. Akiba alone had survived this perilous spiritual experiment, the kabbalists claimed that their exegesis, which they called *pardes*, derived from him and was the only safe form of mysticism.[38] They found that their method of studying Torah carried them daily to 'paradise'.[39] PaRDeS was an anagram for the four senses of scripture: *peshat*, the literal sense; *remez*, allegory; *darash*, the moral, homiletic sense; and *sod*, the mystical culmination of Torah study. *Pardes* was a rite of passage which began with *peshat* and rose to the ineffable heights of *sod*. As the original *Pardes* story made clear, this journey was not for everybody but only for a properly initiated elite. The first three forms of midrash – *pardes, remez* and *darash* – had all been used by Philo, the rabbis and the philosophers, so the kabbalists implied that their new spirituality was in line with tradition, while at the same time suggesting that their own speciality – *sod* – was its fulfilment. Their experience probably seemed so self-evidently Jewish that they may have been entirely unaware of any conflict with the mainstream.[40]

The kabbalists created a powerful synthesis.[41] They revived the mythical element in ancient Israelite tradition, which the rabbis and the philosophers had downplayed or tried to eradicate. They were also inspired by the Gnostic tradition, which had surfaced again in various mystical movements in the Muslim world with which they were probably familiar. Finally, the kabbalists drew upon the ten emanations envisaged by the philosophers in which every element in the chain of being was connected. Revelation no longer had to bridge an ontological abyss, but occurred continuously within each individual, and creation had not happened once in the distant past but was a timeless event in which we could all participate.

Kabbalah was probably more scripturally based than any other form of mysticism. Its 'bible' was the *Zohar*, 'The Book of Splendour', which was probably the work of Moses of Leon, but took the form of a second-century novel about the mystical revolutionary R. Simeon ben Yohai, who wandered around Palestine, meeting with his companions to discuss the Torah, which, as a result of their exegesis 'opened' directly on to the divine world. By studying scripture, the kabbalist descended into the text and into himself, layer by layer, and found that he was at the same time ascending to the source of all being. The kabbalists agreed with the philosophers that words could not convey the incomprehensible transcendence of God, but believed that even though God could not be known, he could be experienced in the symbols of scripture. They were convinced that God had left hints about his inner life in the biblical text. In their mystical exegesis, kabbalists built on these, creating mythical stories and dramas which broke the *peshat* text open. Their mystical interpretation found an esoteric meaning in every single verse of scripture that described the mysteries of the divine being.

The kabbalists called the innermost essence of God *En Sof* ('without end'). En Sof was incomprehensible and was not even mentioned in the Bible or the Talmud. It was not a personality, so it was more accurate to call En Sof 'it' rather than 'he'. But the incomprehensible En Sof had revealed itself to humanity at the same time as it had created the world. It had emerged from its impenetrable concealment like a massive tree sprouting a trunk, branches and leaves. The divine life spread in ever wider spheres until it filled everything that is, while En Sof itself remained hidden. It was the root of the tree, source of its stability and vitality but forever invisible. What the philosophers called God's attributes – his Power, Wisdom, Beauty and Intelligence – thus became manifest, but the kabbalists transformed these abstract qualities into dynamic potencies. Like the philosophers' ten emanations, they revealed aspects of the unfathomable En Sof and became more concrete and more comprehensible as they approached the material world. The kabbalists called these ten potencies, the inner dimensions of the divine psyche, *sefiroth* ('numerations'). Each *sefirah* had its own symbolic name and represented a stage in En Sof's unfolding revelation, but they were not 'segments' of God but together formed one great Name not known to human beings. Each *sefirah* encapsulated the entire mystery of God under a particular heading.

The kabbalists interpreted the first chapter of Genesis as a parable of the emergence of the *sefiroth*. *Bereshit* ('the beginning'), the very first word of the Bible, revealed the moment when Kether Elyon (the 'Supreme Crown'), the first *sefirah*, broke through the unfathomable mystery of En Sof as a 'dark flame'. As yet nothing had been revealed, because there was nothing about this first *sefirah* that human beings could understand. 'It could not be recognized at all,' the *Zohar* explained, 'until a hidden, supernal point shone forth under the impact of the final breaking through.' This 'point' was the second *sefirah*, Hokhmah ('Wisdom'), the divine masterplan of creation that represented the limit of human understanding. 'Beyond this nothing can be known,' the *Zohar* continued. 'Therefore is it called *reshit*, beginning.' Next Hokhmah penetrated the third *sefirah*, Binah, the divine Intelligence whose 'unknowable radiance' was of a slightly 'lesser subtility and translucency than the primal point'. After this 'beginning', the seven 'lower' *sefiroth* followed, one after the other, 'extension upon extension, each constituting a vesture to the one before, as a membrane to the brain'.[42]

This *mythos* was designed to throw light on the indescribable process in which the unknowable God made itself known to human beings and brought the cosmos into being. There was always a strong sexual element in Kabbalah. Binah was also known as the Supernal Mother, whose womb, once penetrated by the 'primal point' gave birth to the lower *sefiroth*, which reflected aspects of the divine that were more accessible to human beings and, in the first chapter of Genesis, were symbolized by the seven days of creation. Human beings could discern these 'powers' of God in the world and in scripture: *Rakhamin* (Compassion) – also called *Tifereth* (Grace); *Din* (Stern Judgement) which should always be balanced by *Hesed* (Mercy); *Netsakh* (Patience), *Hod* (Majesty), *Yesod* (Stability) and finally *Malkuth* (Kingdom), also called *Shekhinah*, whom the kabbalists imagined as a female personality.

The *sefiroth* should not be seen as a ladder linking the Godhead with humanity. They informed our world and enclosed it, so that we were embraced and pervaded by this dynamic, multifarious divine activity. Because they were also present in the human psyche, the *sefiroth* also represented the stages of human consciousness through which the mystic ascended to the Godhead. The emanation of the *sefiroth* depicted the process whereby impersonal En Sof became the personal God of the Bible. As the three 'higher' *sefiroth* emerged, the 'it' of En Sof became 'he'. In the next six *sefiroth*, 'he' became 'you', a reality to whom human beings could relate. In the Shekhinah, the divine presence in our world, 'you' became 'I', because God was also present in each individual. In the course of the *pardes* exegesis, kabbalists gradually became aware of the divine presence in the deepest recesses of the psyche.

Kabbalists took the doctrine of creation *ex nihilo* very seriously, but turned it on its head. This 'nothing' could not be outside the Godhead which constituted the whole of reality. The abyss was within En Sof and was – somehow – overcome in creation. The kabbalists also called the first *sefirah*, the dark flame that started the revelatory/creative process, 'Nothing', because it did not correspond to any reality that we could conceive. Creation was truly *ex nihilo*. The kabbalists noticed that there were two accounts of the creation of Adam. In Chapter One of Genesis, God created *adam* ('humankind'), which, the mystics decided, was primordial humanity (*adam kadmon*), the climax of the creative process, made in God's image: the divine became manifest in the archetypal human being, the *sefiroth* forming his body and limbs.

In Chapter Two, when God created Adam from dust, he brought earthbound humanity as we know it into being. This mundane Adam was supposed to contemplate the entire mystery of the Godhead on the first Sabbath, but he took the easier option and meditated only on the Shekhinah, the nearest and most accessible *sefirah*. This – not the act of disobedience – was the reason for Adam's fall, which shattered the unity of the divine world, separating the Tree of Life from the Tree of Knowledge, and tearing the fruit from the tree to which it was supposed to cling. The Shekhinah was ripped away from the tree of *sefiroth* and has remained in exile from the divine world.

The kabbalists, however, had the power to reunite the Shekhinah with the rest of the *sefiroth* by performing the task assigned to Adam. In their *pardes* exegesis, they could contemplate the entire divine mystery in all its complexity and the whole of scripture became a coded reference to the interaction of the *sefiroth*. Abraham's binding of Isaac showed how *Din* and *Hesed* – Judgement and Mercy – must act together, each tempering the other. The story of Joseph, who resisted sexual temptation and rose to power as the provider of food in Egypt, showed that in the divine psyche, restraint (*Din*) was always balanced by grace (*Tifereth*). The Song of Songs symbolized the yearning for harmony and unity that throbs through all levels of existence.[43]

Just as En Sof devolved, exteriorized and constricted itself in the progressive emanation of the *sefiroth*, so too the Godhead expressed itself in the limited human words of the Torah. The kabbalists learned to explore the different levels of the Bible in the same way as they contemplated the layers of divinity. In the *Zohar*, the Torah was compared to a beautiful maiden, secluded in a palace, who had a secret lover. She knew that he was forever walking up and down the street outside her chamber in the hope of seeing her, so she opened a door to show him her face – just for a second – and then withdrew. Only her lover understood the significance of her fleeting appearance. This was the way Torah revealed herself to a mystic. First she gave him a sign; next she spoke with him 'from behind the veil which she has hung before her words, so that they suit the manner of understanding in order that he may progress gradually'.[44] Very slowly, the kabbalist progressed from one level of scripture to another – through the moral reflections of *darash* and the riddles and allegories of *remez*. The veils became thinner and less opaque, until at last, as he reached the culminating insight of *sod*, the beloved 'stands disclosed, face to face with him, and holds converse with him concerning all of her secret mysteries, and all the secret ways which have been hidden in her heart from immemorial time'.[45] The mystic must strip away the surface meaning of the Bible – all the stories, laws and genealogies – as a lover unveils his beloved and learns to recognize not only her body but her soul.

> People without understanding see only the narratives, the
> garment; those somewhat more penetrating see also the
> body. But the truly wise, those who serve the most high King
> and stand on Mount Sinai, pierce all the way through to the
> soul, to the true Torah, which is the root principle of all.[46]

Anybody who simply read the Bible literally 'as a book presenting narratives and everyday matters', had missed the point. There was nothing special about the literal Torah: anybody could write a better book – even the gentiles had produced greater works.[47]

Kabbalists combined their mystical meditations on scripture with vigils, fasts and constant self-examination. They had to live together in fellowship, repressing selfishness and egotism because anger entered into the psyche like an evil spirit and shattered the divine harmony of his soul. It was impossible to experience the unity of the *sefiroth* in such a divided state.[48] The love of friends was fundamental to the *ekstasis* of Kabbalah. In the *Zohar*, one of the signs of a successful piece of exegesis is the cry of joy uttered by the interpreter's colleagues when they have heard what they experience as divine truth or when the exegetes kiss one another before they resume their mystical journey.

Kabbalists believed that the Torah was flawed, incomplete and presented relative rather than absolute truth. Some thought that two whole books were missing from our Torah or that our alphabet lacked one of its letters, so that language itself had been dislocated. Others developed a version of the myth of the Seven Ages of Man, each of which lasted seven thousand years and was ruled by one of the seven 'lower' *sefiroth*. The First Age had been governed by *Rekhamim/ Tifereth* (Grace and Compassion). All creatures had lived together in harmony and their Torah never spoke of the serpent, the Tree of Knowledge or death because these realities did not exist. But we were living in the Second Age of *Din*, the Stern Judgement that reflects the darker side of God, so our Torah spoke of constant conflict between good and evil, was full of laws, judgements and prohibitions, and its stories were often violent and cruel. But in the Third Cycle, under *Hesed* (Mercy), the Torah would be good and holy once more.

Kabbalah began as a tiny, esoteric movement, but it would

become a mass movement in Judaism and its mythology would influence even those who had no mystical talent. As their history became more tragic, Jews found the dynamic God of the mystics more sympathetic than the remote God of the philosophers, and felt increasingly that the plain sense of scripture was unsatisfactory and could shed no light without the interpretation of an inherited tradition (*kaballah*).

In Europe, however, Christians were coming to the opposite conclusion. The Franciscan scholar Nicholas of Lyre (1270–1340) combined the older methods of interpretation with the new insights of the scholastics. He defended the use of the three 'spiritual senses' of the Bible, but preferred the plain sense of historical exegesis. He had taught himself Hebrew, was familiar with the work of Rashi and proficient in Aristotelian philosophy. His *Postillae,* a literal exegesis of the whole of the Bible, became a standard textbook.

Other developments revealed a growing dissatisfaction with the traditional interpretation. Roger Bacon (1214–92), an English Franciscan, had no patience with scholastic theology and urged scholars to study the Bible in the original languages. Marsilio of Padua (1275–1342) was incensed by the growing power of the established Church and challenged papal claims to be the supreme guardian of the Bible. Henceforth all reformers would link their dislike of popes, cardinals and bishops with a rejection of their claim to be the arbiters of exegesis. John Wycliffe (1329–84), an Oxford academic, became enraged by the corruption of the Church and argued that the Bible should be translated into the vernacular, so that the common people did not have to rely on the priesthood but could read the Word of God for themselves. 'Crist seith that the gospel shold be prechid in al the world,' he insisted: 'Holi writ is the scripture of pupilis for it is maad that alle pupilis shulden knowe it.'[49] And William Tyndale (c. 1494–1536), who translated the Bible into English, raised the same issues: should the authority of the Church be greater than that of the gospel or should the gospel be elevated above the Church? By the sixteenth century this discontent would erupt in a biblical revolution that urged the faithful to rely on scripture alone.

CHAPTER 7

Sola Scriptura

By the sixteenth century, a complex process was under way in Europe that would irrevocably change the way Western people experienced the world. Inventions and innovations, none of which seemed momentous at the time, were occurring simultaneously in many different fields, but their cumulative effect would be decisive. The Iberian explorers had discovered a new world, astronomers were opening up the heavens, and a new technical efficiency was giving Europeans more control over their environment than ever before. A pragmatic, scientific spirit was very slowly beginning to undermine medieval sensibility. A series of catastrophes had left people feeling helpless and anxious. During the fourteenth and fifteenth centuries, the Black Death had killed a third of the population of Europe, the Ottoman Turks had conquered Christian Byzantium in 1453, and the papal scandals of the Avignon captivity and the Great Schism, when as many as three pontiffs had claimed the See of Peter, had alienated many from the established Church. People would soon find it impossible to be religious in the traditional way and this would affect their reading of the Bible.

The West was about to create a civilization that had no precedent in world history, but on the threshold of this new era, many wanted to return *ad fontes*, 'to the wellsprings' of their culture, to the classical world of Greece and Rome as well as to early Christianity. The philosophers and humanists of the Renaissance were highly critical of much medieval piety, especially of scholastic theology, which they found too dry and abstract, and wanted to go back to the Bible and the fathers of the Church.[1] Christianity, they believed, should be an experience rather than a body of doctrines. But the humanists had also imbibed the scientific spirit of the age and began to study the biblical text more objectively. The Renaissance is usually remembered for its rediscovery of classical paganism, but it also had a strong biblical character, which was in part inspired by a wholly new enthusiasm for the study of Greek. The humanists had started to read Paul as well as Homer in the original language and found the experience electrifying.

Very few Western people had been familiar with Greek in the Middle Ages, but Byzantine refugees from the Ottoman wars had fled to Europe in the fifteenth century and hired themselves out as tutors. In 1519, the Dutch humanist Desiderius Erasmus (1466–1536) published the Greek text of the New Testament, which he had translated into an elegant Ciceronian Latin that was very different from the Vulgate. The humanists valued style and rhetoric above all else. They were also concerned about the errors that had accumulated in the text over the centuries, and wanted to liberate the Bible from the accretions and baggage of the past.

The fact that the invention of the printing press made it possible for Erasmus to publish his translation was of immense importance. Anybody who knew Greek could now immediately read the gospels in the original. Other scholars could review the translation more quickly than ever before and suggest improvements. Erasmus profited from these suggestions and published several more editions of his New Testament before he died. He had been greatly influenced by the Italian humanist Lorenzo Valla (1405–57), who had produced an anthology of the main New Testament 'proof texts' used to support Church doctrine; but he had placed the Vulgate version alongside the original Greek, pointing out that these texts did not always 'prove' what they claimed because the Vulgate was so inaccurate. But Valla's *Collatio* had appeared only in manuscript; Erasmus had it printed and immediately it reached a far wider audience.

It would now be de rigueur to read the Bible in the original languages, and this scholarly requirement encouraged a more detached, historical attitude towards biblical antiquity. Hitherto, exegetes had viewed the Bible as a single work rather than a collection of diverse books. They may never have physically seen the scriptures in a single volume, but the practice of linking disparate texts together had encouraged them to downplay differences of vision and period. Now the humanists began to study the biblical authors as individuals, noting their special talents and idiosyncracies. They were especially drawn to Paul, whose style took on new immediacy in the original *koine* Greek. His passionate quest for salvation seemed a salutary antidote to scholastic rationalism. Unlike humanists today, they were not sceptical about religion, but had become ardent Pauline Christians.

They could particularly empathize with Paul's acute sense of sin. A period of wrenching social change is often characterized by anxiety. People feel lost and impotent; living *in medias res*, they cannot see the direction their society is taking but experience its subterranean transformation in incoherent, sporadic ways. Alongside the enthralling achievements of the early sixteenth century, there was widespread distress. The Protestant reformers Huldrych Zwingli (1484–1531) and John Calvin (1509–64) both felt a sense of acute failure and powerlessness before they found a new religious solution. The Catholic reformer Ignatius Loyola (1491–1556), founder of the Society of Jesus, wept so copiously during Mass that doctors warned him that he could easily lose his sight. And the Italian poet Francesco Petrarch (1304–74) was equally lacrymose: 'With what floods of tears I have sought to wash away my stains so that I can scarce speak of it without weeping, yet hitherto all is vain. God indeed is the best: and I am the worst.'[2]

Few experienced the angst of the age more painfully than a young monk in the Augustinian monastery of Erfurt in Germany:

> Although I lived a blameless life as a monk, I felt I was a
> sinner with an uneasy conscience before God. I also could
> not believe that I had pleased him with my works. Far from

loving that righteous God who punished sinners, I actually
loathed him . . . My conscience would not give me certainty,
but I always doubted and said, 'You did not do that right.
You weren't contrite enough. You left that out of your confession.'[3]

Martin Luther (1483–1546) had been educated in the scholastic philosophy of William of Ockham (c.1287–1347), who had
urged Christians to try to merit God's grace by their good
works.[4] But Luther fell prey to agonizing depression and none
of the traditional pieties could assuage his extreme terror of
death.[5] To escape his fears, he plunged into a frenzy of reform-
ing activity and was especially incensed by the papal policy of
selling indulgences to swell the coffers of the Church.

Luther was rescued from his existential distress by exegesis. The first time he saw a copy of the whole Bible he had
been astonished that it contained so many more writings
than he had realized.[6] He felt that he was seeing it for the
first time.[7] Luther became Professor of Scripture and
Philosophy at the University of Wittenberg and during the
lectures that he gave on the Psalms and Paul's epistles to the
Romans and Galatians (1513–18) he experienced a spiritual
breakthrough that enabled him to break free from his
Ockhamite prison.[8]

The lectures on the Psalms began conventionally enough –
Luther expounded the text verse by verse according to each
of the four senses in turn. But there were two significant
changes. First, Luther asked the university printer Johannes

Gutenberg to produce a custom-made Psalter for him with an ample margin and wide spaces for his own annotations. He had, as it were, wiped the sacred page clean, erasing the traditional gloss in order to start again. Second, he introduced an entirely novel definition of the literal sense. By 'literal' he did not mean the original intention of the author; he meant 'christological'. 'In the whole of scripture,' he claimed, 'there is nothing else but Christ, either in plain words or involved words.'[9] 'Take Christ from the scriptures,' he asked on another occasion, 'and what else will you find there?'[10]

The quick answer to that question is that you will find a great deal. As he grew more familiar with the whole of the Bible, Luther became aware that much of the Bible had very little to do with Christ. Even in the New Testament, there were books that were more Christ-centred than others. This compelled him over the years to invent a new hermeneutics. Luther's solution was to create a 'canon within the canon'. A man of his time, he was especially drawn to Paul, finding his letters describing the Christian experience of the risen Christ far more valuable than the synoptic gospels which were merely about Christ. For the same reason, he privileged John's gospel and the First Epistle of Peter but relegated Hebrews, the epistles of James and Jude, and Revelation to the periphery. He applied the same criteria to the 'Old Testament': he discarded the Apocrypha and had little time for the historical books and the legal sections of the Pentateuch. But he admitted Genesis to his personal canon because Paul quoted it, together with the prophets, who had foreseen the coming of Christ, and the Psalms, which had helped him to understand Paul.[11]

During his lectures on the Psalter, Luther began to ponder the meaning of the word 'righteousness' (Hebrew: *tseddeq*; Latin: *justitia*). Christians had traditionally read the psalms of the royal House of David as direct prophecies of Jesus. Thus, for example, the verse 'God, give your justice to the king, your own righteousness to the royal son'[12] referred to Christ. But Luther's emphasis was different. Understood *literally* – that is, for Luther, christologically – the plea 'In your righteousness, deliver me'[13] was a prayer uttered by Jesus to his Father. But according to the *moral* sense, the words referred to the deliverance of the individual, on whom Christ had bestowed his own righteousness.[14] Luther was gradually moving towards the idea that virtue was not a prerequisite for God's grace but a divine gift, relating the text directly to his own spiritual dilemma: God gave his own justice and righteousness to human beings.

Not long after these lectures on the Psalms, Luther achieved an exegetical breakthrough in his study in the monastery tower. He had been struggling to understand Paul's description of the gospel as a revelation of the righteousness of God: 'In[the gospel], the righteousness of God is revealed, as it is written, *The righteous man shall live through faith*.'[15] His Ockhamite teachers had taught him to understand 'the righteousness (*justitia*) of God' as the divine justice that condemns the sinner. How could this be 'good news'? And what did God's justice have to do with faith? Luther meditated on the text day and night until light dawned: the 'righteousness of God' in the gospel was the divine mercy which clothes the sinner in God's own goodness. All the sinner needed was faith. Immediately Luther's anxieties fell away. 'I felt as though I had been born again, and as though I had entered through open gates into paradise itself.'[16]

After this, the whole of scripture took on new meaning. During Luther's lectures on Romans, there was a marked change. His approach was more informal and less tied to medieval custom. He no longer bothered with the four senses but concentrated on his christological interpretation of the Bible and was openly critical of the scholastics. There was no need for fear. As long as he had 'faith', the sinner could say 'Christ has done enough for me. He is just. He is my defence. He has died for me. He has made his righteousness my right-eousness.'[17] But by 'faith' Luther did not mean 'belief' but an attitude of trust and self-abandonment: 'Faith does not require information, knowledge and certainty, but a free sur-render and a joyful bet on [God's] unfelt, untried and unknown goodness.'[18]

In his lectures on Galatians, Luther expanded on 'justifica-tion by faith'. In this epistle, Paul had attacked those Jewish-Christians who wanted gentile converts to observe the entire law of Moses, when, according to Paul, all that was necessary was trust (*pistis*) in Christ. Luther had begun to develop a dichotomy between Law and Gospel.[19] Law was the means God used to reveal his wrath and the sinfulness of human beings. We encountered the Law in the inflexible commands that we find in scripture, such as the Ten Commandments. The sinner quails before these demands, which he finds impossible to fulfil. But the Gospel revealed the divine mercy that saves us. 'Law' was not confined to the Mosaic law: there was 'Gospel' in the Old Testament (when the prophets looked forward to Christ) and plenty of daunting commandments in the New. Both Law and Gospel came from God, but only the Gospel could save us.

On 31 October 1517, Luther nailed ninety-five theses on the church door in Wittenberg, protesting against the sale of indulgences and the Pope's claim to forgive sins. The very first thesis pitted the authority of the Bible against sacramental tradition: 'When our Lord and Master Jesus Christ said "Repent," he willed the entire life of believers to be one of repentence.' Luther had learned from Erasmus that *metanoia*, which the Vulgate translated *poenitentiam agere* ('do penance'), meant a 'turning around' of the Christian's whole being. It did not mean going to confession. No practice or tradition of the Church could claim divine sanction unless it had the support of the Bible. In his public debate in Leipzig with Johann Eck, theology professor at Ingolstadt (1519), Luther made his controversial new doctrine *sola scriptura* ('scripture alone') explicit for the first time. How could Luther understand the Bible, Eck asked, without the popes, councils and universities? Luther replied: 'A simple layman armed with scripture is to be believed above a pope or a council without it.'[20]

This was an unprecedented claim.[21] Jews and Christians

had always upheld the sacred importance of inherited tradition. For Jews, the oral Torah was essential to the understanding of the written Torah. Before the New Testament had been written, the gospel had been preached by word of mouth and the Christians' scripture had been the Law and the prophets. By the fourth century, when the canon of the New Testament was finalized, the churches relied on their creeds, liturgies and the pronouncements of the church councils as well as upon scripture.[22] Nevertheless, the Protestant Reformation, a deliberate attempt to return to the origins of the faith, made *sola scriptura* one of its most important principles. In fact, Luther himself did not reject tradition. He was happy to use the liturgy and creeds, as long as they did not contradict scripture and he was well aware that the gospel had originally been preached orally. It had only been written down, he explained, because of the danger of heresy and it represented a falling away from the ideal. The gospel must remain a 'loud cry', a vocal summons. The Word of God could not be confined to a written text; it must be brought to life by the human voice in preaching, lectures and the singing of hymns and psalms.[23]

But despite his commitment to the spoken Word, Luther's greatest achievement was probably his translation of the Bible into German. He began with the New Testament, which he translated from Erasmus's Greek text (1522), and then, working at breakneck speed, he completed the Old Testament in 1534. By the time of Luther's death, one German in seventy owned a copy of the vernacular New Testament and Luther's

German Bible became a symbol of German integrity. During the sixteenth and seventeenth centuries, kings and princes throughout Europe started to declare independence of the papacy and form absolute monarchies. The centralized state was an essential part of the modernizing process, and the vernacular Bible became a symbol of the nascent national will. The translation of the Bible into English, which culminated in the King James Bible (1611), was endorsed and controlled at almost every step by the Tudor and Stuart monarchies.

Zwingli and Calvin also based their reforms on the principle of *sola scriptura* but they differed from Luther in several important respects. They were less interested in theology and more concerned with the social and political transformation of the Christian life. They both owed a great deal to the humanists, and insisted on the importance of reading the Bible in the original languages. But they did not approve of Luther's 'canon within the canon'. They both wanted their congregations to be acquainted with the entire Bible. Zwingli's theological seminary in Zurich published excellent biblical commentaries, which were distributed all over Europe, and the Zurich translation of the Bible was published before Luther's. Calvin was convinced that the Bible had been written for simple, unlettered people and had been stolen from them by the scholars. But he realized that they would need guidance. Preachers must be well read in rabbinical and patristic exegesis and acquainted with contemporary scholarship. They must always see a biblical passage in its original context but at the same time they must make the

Bible relevant to the daily needs of their congregations.

Zwingli's study of the Greek and Roman classics had taught him to appreciate other religious cultures:[24] the Bible did not have the monopoly of revealed truth; Socrates and Plato had also been inspired by the Spirit and Christians would meet them in heaven. Like Luther, Zwingli believed that the written Word must be spoken aloud. Because a preacher was guided by the Spirit in the same way as the biblical authors, Zwingli regarded his own sermons as prophetic. His task was to animate the written Word and make it a living force in the community. The Bible was not about what God had done in the past, but what he did here and now.[25]

Calvin, however, had no time for classical culture. He agreed with Luther that Christ was the focus of scripture and the ultimate manifestation of God. But Calvin had a far greater appreciation of the Hebrew Bible. God's revelation had been a gradual, evolutionary process; at each stage of their history, he had adapted his truth to the limited capacity of human beings. The teaching and guidance that God had given to Israel had changed and developed over time.[26] The religion entrusted to Abraham was tailored to the needs of a simpler society than the *torah* bestowed upon Moses or David. The revelation became progressively clearer and more focused on the *christos*, right up to the time of John the Baptizer, who had looked directly into the eyes of Jesus. But the Old Testament was not simply about Christ, as Luther had argued. The covenant with Israel had its own integrity; it came from the same God, and the study of the Torah would help Christians to understand the Gospel. Calvin would become the most influential of the Protestant reformers and make the Jewish scriptures more important to Christians – especially in the Anglo-Saxon world – than ever before.

Calvin never tired of pointing out that in the Bible God condescended to our limitations. The Word was conditioned by the historical circumstances in which it was uttered, so the less edifying stories of the Bible must be seen in context, as a phase in an ongoing process. There was no need to explain them away allegorically. The creation story in Genesis was an example of this divine *balbative* ('baby talk'), which adapted immensely complex processsses to the mentality of uneducated people.[27] It was not surprising that the Genesis story differed from the new theories of learned philosophers. Calvin had great respect for modern science. It should not be condemned simply 'because some frantic persons are wont boldly to reject whatever is unknown to them. For astronomy is not only pleasant but also very useful to be known: it cannot be denied that this art unfolds the admirable wisdom of God.'[28] It was absurd to expect scripture to teach scientific fact; anybody who wanted to learn about astronomy should look elsewhere. The natural world was God's first revelation, and Christians should regard the new geographical, biological and physical sciences as religious activities.[29]

The great scientists shared this view. Nicolaus Copernicus (1473–1543) regarded science as 'more divine than human'.[30] His heliocentric hypothesis was so radical that few people could take it in: instead of being located in the centre of the universe, the earth and the other planets were rotating around the sun; the world appeared to be stable, but was in fact in rapid motion. Galileo Galilei (1564–1642) tested the Copernican theory empirically by observing the planets through his telescope. He was silenced by the Inquisition and forced to recant, but his somewhat aggressive and provocative temperament had also played a part in his condemnation. At first, Catholics and Protestants did not automatically reject the new science. The Pope approved of Copernicus's theory when he first presented it in the Vatican and the early Calvinists and Jesuits were both keen scientists. But some were disturbed by the new theories. How could you reconcile Copernicus's theory with a literal reading of Genesis? If, as Galileo suggested, there was life on the moon, how had these people descended from Adam? How could the revolutions of the earth be squared with Christ's ascension to heaven? Scripture said that the heavens and the earth had been created for man's benefit, but how could this be so if the earth was just another planet revolving round an undistinguished star?[31] The old allegorical exegesis would have made it much easier for Christians to cope with their changing world.[32] But the increasing emphasis on the literal meaning of scripture was the product of early modernity: the scientific bias of early modern thought required people to see truth as conforming to the laws of the external world. It would not be long before some Christians would conclude that unless a book was historically or scientifically demonstrable it could not be true at all.

*

The Jewish people had not yet succumbed to this enthusiasm for the literal: in 1492 they had suffered a disaster, which made many turn to the mystical consolations of Kabbalah. In 1492, Ferdinand and Isabella, the Catholic monarchs of Aragon and Castile, had conquered the kingdom of Granada, the last Muslim stronghold in Europe. Jews and Muslims were given the option of conversion to Christianity or deportation. Many Jews chose exile and took refuge in the new Ottoman empire where a significant number settled in Palestine, which was now an Ottoman province. In Safed in northern Galilee, the saintly mystic Isaac Luria (1534–72) developed a kabbalastic myth that bore no resemblance to the first chapter of Genesis, and yet by the mid-seventeenth century Lurianic Kabbalah had a mass following in Jewish communities from Poland to Iran.[33] Exile had been a central preoccupation for Jews since their deportation to Babylonia. For the Spanish Jews – the Sephardim – the loss of their homeland was the worst disaster to have befallen their people since the destruction of the temple. They felt that everything was in the wrong place and that their entire world had collapsed. Snatched forever from places that were saturated in memories essential to their identity, exiles can feel that their very existence is in jeopardy. When exile is also associated with human cruelty, it raises urgent problems about the nature of evil in a world supposedly created by a just and benevolent God.

In Luria's new myth, God began the creative process by going voluntarily into exile. How could the world exist if God was everywhere? Luria's answer was the myth of *zimzum* ('withdrawal') : the infinite En Sof had, as it were, to evacuate a region within itself to make room for the cosmos. This cosmology was punctuated by accidents, primal explosions and false starts, quite different from the orderly, peaceful creation described in P. But to the Sephardim, Luria's myth seemed a more accurate appraisal of their unpredicatable, fragmented world. At an early stage in the creative process, En Sof had tried to fill the vacuum it had created by *zimzum* with divine light, but the 'vessels' or 'pipes' designed to channel it had broken. So sparks of the primal light fell into the abyss that was not-God. Some of these returned to the divine world, but others remained trapped in the Godless realm dominated by the evil potential of *Din*, which En Sof had – as it were – attempted to purge from itself. After this accident, everything was in the wrong place. Adam could have rectified the situation on the first Sabbath, but he sinned and henceforth the divine sparks remained trapped in matter. The Shekhinah, now in permanent exile, wandered through the world, yearning to be reunited with the rest of the *sefiroth*. Yet there was hope. Jews were not outcasts, but essential to the redemption of the world. Their careful observance of the commandments and the special rituals evolved in Safed could effect the 'restoration' (*tikkun*) of the Shekhinah to the Godhead, the Jews to the Promised Land, and the world to its rightful state.[34]

In Lurianic Kabbalah, the literal, surface meaning of the Bible was a symptom of the primal disaster. Originally the letters of the Torah had been numinous with divine light and had come together to form the *sefiroth*, the secret names of God. When he was first created, Adam had been a spiritual being, but when he sinned his 'great soul' was shattered and his nature became more material. After this catastrophe, humanity needed a different Torah: the divine letters now formed words that related to human beings and earthly events while the commandments required physical actions to separate profane from sacred matter. But when *tikkun* was complete, the Torah would be restored to its original spirituality. 'What pious men now enact in material performance of the commandments,' Luria explained, 'they will then, in the paradisical garment of the soul, so enact as God intended when he created man.'[35]

The restoration of *tikkun* would also redeem the Bible. Kabbalists had long been aware of the flaws in their scriptures. In Lurianic Kabbalah, the God of the Hebrew Bible was one of the 'faces' (*parzufim*) of Adam Kadmon, primordial man, which was composed of six of the 'lower' *sefiroth*: Judgement (*Din*), Mercy, Compassion, Patience, Majesty and Stability. Originally they had been in perfect balance, but after the breaking of the vessels the destructive tendency of *Din* was no longer held in check by the other *sefiroth*. Dominated by *Din*, they became collectively *Zeir Anpin*, 'the Impatient One', the deity revealed in the post-lapsarian Torah. This was why the biblical God often appeared so cruel and irascible.

Separated from the Shekhinah, his female counterpart, he was also irredeemably male.

But there was optimism in this tragic myth. Where Luther felt that he could contribute nothing towards his own salvation, the kabbalists believed that they could transform the world, restore God to his true nature, and reform their scriptures. They did not deny their pain: indeed, the rituals of Safed were designed to help them to face it. They made night vigils, weeping and rubbing their faces in the dust, to identify their own exile with that of the Shekhinah. But Luria was adamant that there must be no wallowing. Kabbalists must work through their sorrow in a purposeful way until they achieved a measure of joy. The vigil always ended with a meditation on the final reunion of the Shekhinah with *Zeir Anpin* in which they imagined that their bodies had become an earthly shrine for the divine presence. They saw visions, shook with wonder and awe, and experienced a rapturous transcendence that transformed the world that had seemed so cruel and alien.[36]

This sense of unity and joy had to be translated into practical action because the Shekhinah could not live in a place of sorrow and pain. Sadness sprang from the forces of evil in the world, so the cultivation of happiness was essential to *tikkun*. To counterbalance the prevalence of *Din*, there must be no anger or aggression in the kabbalists' heart, even for the *goyim* who had oppressed and dispossessed them. There were severe penances for faults that injured others: for sexual exploitation, malicious gossip, humiliating others and dishonouring parents.[37] Luria's mythical rewriting of the creation story helped Jews to develop a spirit of joy and kindness at a time when they could have been overcome by rage and despair.

The new discipline of *sola scriptura* was not able to do this for the Christians of Europe. Even after his great breakthrough, Luther remained terrified of death. He seemed constantly in a state of simmering rage: against the Pope, the Turks, Jews, women, rebellious peasants, scholastic philosophers and every single one of his theological opponents. He and Zwingli engaged in a furious controversy about the meaning of Christ's words when he had instituted the Eucharist at the last supper, saying 'This is my body'.[38] Calvin was appalled by the anger that had clouded the minds of the two reformers and caused an unholy rift that could and should have been avoided: 'Both parties failed altogether to have patience to listen to each other, in order to follow truth without passion, wherever it might be found,' he concluded. 'I deliberately venture to assert that, if their minds had not been partly exasperated by the extreme vehemence of the controversies, the disagreement was not so great that conciliation could easily have been achieved.'[39] It was impossible for interpreters to agree on every single passage of the Bible; disputes must be conducted humbly and with an open mind. Yet Calvin himself did not always live up to these high principles, and was prepared to execute dissenters in his own church.

The Protestant Reformation expressed many of the ideals

of the new culture that was emerging in the West. Instead of being based on a surplus of agricultural produce, like every previous civilization, its economy would be based on the scientific and technological replication of resources and the constant reinvestment of capital. This society had to be productive, and Calvin's theology would be used to support the work ethic. Individuals had to participate, even at a humble level, as printers, factory hands and office clerks, and had, therefore, to acquire a modicum of education and literacy. As a result, they would eventually demand a greater share in the decision-making process of government. There would be political upheaval, revolutions and civil war to establish more democratic regimes. Social, political, economic and intellectual change was part of an interlocking process; each element depended upon the others and religion was inevitably drawn into this spiral of development.

People now read scripture in a 'modern' way. Protestants stood alone before God, relying on the Bible alone. But this would have been impossible before the invention of printing made it feasible for all Christians to own individual copies and before they had the literacy skills to read it. Increasingly, as the pragmatic, scientific ethos of modernity took hold, scripture was read for the information that it imparted. Science depended upon rigorous analysis, and this made the symbolic system of the perennial philosophy incomprehensible. The eucharistic bread – the issue that had divided Luther and Zwingli – was now 'only' a symbol. The words of scripture, once seen as earthly replicas of the divine Logos, had also lost their numinous dimension. But the silent, solitary reading, which freed Christians from the supervision of religious experts, expressed the independence that would become essential to the modern spirit.

Sola scriptura had been a noble, if controversial ideal. But in practice it meant that everybody had a God-given right to interpret these extremely complex documents as they chose.[40] Protestant sects proliferated, each claiming that it alone understood the Bible. In 1534, a radical apocalyptic group in Munster set up an independent theocratic state based on a literal reading of scripture, which licensed polygamy, condemned all violence and outlawed private ownership. This short-lived experiment lasted only a year, but it alarmed the reformers. If there was no authoritative body to control biblical reading, how could anybody know who was right? 'Who will give our conscience sure information about which party is teaching us the pure Word of God, we or our opponents?' asked Luther. 'Is every fanatic to have the right to teach whatever he pleases?'[41] Calvin agreed: 'If everyone has a right to be judge and arbiter in this matter, nothing can be set down as certain and our whole religion will be full of uncertainty.'[42]

Religious liberty was becoming problematic in a political world that increasingly demanded conformity, and was prepared to achieve it by coercive means. In the seventeenth century, Europe was convulsed by wars, which may have been articulated in a religious imagery, but which were really caused by the need for a different kind of political organization in the new Europe. The old feudal kingdoms had to be transformed into efficient, centralized states, initially under absolute monarchs, who could impose unity by force. Ferdinand and Isabella were welding together the old Iberian kingdoms to form a united Spain, but they did not yet have the resources to allow their subjects untrammelled freedom. There was no room for autonomous, self-governing bodies, such as the Jewish communities. The Spanish Inquisition, which hounded these dissidents, was a modernizing institution, designed to create ideological conformity and national unity.[43] As modernization progressed, Protestant rulers in such countries as England were just as ruthless to their Catholic subjects, who were regarded as enemies of state. The so-called Wars of Religion (1618–48) were in fact a thirty-year struggle on the part of the kings of France and the German princes to become politically independent of the Holy Roman Empire and the papacy, even though it was complicated by the confrontation of militant Calvinism and a reinvigorated, reformed Catholicism.

Modernization was progressive and empowering, but it had an inbuilt intolerance: there would always be people who experienced this new Western society as cruel and invasive. Freedom for some meant enslavement for others. In 1620, a party of English settlers made the perilous journey across the Atlantic in the *Mayflower* and arrived in the harbour of Plymouth, Massachusetts. They were English Puritans, radical Calvinists who felt persecuted by the Anglican establishment and decided to migrate to the New World. They had inherited Calvin's interest in the Old Testament and were particularly drawn to the story of the Exodus, which seemed a literal forecast of their own project. England was their Egypt; the transatlantic voyage their sojourn in the wilderness, and they had now arrived in the Promised Land, which they christened New Canaan.[44]

The Puritans gave their colonies biblical names: Hebron, Salem, Bethlehem, Sion and Judaea. When John Winthrop, who would become their leader, arrived on the *Arbella* in 1630, he proclaimed to his fellow passengers that America was Israel; like the ancient Israelites, they were about to take possession of the land but he quoted Moses's words in Deuteronomy: the Puritans would succeed if they kept the Lord's commandments, but would perish if they were disobedient.[45] Appropriating the land brought the Puritans into collision with the native Americans. Here too, they found a mandate in scripture. Like later colonialists, some believed that the indigenous inhabitants deserved their fate: they 'are not industrious, neither have art, science, skill or faculty to cure either the land or the commodities of it,' wrote Robert Cushman, the colony's business agent. 'As the ancient patriarchs therefore removed from straiter places into more roomy, where the land lay waste and idle and none used it . . . so it is lawful now to take a land which none seek to make use of it.'[46] When the Pequots remained hostile, other Puritans compared them with the Amalekites and Philistines 'that did confederate against Israel' and had, therefore, to be destroyed.[47] But some of the settlers believed that the native Americans were the ten lost tribes of Israel, who had been deported by the Assyrians in 722 BCE. Because Paul had predicted that Jews would accept Christianity before the end, the conversion of the Pequot would hasten the Second Coming of Christ.

Many of the Puritans were convinced that their migration to America was a prelude to the last days. Their colony was the 'city on the hill' foreseen by Isaiah, the beginning of a new era of peace and beatitude.[48] In 1654, Edward Johnson published a history of New England:

> Know this is the place where the Lord will create a new
> heaven and new earth, and a new commonwealth together.
> . . . These are but the beginning of Christ's glorious reforma-
> tion and restoration of his churches to a more glorious splen-
> dour than ever. He hath therefore caused the dazzling
> brightness of his presence to be contracted in the burning
> glass of his people's zeal, from whence it begins to be felt in
> many parts of the world.[49]

Not all the American colonists shared the Puritan vision, but it left an indelible impression on the ethos of the United States. The Exodus would remain a crucial text. It was cited by the revolutionary leaders of the War of Independence against Britain. Benjamin Franklin wanted the great seal of the nation to depict the parting of the Sea of Reeds, but the eagle that became America's symbol was not only an ancient imperial emblem but was also linked with the Exodus.[50]

Other migrants drew on the Exodus story in the same way: the Mormons, the Afrikaaners of South Africa, and the Jews who fled persecution in Europe and found refuge in the United States. God had saved them from oppression and established them in a new land – sometimes at the expense of others. Many Americans still regard themselves as a chosen people with a manifest destiny, and see their nation as a beacon to the rest of the world. There has been a tradition of American reformers making an 'errand into the wilderness' in order to make a new start. As we shall see in the next chapter, a significant number of American Protestants continued to be preoccupied by the last days and felt a strong identity with Israel. Yet even though Americans were committed to liberation and freedom, for two hundred years there was an enslaved Israel in their midst.

In 1619, the year before the *Mayflower* arrrived in Plymouth, a Dutch frigate had cast anchor off the shore of Virginia, with twenty 'negars' who had been captured in West Africa and forcibly conveyed to America. By 1660, the status of such Africans had been defined. They were slaves, who could be bought and sold, flogged, fettered and separated from their tribes, wives and children.[51] They were introduced to Christianity as slaves, and the Exodus became their story. At first they probably retained their traditional religion: slave masters were wary of their conversion, lest they used the Bible to demand freedom and basic human rights. But Christianity would have seemed grossly hypocritical to the slaves, since preachers quoted scripture to justify their enslavement. They cited Noah's curse of his grandson Canaan, the son of Ham, ancestor of the African peoples: 'He shall be his brothers' meanest slave.'[52] They referred to Paul's instructions that slaves be obedient to their masters.[53] Yet by the 1780s, African American slaves had redefined the Bible on their own terms.

Central to their Christianity was the 'spiritual', a song based on a biblical theme, accompanied by the stamping, sobbing, clapping and shrieking that had characterized African worship. Only about 5 per cent of the slaves could read, so the spirituals focused on the essence of the biblical story instead of the literal sense of the words. Like Luther, they created their own 'canon within the canon', concentrating on stories that spoke directly to their own condition: Jacob wrestling with the angel, Joshua entering the Promised Land, Daniel in the Lion's Den, and the suffering and resurrection of Jesus. But the most important narrative was the Exodus: the slaves' Egypt was America, but one day God would liberate them:

> When Israel was in Egypt's land,
>   O let my people go!
> Oppressed so hard they could not stand,
>   O let my people go!
> *Chorus:* O go down, Moses
> Away to Egypt's land,
> And tell King Pharaoh
> To let my people go!

The slaves used the Exodus story to raise their consciousness, to help them endure the dehumanizing conditions in
which they lived, and to demand justice. The spirituals per-
sisted long after the abolition of slavery by Abraham Lincoln;
the Exodus story inspired Martin Luther King Jr during the
civil rights movement in the 1960s, and after the assassina-
tions of King (1968) and Malcolm X (1965), the black liberation
theologian James Hal Cone argued that Christian theology
must become black theology, wholly identified with the cause
of the oppressed and affirmative of the divine character of
their struggle for freedom.[54]

A single text could be interpreted to serve diametrically
opposed interests. The more people were encouraged to
make the Bible the focus of their spirituality, the more difficult it became to find a core message. At the same time as
African Americans drew on the Bible to develop their theology of liberation, the Ku Klux Klan used it to justify their
lynching of blacks. But the Exodus story did not mean liberation for everybody. Israelites who rebelled against Moses
in the wilderness were exterminated; the indigenous
Canaanites were massacred by Joshua's armies. Black femi-
nist theologians have pointed out that the Israelites owned
slaves; that God had permitted them to sell their daughters
into slavery; and that God actually ordered Abraham to
abandon the Egyptian slave girl Hagar in the wilderness.[55]
Sola scriptura could point people in the direction of the Bible,
but it could never provide an absolute mandate: people
could always find alternative texts to support an opposing

point of view. By the seventeenth century, religious people were becoming acutely aware that the Bible was a very confusing book, and this at a time when clarity and rationality were prized as never before.

CHAPTER 8

Modernity

By the late seventeenth century, Europeans had entered the age of reason. Instead of relying on sacred tradition, scientists, scholars and philosophers were becoming future-oriented, ready to jettison the past and start again. Truth, they were beginning to discover, was never absolute, since new discoveries habitually undermined old certainties. Increasingly, truth had to demonstrated empirically and objectively, assessed by its efficiency in and fidelity to the external world. Consequently, the more intuitive modes of thought became suspect. Instead of conserving what had been achieved, scholars were becoming pioneers and specialists. The 'renaissance man', with an encyclopaedic grasp of knowledge, belonged to the past. It would soon be almost impossible for an expert in one field to be truly competent in another. The rationality of the philosophical movement known as the Enlightenment encouraged an analytic mode of thought: instead of trying to see things whole, people were learning to dissect a complex reality and study its component parts. All this would have a profound effect on the way they read the Bible.

In his seminal treatise, the *Advancement of Learning* (1605),

Francis Bacon (1561–1626), counsellor to King James I of England, was one of the first to argue that even the most sacred doctrines must be subjected to the stringent methods of empirical science. If these beliefs contradicted the evidence of our senses, they had to go. Bacon was enthralled by science, convinced that it would save the world and inaugurate the millennial kingdom foretold by the prophets. Its progress must not, therefore, be impeded by timorous, simple-minded clergymen. But Bacon was convinced that there could be no conflict between science and religion, since all truth was one. Bacon's view of science was, however, different from our own. For Bacon, the scientific method consisted of assembling proven facts; he did not appreciate the importance of guess-work and hypothesis in scientific research. The only information upon which we could rely came from our five senses; anything that could not be demonstrated empirically – philosophy, metaphysics, theology, art, mysticism and mythology – was irrelevant. His definition of truth would become extremely influential, not least among the more conservative champions of the Bible.

The new humanism was increasingly antagonistic to religion. The French philosopher René Descartes (1596–1650) maintained that there was no need for revealed scripture, since reason provided us with ample information about God. The British mathematician Isaac Newton (1642–1727) scarcely mentioned the Bible in his copious writings, because he derived his knowledge of God from an intensive study of the universe. Science would soon clear up the irrational 'mysteries' of traditional faith. The new religion of Deism, espoused by John Locke (1632–1704), one of the founders of the Enlightenment, was rooted in reason alone. Immanuel Kant (1724–1804) was convinced that a divinely revealed Bible violated the autonomy and freedom of the human being. Some thinkers went further. The Scottish philosopher David Hume (1711–76) argued that there was no reason to believe that anything lay beyond the experience of our senses. Denis Diderot (1713–84), philosopher, critic and novelist, simply did not care whether God existed or not, while Paul Heinrich, Baron of Holbach (1723–89) argued that belief in a supernatural God was an act of cowardice and despair.

Yet many of the men of reason were in love with the classics of Graeco-Roman antiquity, which seemed to fulfil many of the functions of scripture.[1] When Diderot read the classics, he experienced 'transports of admiration ... thrills of joy ... divine enthusiasm'.[2] Jean-Jacques Rousseau (1712–72) declared that he would study the Greek and Roman authors again and again.'I took fire!' he cried on reading Plutarch.[3] When the English historian Edward Gibbon (1737–94) visited Rome for the first time, he found that he could not proceed with his reasearch because he was 'agitated' by such 'strong emotions' and experienced a quasi-religious 'intoxication' and 'enthusiasm'.[4] They all invested these ancient works with their deepest aspirations, allowed them to shape their minds, inform their interior world, and found that, in return, the texts gave them moments of transcendence.

*

Other scholars applied their sceptically critical skills to the Bible. Baruch Spinoza (1632–77), a Sephardic Jew of Spanish descent born in the liberal city of Amsterdam, had studied mathematics, astronomy and physics and found them incompatible with his religious beliefs.[5] In 1655 he started to voice doubts that unsettled his community: the manifest contradictions in the Bible proved that it could not be of divine origin; the idea of revelation was a delusion; and there was no supernatural deity – what we called 'God' was simply nature itself. On 27 July 1656 Spinoza was excommunicated from the synagogue and became the first person in Europe to live successfully beyond the reach of established religion. Spinoza dismissed conventional faith as 'a tissue of meaningless mysteries'; he preferred to get what he called 'beatitude' from the untrammelled exercise of his reason.[6] Spinoza studied the historical background and literary genres of the Bible with unprecedented objectivity. He agreed with Ibn Ezra that Moses could not have written the entire Pentateuch but went on to claim that the extant text was the work of several different authors. He had become the pioneer of the historical-critical method that would later be called the Higher Criticism of the Bible.

Moses Mendelssohn (1729–86), the brilliant son of a poor Torah scholar in Dessau, Germany, was less radical. He had fallen in love with modern secular learning, but, like Locke, had no difficulty in accepting the idea of a benevolent God, which seemed to him a matter of common sense. He created the *Haskalah*, a Jewish 'enlightenment' which presented

Judaism as a rational faith well suited to modernity. On Mount Sinai, God had revealed himself in a law code, not a set of doctrines, so Jewish religion was concerned only with ethics and left the mind entirely free. Before they accepted the authority of the Bible, Jews must convince themselves rationally of its claims. It is difficult to recognize this as Judaism. Mendelssohn had tried to force it into a rationalistic mould that was alien to spirituality. Nevertheless many Jews, who became known as the *maskilim* (the 'enlightened ones'), were ready to follow him. They were eager to escape the intellectual constraints of the ghetto, move in gentile society, study the new sciences, and keep their faith a private matter.

But this rationalism was countered by a mystical movement among the Jews of Poland, Galicia, Belorusssia and Lithuania that amounted to a rebellion against modernity.[7] In 1735, Israel ben Eliezer (1698–1760), a poor Jewish tavernkeeper in south-eastern Poland, announced that he had become a *baal shem*, a 'Master of the Name', one of the many faith-healers who wandered through the rural districts of Eastern Europe, preaching in the name of God. This was a dark time for Polish Jewry. During a peasant uprising against the nobility (1648–67), Jews had been massacred in large numbers and were still vulnerable and economically deprived. There was an ever-widening gap between rich and poor, and many of the rabbis had simply retreated into Torah study and neglected their congregations. Israel ben Eliezer initiated a reform movement and became known as the *Baal Shem Tov* – or the 'Besht' – a master of exceptional status. By the end of his life, there were about forty thousand of his *Hasidim* ('pious ones').

The Besht claimed that he had not been singled out by God because he had studied the Talmud, but because he recited the traditional prayers with such fervour and concentration that he achieved ecstatic union with God. Unlike the rabbis of the Talmudic age, who believed that Torah study took precendence over prayer,[8] the Besht insisted on the primacy of contemplation.[9] A rabbi must not bury himself in his books and neglect the poor. Hasidic spirituality was based on Isaac Luria's myth of the divine sparks trapped in the material world, but the Besht transformed this tragic vision into a positive appreciation of the ubiquitous presence of God. A spark of the divine could be found in any material object, however lowly, and no activity – eating, drinking, making love or conducting business – was profane. By the constant practice of *devekut* ('attachment'), a Hasid cultivated a perpetual awareness of God's presence. Hasidim expressed this enhanced consciousness in ecstatic, noisy and tumultuous prayer, accompanied by extravagant gestures – such as turning somersaults that symbolized a total reversal of vision – that helped them to throw their whole being into their worship.

Just as the Hasidim looked through the veil of matter to see the divine spark latent within the most commonplace object, so too they learned to penetrate the words of the Bible and glimpse the divinity hidden beneath the surface. The words and letters of the Torah were vessels that contained the light of En Sof, so a Hasid must not concentrate on the purely literal sense of the text but on the spiritual reality it enclosed.[10] He must cultivate a receptive attitude and allow the Bible to speak to him by reining in his mental powers. One day, the Besht was visited by Dov Ber (1716–72), a learned kabbalist who would eventually succeed him as leader of the Hasidic movement. The two men studied Torah together and became immersed in a text about the angels. Dov Ber approached the passage in a rather abstract way and the Besht asked him to show respect for the angels they were discussing by standing up. As soon as he rose to his feet, 'the whole house was suffused with light, a fire burned all around, and they [both] sensed the presence of the angels'. 'The simple reading is as you say,' the Besht told Dov Ber, 'but your manner of studying lacked soul.'[11] A commonsense reading, without the attitudes and gestures of prayer, would not yield a vision of the unseen.

Without such prayer, Torah study was useless. As one of Dov Ber's disciples explained, Hasidim must read scripture 'with burning enthusiasm of the heart, with a coercion of all man's psychological faculties in the direction of clear and pure thoughts on God constantly, and in separation from every pleasure'.[12] The Besht told them that if they approached the story of Mount Sinai in this way, they would 'always hear God speak to them, as he did during the revelation on Sinai, because it was Moses's intention that all Israel be worthy of attaining the same level as he did'.[13] The point was not to read *about* Sinai but to experience Sinai itself.

When Dov Ber became the Hasidic leader, his scholarly

reputation attracted many rabbis and scholars to the movement. But his exegesis was no longer dry and academic. One
of his disciples recalled that 'When he opened his mouth to
speak words of Truth, he looked as if he was not of this world
at all and the Divine Presence spoke out of his throat.'[14]
Sometimes, in the middle of a word, he would pause and wait
for a while in silence. The Hasidim were evolving their own
lectio divina, making a quiet place for scripture in their hearts.
Instead of analysing a text and pulling it apart, the Hasid had
to still his critical faculties. 'I will teach you the way Torah is
best taught,' Dov Ber used to say: 'not to feel [conscious of]
oneself at all, but to be like a listening ear that hears the world
of sound speaking but does not speak itself.'[15] The exegete had
to make himself a vessel for the divine presence. The Torah
must act upon him, as though he were its instrument.[16]

Hasidism aroused fierce opposition from orthodox Jews,
who were appalled by the Besht's apparent denigration of the
scholarly study of Torah. They became known as the *Misnagdim* ('opponents'). Their leader was Elijah ben Solomon
Zalman (1720–97), head (*gaon*) of the academy of Vilna in
Lithuania. Torah study was the Gaon's chief passion, but he
was also proficient in astronomy, anatomy, mathematics and
foreign languages. Even though he studied scripture more
aggressively than the Hasidim, the Gaon's method was in its
own way mystical. He relished what he called the 'effort' of
study, an intense mental activity that tipped him into a new
level of consciousness, and kept him at his books all night, his
feet immersed in icy water to prevent him from falling asleep.

When he did allow himself to doze off, the Torah penetrated his dreams and he experienced an ascent to the divine. 'He who studies Torah communes with God,' one of his disciples claimed, 'for God and the Torah are one.'[17]

In Western Europe, however, it was becoming increasingly difficult to find God in scripture. The ethos of the Enlightenment had inspired more scholars to study the Bible critically, but it was impossible to experience its transcendent dimension without the gestures and disposition of prayer. In England, some of the more radical deists used the new scholarly methods to undermine the Bible.[18] The mathematician William Whiston (1667–1752) believed that early Christianity had been a more rational faith. In 1745 he published a version of the New Testament from which he had erased every reference to the Incarnation and the Trinity, doctrines that, he claimed, had been foisted on the faithful by the fathers of the Church. The Irish deist John Toland (1670–1722) tried to replace the New Testament with a manuscript that purported to be the long-lost Jewish-Christian gospel of Barnabas, which denied the divinity of Christ. Other sceptics argued that the text of the New Testament was so corrupt that it was impossible to determine what the Bible actually said. But the distinguished classicist Richard Bentley (1662–1742) mounted a scholarly campaign in the Bible's defence. Using the critical techniques now applied to Graeco-Roman literature, he showed that it was possible to reconstruct the original manuscripts by collating and analysing the variants.

In Germany the Pietists, who wanted to get beyond the arid doctrinal polemics of the competing Protestant sects, also seized on these analytic methods to reinstate the Bible, convinced that the biblical critic should be above denominational loyalty.[19] The Pietists' aim was to liberate religion from theology and recover a more personal experience of the divine. In 1694, they founded a university at Halle to bring the new scholarship to the laity in a non-sectarian guise and Halle became the centre of a biblical revolution.[20] Between 1711 and 1719, its press printed 100,000 copies of the New Testament and 80,000 complete Bibles. Halle scholars also produced the *Biblia Pentapla* to encourage a trans-denominational reading of scripture: five different translations were printed side by side, so that Lutherans, Calvinists and Catholics could read the version of their choice but could consult the wording in another column if they encountered a difficulty. Others translated the Bible in a wholly literal way to show that even in the vernacular the Word of God was far from clear. Theologians should be more reticent in their use of 'proof texts' that could not bear the weight of theological interpretation imposed upon them. If the original could not be rendered into elegant German, the Bible sounded strange and unfamiliar and this was a salutary reminder that it was always difficult to understand God's Word.[21]

By the end of the eighteenth century, German scholars led the way in biblical studies and were taking Spinoza's historical-critical method to new lengths. They agreed that Moses had certainly not written the entire Pentateuch, which seemed to have a number of different authors who all wrote in a distinctive style. One favoured the divine title 'Elohim'; another preferred to call God 'Yahweh'. There were duplicate narratives, obviously by different hands, such as the two creation accounts in Genesis.[22] So Jean Astruc (1684–1766), a Paris physician, and Johann Gottfried Eichhorn (1752–1827), Professor of Oriental Languages at Jena University, argued that there were two main documents in Genesis: the 'Yahwist' and the 'Elohist'. But in 1798, Karl David Igen, Eichhorn's successor, claimed that the Elohist material derived from two separate sources. Other scholars, including Johann Severin Vater (1771–1826) and Wilhelm DeWette (1780–1849) believed that this was too simplistic: the Pentateuch consisted of numerous, separate fragments that had been put together by a redactor.

By the nineteenth century, it was generally agreed by the scholars of the Higher Criticism that the Pentateuch was a combination of four originally independent sources. In 1805, DeWette argued that Deuteronomy ('D') was the latest book of the Pentateuch and was probably the *sefer torah* discovered in the time of Josiah. Hermann Hupfeld (1796–1866), a professor at Halle, agreed with Igen that the 'Elohist' source consisted of two separate documents: E1 (a priestly work) and E2. E1, he believed, was the earliest source, followed by E2, J and D, in that order. But Karl Heinrich Graf (1815–69) made an important breakthrough when he argued that the priestly document (E1) was in fact the latest of the four sources.

Julius Wellhausen (1844–1918) seized upon Graf's theory because it solved a problem that had long troubled him. Why did the prophets never refer to the Mosaic law? And why was the Deuteronomist, who was clearly familiar with the work of the Yahwist and Elohist, ignorant of the priestly document? All this could be explained if the priestly source (E1) was indeed a late composition. Wellhausen also showed that the four-document theory was too simplistic; there had been additions to all four sources before they had been combined into a single narrative. His work was regarded by his contemporaries as the culmination of the critical method, but Wellhausen himself realized that research had only just begun – and, indeed, it continues to the present day.

How would these discoveries affect the religious lives of Jews and Christians? Some Christians embraced the insights of the Enlightenment. Friedrich Schleiermacher (1768–1834) was initially disturbed that the Bible seemed such a flawed document.[23] His response was to promote a spirituality based on an experience that was fundamental to all religion, but which Christianity had expressed in a distinctive way. He defined this experience as 'the feeling of absolute dependence'.[24] This was no abject servility but a sense of reverence and awe before the mystery of life, which made us aware that we were not the centre of the universe. The gospels showed that Jesus perfectly embodied this attitude of wonder and surrender, and the New Testament described the impact of his personality on the disciples who founded the early church.

Scripture was, therefore, essential to the Christian life

because it provided us with our only access to Jesus. But because its authors were conditioned by the historical circumstances in which they lived, it was legitimate to subject their testimony to critical scrutiny. The life of Jesus had been a divine revelation, but the writers who recorded it were ordinary human beings, subject to sin and error. It was quite possible that they had made mistakes. But the Holy Spirit had guided the Church in its selection of canonical books, so Christians could put their trust in the New Testament. The scholar's task was to peel away its cultural shell to reveal the timeless kernel within. Not every word of scripture was authoritative, so the exegete must distinguish marginal ideas from the gospel's main thrust.

The Law and the prophets had been the scripture of the New Testament authors. But Schleiermacher believed that the Old Testament was not as authoritative as the New for Christians. It had different views of God, sin and grace and relied on law rather than spirit. In time, the Old Testament might even be relegated to an appendix. Schleiermacher's biblical theology gave birth to a new Christian movement known as Liberalism, which looked for the universal religious message in the gospels, discarded what seemed peripheral, and tried to express these essential truths in a way that would engage a modern audience.

In 1859, Charles Darwin (1809–82) published *On the Origin of Species by Means of Natural Selection*, which marked a new phase in the history of science. Instead of merely collecting facts, Baconian-style, Darwin put forward an hypothesis:

animals, plants and human beings had not been created fully formed but had developed slowly in a long period of evolutionary adaptation to their environment. In *The Descent of Man*, a later work, he suggested that *Homo sapiens* had evolved from the same proto-ape as the gorilla and chimpanzee. The *Origin* was a sober, careful exposition of a scientific theory that attracted a large popular audience: 1,400 copies were sold on the day of publication.

Darwin did not intend to attack religion and at first the religious response was muted. There was far greater outcry when seven Anglican clergymen published *Essays and Reviews* (1861), which made the Higher Criticism accessible to the general reader.[25] The public were now informed that Moses had not written the Pentateuch nor David the Psalms. Biblical miracles were simply literary tropes and should not be understood literally, and most of the events described in the Bible were clearly not historical. The authors of *Essays and Reviews* argued that the Bible should not be given special treatment but must be approached with the same critical rigour as any other ancient text.

At the end of the nineteenth century, the Higher Criticism rather than Darwinism was the main bone of contention between liberal and conservative Christians. Liberals believed that in the long term the critical method would lead to a deeper understanding of the Bible. But for conservatives, the Higher Criticism symbolized everything that was wrong with the post-Enlightenment world that was sweeping old certainties away.[26] In 1888, the British novelist Mrs Humphry Ward published *Robert Elsmere*, the story of a young clergyman whose faith was destroyed by the Higher Criticism. It became a bestseller, indicating that many people sympathized with Robert's dilemma. As his wife said: 'If the Gospels are not true as fact, as history, I cannot see that they are true at all, or of any value.'[27] It is a sentiment that many would share today.

The rational bias of the modern world made it difficult – if not impossible – for an increasing number of Western Christians to appreciate the role and value of mythology. There was, therefore, a growing sense that the truths of religion must be factual and a deep fear that the Higher Criticism would leave a dangerous void. Discount one miracle and consistency demanded that you reject them all. If Jonah did not spend three days in the whale's belly, asked a Lutheran pastor, did Jesus really rise from the tomb?[28] Clergymen blamed the Higher Criticism for widespread drunkenness, infidelity, and the rising crime and divorce rates.[29] In 1886, the American revivalist preacher Dwight Moody (1837–99) founded the Moody Bible Institute in Chicago to combat the Higher Criticism. His aim was to create a cadre of true believers to fight the false ideas that, he was convinced, had brought the nation to the brink of destruction. The Bible Institute would become a crucial fundamentalist phenomenon, representing a safe and sacred haven in a Godless world.

Conservatives who felt outnumbered by the liberals in the denominations started to band together. In the last years of the nineteenth century, the Bible Conference, where conservatives could read scripture in a literal, no-nonsense manner and purge their minds of the Higher Criticism, became increasingly popular in the United States. There was a widespread hunger for certainty. People now expected something entirely new from the Bible – something it had never pretended to offer hitherto. In his book, tellingly entitled *Many Infallible Proofs* (1895), the American Protestant Arthur Pierson wanted the Bible discussed 'in a truly impartial and scientific spirit':

> I like Biblical theology that . . . does not begin with an
> hypothesis and then wraps the facts and the philosophy to
> fit the crook of our dogma, but a Baconian system, which
> first gathers the teachings of the word of God and then seeks
> to deduce some general law upon which the facts can be
> arranged.[30]

At a time when so many traditional beliefs were being eroded, this was an understandable desire but the myths of the Bible could not possibly provide the scientific certainty that Pierson expected.

The Presbyterian seminary at Princeton, New Jersey, became the bastion of this 'scientific' Protestantism. The term 'bastion' is appropriate, because this quest for a wholly rationalistic interpretation of the Bible seemed chronically defensive. 'Religion has to fight for its life against the large class of scientific men,' wrote Charles Hodge (1797–1878), Princeton professor of theology.[31] In 1871, Hodge published the first volume of his *Systematic Theology*. The title alone revealed its

Baconian bias. The theologian, Hodge argued, was not to look for a meaning beyond the words of scripture but should simply arrange the teachings of the Bible into a system of general truths – a project that would involve a good deal of misplaced effort, because this type of system was entirely alien to the Bible.

In 1881, Archibald A. Hodge, Charles's son, published a defence of the literal truth of the Bible with his younger colleague Benjamin Warfield. It became a classic: 'The scriptures not only contain but are the Word of God, and hence all their elements and all their affirmations are absolutely errorless and binding on the faith and obedience of men.' Every biblical statement – on any subject – was absolute 'truth to the facts'.[32] The nature of faith was changing. It was now no longer 'trust' but intellectual submission to a set of beliefs. But for Hodge and Warfield, this required no suspension of disbelief because Christianity was entirely rational. 'It is solely by reasoning that it has come thus far on its way,' Warfield argued in a later article, 'And it is solely by reasoning that it will put its enemies under its feet.'[33]

This was an entirely new departure. In the past, some interpreters had favoured the study of the literal sense of the Bible but they had never believed that every single word of scripture was factually true. Many had admitted that, if we confined our attention to the letter, the Bible was an impossible text. The belief in biblical inerrancy, pioneered by Warfield and Hodge, would, however, become crucial to Christian fundamentalism and would involve considerable denial. Hodge and Warfield were responding to the challenge of modernity but in their desperation were distorting the scriptural tradition they were trying to defend.

The same was true of the new apocalyptic vision that gripped conservative American Protestants in the late nineteenth century. This was the creation of an Englishman, John Nelson Darby (1800–82), who found few followers in Britain but toured the United States to great acclaim between 1859 and 1877.[34] He was convinced, on the basis of a literal reading of Revelation, that God would shortly bring this era of history to an end in an unprecedentedly terrible disaster. Antichrist, the fake redeemer whose coming before the end had been foretold by St Paul,[35] would initially be welcomed and would deceive the unwary. He would then inflict seven years of tribulation, war and massacre upon humanity, but eventually Jesus would descend to earth and defeat him on the plain of Armageddon outside Jerusalem. Christ would then rule on earth for a thousand years until the Last Judgement brought history to a close. The attraction of this theory was that true believers would be spared. On the basis of a chance remark of St Paul, who suggested that at the Second Coming Christians would be 'taken up in the clouds' to meet Jesus,[36] Darby maintained that shortly before Tribulation, there would a 'rapture', a 'snatching' of born-again Christians, who would be whisked up to heaven and would thus escape the sufferings of the end time.

Bizarre as it sounds, this Rapture theory was in line with aspects of nineteenth-century thought. Darby spoke of historical eras or 'dispensations', each of which had ended in destruction; this was not dissimilar to the successive epochs that geologists had found in the strata of fossils in rocks and cliffs – each one of which, some thought, had ended in catastrophe. In line with the modern spirit, Darby's theory was literal and democratic. There was no hidden truth, accessible only to a learned elite. The Bible meant exactly what it said. A millennium meant ten centuries; if the prophets spoke of 'Israel' they meant Jews not the Church; if Revelation prophesied a battle outside Jerusalem, that was exactly what would happen.[37] This reading of scripture would become even easier after the publication of *The Scofield Reference Bible* (1909), which became an instant bestseller. Cyrus I. Scofield explained the Rapture theory in detailed notes – a gloss, which for many Christian fundamentalists has become almost as authoritative as the Bible itself.

The Jewish world was also divided between those who wanted to embrace modernity and those determined to fight it. In Germany, the *maskilim* who had embraced the Enlightenment believed that they could be a bridge between the ghetto and the modern world. In the early years of the nineteenth century, some decided to reshape the religion itself. Reform Judaism, whose worship was conducted in German, with choral singing and mixed choirs, seemed more Protestant than Jewish. To the disgust of the orthodox rabbis, synagogues – now called 'temples' – were established in

Hamburg and Berlin. In America, the playwright Isaac Harby founded a reformed temple in Charleston, and by 1870 a substantial proportion of the two hundred synagogues in the United States had adopted at least some Reform practices.[38]

The Reformers belonged to the modern world. They had no time for the irrational, the mystical or the mysterious. By the 1840s, some Reform scholars who had embarked on a critical study of Jewish history founded a school aptly known as the Science of Judaism. They were influenced by the philosophies of Kant and Georg Wilhelm Friedrich Hegel (1770–1831), who had argued in *The Phenomenology of Mind* (1807) that God, which he called the universal Spirit, could achieve its full potential only if it came down to earth and was most fully realized in the human mind. Both Hegel and Kant had seen Judaism as the epitome of bad religion: the Jewish God, Hegel argued, was a tyrant, who required unquestioning submission to his intolerable laws. Jesus had tried to liberate humans from this base servitude, but Christians had reverted to the old tyranny.

The scholars of the Science of Judaism all rewrote the biblical story in Hegelian terms to correct this prejudice. In their work, the Bible recorded the spiritualizing process whereby Judaism attained self-consciousness.[39] In *The Religion of the Spirit* (1841), Solomon Formstecher (1808–89) argued that Jews had been the first to arrive at a Hegelian notion of God. The Hebrew prophets had initially imagined that their inspiration had come from an external force, but eventually understood that it was due to their own Spirit-nature. The exile had weaned Jews away from external props and controls so that they were now able to approach God in freedom. Samuel Hirsch (1815–89) argued that Abraham had been the first human being to abandon pagan fatalism and dependence to stand alone in God's presence in total control of himself, whereas Christianity had reverted to the superstition and irrationality of heathenism. Nachman Krochmal (1785–1840) and Zachariah Frankel (1801–75) agreed that the whole of the written Torah had been revealed to Moses on Sinai, but denied the divine inspiration of Oral Law, which was entirely man-made and could be altered to meet the demands of the present. Abraham Geiger (1810–74), an out-and-out rational-ist, believed that the naive, creative and spontaneous period of Jewish history, which had begun in biblical times, had come to an end. With the Enlightenment, a higher stage of reflective contemplation was under way.

But some of these historians could see the value of ancient rituals, such as the wearing of phylacteries or the dietary laws, that the Reformers wanted to abolish. Frankel and Leopold Zunz (1794–1886) both believed that there was great danger in wholesale abolition of tradition. Those practices had become an essential part of the Jewish experience and without them, Judaism could degenerate into a system of abstract, lifeless doctrines. Zunz in particular feared that the Reform was losing touch with the emotions: reason alone could not produce the delight and joy that characterized Judaism at its best. It was an important point. In the past, the reading of the Bible had always been accompanied by rituals

– by liturgy, exercises in concentration, silence, fasting, chanting and ceremonial gestures – which had brought the sacred page to life. Without this ritual context, the Bible could be reduced to a document that provided information but no spiritual experience. Eventually Reform Judaism would recognize the truth of Zunz's critique and restore some of the rites that it had discarded.

As they watched their fellow Jews assimilating, many Jews were deeply concerned for the loss of tradition and the more orthodox felt increasingly embattled. In 1803, R. Hayyim Volozhiner, a disciple of the Gaon of Vilna, took a decisive step when he founded the Etz Hayyim yeshiva in Volozhin, Lithuania. Similar yeshivoth were founded in other parts of Eastern Europe during the nineteenth century and became the Jewish equivalents of the American Bible colleges. In the past, a yeshivah had simply consisted of a few rooms for the study of Torah and Talmud behind the synagogue. Etz Hayyim, where hundreds of gifted students from all over Europe gathered to study with experts, was quite different. R. Hayyim taught Torah and Talmud in the method he had learned from the Gaon, analysing the text logically but in a way that produced a spiritual experience. Students were not there to learn *about* Torah; the process of rote-learning, preparation, and lively, heated discussion were rituals that were just as important as any conclusion reached in class. This method was a form of prayer, and its intensity reflected the spirituality of the Gaon. The curriculum was demanding, the hours long, and the young men were separated from family and friends. Some were allowed to spend a little time on secular subjects, but these were secondary, regarded as stealing time from Torah.[40]

The original purpose of Etz Hayyim had been to counter Hasidism and reinstate rigorous study of Torah. But as the nineteenth century progressed the threat of the Jewish Enlightenment became a more pressing danger, and Hasidim and *misnagdim* joined forces against the *maskilim*, whom they saw as a sort of Trojan horse, smuggling the evils of secular culture into the Jewish world. Gradually the new yeshivoth became bastions of orthodoxy to ward off this encroaching peril. Jews were developing their own type of fundamentalism, which rarely begins as a battle with an external foe, but rather as an internal struggle in which traditionalists fight their co-religionists. Fundamentalist institutions respond to modernity by creating an enclave of pure faith – the yeshiva or the Bible college – where the faithful can reshape their lives. It is a defensive move, which has the potential for a future counter-offensive. The students of a yeshiva, madrasah or Bible college are likely to become a cadre, with a shared training and ideology, in their local communities.

By the end of the nineteenth century the world could indeed seem a Godless place. Instead of being a shunned minority, as in the past, atheists were beginning to take the high moral ground. Hegel's pupil Ludwig Feuerbach (1804–72) argued that the idea of God diminished and devalued our humanity.

For Karl Marx (1818–83), religion was the symptom of a sick society, an opiate that made the diseased social system bearable and removed the will to find a cure. And radical Darwinists fired the first shots in a war between scripture and science that continues to the present day. In England, Thomas H. Huxley (1825–95) and on the Continent, Karl Vogt (1817–95), Ludwig Buchner (1824–99), Jakob Moleschott (1822–93) and Ernst Haeckel (1834–1919) popularized evolutionary theory to prove that religion and science were utterly incompatible. For Huxley, there could be no compromise between science and traditional religion: 'one or the other must go after a struggle of unknown duration'.[41]

If religious people felt embattled by the twentieth century, that is because they were indeed under attack. Jews were imperilled by a new 'scientific' racism, which defined the essential biological and genetic characteristics of the peoples of Europe so narrowly that the Jew became 'other'.[42] In Eastern Europe, a new wave of pogroms at the turn of the twentieth century led some non-religious Jews to create Zionism, a political movement to establish a Jewish homeland in Palestine. Even though it used the biblical symbol of the Land of Israel, the Zionists were not motivated by religion but by secular modern thought: nationalism, colonialism and socialism.

Secular modernity was in many ways benign, but it was also violent and tended to romanticize armed struggle. Between 1914 and 1945, seventy million people in Europe and the Soviet Union died as the result of war and conflict.[43] There were two world wars, brutally efficient ethnic cleansing and

acts of genocide. Some of the worst atrocities had been perpetrated by the Germans, who had created one of the most cultivated societies in Europe. It was no longer possible to assume
that a rational education would eliminate barbarism. The
sheer scale of the Nazi Holocaust and the Soviet Gulag reveals
their modern origins. No previous society had the technology
to implement such grandiose schemes of extermination. The
horrors of the Second World War (1939–45) ended with the
explosion of the first atomic bombs over the Japanese cities of
Hiroshima and Nagasaki. For centuries, men and women had
dreamed of a final apocalypse wrought by God. Now they
had used their prodigious learning to find the means of doing
this very efficiently for themselves. The death camp, the
mushroom cloud, and – today – the wanton destruction of the
environment reveal a nihilistic ruthlessness at the heart of
modern culture. The interpretation of the Bible had always
been affected by historical conditions, and during the twentieth century Jews and Christians, as well as Muslims, began to
develop scripturally based ideologies that had absorbed the
violence of modernity.

During the First World War, an element of terror entered
conservative Protestantism in the United States: the unprecedented slaughter was on such a scale that, they reasoned,
these must be the battles foretold in Revelation. Because conservatives now believed that every word of the Bible was literally true, they began to view current events as the fulfilment
of precise biblical predictions. Hebrew prophets had declared
that the Jews would return to their land before the end, so

when the British government issued the Balfour Declaration (1917), pledging support for a Jewish homeland in Palestine, Christian fundamentalists felt a mixture of awe and exultation. Cyrus Scofield had suggested that Russia was 'the power from the North'[44] that would attack Israel before Armaggedon: the Bolshevik Revolution (1917), which made atheistic communism the state ideology, seemed to confirm this. The creation of the League of Nations after the war obviously fulfilled the prophecy of Revelation 16:14. This was the revived Roman empire that would shortly be led by the Antichrist. What had once been a purely doctrinal dispute with the liberals was becoming a struggle for the future of civilization. When they read the Bible, Christian fundamentalists saw – and still see – themselves on the frontline against satanic forces that will shortly destroy the world. The wild tales of German atrocities circulating during and after the war seemed to prove the corrosive effects of the Higher Criticism on the nation that had spawned it.[45]

It was a vision inspired by deep fear. Christian fundamentalists were now ambivalent about democracy, which could lead to the 'most devilish rule this world has ever seen'.[46] Peace-keeping institutions such as the League of Nations – and, today, the United Nations – would always be associated with absolute evil: the Bible said that there would be war, not peace at the end, so the League was dangerously on the wrong track. Indeed, Antichrist himself, whom Paul had described as a plausible liar, would probably be a peace-maker.[47] Jesus was no longer a loving saviour, but the warlike

Christ of Revelation, who, said Isaac Haldemann, one of the leading Rapture ideologues, 'comes forth as one who no longer seeks either friendship or love ... His garments are dipped in blood, the blood of others. He descends that he may shed the blood of men.'[48] In the past, exegetes had tried to see the Bible as a whole. Now the selection of one text at the expense of others – the fundamentalist 'canon within the canon' – led to a shocking distortion of the gospel.

In 1920, the Democratic politician William Jennings Bryan (1860–1925) launched a crusade against the teaching of evolution in the public schools. In his view, although the two were linked, it was not the Higher Criticism but Darwinism that had been responsible for the atrocities of the Great War.[49] Bryan's research had convinced him that the Darwinian conviction that only the strong should survive had 'laid the foundation for the bloodiest war in history'. It was no accident that 'the same science that manufactured poisoned gases to suffocate soldiers is preaching that man has a brutal ancestry and eliminating the miraculous and supernatural from the Bible'.[50] For Bryan, evolution was surrounded by a nimbus of evil, which symbolized the ruthless potential of modernity.

Bryan's conclusions were naive and incorrect but people were ready to listen to him. The war had ended the honeymoon period with science and they wanted it kept within due bounds. Those who espoused plain-speaking Baconian religion found it in Bryan, who singlehandedly pushed the topic of evolution to the top of the fundamentalist agenda, where it has remained. But it might never have replaced the Higher

Criticism had it not been for a dramatic development in Tennessee.

The southern states had hitherto taken little part in the fundamentalist movement but they were worried about the teaching of evolution. Bills were introduced into the state legislatures of Florida, Mississippi, Louisiana and Arkansas to ban the teaching of Darwinian theory. The anti-evolutionary laws in Tennessee were particularly strict and John Scopes, a young teacher in the small town of Dayton, decided to strike a blow for freedom of speech and confessed that he had broken the law when he had taken a biology class in place of his principal. In July 1925 he was brought to trial. The new American Civil Liberties Union (ACLU) sent a team of lawyers to defend him, headed by the rationalist campaigner Clarence Darrow. Bryan agreed to support the law. Immediately the trial became a contest between the Bible and science.

Bryan was a disaster on the stand and Darrow emerged from the trial as the champion of rational thought. The press gleefully denounced the fundamentalists as hopeless anachronisms, who could take no part in the modern world. This had an effect that is instructive to us today. When fundamentalist movements are attacked they usually become more extreme. Before Dayton, the conservatives were wary of evolution, but very few had espoused 'creation science', which maintained that the first chapter of Genesis was factually true in every detail. After Scopes, however, they became more vehemently literal in their interpretation of scripture, and creation science became the flagship of their movement. Before

Scopes, fundamentalists had been willing to work for social reform with people on the left; after Scopes, they swung to the far right of the political spectrum, where they have remained.

After the Holocaust, orthodox Jews felt impelled to rebuild the Hasidic courts and *misnagdic* yeshivoth in the new Jewish state of Israel and the United States as an act of piety to the six million.[51] Torah study was now a lifelong, full-time pursuit. Men would continue at the yeshivah after they married and, supported financially by their wives, had minimal contact with the outside world.[52] These ultra-orthodox Jews, known as the Haredim (the 'trembling ones'),[53] observed the commandments more rigorously than ever before,[54] finding new ways of being punctilious about diet and purification.[55] Before the Holocaust, excessive stringency had been discouraged as divisive. But now the Haredim were creating a Bible-based counter-culture in diametrical opposition to the rationalized efficiency that had helped to slaughter six million Jews. Yeshivah study had nothing in common with the pragmatism of modernity: many of the laws studied, such as the laws of temple service, could no longer be implemented. The repetition of the Hebrew words that God had spoken on Sinai was a form of communion with the divine. Exploring the minutiae of the law was a way of symbolically entering the mind of God. Becoming familiar with the *halakha* of the great rabbis was a way of appropriating the tradition that had so nearly been destroyed.

Zionism had originally been a secular ideology, a rebellion against religious Judaism that was reviled by the Orthodox for profaning the land of Israel, one of the most sacred symbols of Judaism. But during the 1950s and 1960s, a group of young religious Israelis began to develop a religious Zionism based on a literal interpretation of the Bible. God had promised the land to the descendants of Abraham, and this gave Jews a legal title to Palestine. The secular Zionists had never made this claim: they had tried to make the land their own by pragmatic diplomacy, working the land, or by fighting for it. But the religious Zionists saw life in Israel as a spiritual opportunity. In the late 1950s, they found a leader in R. Zvi Yehuda Kook (1891–1982), who was by then almost seventy years old. According to Kook, the secular state of Israel was the kingdom of God *tout court*; every clod of its earth was holy. Like the Christian fundamentalists, he interpreted literally the Hebrew prophecies about the Jews' return to their land: to settle territory now inhabited by the Arabs would hasten the final Redemption and political involvement in the affairs of Israel was an ascent to the pinnacles of holiness.[56] Unless Jews occupied the whole land of Israel, exactly as this was defined in the Bible, there could be no Redemption. The annexation of territory belonging to the Arabs was now a supreme religious duty.[57]

When the Israeli army occupied the West Bank, the Sinai peninsula, the Gaza Strip and the Golan Heights during the June War of 1967, Zionists saw this literal fulfilment of a scriptural imperative as proof positive that the end time had begun. There could be no question of returning the new territories to the Arabs in exchange for peace. Radical Kookists began to squat in Hebron and built a city at nearby Kiryat Arba, even though this contravened Geneva Conventions that forbade settlement in territories occupied during hostilities. This settlement initiative intensified after the October War of 1973. Religious Zionists joined forces with the secular right in opposition to any peace deal. True peace meant territorial integrity and the preservation of the whole land of Israel. As the Kookist rabbi Eleazar Waldman explained, Israel was engaged in a battle against evil, on which hung the prospects of peace for the entire world.[58]

This intransigence sounds perverse, but it was not unlike that of secularist politicians, who also habitually spoke of wars to end all wars and of the grim necessity of going to war to preserve world peace. In another vein, a small group of Jewish fundamentalists formulated a biblical version of the genocidal ethos of the twentieth century, comparing the Palestinians to the Amalekites, a people so cruel that God commanded the Israelites to kill them without mercy.[59] The same tendency was also evident in the movement founded by R. Meir Kahane, whose reading of scripture was so reductionist that it became a deadly caricature of Judaism, giving a biblical rationale to ethnic cleansing. The promise to Abraham was still valid, so the Arabs were usurpers and must go.[60] 'There are not several messages in Judaism,' he insisted. 'There is only one . . . God wanted us to live in a country on our own, isolated, so that we have the least possible contact with what is foreign.'[61]

In the early 1980s, a small group of Kookists plotted to destroy the Muslim shrines on the Haram al-Sharif, which had been built on the site of Solomon's temple and was the third holiest place in the Islamic world. How could the Messiah return when this holy place was polluted? In a literal interpretation of the kabbalistic principle that events on earth could influence the divine, the extremists calculated that by risking all-out war with the entire Muslim world, they would 'force' God to send the messiah to save Israel.[62] Not only could the plot, had it been implemented, have had fatal consequences for the Jewish state, but Washington strategists believed that in the context of the Cold War, when the Soviets supported the Arabs and the United States Israel, it could even have sparked a third world war.[63] Yet this nihilistic project was not out of place in a world where the great powers were prepared to expose their own people to nuclear annihilation in order to defeat the enemy.

Occasionally these pernicious interpretations of scripture have resulted in atrocity. Kahane's ideology inspired Baruch Goldstein, a settler in Kiryat Arba, to shoot twenty-nine Palestinian worshippers in the Cave of the Patriarchs in Hebron on the festival of Purim, 25 February 1994. On 4 November 1995, Yigal Amir, a former student of a Zionist yeshiva, assassinated Prime Minister Yitzhak Rabin during a peace rally in Tel Aviv. His study of Jewish law, he said later, had convinced him that in signing away the sacred land in the Oslo Accords, Rabin was a *rodef* ('pursuer') who endangered Jewish life and was therefore worthy of punishment.

*

In the United States, Protestant fundamentalists had evolved a Christian Zionism that was paradoxically anti-Semitic. The Jewish people had been central to the 'Rapture' vision of John Darby.[64] Jesus could not return unless the Jews were living in the Holy Land.[65] The creation of the State of Israel in 1948 was seen by fundamentalist ideologue Jerry Falwell as the 'greatest single sign indicating the imminent return of Jesus Christ'.[66] Support for Israel was mandatory. But Darby had taught that the Antichrist would slaughter two-thirds of the Jews living in Palestine in the end time, so fundamentalist writers looked forward to a massacre in which Jews would die in ghastly numbers.[67]

Like the Kookists, the Christian fundamentalists were not interested in peace. During the Cold War they were adamantly opposed to any detente with the Soviet Union, the 'enemy from the north'. Peace, said televangelist James Robison was 'against the Word of God'.[68] They were not perturbed by nuclear catastrophe, which had been predicted by St Peter[69] and would not, in any case, affect true believers, who would be raptured before Tribulation. Rapture is still a potent force in the politics of the United States. The Bush administration, which relied on the support of the Christian right, occasionally reverted to Rapture-speak. For a time, after the demise of the Soviet Union, Saddam Hussein filled the role of the 'enemy of the north', and his place was soon taken by Syria or Iran. There is still unqualified support for Israel, which can become pernicious. In January 2006, after Prime Minister Ariel Sharon suffered a massive stroke, fundamentalist leader Pat Robertson claimed that this was God's punishment for withdrawing Israeli troops from Gaza.

Pat Robertson is associated with a form of Christian fundamentalism that is more extreme than Jerry Falwell's Moral Majority. The Reconstruction movement, founded by the Texan economist Gary North and his father-in-law Rousas John Rushdoony, is convinced that the secular administration in Washington is doomed.[70] God will soon replace it with a Christian government run along strictly biblical lines. Reconstructionists are thus planning the Christian commonwealth in which the modern heresy of democracy will be abolished and every single law of the Bible implemented literally: slavery will be re-established, contraception prohibited, adulterers, homosexuals, blasphemers and astrologers will be executed, and persistently disobedient children stoned to death. God is not on the side of the poor: indeed, North explains, there is a 'tight relationship between wickedness and poverty'.[71] Taxes must not be used for welfare, since 'subsidizing sluggards is the same as subsidizing evil'.[72] The Bible forbids all foreign aid to the developing world: its addiction to paganism, immorality and demon worship is the cause of its economic problems.[73] In the past, exegetes tried to bypass these less than humane portions of the Bible or had given them an allegorical interpretation. The Reconstructionists seem to seek these passages out deliberately and interpret them ahistorically and literally. Where other fundamentalists have absorbed the violence of modernity, the Reconstructionists have produced a religious version of militant capitalism.[74]

Fundamentalists grab the headlines but other biblical scholars have tried to revive traditional biblical spirituality in a more eirenic spirit. Writing in the 1940s, the Jewish philosopher Martin Buber (1878–1965) believed that the Bible witnessed to God's presence at a time when he seemed absent. Exegesis could never stand still, since the Bible represented an ongoing dialogue between God and humanity. The study of the Bible must lead to a transformed lifestyle. When we open the Bible, we must be ready to be fundamentally changed by what we hear. Buber was much struck by the fact that the rabbis called scripture a *miqra*, a 'calling out'. It was a summons that did not allow readers to abstract themselves from the problems of the world but trained them to stand fast and listen to the undercurrent of events.

His friend Franz Rosenzweig (1886–1929) agreed that the Bible compelled us to face the crises of the hour. Readers must respond to its *miqra* in the same way as the prophets, crying: '*Hinneni*: "Here I am" – all ready, all soul . . . to the reality at hand.'[75] The Bible was not a preordained script. Our daily lives should illuminate the Bible, and in turn the Bible will help us to discover the sacred dimension of our day-to-day experience. Reading scripture was an introspective process. Rosenzweig knew that modern human beings could not respond to the Bible in the same way as earlier generations. We needed the new covenant described to Jeremiah, when the law would be written within our hearts.[76] The text must be appropriated and interiorized in patient, disciplined study and translated into action in the world.

Michael Fishbane, currently Professor of Jewish Studies at the University of Chicago, believes that exegesis could help us to retrieve the idea of a sacred text.[77] Historical criticism of the Bible makes it impossible for us to read the scriptures synchronistically any longer, linking passages widely separated in time. But modern literary criticism acknowledges that our inner world is created by fragments of many different texts, which live together in our minds, one qualifying another. Our moral universe is shaped by *King Lear*, *Moby Dick* and *Madame Bovary* as well as by the Bible. We rarely absorb texts whole: isolated images, phrases and gobbets live in our minds in myriad, fluid groupings, acting and reacting on one another. Similarly, the Bible does not exist in our minds whole and entire but in fragmentary form. We create our own 'canon within a canon' and should deliberately ensure that our selection is a collection of benign texts. The historical study of the Bible shows that there were many contesting visions in ancient Israel, each claiming – often aggressively – to be the official version of Yahwism. We can read the Bible today as a prophetic commentary on our own world of raging orthodoxies; it can provide us with the compassionate distance to realize the dangers of this strident dogmatism and replace it with a chastened pluralism.

The main thrust of Fishbane's work has been to show how the Bible constantly interpreted and corrected itself. Isaiah had envisaged all the nations making their way to Mount Zion, the city of peace, saying, 'Come, let us go up to the mounain of Yahweh ... that he may teach us his ways ... since the Law will go out from Zion, and the oracle of Yahweh from Jerusalem.'[78] When Micah quoted these words, he also looked forward to a universal peace when the nations would speak gently to one another. But he added an astonishingly daring coda. Each nation, including Israel, 'will go forward, each in the name of its own god'. It is almost as though Micah foresaw our own time of multiple visions converging on a common truth, which for Israel had been expressed by the idea of their god.[79]

Christian exegetes have continued to see Christ at the heart of the Bible. In his biblical theology, the Swiss Jesuit Hans Urs von Balthasar (1905–88) drew on the notion of incarnation. Jesus, like scripture, was God's Word in human form. God is knowable and can express himself in terms that we can understand. But we have constantly to wrestle with these difficult but indispensable texts. The Bible presented archetypal stories of encounters between God and human beings, which helped readers to see the divine as an ideal dimension of their own lives. They can seize the imagination, in the same way as *King Lear* or Michelangelo's *David*. But it was impossible to extract definitive 'essentials' or 'fundamentals' of God's revelation in the Bible. Theology could 'never be more than a reflection in words and concepts, never capable of being brought to a close ... never be completely pinned down'.[80] But scripture was still authoritative, and everybody, including the Pope and the hierarchy, was subject to its summons and critique. Catholics had a duty to challenge the Church if they saw it departing from the spirit of the gospel.

Hans Frei (1922–88), a convert from Judaism who became an episcopal priest and a professor at Yale, noted that in the pre-critical world, most readers assumed that the biblical stories were historical, even if they were chiefly concerned with figurative types of exegesis.[81] But this consensus broke down during the eighteenth century: after the Enlightenment, some saw the biblical narratives as purely factual, forgetting that they were written as stories. The author's use of syntax and vocabulary were supposed to affect the way we understood these tales. Jesus was certainly a historical figure, but when we examine the gospel narratives of the resurrection, for example, it becomes impossible to decide what actually happened. Like the Jewish exegetes, Frei believed that the Bible must be read in conjunction with a sustained reflection on our own times. The juxtaposition of the gospel and current events should not lead to facile interpretations, but enable us to enter more deeply into the complexity of each. The Bible was subversive. These stories must not be used simply to back up the ideology of the establishment, but we should expose the hopes, claims and expectations of our time to the gospel story and examine, deconstruct and refashion them accordingly.

More recently, Wilfred Cantwell Smith (1916–2000), formerly Professor of Comparative Religion at Harvard, stressed the importance of understanding the Bible historically.[82] It was impossible to say what the Bible 'really' meant when any one of its verses was likely to have been interpreted in several different ways. Religious people have all worked out their salvation within the confines of a particular place and time. The Bible has meant different things to Jews and Christians at different stages of their history, and their exegesis was inevitably coloured by their particular circumstances. If an interpretation concentrated only on what the biblical author said, and ignored the way generations of Jews and Christians had understood it, it distorted the significance of the Bible.

EPILOGUE

What is the way forward? This short biography makes it clear that many modern assumptions about the Bible are incorrect. The Bible did not encourage slavish conformity. In the Jewish tradition especially, as we saw with the story of R. Eliezer, not even the voice of God could force an exegete to accept another person's interpretation. From the first, the biblical authors contradicted each other and their conflicting visions were all included by the editors in the final text. The Talmud was an interactive text that, properly taught, compelled a student to find his own answers. Hans Frei was right: the Bible has been a subversive document, suspicious of orthodoxy since the time of Amos and Hosea.

The modern habit of quoting proof-texts to legitimize policies and rulings is out of key with interpretive tradition. As Wilfred Cantwell Smith explained, scripture was not really a text but an activity, a spiritual process that introduced thousands of people to transcendence. The Bible may have been used to back up doctrines and beliefs but that was not its chief function. The fundamentalist emphasis on the literal reflects the modern ethos but is a breach with tradition, which usually preferred some kind of figurative or innovative interpretation. There is, for example, no single doctrine of creation in the Bible and the first chapter of Genesis was rarely read as a factual description of the origins of the cosmos. Many of the Christians who oppose Darwinism today are Calvinists, but Calvin insisted that the Bible was not a scientific document and that those who wanted to learn about astronomy or cosmology should look elsewhere.

We have seen that different texts have been used to support entirely opposed programmes. Athanasius and Arius could both produce quotations to prove their personal beliefs about the divinity of Christ. Because they could find no definitive warrant in scripture to decide this matter, the fathers found theological solutions that owed little to the Bible. Slave-owners interpreted the Bible one way, the slaves in quite another. The same applies today in the Christian debate about ordaining women to the priesthood. Like nearly all pre-modern documents, the Bible is a patriarchal text. Opponents of feminism and women priests can find a host of biblical texts to prove their case, but some of the New Testament authors had very different views and can be cited to show that in Christ there was neither male nor female and that women worked as 'co-workers' and 'co-apostles' in the early Church. Hurling texts around polemically is a sterile pursuit. Scripture is not able to provide certainty on this type of question.

This is also the case with the question of scriptural violence. There is indeed a great deal of violence in the Bible –

far more than there is in the Qur'an. And it is unquestionably true that throughout history people have used the Bible to justify atrocious acts. As Cantwell Smith observed, the Bible and its interpretation must be seen in historical context. The world has always been a violent place and scripture and its exegesis has often fallen prey to contemporary aggression. Joshua was presented by the Deuteronomists fighting with all the ruthlessness of an Assyrian general. The Crusaders ignored the pacifist teachings of Jesus and signed up for an expedition to the Holy Land because they were soldiers, wanted a militant religion and applied their distinctively feudal ethos to the Bible. The same is true in our own time. The modern period has seen violence and slaughter on an unprecedented scale and it is not surprising that this has affected the way some people have read the Bible.

But because scripture has been so flagrantly abused in this way, Jews, Christians and Muslims have a duty to establish a counter-narrative that emphasizes the benign features of their exegetical traditions. Interfaith understanding and coopera-tion are now essential to our survival: perhaps members of the three monotheistic faiths should work together to estab-lish a common hermeneutics. This would consist of a sus-tained critical, moral and spiritual examination of the problematic texts themselves, the way they have been inter-preted throughout history, and an in-depth examination of the exegesis of the people who exploit them today. Their sig-nificance in the tradition as a whole should be defined clearly.

Michael Fishbane's suggestion that we construct a 'canon

within the canon' to moderate the religiously articulated hatred of our time is extremely apposite. The Bible is indeed a witness to the danger of raging orthodoxies – and in our own day, not all these orthodoxies are religious. There is a form of 'secular fundamentalism' that is as bigoted, biased and inaccurate about religion as any Bible-based fundamentalism about secularism. There are good things and bad things in the Bible. The kabbalists were acutely aware of the flaws of their Torah and found inventive ways to qualify the harsh predominance of *Din*. There was a similar debate in the Bible itself. In the Pentateuch, P's message of reconciliation opposed the stridency of Deuteronomy. In the New Testament, the battles of Revelation are juxtaposed with the pacifism of the Sermon on the Mount. In the early fifth century, Jerome railed savagely against his theological opponents, while Augustine pleaded for kindness and humility in biblical debate, just as, later, Calvin was horrified by the polemical diatribes of Luther and Zwingli. The canon that is selected to counter the prevailing enthusiasm for biblical aggression should, as Fishbane suggested, make this alternative Word more audible in our divided world. Buber, Rosenzweig and Frei all argued that the study of the Bible should not be confined to the ivory tower of academe but should be applied rigorously to the contemporary scene. Midrash and exegesis were always supposed to relate directly to the burning issues of the day, and the fundamentalists should not be the only people who attempt this.

Buber and Rosenzweig both stressed the importance of

listening to the Bible. Throughout this biography, we have considered the ways in which Jews and Christians have tried to cultivate a receptive, intuitive approach to scripture. This is difficult for us today. We are a talkative and opinionated society and not always good at listening. The discourse of politics, media and academe is essentially adversarial. While this is undoubtedly important in a democracy, it can mean that people are not really receptive to an opposing viewpoint. It is often apparent during a parliamentary debate or a panel discussion on television that while their opponents are speaking, participants are simply thinking up the next clever thing that *they* are going to say. Biblical discourse is often conducted in the same confrontational spirit, very different from the 'listening ear' proposed by the Hasidic leader, Dov Ber. We also expect immediate answers to complex questions. The soundbite is all. In biblical times, some people feared that a written scripture encouraged a slick, superficial 'knowing'. This is surely an even greater danger in the electronic age, when people are used to finding truth at the click of a mouse.

This makes a truly spiritual reading of the Bible difficult. The achievements of the historical-critical method have been magnificent; it has given us unprecedented knowledge *about* the Bible but has not yet provided us with a spirituality. Fishbane is right: the *horoz* and *pesher* exegesis of the past are no longer an option. Nor are the elaborate allegories of Origen, who was able to find a gospel *miqra* in every word of the Hebrew scriptures. This type of figurative exegesis offends modern academic sensibilities, because it violates the integrity of the original text. But there was a generosity in *alle-goria* that is often lacking in modern discourse. Philo and Origen did not dismiss the biblical texts with disdain but gave them the benefit of the doubt. Modern philosophers of language have argued that 'the principle of charity' is essential for any form of communication. If we truly want to understand the other, we have to assume that he or she is speaking the truth. *Allegoria* was an attempt to find truth in texts that seemed barbarous and opaque and then 'translate' them into a more congenial idiom.[1] The logician N. L. Wilson has argued that a critic who confronts an alien body of texts must apply the 'principle of charity'. He or she must seek interpretation, which 'in light of what it knows of the facts, will maximize truth among the sentences of the corpus'.[2] The linguist Donald Davidson maintains that 'Making sense of the utterance and behaviour of others, even their most aberrant behaviour, requires you to find a great deal of truth and reason in them.'[3] Even though their beliefs may be very different from your own, 'you have to assume that the alien is very much the same as you are,' otherwise you are in danger of denying their humanity. 'Charity is forced upon us,' Davidson concludes. 'Whether we like it or not, if we want to understand others, we must regard them as right in most matters.'[4] In the public arena, however, people are often presumed to be wrong before they are proved right, and this has inevitably affected our understanding of the Bible.

The 'principle of charity' accords with the religious ideal of compassion, the duty to 'feel with' the other. Some of the greatest exegetes of the past – Hillel, Jesus, Paul, Johanan ben Zakkai, Akiba and Augustine – insisted that charity and loving kindness were essential to biblical interpretation. In our dangerously polarized world, a common hermeneutics among the religions should surely emphasize this tradition. Jews, Christians and Muslims must first examine the flaws of their own scriptures and only then listen, with humility, generosity and charity to the exegesis of others.

What would it mean to interpret the whole of the Bible as a 'commentary' on the Golden Rule? It would first demand an appreciation of other people's scriptures. R. Meir said that any interpretation that spread hatred or denigrated other sages was illegitimate. Today these 'other sages' must include Muhammad, Buddha and the *rishis* of the Rig Veda. In the spirit of Michael Fishbane's reading of Micah's coda, Christians must cease regarding the Tanakh as a mere prelude to Christiantiy and learn to value the insights of the rabbis; Jews should acknowledge the Jewishness of Jesus and Paul and learn to appreciate the fathers of the Church.

Augustine claimed that scripture teaches nothing but charity. How then do we interpret the massacres of Joshua, the gospel abuse of the Pharisees and the battles of Revelation? As Augustine advised, these episodes should first be placed in their historical context and studied in the way we have already considered. How have they been interpreted in the past? And do they throw light on the lack of charity in contemporary discourse and the modern political scene?

Today we see too much strident certainty in both the religious and the secular spheres. Instead of quoting the Bible in order to denigrate homosexuals, liberals or women priests, we could recall Augustine's rule of faith: an exegete must always seek the most charitable interpretation of a text. Instead of using a biblical passage to back up a bygone orthodoxy, modern hermeneutics could bear in mind the original meaning of midrash: 'to go in search of'. Exegesis is a quest for something new. Buber said that each reader should stand before the Bible as Moses stood before the burning bush, listening intently and preparing for a revelation that will force him or her to lay aside former preconceptions. If this offends the religious establishment, we might remind them, with Balthasar, that the authorities are also accountable to the *miqra* of scripture.

The major religions all insist that the practice of daily, hourly compassion will introduce us to God, Nirvana and the Dao. An exegesis based on the 'principle of charity' would be a spiritual discipline that is deeply needed in our torn and fragmented world. The Bible is in danger of becoming a dead or an irrelevant letter; it is being distorted by claims for its literal infallibility; it is derided – often unfairly – by secular fundamentalists; it is also becoming a toxic arsenal that fuels hatred and sterile polemic. The development of a more compassionate hermeneutics could provide an important counter-narrative in our discordant world.

GLOSSARY OF KEY TERMS

Allegory (Greek, *allegoria*) A discourse that describes one thing under the guise of another.

Anagogy; anagogical (Greek) The mystical or eschatological meaning of a biblical text.

Apatheia (Greek) Indifference to earthly conditions, impassibility, serenity, selflessness and invulnerability.

Apocalypse (Greek, *apokalypsis*) Literally, 'unveiling' or revelation. Often used to refer to a revelation about the last days or the end time.

Apologia (Latin) A rational explanation. Christian apologists tried to give a reasonable account of their faith to convince their pagan neighbours.

Apophatic (Greek) Silent; an experience beyond the reach of speech. Greek Christians came to believe that all theology should have an element of stillness, paradox and restraint in order to emphasize the ineffability and mystery of God.

Bavli The Babylonian Talmud (q.v.)

Binah (Hebrew) Intelligence; the third *sefirah* (q.v.) in the kabbalistic myth of creation and redemption. Binah is also known as 'the Supernal Mother', the womb which, once penetrated by *Hokhmah* (q.v.), gave birth to seven 'lower' *sefiroth* and thence to all that is.

Breaking of the Vessels A term in Lurianic Kabbalah (q.v.) describing the primal catastrophe, when sparks of divine light fell to earth and were trapped in matter.

Canon Literally, a rule or decree; the list of officially accepted books in the Hebrew and Christian Bible.

Christ (Greek, *christos*) A Greek translation of the Hebrew *meshiah* ('anointed one') (q.v.); a title applied by the early Christians to Jesus of Nazareth.

Coincidentia Oppositorum (Latin) 'An agreement of opposites'; the term applied to an ecstatic experience, when divisions and contradictions fade in an apprehension of the unity of all things; a numinous intimation of harmony and wholeness.

Darash (Hebrew) 'To study', 'to investigate', 'to go in search of'. The term was also used by kabbalists to describe the moral or homiletic sense of scripture in *Pardes* exegesis (q.v.).

Demiourgos (Greek) 'Craftsman'. In Plato's *Timaeus*, the demiourgos was the divine craftsman, the subordinate of the Supreme God, who gave shape and coherence to the material world, making it conform to the eternal forms. The Gnostics used the term *demiourgos* to describe the God of the Jewish Bible, who was responsible for the creation of the evil world of matter.

Deuteronomy; Deuteronomist (Greek, *deuteronomion*: 'second law') Originally the term implied to Moses's final discourse before his death on Mount Nebo, which is described in the fifth book of the Pentateuch. The term is also used of the reformers who composed the book of Deuteronomy and the historical books of Samuel and Kings in the seventh century BCE.

Devekut (Hebrew) 'Attachment' to God; the perpetual consciousness of the divine to which the Hasidim aspired.

Din (Hebrew)   Stern Judgement; the fifth *sefirah* (q.v.) in the kabbalistic myth of creation and revelation. In Lurianic Kabbalah (q.v.), *Din* represented the evil potential within the divine, which became predominant after the primal catastrophe of the 'breaking of the vessels' (q.v.).

Dogma (Greek)   Term used by Greek-speaking Christians to describe the hidden, ineffable traditions of the Church, which could only be understood mystically and expressed symbolically. In the West, 'dogma' has come to mean a body of opinion, categorically and authoritatively stated.

Dynameis (Greek)   The 'powers' of God, a term used by the Greeks to denote God's activity in the natural world and as described in the Bible; it was to be regarded as quite distinct from God's inaccessible *ousia* (q.v.), 'essence'.

Economy   The divine government of the world; the divine dispensation; the system that underlies the whole of reality.

Ekstasis (Greek, 'stepping outside')   An ecstasy that takes the worshipper beyond the self and outside mundane experience.

Ekklesia (Greek)   Congregation, Church.

Emanation   A process whereby the various grades of reality were imagined to flow from a single, primal source, which Jews, Christians and Muslims identified with God; some preferred to use the metaphor of emanation to describe the origins of life rather than creation *ex nihilo* (q.v.), the instantaneous creation of all things at a given moment in time.

En Sof (Hebrew, 'without end')   The inscrutable, inaccessible and unknowable essence of God in the mystical philosophy of Kabbalah; the Godhead, the hidden source or root of the divine.

Energeiaei (Greek, 'energies')   God's 'activities' in the world, which enable us to catch a glimpse of him. Like *dynameis* (q.v.), the term is used to distinguish the human conception of God from the ineffable and incomprehensible reality itself.

Epithalamium: (Latin derivation)   A marriage song, describing the union of bride and groom.

Eschatology   Derived from the Greek, *eskaton:* 'the end'. The study of the last days and the end time.

Ex nihilo (Latin, 'out of nothing')   The phrase used to describe God's creation of the universe from nothing in a free, spontaneous and unique act in time. Some philosophers found this an impossible notion, because in Greek rational theology the universe is eternal and God is impassible and not subject to sudden actions and change.

Exegesis (Greek)   To 'lead or guide out'; the art of interpreting and explaining the biblical text.

Father: The title Jesus seems to have used when he spoke to God; later identified with Christians as the first of the *dynameis* (q.v.) of the Trinity.

Gaon (Hebrew)   The 'head' or principal of a rabbinical academy.

Gemara (Hebrew)   Exegesis. In the Talmud (q.v.) it refers to the commentary on the Mishnah (q.v.)

Gentile   A non-Jew; derived from the Latin *gentes,* a translation of the Hebrew *goyim* (q.v.), the 'foreign nations'.

Gnostic (Greek)   A form of Christianity that emphasized the importance of *gnosis*, a redeeming 'knowledge', and distinguished between the wholly spiritual Supreme God, who had sent Jesus as his envoy, and the *demiourgos* (q.v.), revealed in the Jewish Bible, who had created the evil world of matter.

Godfearer   A gentile pagan sympathizer, who was an honorary member of the synagogue, with varying degrees of commitment.

Godhead   The source of divinity; the hidden root of the divine; *En Sof* (q.v.)

Gospel   Literally 'good news' (from the Anglo-Saxon *god spel*). The proclamation (Greek, *evangelion*) of the early Church. The term is also applied to the various biographies of Jesus.

Goyim (Hebrew)   The foreign nations; the gentiles.

Halakah; halakoth (Hebrew)   A rabbinical legal ruling.

Haredim (Hebrew, 'the trembling ones')   A term derived from Isaiah 66:5, which refers to devout Israelites who 'tremble' at God's word and which was applied to ultra-orthodox Jews.

Hasid (Hebrew, 'pious one'); **Hasidim**   The Jewish mystical reform movement founded in the eighteenth century by the Baal Shem Tov.

Haskalah (Hebrew)   The Jewish enlightenment founded by Moses Mendelssohn.

Hermeneutics (Greek)   The art of interpretation, especially of scripture.

Hesed (Hebrew)   Originally tribal or cultic 'loyalty'; later 'love' or 'mercy'. The sixth *sefirah* (q.v.) in the kabbalistic myth of creation and revelation, paired with *Din* (q.v.); *hesed* must always moderate the Stern Judgement of God.

Hod (Hebrew, 'Majesty')   The eighth *sefirah* (q.v.) in the kabbalistic myth of creation and revelation.

Holy Spirit   Term used by rabbis in the Talmudic age, often interchangeably with *Shekhinah* (q.v.) to denote God's presence on earth; a way of distinguishing the God we experience from the utterly transcendent divinity which forever eluded us. In Christianity, this divine presence became one of the three *dynameis* (q.v) recounted in scripture, which – along with Father and Logos – constituted the revelation of God as Trinity.

Hokhmah (Hebrew, 'Wisdom')   In the Bible, Wisdom is the blueprint of creation, the divine plan that governs the universe, which was eventually identified with the Torah (q.v.). *Hokhmah* is also the second *sefirah* (q.v.) of the kabbalistic myth of creation and revelation, which merges with the first *sefirah* as a 'point' that penetrates the womb of *Binah* (q.v.).

Horoz (Hebrew, 'enchaining') The rabbinic practice of 'linking' separate biblical quotations together in a 'chain' that yielded the ecstatic experience of *coincidentia oppositorum* (q.v.).

Hypothesis (Greek, 'underlying argument') Originally a subtext, the message that lies hidden beneath the surface meaning of the Bible. Later, a scientific theory put forward as a conjecture for empirical demonstration.

Incarnation (Latin derivation) The 'embodiment' of a spiritual reality in an earthly form; in Christianity it refers specifically to the descent of the Logos (q.v.), which was 'made flesh' in the human body of Jesus.

Kabbalah (Hebrew, 'inherited tradition') The mystical tradition of Judaism.

Kerygma (Greek) A term used by Greek Christians to denote the public teaching of the Church, based on scripture, which can be expressed adequately in words, as opposed to dogma (q.v.), which could not.

Kether Elyon (Hebrew, 'Supreme Crown') The first *sefirah* (q.v.) in the kabbalistic myth of creation and revelation, which emerges from the unfathomable depths of *En Sof* (q.v.) as a 'dark flame'. It is also known as 'Nothing', because it does not correspond to any category intelligible to human beings.

Kethuvim (Hebrew) The Writings, the third category of the Hebrew Bible; the canon of the Writings included Chronicles,

Ezra, Nehemiah, Esther, Job, and the Wisdom books attributed to Solomon: Proverbs, Ecclesiastes and the Song of Songs.

Lectio Divina (Latin) 'Sacred Study': the monastic practice of reading the Bible slowly and meditatively, identifying with the action and experiencing moments of *ekstasis* (q.v.)

Logos (Greek) 'Reason', 'definition', 'word'. God's Logos was identified with the Wisdom (q.v.) and Word of God which brought everything into being, and had communicated with human beings throughout history. The prologue of John's gospel claimed that the Word had become incarnate in Jesus of Nazareth.

Lurianic Kabbalah The form of Kabbalah (q.v.) initiated by Isaac Luria in the sixteenth century, based on the myth of *Zimzum* (q.v.).

Malkuth (Hebrew, 'kingdom') The last of the *sefiroth* (q.v.) in the kabbalistic myth of creation and revelation; it is also called *Shekhinah* (q.v.), the divine presence on earth.

Maskilim (Hebrew, 'the enlightened ones') Followers of the Jewish Enlightenment, who wanted to privatize their religion, make it a rational faith, and participate in gentile (q.v.) culture.

Messiah (Hebrew *meshiah*, 'anointed one') Originally the term applied to anybody who was given a special task by God – notably the king, who was anointed at his coronation and became a 'son of God'. But the term was also used of prophets and priests, and also of Cyrus, king of Persia, who permitted the Jews to return to Judah and rebuild their temple after their long exile in Babylon. Later some Jews in the first century CE expected a *meshiah* to redeem Israel, assist Yahweh during the last days, and establish his reign on earth. The Christians believed that Jesus was this messiah.

Midrash (Hebrew)   Derived from *darash* (q.v.); exegesis; interpretation, with connotations of investigation, quest.

Mishnah (Hebrew, 'learning by repetition')   A Jewish scripture composed between 135 and 200 CE that consisted of a collection of oral traditions and rabbinic legal rulings.

Misnagdim (Hebrew)   The 'opponents' of the Hasidim (q.v.).

Mythos (Greek, 'myth')   A story that was not meant to be historical or factual, but which expressed the meaning of an event or narrative and encapsulated its timeless, eternal dimension. A myth can be described as an occurrence that in some sense happened once, but which also happens all the time. Myth has also been described as an early form of psychology, which described the labyrinthine and mysterious world of the psyche.

Netsakh (Hebrew, 'patience')   The seventh *sefirah* (q.v.) in the kabbalistic myth of creation and revelation.

Neviim (Hebrew)   The 'Prophets', the second category of the Hebrew Bible.

Ousia (Greek)   The 'essence' of God, which is beyond our comprehension, remains utterly unknowable by human beings, and is not mentioned in the Bible. It is not dissimilar to *En Sof* (q.v.). Nevertheless, in the scriptures, God revealed itself in the three *dynameis* (q.v.): Father (q.v.), Logos (q.v.) and Holy Spirit (q.v.).

Pardes   Originally a Persian word denoting 'orchard' but which indicated a high mystical state associated with 'paradise'. Later *Pardes* became a method of kabbalistic exegesis of scripture, which interpreted scripture according to the *Peshat* (literal), *Remez* (allegorical), *Darash* (moral) and *Sod* (mystical) senses (q.v.) and achieved a spiritual ascent to the divine.

Pentateuch   The first five books of the Bible, also called the Torah: Genesis, Exodus, Leviticus, Numbers and Deuteronomy.

Peshat (Hebrew)   The literal sense of scripture in the kabbalistic exegesis of *Pardes*.

Pesher (Hebrew, 'deciphering')   A form of exegesis used by the Qumran sect and the early Christians, which saw the whole of scripture as a code, referring to their own community in the last days.

Pistis (Greek)   The virtue of 'trust', often translated 'faith'.

Polis (Greek)   A city state.

Rachamin (Hebrew, 'compassion')   The fourth *sefirah* (q.v.) in the kabbalistic myth of creation and revelation. It is sometimes called *Tifereth* ('grace') (q.v.).

Remez (Hebrew, 'allegory')   The second sense of scripture in kabbalistic *Pardes* exegesis.

Sefer Torah (Hebrew)   The 'scroll of the law' discovered by the seventh-century reformers in the time of Josiah, which purported to be the document given to Moses on Mount Sinai.

Sephardim (Hebrew)   The Jews of Spain (*Sepharad*).

Sefirah; Sefiroth (Hebrew, 'numerations')   The inner dimensions of the divine psyche; the attributes of God which were not remote abstractions but dynamic potencies. In kabbalistic myth, the ten *sefiroth* were the ten emanations (q.v) or stages of God's revelation of himself. The ten sefiroth consisted of

- the 'higher' sefiroth: Kether Elyon (q.v.); Hokhmah (q.v.) and Binah (q.v)
- the seven 'lower' sefiroth: Rachamin/Tifereth (q.v.), Din (q.v), Hesed (q.v.), Netsakh (q.v.) Hod (q.v.), Yesod (q.v.) and Malkuth/Shekhinah (q.v.).

Shalom (Hebrew)   Often translated 'peace' but more accurately 'wholeness, completeness'.

Shekhinah (Hebrew)   Deriving from the verb *shakan*: to pitch one's tent; to live as a tent-dweller. The divine presence on earth, a term used by the rabbis to distinguish a Jew's experience of God from the ineffable reality itself. The kabbalists saw the *Shekhinah* as the tenth *sefirah*, and a female personality, who had been exiled from the rest of the *sefiroth* and wandered perpetually on earth.

Sola Scriptura (Latin)   'Scripture alone!', the watchword of the Protestant reformation.

Synoptics (Greek, 'seeing together')   The three gospels of Mark, Matthew and Luke, who shared more or less the same theology and vision of Jesus.

Sod (Hebrew)   The 'mystical' sense of scripture in the kabbalistic *Pardes* exegesis.

Tanna; Tannaim (Hebrew, 'reciters, repeaters')   The rabbinic scholars who collated the Mishnah (q.v.)

Talmud (Hebrew, 'teaching study')   The term refers to two scriptures, the Yerushalmi, the Jerusalem Talmud, completed in the early fifth century CE, and the Bavli, the Babylonian Talmud, completed in the sixth century. Both took the form of a *gemara* ('commentary') (q.v.) on the Mishnah (q.v.).

Tanakh (Hebrew acronym)   The Hebrew Bible, which consisted of the Torah (q.v), the Neviim (q.v.) and the Kethuvim (q.v.) – the Law, the Prophets and the Writings.

Text (Latin, *textus*)   A piece of writing 'woven' of myriad intertwining strands, meanings and realities.

Theophany (Greek)   A revelation of God.

Theoria (Greek)   Contemplation, meditation.

Tifereth (Hebrew, 'grace', beauty)   The fourth *sefirah* (q.v.) in the

kabbalistic myth of creation and revelation; often called
Rachamin (q.v.).

Tikkun (Hebrew)   The 'restoration' of the *Shekhinah* (q.v.) to the
rest of the *sefiroth* (q.v.), the Jews to their homeland, the world
to its rightful state, and scripture to its original spirituality and
grace. *Tikkun* could be effected by Jews by means of the
dedicated observance of Torah, *Pardes* exegesis (q.v.) and
kabbalistic rituals.

Torah (Hebrew)   Often simply translated 'law', it derives from a
verb meaning to instruct, teach or guide. In the Bible, Torah
included the fact of God's guidance in the world and the words
he used to formulate it. Thus the Torah often refers to the
Pentateuch, which consists of narratives that reveal God's care
and tutelage as well as legislation. Later, Torah was linked
with God's Wisdom (*Hokhmah*) (q.v.) and the Word that
brought the world into being: it thus became synonymous with
the highest knowledge and with transcendent goodness.

Wisdom   see *Hokhmah*.

Yerushalmi   The Jerusalem Talmud (q.v.).

Yeshivah; Yeshivoth (Hebrew)   Derives from the verb *shivah* 'to
sit'. A house of studies; a series of rooms attached to a
synagogue, where Jews could study Torah (q.v.) and Talmud
(q.v.).

Yesod (Hebrew, 'stability')   The ninth *sefirah* (q.v.) in the
kabbalistic myth of creation and revelation.

Zeir Anpin (Hebrew, 'the Impatient One')   In Lurianic Kabbalah
(q.v.), the God revealed in the Hebrew Bible, which consisted
of six of the lower *sefiroth* (q.v.). Because *Din* (q.v.) had become
predominant after the 'breaking of the vessels' (q.v.) and was

no longer moderated and balanced by *hesed* (q.v.), God often seemed irascible and even violent in scripture. Separated from the *Shekhinah*, Zeir Anpin was also now unmistakably masculine.

Zimzum (Hebrew, 'withdrawal')   The process in Lurianic Kabbalah (q.v.), whereby *En Sof* (q.v.) shrank into itself at the beginning of the creative process in order to make room for the cosmos.

NOTES

Introduction

1   Margaret Barker, *The Gate of Heaven: The History and Symbolism of the Temple in Jerusalem*, London, 1991, pp. 26–9; R. E. Clements, *God and Temple*, Oxford, 1965, p. 65.

Chapter 1

1   Ezekiel 1.

2   Ezekiel 3: 1–3.

3   Ezekiel 40–8; Psalm 137.

4   Geo Widengren, *The Ascension of the Apostle and the Heavenly Book*, Uppsala and Leipzig, 1950, *passim*; Wilfred Cantwell Smith, *What Is Scripture? A Comparative Approach*, London, 1993, pp. 59–61.

5   Deuteronomy 26: 5–9. This very early text was probably recited at one of the covenant festivals.

6   Joshua 3; 24.

7   For example, Psalms 2, 48, 87 and 110.

8   Frank Moore Cross, *Canaanite Myth and Hebrew Epic: Essays in the History of the Religion of Israel*, Cambridge, Mass., and London, 1973, pp. 148–50, 162–3.

9   William M. Schniedewind, *How the Bible Became a Book: The*

Textualization of Ancient Israel, Cambridge, 2004, pp. 35–47.

10 Frank Moore Cross, *From Epic to Canon: History and Literature in Ancient Israel*, Baltimore and London, 1998, pp. 41–2.

11 Judges 5:4–5; Habakkuk 3:4–8. These are very ancient texts, dating back to the tenth century BCE.

12 George W. Mendenhall, *The Tenth Generation: The Origins of Biblical Tradition*, Baltimore and London, 1973; N. P. Lemche, *Early Israel: Anthropological and Historical Studies on the Israelite Society Before the Monarchy*, Leiden, 1985; D. C. Hopkins, *The Highlands of Canaan*, Sheffield, 1985; James D. Martin, 'Israel as a Tribal Society' in R. E. Clements (ed.), *The World of Ancient Israel: Sociological, Anthropological and Political Perspectives*, Cambridge, 1989, pp. 94–114; H. G. M. Williamson, 'The Concept of Israel in Transition' in Clements, *The World of Ancient Israel*, pp. 141–63.

13 Deuteronomy 32: 8–9.

14 Psalm 82.

15 Psalms 47–48, 96, 148–51.

16 Psalm 89: 5–8; Mark S. Smith, *The Origins of Biblical Monotheism: Israel's Polytheistic Background and the Ugaritic Texts*, New York and London, 2001, p. 9.

17 Mark S. Smith, *The Early History of God: Yahweh and the Other Deities in Ancient Israel*, New York and London, 1990, pp. 44–9.

18 R. E. Clements, *Abraham and David*, London, 1967.

19 David S. Sperling, *The Original Torah: The Political Intent of the Bible's Writers*, New York and London, 1998, pp. 89–90.

20 Exodus 24: 9–31; 18. Schniedewind, *How the Bible Became a Book*, pp. 121–34.

21 Exodus 24:9, 11. Smith, *The Origins of Biblical Monotheism*, p. 86.

22 Hosea 6: 6.

23 Hosea 11: 5–6.

24 Amos 1: 3–5; 6 : 13; 2: 4–16.

25 Amos 5 : 24.

26 Isaiah 6: 1–9.

27 Isaiah 6 : 11–13.

28 Isaiah 6 : 3.

29 Isaiah 2 : 10–13; 10: 5–7. cf. Psalm 46: 5–6.

30 William G. Dever, *What Did the Biblical Writers Know and When Did They Know It? What Archaeology Can Tell Us About the Reality of Ancient Israel*, Grand Rapids, Mich., and Cambridge, UK, 2001, p. 280.

31 Isaiah 7 : 14. This is a literal translation of the verse, and does not follow the traditional version of the Jerusalem Bible.

32 Isaiah 9 : 1.

33 Isaiah 9: 5–7.

34 2 Kings 21: 2–7; 23 : 11; 23 : 10; Ezekiel 20 : 25–6; 22 : 30.

35 Cf. Psalms 68 : 18; 84 : 12. Gosta W. Ahlstrom, *The History of Ancient Palestine*, Minneapolis, 1993, p. 734.

36 2 Kings 22.

37 Exodus 24 : 3.

38 Exodus 24: 4–8. This is the only other place in the Bible where the phrase *sefer torah* is found. Schniedewind, *How the Bible Became a Book*, pp. 124–6.

39 2 Kings 23: 4–20.

40 Deuteronomy 12–26.

41 Deuteronomy 11: 21.

42 R. E. Clements, *God and Temple*, Oxford, 1965, pp. 89–95; Sperling, *The Original Torah*, pp. 146–7.

43 1 Kings 8: 27.

44 Judges 2: 7.

45 1 Kings 13: 1–2; 2 Kings 23: 15–18; 2 Kings 23: 25.

46 Jeremiah 8: 8–9; Schniedewind, *How the Bible Became a Book*, pp. 114–17.

47 Haym Soloveitchik, 'Rupture and Reconstruction: The Transformation of Contemporary Orthodoxy', *Tradition*, 28, 1994.

48 Deuteronomy 12: 2–3.

49 Joshua 8: 24–5.

50 2 Kings 21: 10–15.

51 Cross, *Canaanite Myth and Hebrew Epic*, pp. 321–5.

52 Leviticus 17–26.

53 Leviticus 25–7; 35–8; 40.

54 Exodus 29: 11, 45–6.

55 Cross, *Canaanite Myth and Hebrew Epic*, p. 321.

56 Exodus 40: 34, 36–8.

57 Cross, *Canaanite Myth and Hebrew Epic*, p. 421.

58 Peter Ackroyd, *Exile and Restoration: A Study of Hebrew Thought in the Sixth Century BC*, London, 1968, pp. 254–5.

59 Leviticus 19: 2; *qaddosh* (holy) means 'separate; other'.

60 Leviticus 26: 12; trans. Cross, *Canaanite Myth and Hebrew Epic*, p. 298.

61 Leviticus 25.

62 Leviticus 19: 33–4.

63 Genesis 2: 5–17.

64 Smith, *Origins of Biblical Monotheism*, pp. 167–71.

65 Psalms 89: 10–13; 93: 1–4; Isaiah 27: 1; Job 7: 12; 9: 8; 26: 12; 38: 7–11.

66 Genesis 1: 31.

67 Isaiah 44: 28.

68 Isaiah 41: 24.

69 Isaiah 45 : 5.

70 Isaiah 51 : 9–10.

71 Isaiah 42 : 1–4; 49 : 1–6; 50 : 4–9; 52 : 13; 53 : 12.

72 Isaiah 49 : 6.

Chapter 2

1   Malachi 1: 6–14; 2: 8–9.

2   It is very difficult to date this period accurately. See Gosta W.
    Ahlstrom, *The History of Ancient Palestine*, Minneapolis, 1993,
    pp. 880–83; Elias J. Bickerman, *The Jews in the Greek Age*,
    Cambridge, Mass., 1988, pp. 29–32; W. D. Davies and Louis
    Finkelstein (eds), *The Cambridge History of Judaism*, 2 vols,
    Cambridge, UK, 1984, vol. I, pp. 144–53.

3   The tribe of Levi had originally been singled out to serve
    Yahweh in the desert tabernacle (Numbers 1 : 48–53; 3: 5–40).
    But after the exile, they had become second-class priests,
    subject to those priests who were direct descendants of Aaron,
    Moses's brother.

4   Nehemiah 8: 7–8.

5   Nehemiah 8 : 12–16.

6   Michael Fishbane, *The Garments of Torah, Essays in Biblical
    Hermeneutics*, Bloomington and Indianapolis, 1989, pp. 64–5;
    Gerald L. Bruns, 'Midrash and Allegory; The Beginnings of
    Scriptural Interpretation', in Robert Alter and Frank
    Kermode (eds), *The Literary Guide to the Bible*, London, 1978,
    pp. 626–7.

7   Ezra 1 : 6. Fishbane translation in *Garments of Torah*, p. 65.

8   Ezra 1 : 10. Fishbane translation, ibid., p. 66.

9   Ezra 1 : 6, 9; cf. Ezekiel 1 : 3.

10 1 Samuel 9: 9; 1 Kings 22 : 8, 13, 19; cf. Nehemiah 7 : 65.

11 Wilfred Cantwell Smith, *What Is Scripture? A Comparative Approach*, London, 1993, p. 290.

12 Ezra 10.

13 Fishbane, *Garments of Torah*, p. 64.

14 Bruns, 'Midrash and Allegory', pp. 626–7.

15 Proverbs 29: 4–5.

16 I Kings 5: 9–14.

17 Job 42: 3.

18 Ben Sirah 24: 1–22. (This book is also called Ecclesiasticus.)

19 Ben Sirah 24: 23.

20 Proverbs 8: 22, 30–31.

21 Ben Sirah 24: 20.

22 Ben Sirah 24: 21.

23 Ben Sirah 24: 28–9.

24 Ben Sirah 35: 1–6.

25 Ben Sirah 35: 7–11.

26 Ben Sirah 24: 33.

27 Fishbane, *Garments of Torah*, pp. 67–9; Donald Harman Akenson, *Surpassing Wonder, The Invention of the Bible and the Talmuds*, New York, San Diego and London, 1998, pp. 89–90.

28 Ezekiel 14: 14; 28: 15.

29 Daniel 1: 4.

30 Daniel 1: 18.

31 Daniel 7: 25.

32 Daniel 11: 31.

33 Daniel 7: 13–14.

34 Jeremiah 25: 11–12; Daniel 9: 3.

35 Daniel 9: 3.

36 Daniel 10: 3.

37 Daniel 9: 21; 10: 16 cf. Isaiah 6: 6–7; Daniel 10: 4–6 cf. Ezekiel 1: 1, 24, 26–8.

38 Daniel 11: 35; 12: 9–10.

39 Akenson, *Surpassing Wonder*, pp. 160–67.

40 Jacob Neusner, 'Judaism and Christianity in the First Century', in Philip R. Davies and Richard T. White (eds), *A Tribute to Geza Vermes; Essays in Jewish and Christian Literature and History*, Sheffield, 1990, pp. 256–7.

41 Fishbane, *Garments of Torah*, pp. 73–6.

42 Bruns, 'Midrash and Allegory', p. 634.

43 Flavius Josephus, *The Jewish Antiquities*, 18.21. Scholars give different estimates of the population of Palestine at this time; some put it at 2.5 million; others at 1 million; some at a mere 500,000.

44 Jacob Neusner, 'Varieties of Judaism in the Formative Age', in Arthur Green (ed.), *Jewish Spirituality*, 2 vols, London, 1986, 1988, p. 185; E. P. Sanders, *Judaism: Practice and Belief, 63* BCE *to 66 CE*, London and Philadelphia, 1992, pp. 342–7.

45 Josephus, *Jewish Antiquities*, 17.42.

46 Akenson, *Surpassing Wonder*, pp. 144–70.

47 Ibid., pp. 171–89.

48 Psalms of Solomon, 17: 3. Akenson translation.

49 Florentino Garcia Martinez (ed.), *The Dead Sea Scrolls Translated*, Leiden, 1994, p. 138.

50 Josephus, *The Jewish War*, translated by G. A. Williamson, Harmondsworth, 1959, 2: 258–60; Josephus, *Jewish Antiquities*, 20: 97–9, cf. Acts of the Apostles 5: 36.

51 Matthew 3: 1–2.

52 Luke 3: 3–14; Josephus, *Jewish Antiquities*, 18: 116–19.

53 Mark 1: 14–15. The terms 'Kingdom of God' and 'Kingdom of

Heaven' were used interchangeably. Some Jews felt it more respectful to avoid the word 'God' and preferred 'Heaven' instead.

54 Jaroslav Pelikan, *Whose Bible Is It? A History of the Scriptures Through the Ages*, New York, 2005, pp. 36–44; Akenson, *Surpassing Wonder*, pp. 124–5; Cantwell Smith, *What Is Scripture?*, p. 58; Bruns, 'Midrash and Allegory', pp. 636–7.

55 Moses Hadas (ed. and trans.), *Aristeas to Philcrates*, New York, 1951, pp. 21–3.

56 Philo, *The Life of Moses* in *Philo*, translated by F. H. Colson, Cambridge, Mass., 1950, 6 : 476.

57 Beryl Smalley, *The Study of the Bible in the Middle Ages*, Oxford, 1941, pp. 3–4; Bruns, 'Midrash and Allegory', pp. 637–42; Burton L. Mack, *Who Wrote the New Testament? The Making of the Christian Myth*, San Francisco, 1995, pp. 254–6; Akenson, *Surpassing Wonder*, pp. 128–32; Pelikan, *Whose Bible Is It?*, pp. 46–7.

58 Philo, *The Migration of Abraham*, l.16, in *Philo in Ten Volumes*, translated by F. H. Colson and G. H. Whitaker, Cambridge, Mass, and London, 1958, vol. II.

59 Bruns, 'Midrash and Allegory', pp. 638–9.

60 Philo, *On the Birth of Abel and the Sacrifices Offered by Him and His Brother Cain*, vol. II, ll. 95–7. Colson and Whitaker translation.

61 Philo, *Special Laws*, 1 : 43. Colson and Whitaker translation.

62 Philo, *On the Confusion of Tongues*, ll. 146–7.

63 Philo, *Abraham*, l. 121. Colson and Whitaker translation.

64 Philo, *On the Confusion of Tongues*, l. 147. Colson and Whitaker translation.

65 Philo, *The Migration of Abraham*, ll. 34–5. Colvin and Whitaker translation.
66 Dio Cassius, *History*, 66: 6; Josephus, *Jewish War*, 6: 98.

Chapter 3

1   Donald Harman Akenson, *Surpassing Wonder, The Invention of the Bible and the Talmuds*, New York, San Diego and London, 1998, pp. 212–13.
2   Josephus, *The Jewish War*, translated by G. A. Williamson, Harmondsworth, 1959, 6: 312–13; Tacitus, *Histories*, 5: 13; Suetonius, *Vespasian*, 4. Paula Fredricksen, *Jesus of Nazareth, King of the Jews. A Jewish Life and the Emergence of Christianity*, London, 2000, p. 246.
3   Mark 8: 27–33.
4   Mark 5: 12; Matthew 27: 17, 22; cf. Josephus, *Jewish Antiquities* 18: 63–4.
5   1 Corinthians 15: 20.
6   Akenson, *Surpassing Wonder*, p. 94; Fredricksen, *Jesus*, pp. 262–3.
7   Matthew 19: 28.
8   Luke 24: 53; Acts 2: 46.
9   Matthew 26: 29; Mark 14: 25.
10 Acts 4: 32–5.
11 Matthew 5: 3–12; Luke 6: 20–23; Matthew 5: 38–48; Luke 6: 27–38; Romans 12: 9–13, 14; 1 Corinthians 6: 7; Akenson, *Surpassing Wonder*, p. 102; Fredricksen, *Jesus*, p. 243.
12 Matthew 12: 17; Romans 13: 6–7.
13 Matthew 5: 17–19; Luke 16: 17.
14 Luke 23: 56.
15 Galatians 2: 11–12.

16 Matthew 7: 12; Luke 6: 31; cf Romans 13: 10 and Shabbat 31a.

17 Mark 13: 1–2.

18 1 Corinthians 1: 22.

19 Matthew 21: 31.

20 Acts 8: 1, 18; 9:2; 11: 19.

21 Fredricksen, *Jesus*, pp. 60–61.

22 Galatians 2: 1–10; 5: 3; Acts 15.

23 Acts 10–11.

24 Acts 11: 26.

25 Thus Romans 1:20–32.

26 In the ancient world, people did not usually eat red meat that had not been sacrificed and consecrated in a temple.

27 Isaiah 2: 2–3; Zephaniah 3: 9; Tobit 14: 6; Zechariah 8: 23.

28 Galatians 1: 1–16.

29 The authorship of the first epistle to the Thessalonians is disputed; it may not have been written by Paul.

30 1 Thessalonians 1:9; 1 Corinthians 5: 1–13; 8: 4–13; 10: 4.

31 Joel 3: 1–5; Acts 2: 14–21.

32 Romans 8: 9; Galatians 4: 16; Fredricksen, *Jesus*, pp. 133–5.

33 Romans 9: 1–33.

34 Julia Galambush, *The Reluctant Paring. How the New Testament's Jewish Writers Created a Christian Book*, San Francisco, 2005, p. 148.

35 Psalm 69: 9; Romans 15: 3.

36 Romans 15: 4. Jaroslav Pelikan, *Whose Bible Is It? A History of the Scriptures Through the Ages*, New York, 2005, p. 72. My italics.

37 2 Corinthians 3: 9–18. Galambush, *Reluctant Parting*, pp. 145–6.

38 Romans 5: 12–20; cf. 1 Corinthians 15: 45.

39 Genesis 15: 6.

40 Romans 4: 22–4. My italics.

41 Galatians 3 : 8; Genesis 12 : 3.

42 Galatians 4 : 22–31.

43 Hebrews 3: 1–6.

44 Hebrews 4 : 12–9 : 28.

45 Hebrews 11 : 1.

46 Hebrews 11 : 32.

47 Hebrews 11 : 40.

48 Akenson, *Surpassing Wonder*, p. 213.

49 2 Peter 3 : 15; Ignatius of Antioch, *Letter to the Ephesians* 2 : 12.

50 A collection of these Gnostic gospels was discovered at Nag Hammadi in Egypt in 1945.

51 Akenson, *Surpassing Wonder*, pp. 229–43.

52 See, for example, Mark 14 : 61–4.

53 Philippians 2: 6–11.

54 Daniel 7 : 13; Matthew 24 : 30; 26 : 65; Mark 13 : 26; 14 : 62; Luke 17 : 22; 21 : 25; 22 : 69.

55 John 1 : 1–14; Hebrews 1: 2–4.

56 Luke 2 : 25; Matthew 12 : 14–21; 26 : 67; Acts 8 : 32–4; 1 Peter 2 : 23–4.

57 Psalms 69 : 21; 31 : 6; 22 : 18; Matthew 33–6.

58 Isaiah 7 : 14; Matthew 1 : 22–3.

59 David Flusser, *Jesus*, New York, 1969, p. 72.

60 Fredricksen, *Jesus*, p. 19.

61 There is a widespread belief that Luke was a gentile, but there is no hard evidence for this.

62 Mark 13 : 9–19, 13.

63 Mark 4: 3–9; 8 : 17–18.

64 Mark 2 : 21–2.

65 Mark 13 : 33–7.

66 Mark 14 : 58–61; 15 : 29.

67 Mark 13: 5–27.

68 Mark 13: 14; Daniel 9: 27.

69 Mark 11: 15–19; Isaiah 56: 7; Jeremiah 7: 11.

70 Mark 14: 21, 27.

71 Psalm 41: 8.

72 Zechariah 13: 7.

73 Mark 16: 8. In the earliest manuscripts Mark's gospel ends here. The next twelve verses describing Jesus's resurrection appearances were almost certainly added later.

74 Mark 1: 15. This is a literal translation of the Greek and does not follow the Jerusalem Bible.

75 Matthew 13: 31–50.

76 Matthew 5: 17.

77 Matthew 5: 11; 10: 17–23.

78 Matthew 24: 9–12.

79 Genesis 16: 11; Judges 13: 3–5; Genesis 17: 15–21.

80 Matthew 8: 17; Isaiah 53: 4.

81 Matthew 5: 1.

82 Matthew 5: 19.

83 Matthew 5: 21–39.

84 Matthew 5: 38–48.

85 Matthew 9: 13; Hosea 6: 6; cf. Aboth de Rabbi Nathan 1.4.11a.

86 Matthew 7: 12; cf. B. Shabbat, 31a.

87 Matthew 12: 16, 41, 42.

88 M. Pirke Avoth, 3: 3, in C. C. Montefiore and H. Loewe (eds), *A Rabbinic Anthology*, New York, 1974, p. 23.

89 Matthew 18: 20; Galambush, *Reluctant Parting*, pp. 67–8.

90 Luke 24: 13–35; Galambush, *Reluctant Parting*, pp. 91–2; Gabriel Josipovici, 'The Epistle to the Hebrews and the Catholic Epistles', in Robert Alter and Frank Kermode (eds), *The*

Literary Guide to the Bible, London, 1987, pp. 506–7.

91 John 1: 1–5.

92 John 1: 30.

93 1 John 4: 7–12; John 15: 12–13.

94 John 15: 18–27; 1 John 3: 12–13.

95 John 6: 60–66.

96 1 John 2: 18–19.

97 1 John 4: 5–6.

98 John 7: 34; 8: 19–21.

99 John 2: 19–21.

100 John 8: 57.

101 M. Sukkah 4: 9; 5: 2–4; John 7: 37–39; 8: 12.

102 John 6: 32–6.

103 John 8: 58. The phrase *Ani Waho*: I Am, was used in the
     Sukkoth rituals and was probably a term for the *Shekhinah*;
     W. D. Davies, *The Gospel and the Land: Early Chrisitainity and
     Jewish Territorial Doctrine*, Berkeley, 1974, pp. 294–5.

104 Galambush, *Reluctant Parting*, pp. 291–2.

105 Revelation 21: 22–4.

106 Luke 18: 9–14.

107 Matthew 27: 25.

108 Matthew 23: 1–33.

109 John 11: 47–53; 18: 2–3. The one honourable exception is the
     Pharisee Nicodemus, who comes secretly to Jesus for private
     instruction (John 3: 1–21).

Chapter 4

1 Donald Harman Akenson, *Surpassing Wonder, The Invention of
   the Bible and the Talmuds*, New York, San Diego and London,
   1998), pp. 319–25.

2   B. Berakhot 8b; 63b; B. Avodah Zarah 3b.

3   Pesikta Rabbati 14: 9 in William Braude (trans.), *Pesikta Rabbati: Discourses for Feasts, Fasts and Special Sabbaths*, 2 vols, New Haven, 1988; Gerald L. Bruns, 'Midrash and Allegory: The Beginnings of Scriptural Interpretation', in Robert Alter and Frank Kermode (eds), *The Literary Guide to the Bible*, London, 1987, p. 630.

4   Bruns, 'Midrash and Allegory', p. 629.

5   B. Shabbat, 31a in A. Cohen (ed.), *Everyman's Talmud*, New York, 1975, p. 65.

6   Sifra on Leviticus 19: 11.

7   Genesis 5: 1; C. G. Montefiore, 'Preface' in C. G. Montefiore and H. Loewe (eds), *A Rabbinic Anthology*, New York, 1974, p. xl.

8   Aboth de Rabbi Nathan, 1.4.11a in Montefiore and Loewe (eds), *A Rabbinic Anthology*, pp. 430–1. Hosea 6: 6.

9   Michael Fishbane, *The Garments of Torah, Essays in Biblical Hermeneutics*, Bloomington and Indianapolis, 1989, p. 37.

10 Ben Sirah, 50.

11 M. Pirke Avoth, 1: 2.

12 Psalm 89: 2; Aboth de Rabbi Nathan, 1.4.11a in Montefiore and Loewe (eds), *A Rabbinic Anthology*, p. 430.

13 B. Menahoth, 29b.

14 M. Rabbah, Numbers 19: 6.

15 M. Avoth, 5: 25; Fishbane, *Garments of Torah*, p. 38.

16 Eliyahu Zatta, 2.

17 Sifra on Leviticus 13.47 in Fishbane, *Garments of Torah*, p. 115.

18 John Bowker, *The Targums and Rabbinic Literature, An Introduction to Jewish Interpretations of Scripture*, Cambridge, 1969, pp. 54–5.

19 Bruns, 'Midrash and Allegory', p. 629.

20 Fishbane, *Garments of Torah*, pp. 22–32.

21 Deuteronomy 21: 23.

22 M. Sanhedrin, 6: 4–5.

23 Fishbane, *Garments of Torah*, p. 30.

24 Sifre Benidbar, Pisqa 84; Zechariah 2: 12; Fishbane translation, *Garments of Torah*, pp. 30–31.

25 Deuteronomy 30:12.

26 Exodus 33: 2, as interpreted in the midrash.

27 Baba Metziah, 59b in Montefiore and Loewe (eds), *A Rabbinic Anthology*, pp. 340–41.

28 Genesis Rabbah 1: 14.

29 B. Sanhedrin, 99b.

30 Ibid.

31 Jeremiah 23: 29.

32 M. Song of Songs Rabbah 1.10.2; Bruns, 'Midrash and Allegory', p. 627; Fishbane, 'Midrash and the Nature of Scripture', p. 19.

33 B. Hagigah 14b; T. Hagigah 2: 3–4; J. Hagigah 2: 1, 77a.

34 M. Tohorot; Yadayim 3: 5, translated by Wilfred Cantwell Smith, *What is Scripture? A Comparative Approach*, London, 1993, p. 253.

35 Leviticus Rabbah 8: 2; Sotah 9b.

36 J. Hagigah 2: 1.

37 T. Sanhedrin 11: 5; T. Zabiim 1: 5; T. Maaser Sheni 2: 1; Bowker, *The Targums*, pp. 49–53.

38 Dio Cassius, *History*, 69: 2.

39 Traditionally this is believed to have happened at Yavneh, but there are good arguments for assigning this development to the Usha period, which was more committed to written scripture.

40 Akenson, *Surpassing Wonder*, pp. 324–5.

41 In M. Yadayim 4 : 3; M. Edayyoth 8 : 7; M. Peah 2 : 6; M. Rosh Hashanah 2 : 9 the Mishnah gives a Mosaic reference to its *halakoth*, but does not claim to derive them from Moses or Sinai; Akenson, *Surpassing Wonder*, pp. 302–303.

42 Cantwell Smith, *What Is Scripture?*, pp. 116–17.

43 Jacob Neusner, *Medium and Message in Judaism*, Atlanta, 1989, p. 3; 'The Mishnah in Philosophical Context and Out of Canonical Bounds', *Journal of Biblical Literature*, 11, Summer 1993; Akenson, *Surpassing Wonder*, pp. 305–20.

44 Jacob Neusner, *Judaism. The Evidence of the Mishnah*, Chicago, 1981, pp. 87–91, 97–101, 132–1–37, 150–53.

45 B. Menahoth, 110a.

46 Akenson, *Surpassing Wonder*, pp. 329–39.

47 This is a body of doubtful historicity, not mentioned in the Mishnah.

48 Joshua 24 : 51.

49 Gershom Scholem, *On the Kabbalah and Its Symbolism*, New York, 1995, p. 46.

50 Pirke Avoth, 1 : 1; 3 : 13 in Jacob Neusner (trans.), *The Mishnah, A New Translation*, New Haven, 1988.

51 Akenson, *Surpassing Wonder*, pp. 361–2.

52 Ibid., pp. 366–95.

53 Jaroslav Pelikan, *Whose Bible Is It? A History of the Scriptures Through the Ages*, New York, 2005, pp. 67–8.

54 B. Yoma, 81a.

55 Davod Kraemer, *The Mind of the Talmud. An Intellectual History of the Bavli*, New York and Oxford, 1990, p.151.

56 B. Zebatim, 99a.

57 B. Baba Batara, 12a.

58 Cantwell Smith, *What Is Scripture?*, pp. 102–4; Pelikan, *Whose Bible Is It?*, p. 66.

59 Louis Jacobs, *The Talmudic Argument. A Study in Talmudic Reasoning and Methodology*, Cambridge, 1984, pp. 20–23; 203–13.

60 Akenson, *Surpassing Wonder*, p. 379.

61 Mekhilta de R. Ishmael, Beshalah, 7; Fishbane, *Garments of Torah*, p. 124.

62 B. Qedoshim, 49b; Cantwell Smith, *What Is Scripture?*, pp. 116–17.

63 William G. Braude (ed. and trans.), *Pesikta Rabbati Discourses for Feasts, Fasts and Special Sabbaths*, 2 vols, New Haven, 1968, *Piska* 3 : 2.

Chapter 5

1   Burton L. Mack, *Who Wrote the New Testament? The Making of the Christian Myth*, San Francisco, 1995, pp. 266–73.

2   Justin, *Apology*, 1.36; Mack, *Who Wrote the New Testament?*, p. 269.

3   Apologia 1 : 63.

4   Irenaeus, *Against Heresies*, 4 : 23.

5   R. R. Reno, 'Origen', in Justin S. Holcomb (ed.), *Christian Theologies of Scripture: A Comparative Introduction*, New York and London, 2006, pp. 23–4; R. M. Grant, *Irenaeus of Lyon*, London, 1997, pp. 47–51.

6   Ephesians 1 : 10, Revised Standard Version. Ephesians was probably not written by Paul himself.

7   David S. Pacini, 'Excursus: Reading Holy Writ: the Locus of Modern Spirituality', in Louis Dupre and Don E. Saliers, *Christian Spirituality: Post Reformation and Modern*, London and New York, 1989, p. 177.

8   Irenaeus, *Against Heresies*, 1: 8–9.

9   Mack, *Who Wrote the New Testament?* pp. 285–6.

10 Matthew 13: 38–44.

11 Irenaeus, *Against Heresies*, 4.26.1; Reno, 'Origen', p. 24.

12 Eusebius, *Demonstratio* Evangelium, 4: 15 in J. P. Migne (ed.), *Patrologia Graeca*, Paris, 1857–66, vol. 22, p. 296. My italics.

13 Ibid.

14 Reno, 'Origen'; David W. Kling, *The Bible in History: How the Texts Have Shaped the Times*, Oxford and New York, 1994, pp. 89–91; Jaroslav Pelikan, *Whose Bible Is It? A History of the Scriptures Through the Ages*, New York, 2005, pp. 61–2.

15 R. B. Tollington (trans.), *Selections from the Commentaries and Homilies of Origen*, London, 1929, p. 54. Gerald L. Bruns, 'Midrash and Allegory: The Beginnings of Scriptural Interpretation', in Robert Alter and Frank Kermode (eds), *A Literary Guide to the Bible*, London, 1987, p. 365.

16 Matthew 5: 29.

17 Origen, *On First Principles*, 4.3.1. He is commenting on a verse as translated in the Septuagint.

18 Exodus 25–31; 35–40.

19 Genesis 3: 8.

20 Matthew 10: 9.

21 *On First Principles*, 4.3.1 in G. W. Butterworth (trans.), *Origen; On First Principles*, Gloucester, Mass., 1973.

22 Homilies on Ezekiel 1: 2 quoted in Jaroslav Pelikan, *Whose Bible Is It? A History of the Scriptures Through the Ages*, New York, 2005, p. 60.

23 Genesis 20.

24 Exodus 12: 37.

25 Matthew 6: 20.

26 Exodus 13: 21.

27 1 Corinthians 10: 1–4.

28 Ibid., cf. John 6: 51.

29 Matthew 6: 20.

30 Matthew 19: 21.

31 Ronald E. Haine (trans.), *Origen: Homilies on Genesis and Exodus*, Washington DC, 1982, p. 277; Reno, 'Origen', pp. 25–6.

32 Reno, 'Origen', p. 29.

33 Mircea Eliade, *The Myth of the Eternal Return, or, Cosmos and History*, translated by Willard R. Trask, New York, 1959.

34 Origen, *On First Principles*, Preface, para. 8. Butterworth translation.

35 Ibid., 4.2.3.

36 Ibid., 2.3.1.

37 Ibid., 4.2.9.

38 Ibid.

39 Ibid., 4.2.3.

40 Ibid., 4.2.7.

41 Ibid., 4.1.6.

42 R. P. Lawson (trans.), *Origen, The Song of Songs: Commentary and Homilies*, New York, 1956, p. 44.

43 Song of Songs 1: 2.

44 Ephesians 5: 23–32.

45 Lawson, *Song of Songs*, p. 60.

46 Ibid., p. 61.

47 Origen, *Commentary on John*, 6: 1 in Reno, 'Origen', p. 28.

48 Matthew 19: 21.

49 Douglas Burton Christie, *The Word in the Desert: Scripture and the Quest for Holiness in Early Christian Monasticism*, New York and Oxford, 1993, pp. 297–8; Kling, *Bible in History*, pp. 23–40.

50 Beldon C. Lane, *The Solace of Fierce Landscapes: Exploring Desert and Monastic Spirituality*, New York and Oxford, 1998, p. 175.

51 Jaroslav Pelikan, *The Christian Tradition, A History of the Development of Doctrine.1. The Emergence of Catholic Tradition (100–600)*, Chicago and London, 1971, pp. 191–200.

52 Matthew 26: 39; 24: 36; 17: 5.

53 Basil, *On the Holy Spirit*, 28: 66.

54 Basil, *Epistle*, 234: 1.

55 Denys the Areopagite was the name of St Paul's first convert in Athens.

56 Denys, *Mystical Theology*, 3 in Paul Rosea, 'The Uplifting Spirituality of Pseudo-Dionysius' in Bernard McGinn and John Meyendorff (eds), *Christian Spirituality: Origins to the Twelfth Century*, London, 1985, p. 142.

57 Maximus, *Ambigua*, in Migne, *Patrologia Graeca*, vol. 91, p. 1085.

58 Romans 13: 13–14.

59 Augustine, *Confessions*, 8.12.29, in Philip Burton (trans.), *Augustine, The Confessions*, London, 2001.

60 Ibid., *Confessions*, 7.18.24.

61 Ibid., *Confessions*, 13.15.18. Pamela Bright, 'Augustine', in Holcomb (ed.), *Christian Theologies of Scripture*, pp. 39–50.

62 Exodus 33: 23. Augustine, *The Trinity*, 2.16.27; G. R. Evans, *The Language and Logic of the Bible: The Earlier Middle Ages*, Cambridge, 1984, pp. 3–6.

63 Augustine, *Confessions*, 12.25.35.

64 Ibid., Burton translation.

65 Deuteronomy 6: 5; Matthew 22: 37–9; Mark 23: 30–31; Luke 10: 17.

66 John 5: 10. Augustine, *Confessions*, 12.25.35.

67 Augustine, *Confessions*, 12.25.34–5, in Philip Burton (trans.)
    Augustine, The Confessions, London, 1907.

68 Deuteronomy 6 : 5; Matthew 22 : 37–9; Mark 12 : 30–31; Luke
    10 : 17; Augustine, *Confessions*, 12.25.35, Burton translation.

69 Beryl Smalley, *The Study of the Bible in the Middle Ages*, Oxford,
    1941, p. 11.

70 D. W. Robertson (trans.), *Augustine: On Christian Doctrine*,
    Indianapolis, 1958, p. 30.

71 Ibid.

72 Augustine, On Psalm 98 : 1 in Michael Cameron. 'Enerrationes
    in Pslamos', in Allen D. Fitzgerald (ed.), *Augustine Through the
    Ages*, Grand Rapids, 1999, p. 292.

73 1 Corinthians 12 : 27–30; Colossians 1 : 15–20. Charles
    Kannengiesser, 'Augustine of Hippo', in Donald Mc.Kim (ed.),
    Major Biblical Interpreters, Downers Grove, Ill., 1998, p. 22.

Chapter 6

1 John Cassian, *Collationes*, 1.17.2.

2 Ewart Cousins, 'The Humanity and Passion of Christ', in Jill
   Raitt (ed.), with Bernard McGinn and John Meyendorff,
   Christian Spirituality: High Middle Ages and Reformation, London,
   1988, pp. 377–83.

3 Gregory, *Homilies on Ezekiel*, 2.2.1.

4 Gregory, *Morals on Job*, 4.1.1. G. R. Evans, *The Language and
   Logic of the Bible: The Earlier Middle Ages*, Cambridge, 1984,
   pp. 56, 143, 164.

5 Gregory, *On the First Book of Kings*, 1.

6 James F. McCrae, 'Liturgy and Eucharist: West', in Raitt,
   Christian Spirituality, pp. 428–9.

7 Luke 14 : 27.

8   Jonathan Riley-Smith, 'Crusading as an Act of Love', *History*, 65, 1980.

9   Evans, *Language and Logic*, pp. 37–47; Beryl Smalley, *The Study of the Bible in the Middle Ages*, Oxford, 1941, pp. 31–57.

10 Ibid., pp. 121–7. Jaroslav Pelikan, *Whose Bible Is It? A History of the Scriptures Through the Ages*, New York, 2005, p. 106.

11 Smalley, *Study of the Bible*, p. 123.

12 Joseph Bekhor Shor, *Commentary on Exodus*, 9: 8.

13 Hugh of St Victor, *Didascalion*, 8–11; Smalley, *Study of the Bible*, pp. 69–70.

14 Smalley, *Study of the Bible*, pp. 86–154.

15 Ibid., p. 139.

16 Evans, *Language and Logic*, pp. 17–23.

17 Anselm, *Cur Deus Homo*, 1: 11–12; 1: 25; 2: 4; 2: 17.

18 Evans, *Language and Logic*, pp. 70–71; 134–41.

19 Bernard, *Epistle,* 191.1 in J. P. Migne (ed) *Patrologia Latina*, Paris, 1878–90, vol. 182, p. 357.

20 Cf. 1 Corinthians 13: 12. Quoted in Henry Adams, *Mont St Michel and Chartres*, London, 1986, p. 296.

21 Wilfred Cantwell Smith, *What Is Scripture? A Comparative Approach*, London, 1993, pp. 29–37; David W. Kling, *The Bible in History: How the Texts Have Shaped the Times*, Oxford and New York, 2004, pp. 96–112.

22 Irene M. Edmonds and Killian Walsh (trans.), *The Works of Bernard of Clairvaux: On the Song of Songs,* 4 vols, vol. 1, Spencer, Mass.; vols 2–4, Kalamazoo, Michigan, 1971–1980, vol. 1, p. 54.

23 Ibid., vol. 2, p. 28.

24 Ibid., vol. 2, pp. 30–32.

25 Ibid., vol. 1, p. 2.

26 Ibid., vol. 4, p. 86.

27 Ibid., p. 4.

28 Kling, *The Bible in History*, p. 103.

29 Edmonds and Walsh, *On the Song of Songs*, vol. 1, p. 16.

30 Evans, *Language and Logic*, pp. 44–7.

31 Henry Malter, *Saadia Gaon, His Life and Works*, Philadelphia, 1942.

32 Abraham Cohen, *The Teachings of Maimonides*, London, 1927; David Yellin and Israel Abrahams, *Maimonides*, London, 1903.

33 Moses Friedlander, *Essays on the Writings of Abraham Ibn Ezra*, London, 1877; Louis Jacobs, *Jewish Biblical Exegesis*, New York, 1973, pp. 8–21.

34 Deuteronomy 1: 1; my italics. This does not follow the Jerusalem Bible but is a literal translation of the Hebrew, as read by Ibn Ezra.

35 Hyam Maccoby, *Judaism on Trial: Jewish–Christian Disputation in the Middle Ages*, London and Toronto, 1982, pp. 95–150; Solomon Schechter, *Studies on Judaism*, Philadelphia, 1945, pp. 99–141.

36 Moshe Idel, 'PaRDeS: Some Reflections on Kabbalistic Hermeneutics', in John J. Collins and Michael Fishbane (eds), *Death, Ecstasy and Other-Worldly Journeys*, Albany, 1995, pp. 251, 255–6.

37 See Chapter 4, p. 90.

38 Collins and Fishbane, *Death, Ecstasy and Other-Worldly Journeys*, p. 249–57; Michael Fishbane, *The Garments of Torah, Essays in Biblical Hermeneutics*, Bloomington and Indianapolis, 1989, pp. 113–20.

39 Cantwell Smith, *What Is Scripture?*, p. 112.

40 Gershom Scholem, 'The Meaning of Torah in Jewish
    Mysticism', in *On the Kabbalah and Its Symbolism*, translated by
    Ralph Manheim, New York, 1965, p. 33.

41 Ibid., pp. 11–158; Gershom Scholem, *Major Trends in Jewish
    Mysticism*, New York, 1995 edn, pp. 1–79, 119–243; Michael
    Fishbane, *The Exegetical Imagination: On Jewish Thought and
    Theology*, Cambridge, Mass., and London, 1998, pp. 99–126;
    Fishbane, *Garments of Torah*, pp. 34–63.

42 Zohar, 1.15.a in Gershom Scholem (trans. and ed.), *Zohar, The
    Book of Splendor; Basic Readings from the Kabbalah*, New York,
    1949, pp. 27–8.

43 Fishbane, *The Exegetical Imagination*, pp. 100–1.

44 Zohar, II.94b in Scholem, *Zohar,The Book of Splendor*, p. 90.

45 Ibid.

46 Ibid., p. 122.

47 Zohar, III. 152a in Scholem, *Zohar,The Book of Splendor*, p. 121.

48 Zohar, II. 182a

49 A. Hudson, *Selections from English Wycliffite Writings*,
    Cambridge, 1978, pp. 67–8.

Chapter 7

1   Jerry S. Bentley, *The Humanists and Holy Writ; New Testament
    Scholarship in the Renaissance*, Princeton, 1983; Debora Kuller
    Shuger, *The Renaissance Bible, Scholarship, Sacrifice,
    Subjectivity*, Berkeley, Los Angeles and London, 2004);
    Jaroslav Pelikan, *Whose Bible Is It? A History of Scripture
    Through the Ages*, New York, 2005, pp. 112–28; William J.
    Bouwsma, 'The Spirituality of Renaissance Humanism', in Jill
    Raitt (ed.) with Bernard McGinn and John Meyendorff,
    Christian Spirituality: High Middle Ages and Reformation,

London, 1988; James D. Tracy, 'Ad Fontes, The Humanist Understanding of Scripture', in Raitt (ed.), *Christian Spirituality*.

2 Charles Trinkaus, *The Poet as Philosopher, Petrarch and the Formation of Renaissance Consciousness*, New Haven, 1977, p. 87.

3 Quoted in Alastair McGrath, *Reformation Thought, An Introduction*, Oxford and New York, 1988, p. 73.

4 Marc Leinhard, 'Luther and the Beginnings of the Reformation', in Raitt (ed.), *Christian Spirituality*, p. 269.

5 Richard Marius, *Martin Luther: The Christian between God and Death*, Cambridge, Mass., and London, 1999, pp. 73–4, 213–15, 486–7.

6 G. R. Evans, *The Language and Logic of the Bible: the Road to Reformation*, Cambridge, 1985, p. 8.

7 Ibid., p. 100.

8 David W. Kling, *The Bible in History: How the Texts Have Shaped the Times*, Oxford and New York, 2004, pp. 120–49.

9 Philip S. Watson, *Let God Be God! An Interpretation of the Theology of Martin Luther*, Philadelphia, 1947, p. 149.

10 Martin Luther, *Luther's Works* (*LW*), 55 vols, edited by Jaroslav Pelikan and Helmut Lehmann, Philadelphia and St Louis, 1955–86, vol. 33, p. 26.

11 Emil G. Kraeling, *The Old Testament Since the Reformation*, London, 1955, pp. 145–6.

12 Psalm 72 : 1

13 Psalm 71 : 2.

14 Leinhard, 'Luther and the Beginnings of the Reformation', p. 22.

15 Romans 1 : 17, quoting Habakkuk 2 : 4.

16 McGrath, *Reformation Thought*, p. 74.

17 *LW*, vol. 25, pp. 188–9.

18 Martin Luther, *Sermons*, 25 : 7; *LW*, vol. 10, p. 239.

19 Mickey L. Mattox, 'Martin Luther', in Justin S. Holcomb (ed.), *Christian Theologies of Scripture*, New York and London, 2006, p. 101; Jaroslav Pelikan, *The Christian Tradition: Volume 4: Reformation of Church and Dogma*, Chicago and London, 1984, pp. 168–71; Leinhard, 'Luther and the Beginnings of the Reformation', p. 274–6.

20 Scott H. Hendrix, *Luther and the Papacy: Stages in a Reformation Conflict*, Philadelphia, 1981, p. 83; Roland H. Bainton, *Here I Stand: A Life of Martin Luther*, New York, 1950, p. 90.

21 Bernard Lohse, *Martin Luther: An Introduction to His Life and Work*, translated by Robert C. Schultz, Philadelphia, 1988, p. 154.

22 Wilfred Cantwell Smith, *What Is Scripture? A Comparative Approach*, London, 1993, pp. 204–5; Pelikan, *Whose Bible Is It?*, p. 145.

23 Leinhard, 'Luther and the Beginnings of the Reformation', pp. 276–86; Pelikan, *The Christian Tradition*, pp. 180–81.

24 He found biblical support for his belief in John 3 : 8.

25 Fritz Buster, 'The Spirituality of Zwingli and Bullinger in the Reformation of Zurich', in Raitt (ed.), *Christian Spirituality*; Kraeling, *The Old Testament*, pp. 21–2.

26 Kraeling, *The Old Testament*, pp. 30–32; Randall C. Zachman, 'John Calvin', in Holcomb (ed.), *Christian Theologies*, pp. 117–29.

27 Alastair McGrath, *A Life of John Calvin, A Study in the Shaping of Western Culture*, Oxford, 1990, p. 131; Zachmann, 'John Calvin', p. 129.

28 Commentary on Genesis 1 : 6 in *The Commentaries of John Calvin on the Old Testament*, 30 vols, Calvin Translation Society,

1643–48, vol. 1, p. 86.

29 Bernard Lohse, *Martin Luther: An Introduction to His Life and Work*, translated by Robert C. Schultz, Philadelphia, 1988, p. 154.

30 Quoted in Richard Tarnas, *The Passion of the Western Mind; Understanding the Ideas that have Shaped Our World View*, New York and London, 1990, p. 300.

31 William R. Shea, 'Galileo and the Church', in David C. Lindberg and Ronald E. Numbers (eds), *God and Nature; Historical Essays on the Encounter Between Christianity and Science*, Berkeley, Los Angeles and London, 1986, pp. 124–5.

32 Pelikan, *Whose Bible Is It?*, p. 128.

33 Gershom Scholem, *Sabbetai Sevi, The Mystical Messiah*, London and Princeton, pp. 30–45; Gershom Scholem, *Major Trends in Jewish Mysticism*, New York, 1995 edn, pp. 245–80; 'The Messianic Idea in Kabbalism' in Scholem, *The Messianic Idea in Judaism and Other Essays in Jewish Spirituality*, New York, 1971, pp. 43–8; 'The Meaning of the Torah in Jewish Mysticism' in Scholem, *On the Kabbalah and Its Symbolism*, translated by Ralph Manheim, New York, 1965; 'Kabbalah and Myth' in Scholem, *On the Kabbalah*, pp. 90–117.

34 Scholem, *Sabbetai Sevi*, pp. 37–42.

35 As reported in Hyam Vital, *Sh'ar Ma'amar Razal* 16c, in Scholem, 'The Meaning of the Torah in Jewish Mysticism', pp. 72–5.

36 R. J. Wenlowsky, 'The Safed Revival and Its Aftermath' in Arthur Green (ed.), *Jewish Spirituality*, 2 vols, London, 1986, 1989, vol. 2, pp. 15–17; Louis Jacobs, 'The Uplifting of the Sparks', in ibid., pp. 108–11.

37 Laurence Fine, 'The Contemplative Practice of Yehudim in Lurianic Kabbalah' in Green (ed.), *Jewish Spirituality*, vol. 2,

pp. 73–8.

38 Matthew 26: 26.

39 John W. Fraser (trans.), *John Calvin: Concerning Scandals*, Grand Rapids, MI, 1978, p. 81.

40 Pelikan, *Whose Bible Is It?*, p. 132.

41 *LW*, vol. 36, p. 67.

42 Calvin, *Commentaries*, translated and edited by J. Harontinian and L. P. Smith, London, 1958, p. 104.

43 Yirmanyahu Yovel, *Spinoza and Other Heretics*, 2 vols, Princeton, 1989, vol. 1, p. 17.

44 Kling, *Bible in History*, pp. 205–7; Alan Heimert and Andrew Delbanco (eds), *The Puritans in America: A Native Anthology*, Cambridge, Mass., 1988.

45 Deuteronomy 30: 15–17; John Winthrop, 'A Model of Christian Charity', in Perry Miller, *The American Puritans: Their Prose and Poetry*, Garden City, NY, 1956, p. 83.

46 Robert Cushman, 'Reasons and Considerations' in Heimert and Delbanco (eds), *The Puritans in America*, p. 44.

47 Regina Sharif, *Non-Jewish Zionism: Its Roots in Western History*, London, 1983, p. 90.

48 Isaiah 2: 1–6.

49 Edward Johnson, 'Wonder-Working Providence of Sion's Savior in New England', in Heimert and Delbanco (eds), *The Puritans in America*, p. 115–16.

50 Exodus 19: 4; Kling, *Bible in History*, pp. 206–7.

51 Kling, *Bible in History*, pp. 207–29; Theophilus H. Smith, 'The Spirituality of Afro-American Traditions', in Louis Dupre and Don E. Saliers, *Christian Spirituality: Post Reformation and Modern*, New York and London, 1989; Lewis V. Baldwin and Stephen W. Murphy, 'Scripture in the African-American

Christian Tradition', in Holcomb (ed.), *Christian Theologies*; Sterling Stuckey, *Slave Culture: Nationalist Theory and the Foundations of Black America*, New York and Oxford, 1987.

52 Genesis 9: 25.

53 Ephesians 6: 5.

54 James Hal Cone, *A Black Theology of Liberation*, Philadelphia, 1970, pp. 18–19, 26.

55 Exodus 21: 7–11; Genesis 16; 21: 8–21. Delores S. Williams, *Sisters in the Wilderness: The Challenge of Womanist God-Talk*, Maryknoll, NY, 2003, pp. 144–9.

Chapter 8

1 Wilfred Cantwell Smith, *What Is Scripture? A Comparative Approach*, London, 1993, pp. 184–94.

2 Diderot, Letter to Falconet, 1766, in Diderot, *Correspondence*, edited by Georges Roth, 16 vols, Paris, 1955–70, vol. VI, p. 261.

3 Rousseau, *Confessions*, Part I; Book I, in G. Petain (ed.), *Oeuvres complete de J. J. Rousseau*, 8 vols, Paris, 1839, vol. I. p. 19.

4 Edward Gibbon, *Memoirs of My Life*, edited by Georges A. Bonnard, London, 1966, p. 134.

5 Julius Guttman, *Philosophies of Judaism*, London and New York, 1964, pp. 265–85; R. M. Silverman, *Baruch Spinoza: Outcast Jew, Universal Sage*, Northwood, UK, 1995; Leo Strauss, *Spinoza's Critique of Religion*, New York, 1982; Yovel Yirmanyahu, *Spinoza and Other Heretics*, 2 vols, Princeton, 1989.

6 Spinoza, *A Theologico-Political Treatise*, translated by R. H. M. Elwes, New York, 1951, p. 7.

7 Gershom Scholem, *Major Trends in Jewish Mysticism*, New York, 1995 edn, pp. 327–429; Gershom Scholem, *The Messianic Idea in Judaism and Other Essays on Jewish Spirituality*, New York, 1971,

pp. 189–227; Gerschon David Hundert (ed.), *Essential Papers on Hasidism: Origins to Present*, New York and London, 1991.

8 B. Shabbat, 10a; 11a.

9 Louis Jacobs, 'Hasidic Prayer', in Hundert (ed.), *Essential Papers*, p. 330.

10 Scholem, *Messianic Idea in Judaism*, p. 211.

11 Quoted in Simon Dubnow, 'The Maggid of Miedzyryrecz, His Associates and the Center in Volhynia', in Hundert (ed.), *Essential Papers*, p. 61.

12 R. Meshullam Phoebus of Zbaraz, *Devekh emet*, n.p., n.d. in Jacobs, 'Hasidic Prayer', p. 333.

13 Benzion Dinur, 'The Messianic-Prophetic Role of the Baal Shem Tov', in Marc Saperstein (ed.), *Essential Papers on Messianic Movements and Personalities in Jewish History*, New York and London, 1992, p. 381.

14 Dubnow, 'The Maggid', p. 65.

15 Ibid.

16 Ibid.

17 Louis Jacobs (ed. and trans.), *The Jewish Mystics*, London, 1990; New York, 1991, pp. 208–15.

18 Jonathan Sheehan, *The Enlightenment Bible; Translation, Scholarship, Culture*, Princeton and Oxford, 2005, pp. 28–44.

19 Ibid., pp. 95–136.

20 Ibid., pp. 54–84.

21 Ibid., p. 68.

22 Ernest Nicholson, *The Pentateuch in the Twentieth Century: The Legacy of Julius Wellhausen*, Oxford, 1998, pp. 3–61.

23 John R. Franke, 'Theologies of Scripture in the Nineteenth and Twentieth Centuries', in Holcomb (ed.), *Christian Theologies of Scripture A Comparative Introduction*, New York and London, 2006;

Jeffrey Hensley, 'Friedrich Schleiermacher' in Holcomb (ed.), ibid.

24 Friedrich Schleiermacher, *The Christian Faith*, translated by H. R. Mackintosh and J. S. Steward, Edinburgh, 1928, p. 12.

25 James R. Moore, 'Geologists and Interpreters of Genesis in the Nineteenth Century', in David C. Lindberg and Ronald E. Numbers (eds), *God and Nature; Historical Essays on the Encounter Between Christianity and Science*, Berkeley, Los Angeles and London, 1986, pp. 341–3.

26 Ferenc Morton Szasz, *The Divided Mind of Protestant America, 1880–1930*, University, Alabama, 1982, pp. 16–34, 37–41; Nancy Ammerman, 'North American Protestant Fundamentalism', in Martin E. Marty and R. Scott Appleby (eds), *Fundamentalisms Observed*, Chicago and London, 1991, pp. 11–12.

27 Mrs Humphry Ward, *Robert Elsmere*, Lincoln, Neb., 1969, p. 414.

28 *New York Times*, 1 February 1897.

29 Ibid., 18 April 1899.

30 George M. Marsden, *Fundamentalism and American Culture: The Shaping of Twentieth-Century Evangelicalism, 1870–1925*, New York and Oxford, 1980, p. 55.

31 Charles Hodge, *What is Darwinism?*, Princeton, 1874, p. 142.

32 A. A. Hodge and B. B. Warfield, 'Inspiration', *Presbyterian Review*, 2, 1881.

33 B. B. Warfield, *Selected Shorter Writings of B. B. Warfield*, 2 vols, edited by John B. Meeber, Nutley, NJ, 1902, pp. 99–100.

34 Paul Boyer, *When Time Shall Be No More: Prophecy Belief in Modern American Culture*, Cambridge, Mass., and London, 1992, pp. 87–90; Marsden, *Fundamentalism*, pp. 50–58.

35 2 Thessalonians 2: 3–8.

36 1 Thessalonians 4:16.

37 Marsden, *Fundamentalism*, pp. 57–63.

38 David Rudavsky, *Modern Jewish Religious Movements: A History of Emancipation and Adjustment*, rev. edn, New York, 1967, pp. 157–64, 286–90.

39 Guttman, *Philosophies of Judaism*, pp. 308–51; A. M. Eisen, 'Strategies of Jewish Faith', in Arthur Green (ed.), *Jewish Spirituality*, 2 vols, London, 1986, 1989, vol. II, pp. 291–87.

40 Samuel C. Heilman and Menachem Friedman, 'Religious Fundamentalism and Religious Jews', in Marty and Appleby (eds), *Fundamentalisms Observed*, pp. 211–15; Charles Selengut, 'By Torah Alone: Yashiva Fundamentalism in Jewish Life', in Martin E. Marty and R. Scott Appleby (eds), *Accounting for Fundamentalisms*, Chicago and London, 1994; Menachem Friedman, 'Habad as Messianic Fundamentalism' in ibid., p. 201.

41 Quoted in Peter Gay, *A Godless Jew: Freud, Atheism, and the Making of Psychoanalysis*, New Haven and London, 1987, pp. 6–7.

42 Zygmunt Bauman, *Modernity and the Holocaust*, Ithaca, NY, 1989, pp. 40–77.

43 George Steiner, *In Bluebeard's Castle: Some Notes Towards the Re-definition of Culture*, London and New Haven, 1971, p. 33.

44 Daniel 11:15; Jeremiah 1:14.

45 Robert C. Fuller, *Naming the Antichrist: The History of an American Obsession*, Oxford and New York, 1995, pp. 115–17; Paul Boyer, *When Time Shall Be No More*, pp. 101–5; Marsden, *Fundamentalism*, pp. 141–4; 150; 157; 207–10.

46 Boyer, *When Time Shall Be No More*, p. 119; Marsden, *Fundamentalism*, pp. 90–92.

47 Boyer, *When Time Shall Be No More*, p. 192; Marsden,

Fundamentalism, pp. 154–5.

48 Szasz, *The Divided Mind*, p. 85.

49 Ammerman, 'North American Protestant Fundamentalism',
    p. 26; Marsden, *Fundamentalism*, pp. 69–83; Ronald L.
    Numbers, *The Creationists: The Evolution of Scientific Creationism*,
    Berkeley, Los Angeles and London, 1992, pp. 41–4; Szasz,
    The Divided Mind, pp. 107–18.

50 To J. Baldon, Mark 27, 1923, in Numbers, *The Creationists*, p. 41.

51 Heilman and Friedman, 'Religious Fundamentalism and
    Religious Jews', p. 220.

52 Michael Rosenek, 'Jewish Fundamentalism in Israeli Education',
    in Martin E. Marty and R. Scott Appleby (eds), *Fundamentalisms
    and Society*, Chicago and London, 1993, pp. 383–4.

53 The name is derived from Isaiah 66 : 5: 'Listen to the word of
    Yahweh, you who tremble at his word.'

54 Menachem Friedman, 'The Market Model and Religious
    Radicalism', in Laurence J. Silberstein (ed.), *Jewish
    Fundamentalism in Comparative Perspective: Religion, Ideology and
    the Crisis of Modernity*, New York and London, 1993, p. 194.

55 Heilman and Friedman, 'Religious Fundamentalism and
    Religious Jews', pp. 229–31.

56 Gideon Aran, 'The Roots of Gush Emunim', *Studies in
    Contemporary Judaism*, 2, 1986; Gideon Aran, 'Jewish Religious
    Zionist Fundamentalism' in Marty and Appleby (eds),
    Fundamentalisms Observed, pp. 270–71; 'The Father, the Son and
    the Holy Land', in R. Scott Appleby (ed.), *Spokesmen for the
    Despised, Fundamentalist Leaders in the Middle East*, Chicago,
    1997, pp. 318–20; Samuel C. Heilman, 'Guides of the Faithful,
    Contemporary Religious Zionist Rabbis', in ibid., pp. 329–38.

57 Ian S. Lustick, *For the Land and the Lord: Jewish Fundamentalism*

in Israel, New York, 1988, p. 84.

58 Eleazar Waldman, *Artzai*, 3, 1983, in Lustick, *For the Land and the Lord*, pp. 82–3.

59 1 Samuel 15 : 3; R. Israel Hess, 'Genocide: A Commandment of the Torah', in *Bat Kol*, 26 February 1980; Haim Tzuria, 'The Right to Hate', *Nekudah*, 15; Ehud Sprinzak, 'The Politics, Institutions and Culture of Gush Eminim', in Silberstein (ed.), *Jewish Fundamentalism*, p. 127.

60 Ehud Sprinzak, *The Ascendance of Israel's Far Right*, Oxford and New York, 1991, pp. 233–5.

61 Raphael Mergui and Philippe Simonnot, *Israel's Ayatollahs: Meir Kahane and the Far Right in Israel*, London, 1987, p. 45.

62 Aviezer Ravitsky, *Messianism, Zionism and Jewish Religious Radicalism*, translated by Michael Swirsky and Jonathan Chipman, Chicago and London, 1983, pp. 133–4; Sprinzak, *Ascendance of Israel's Radical Right*, pp. 94–8.

63 Aran, 'Jewish Religious Zionist Fundamentalism', pp. 267–8.

64 John N. Darby, *The Hopes of the Church of God in Connexion with the Destiny of the Jews and the nations as Revealed in Prophecy*, 2nd edn, London, 1842.

65 Boyer, *When Time Shall Be No More*, pp. 187–8.

66 Jerry Falwell, *Fundamentalist Journal*, May 1968.

67 John Walvoord, *Israel and Prophecy*, Grand Rapids, Mich., 1962.

68 Boyer, *When Time Shall Be No More*, p. 145.

69 2 Peter 3 : 10.

70 Ammerman, 'North American Protestant Fundamentalism', pp. 49–53; Michael Liensesch, *Redeeming America: Piety and Politics in the New Christian Right*, Chapel Hill, NC, and London, 1995, p. 226.

71 Gary North, *In the Shelter of Plenty: The Biblical Blueprint for*

Welfare, Fort Worth, Tex., 1986, p. xiii.

72 Ibid., p. 55.

73 Gary North, *The Sinai Strategy: Economics and the Ten Commandments*, Tyler Tex., 1986, pp. 213–14.

74 Ammerman, 'North American Protestant Fundamentalism', pp. 49–53; Liensesch, *Redeeming America*, p. 226.

75 Franz Rosenzweig, *The Star of Redemption*, translated by William W. Hallo, New York, 1970, p. 176.

76 Jeremiah 31 : 31–3.

77 Fishbane, 'The Notion of a Sacred Text', in *The Garments of Torah, Essays in Biblical Hermeneutics*, Bloomington and Indianapolis, 1989, pp. 122–32.

78 Isaiah 2: 1–4.

79 Fishbane, 'The Notion of a Sacred Text', p. 131.

80 Hans Urs von Balthasar, *The Glory of the Lord: A Theological Aesthetic*, vol VII, *Theology: the New Covenant*, edited by John Riches, translated by Brian McNeill C.R.V., San Francisco, 1989, p. 202.

81 Hans Frei, *The Eclipse of Biblical Narative*, New Haven, 1974.

82 Smith, *What Is Scripture?*

Epilogue

1   Gerald L. Bruns, 'Midrash and Allegory: The Beginnings of Scriptural Interpretation', in Robert Alter and Frank Kermode (eds), *The Literary Guide to the Bible*, London, 1987, pp. 641–2.

2   Quoted by Ian Hacking, *Why Does Language Matter to Philosophy?*, Cambridge, 1975, p. 148.

3   Donald Davidson, *Inquiries into Truth and Interpretation*, Oxford, 1984, p. 153.

4   Ibid.

INDEX OF BIBLICAL CITATIONS

Indexes compiled by Meg
Davies (Fellow of the Society of
Indexers)

SUGAR STREET
Book 1 in the Sugar Street Series
Copyright © 2018 by Amada Pullen Turetsky

Published by Freshwater Ink

Cover Design and Interior Format

Sugar Street

A NOVEL

M.J. PULLEN

For the neighbors.

1

JESS

City Jail, Sugar Mills, Georgia

TO BE HONEST, HER FIRST trip to jail was not living up to Jess Rodriguez's expectations. Years of *Law and Order* had led her to believe the cells at the Sugar Mills Jail would be larger, more open to the rest of the police station. She hadn't spent much time considering the small suburban jail, despite driving past it at least once a day. It was tucked on the ground floor of City Hall, which in turn was set back from the main thoroughfare through the historic center of Sugar Mills. Once a quaint northern outpost on the Chattahoochee River, where a wealthy sugar cane processor gave the town its livelihood and name, Sugar Mills was now another chunk of increasingly homogenous suburban Atlanta sprawl.

Before arriving tonight, she'd assumed there would be bars along one wall, maybe facing the guard station so she and her companions in the women's holding cell could call out if they needed something. But there were no bars. Concrete walls and a heavy institutional door, with an electronic lock and speaker next to it. This door had a long, narrow slit in the middle. In case the speaker quit working in a power outage?

Oh, God. What if there were a power outage?

What if they were locked in and couldn't get out? What if they needed something? Jess was suddenly thirsty. Not that she wanted to drink, and be forced to use the weird metal toilet in the far corner. But still. She'd sort of assumed that when you were in a small-town jail at night, you'd lie on a scratchy blanket and talk to the guards while they watched a tiny desk-sized television. Come to think of it, her primary impressions of jail might be from *The Andy Griffith Show*.

"Stop." Delia Cargill moaned from her folded-over position on the bench across from Jess. Her normally perfectly coiffed friend was dressed in a see-through black top, gray sweatpants that were too large, and cheap pink flip-flops. Of the three of them—Jess, Delia, and Maizy Henriksson—Delia was the only one whose shoelaces the guards hadn't had to confiscate.

"Stop what?" Jess said.

"You're making a whining noise. It's incessant."

"I am? No, I'm not."

"You *are*," Maizy agreed from her spot on the third wall. Maizy was sitting cross-legged with her eyes closed, like fucking Buddha instead of the president of the PTA. She was a few feet away from the cell's fourth occupant: a lady who smelled like urine and cheap liquor and had been snoring loudly since Jess and the other two had arrived. "And it's seriously irritating."

"Well, it's nice to see the two of you agreeing on something for once," Jess said flatly.

"Shut up," Maizy and Delia said simultaneously.

Fine. Jess closed her eyes, trying to mimic Maizy's calm position. She *sucked* at meditation. And she was not good in situations like this. Jess was not a crisis girl.

Carras—who had not been arrested with the other three— seemed like a crisis girl. Maybe it was her Caribbean roots—she had that whole chill, Bobby McFerrin thing going—or her years in front of crowds on the tennis court, or her training as a therapist. Maybe because she was the only one of the four of them who hadn't yet had her sanity destroyed by motherhood. Whatever it was, Carras always seemed to be the calm one. Jess could use some of that calm right about now. *Was it weird that Carras hadn't been brought in yet?*

"For God's sake, Jess, stop!" Delia snapped.

Now she heard it. The whining noise came from her own chest, as though it belonged to someone else. "Sorry." Feeling the need to fill the silence with something else, she added, "I was thinking that if Carras isn't here yet, maybe she can get us help. Reach one of the guys."

"Let's hope." Delia sighed.

Poor Delia. Gage was on an international flight—little chance of reaching him for hours. At least Tom was only in Boston, covering a game at Fenway Park. How was it they had managed to get arrested when three out of their four husbands were out of town?

How was it they had managed to get arrested at all?

"I never wanted this," Jess said, barely aware she was speaking aloud. "I tried to say no."

Delia's head snapped toward her. "You're saying that I did want this?" Her usually refined, Southern parlor accent slipped into the hillbilly drawl that Delia only let fly when she was angry. "You're saying that I talked you into it against your will? Okay, fine. I'm a horrible person. I've ruined all our lives. Happy?"

"Delia, that's not what I meant. But my marriage isn't like yours and Gage's—"

"You didn't ruin anyone's life," Maizy interrupted. "We're adults and we can take our medicine with our big-girl panties on."

Delia shot Maizy a baffled glance. Before they could say more, however, the electronic lock buzzed on the cell door, and Jess's brief hope that Carras was working to get them out died. Carras came in with her head down, wearing athletic shorts and sandals, and a black T-shirt with a faded red mask in the middle—probably some comic book character Jess wouldn't know if she met in an alley. Carras looked despondent: her normally glowing onyx skin was ashen and hollow. "Sorry," she said. "I called everyone I could before the officer came to my house. I had to leave messages."

The deputy who'd escorted Carras in pulled the metal door closed, and Jess felt the slamming sound reverberate in her skull for long after the noise itself had stopped. Carras had been their last hope.

Carras dropped onto the cold metal bench next to Jess, and the air in the room seemed to deflate with her. There was nothing else. All they could do now was wait for their fate to be decided.

2

JESS

Two Months Earlier

SHE SHOULD HAVE KNOWN SOMETHING was up when
Delia invited them to play tennis. Or in Jess's case, *pretend* to
play tennis.

Technically, Jess was half the doubles team soundly defeating
her friend Delia and Belinda Hayes-Currington, the iconic head
of the Sugar Mills Country Club Membership Committee. In reality, very little of that achievement could be attributed to Jess
herself, considering her teammate was two-time women's NCAA
champion Carras Lightbourne Prather. If Jess's husband Tom and
Carras's husband Stuart hadn't been longtime friends, Carras surely would never have accepted an invitation that included Jess as a
doubles partner, even for a casual neighborhood match.

Carras made a pick-up tennis match appear as hard as watching Netflix on her couch. Jess watched in awe, panting, as Carras
floated back and forth across their side of the court; her dark, muscular legs flexed with effort that didn't show on her face. She had
Delia and Belinda running all over the court, both wiping their
foreheads beneath embroidered Sugar Mills Country Club tennis
visors. Carras, meanwhile, had scarcely broken a sweat.

"You're not even *trying*," Delia complained, when she and Jess
ended up a few feet from each other at the net while Belinda
chased down an errant ball.

"I don't have to." Jess shrugged. "Carras could beat all three of
us in her sleep."

"Can you ask her to ease up?" Delia glanced furtively toward Belinda's retreating backside. "I finally got Belinda to order from my Pure Indulgences catalog last month, and I am *this close,*" she held her palm an inch from her racket, "to getting her to host a party. If the Club Side women hear that Belinda Hayes-Currington has done it, I could pay off Sadie's braces before the end of the summer."

"Sounds like you can afford to lose, then." Jess grinned. "Besides, you dragged me here, and said to bring a fourth. I have work I could be doing at home. On the *Annex Side.*"

In their neighborhood, "Club Side" referred to the original Sugar Mills Country Club: grand, integration-era houses of the 1960s with sweeping green lawns that surrounded the expansive dome-topped clubhouse, golf course, tennis courts certified by the International Tennis Federation, and Olympic-sized pool, plus a zero-entry children's pool with multiple water slides.

Across Sweet River Road was Sugar Mills Annex, the newer, more modest subdivision where Jess, Delia, and Carras lived. Annex residents could pay a reduced annual fee for a limited club membership, which allowed them to reserve tee times and tennis courts, and sign their kids up for the swim team. They could even make reservations at the club's restaurant during off-peak hours, so long as they paid their tabs in cash (Club Side members retained the privilege of being billed monthly with their dues).

For her part, Jess thought the whole thing was rather absurd. It had been Tom who'd insisted they move here ten years earlier, when the real estate crash made prices almost affordable, and their daughter Mina was on the way. It had been a "most house for the money" kind of decision at a time when Jess was already overwhelmed by impending motherhood. Now she'd grown comfortable in their house and (mostly) in suburban utopia, but the cachet of living in Sugar Mills still meant nothing to her.

Delia Cargill, on the other hand, seemed to long for the mysterious exclusivity of the Club Side. Jess enjoyed her friendship with her spunky blonde neighbor Delia, and their proximity across the cul-de-sac had thrown them together despite being different in almost every way. Delia's desperation to fit in with the club, and to court Belinda Hayes-Currington's friendship, Jess would never fully understand.

"Better hustle!" she called, teasing, as Delia scrambled to hit Carras's drop shot. Delia glared as she lobbed the ball back over the net. Jess grunted with feigned effort to get to it, but actually veered off long before she got there. Carras expertly took the ball out of the air for a winning overhead from much farther away.

To be fair, Carras had been a tennis star in college, and played semipro for a while afterward before deciding to settle down with Tom's college roommate, Stuart Prather, and work as a therapist for teenagers. It had been somewhat cruel to bring Carras as her fourth, but what did Delia expect, dragging Jess out last minute like this?

Carras smashed a volley at Delia's feet. Seconds later, she whipped a fireball shot past Belinda to end the game. *Thank goodness.* As the women wiped their brows and congratulated one another at the net, Carras was polite enough to congratulate Jess, as though she'd had anything to do with their victory. Jess laughed.

"Great game, ladies." Belinda's pristine white teeth shone brightly, along with most of her gums. She shouldered her Tory Burch tennis bag, which probably cost a month's worth of groceries at Jess's house. "Lunch up the hill. My treat."

Without waiting for agreement, Belinda started up the hill toward the club café. As they shuffled behind her, Jess leaned in to Delia. "You owe me for this. I have a huge stack of proposals due tomorrow."

Delia knocked Jess with her shoulder. "Like you can't do those things in your sleep by now. Besides, what are they going to do, fire you?"

A valid point. Jess had been doing contract work for her old management consulting firm ever since Mina was born nine years ago. She was their most reliable editor of proposals and presentations, all the stuff the consultants hated doing themselves. She could probably tell them she wanted two months off and to be paid in blueberry pancakes, and they still wouldn't fire her.

"Fine. But you know I hate these 'ladies who lunch' things," Jess complained. "The conversation always devolves into hyper-achieving parent one-upmanship."

"You'll be fine. You're a great mom with nothing to prove, and

I am going to get Belinda to host a party and invite all her up-per-crust friends with disposable income. It will be fabulous."

Jess rolled her eyes. Still, it was a relief to get off the court and into the shade of an umbrella at the café. Belinda signaled to a waiter in shorts and a polo as they dropped their bags and settled onto the warm iron patio furniture.

"You have to excuse my destroyed manicure," Belinda said, even though Jess could see nothing wrong with her pale pink, shiny nails. "Sewing all these costumes for the play is murder."

"Are all three of your kids in the play?" Delia asked. "You have such a talented family."

"Couldn't talk them out of it," Belinda lamented. Jess found this hard to believe, because Orson the Fifth—O5, Belinda's young-est—was a white-blond boy in Dash's class, whom she had never heard utter a single word voluntarily. "And you know I've taken on the costumes for half the cast—people don't know how to sew anymore."

"Mina has a small part," Jess said, fully aware she was one of those people. "I bought something at the dollar store to throw over tights. The teacher said it was fine."

Belinda patted her hand. "You working moms. I don't know how you do it. Don't worry, I'm sure they'll put Mina in the back of the ensemble. She'll blend right in."

Jess opened her mouth to respond, but couldn't figure out how to do it without swearing.

Belinda didn't notice. "Personally, I can't imagine how I would have time to hold down a job. Allegra made the all-state gymnas-tics team again this year, and her coach wants her to anchor the dance competition as well. Emma's joined the travel soccer team, and she plays lacrosse, and they both want voice lessons this sum-mer... Remember, Delia, I told you about that talent scout who found us on our cruise last year?"

Jess raised an eyebrow at Delia, who avoided her gaze. Carras, exempt from the conversation thanks to her non-parent status, said nothing. Before they had to suffer Belinda's rendition of how the Currington girls got "discovered," however, the waiter returned with a pitcher of white peach sangria and five frosted glasses.

"Is someone joining us?" Delia glanced at the fifth glass.

"I hope you don't mind," Belinda trilled. "I have a friend coming. My…tennis instructor."

Carras's eyes went wide and Jess saw her glance away. Belinda's tennis skills didn't exactly scream professional tutelage, even to Jess's inexperienced eye.

Jess checked her watch. The kids would be getting off the bus in three hours. She had four proposals, one presentation, and three loads of laundry to finish by the weekend, on top of getting Mina to the auditorium for four showings of the school play, with no help from Tom until Sunday afternoon.

But before Belinda could explain why her tennis coach was meeting her at lunch rather than on the court, her face lit. "Here he is! Parker! Yoo-hoo!"

Across the patio, a well-built Asian man in his twenties spotted Belinda and crossed to their table, smiling wide. He wore white shorts with a lime-green athletic polo that strained across his substantial chest and arm muscles. *Yum.* Jess sat up straighter, suddenly worried that the soft roll of fat on her lower belly might be showing.

Parker took the seat next to Belinda, kissing her hand. Already flushed from their match, Belinda reddened prettily. A harmless enough gesture, Jess supposed. But she couldn't shake the feeling that she was intruding on an intimate moment. It was a surprise to think of Belinda that way: she was one of those super-moms who served on every committee imaginable for her three gorgeous, towheaded children. To think of her as a sexual creature was a bit jarring.

"Parker, these are the girls I was telling you about," Belinda said. "Delia, Jess, and Carrie."

"Carras."

"Right. Carras is a tennis player, too."

Parker leaned in. "I thought I recognized you. Carras Lightbourne, right?" He turned to Belinda. "You didn't tell me you had a semipro tennis player on your list."

"I didn't know." Belinda spoke brightly, through her teeth. "So you know each other?"

"Carras probably doesn't remember me." Parker had a charming smile, Jess noticed. "But we all used to really admire her. I was a few years behind you on the Junior Nationals circuit. Parker Yung."

"Of course. Nice to see you, Parker." Jess noticed that Carras furrowed her brow, maybe trying to place him. "I didn't realize you were the tennis pro here?"

"Not officially." He smiled. "I'm freelance, but the pro here is a buddy of mine; I do the more advanced lessons. Whatever happened to you? Carras Lightbourne. Damn. You were, like, kind of successful, weren't you?"

"It's Carras Prather now." If she was offended by Parker's characterization, Carras didn't show it. "And I wouldn't say successful. My eligibility ran out after undergrad and I really wanted a master's degree, so I went semipro to pay for it."

Parker nodded. "Education. Great choice. Not for everyone, though. I did two years at Vanderbilt, but it was such a drag. The NCAA won't let you borrow a Kleenex from a booster if you're on scholarship, and I've never been one for the classroom. The money is better out here." He nodded his head at the expansive country club campus.

As Jess and Delia introduced themselves, he greeted them with equally warm smiles, and the small talk began. Tennis, the final weeks of school, summer plans. Belinda and her husband, Orson, were going away on some sort of exotic vacation this summer. Delia pressed her for information, but Jess was unable to focus on the details.

It was warm for April, and the sangria went down faster than Jess intended after the morning on the court. She felt pleasantly disconnected. Up until today, she hadn't been certain Belinda Hayes-Currington knew her name. And now, she was drinking cocktails with her on a school day and this guy was here—cute, smiling, flirty...

When was the last time Jess had a conversation with an attractive young guy, even an innocuous one? Her freelance work had become almost rote. Her former coworkers and their underlings sent her work via six-word emails or texts. There was the occasional Skype call to liven things up, but never an in-person meeting. When Tom was on the road, Jess would bet she went entire weeks without interacting with an adult male who wasn't bagging her groceries or delivering a package. Even then, they pretty much rang the doorbell and ran...

"More sangria, Jess?" Belinda leaned forward to refill Jess's glass, and Parker put a hand on Belinda's back. An unconscious move, the way a man might touch a spouse or...a lover.

"Oh." Jess gaped. She knew she should be subtler, but it was too much information all at once. Jess wasn't naïve, or at least she'd never thought so. Things happened; she knew that. She wasn't a child. It was just...seeing it, with her own eyes. And with someone like Belinda, whose husband was well known in the community... "*Oh.*"

"Jess," Delia hissed.

Jess clamped her mouth closed, embarrassed.

But Belinda's smile held. "It's all right," she said airily as the last of the white sangria dripped into Jess's glass. "There's plenty more where that came from."

She meant the drinks, Jess realized, as Belinda signaled to the waiter for another round. "Oh no, I couldn't. I have work to do..."

"Don't be silly." Belinda stared at Jess as though she had three heads. "You can take a day off, I'm sure."

Jess felt her jaw drop. Before she could respond, Parker cleared his throat and slid his chair back, excusing himself to the restroom.

"How is Orson?" Delia asked as the tennis pro's broad, retreating back disappeared into the clubhouse.

"You know men." Belinda rolled her eyes. "He's always tinkering with something or buying something. Lately it's flying lessons. He's bought a small plane, which of course is terrifying. The man can't park our SUV at the grocery store, but he thinks he's going to fly us both to some horrible Alaskan wilderness? I told him not until the kids are in college, and only if there's a five-star resort at the other end."

"Well, your last trip sounded marvelous," Delia said. "A whole week on a nude beach? How positively *liberating*."

A nude beach? Belinda and Orson? Jess managed to cover her shock with what she hoped was a cool, "oh yes—a nude beach—how adorable—I do that all the time" smile, while Belinda rattled on about private cabanas and couples' massages. Truthfully, it had been years since the beach made Jess think of anything other than bulk quantities of children's sunscreen and sandy PB&J sand-wiches. A solo vacation with Tom—beyond the odd anniversary weekend in downtown Atlanta—was something she didn't even daydream about.

She glanced at Carras, who was staring at the stem of her glass, expression neutral. Carras was from Turks and Caicos originally, so her feelings about nude beaches were probably not so loaded.

"What about Orson's work?" Delia asked. "Didn't you tell me he took you to Paris for Valentine's Day? How does he manage to get away?"

"Oh, he manages." Belinda glided a pink nail down Parker's arm as he returned to the table. "I've made it clear that I have needs and expectations too. And when mama ain't happy…well, I'm worse than a room full of angry stockholders."

Jess watched the woman across the table in awe. Belinda was like a caricature of herself: beautiful and tan and expensive, in the same pink SMCC tennis visor Jess had seen her wear in the elementary school carpool line. But here she was in broad daylight, talking about her sex life as though she were Mae West. Jess picked up her sangria glass, saw it was already half-empty again, and put it down.

Parker rubbed Belinda's tanned shoulder with an impassive smile, seemingly unaffected by the mention of Orson. Maybe Jess was misinterpreting their interaction? Perhaps this Parker was just a physical guy, the kind who would casually touch anyone? She glanced at Delia, but her friend's gaze was over Belinda's shoulder. "Speak of the devil, Belinda. Orson himself's coming this way."

Delia's smooth Southern lilt was a half-octave higher, which told Jess that she shared her concerns about the nature of Parker and Belinda's relationship. As a huffing Orson approached the table, however, Belinda greeted her husband with a smile. "Babe. I thought you were in meetings all day today. You remember Parker, my tennis coach?"

"Sure, sure." Orson extended his hand and shook Parker's. Like his wife, Orson wore a visor, but his was faded maroon with the University of Alabama *A* and a circular sweat stain across the front panel. With his soft beer belly and the way his coarse reddish hair spiked around the visor, he looked more like an aging fraternity boy than the president of his family's beverage company. "Hey, ladies." He greeted the rest of the women as a unit before returning his gaze to his wife. "I snuck out for the afternoon, asked Maria to pick up the kids. I figured we'd go shopping for your birthday a few days early?"

"Orrie, you're sweet, but you know I have my tennis lesson this afternoon." Belinda laid a hand on Parker's muscled arm. "It's so expensive, I can't possibly ask Parker to reschedule at the last minute."

Orson glanced, for a second, at his wife's fingers on the other man's skin. "Parker won't mind, will you, bud? We'll pay the cancelation fee. You can have an extra lesson next week."

"Not a problem," Parker said. "A week off won't hurt your serve, Belinda. Enjoy your birthday."

"I'll make sure she does," Orson said, a low, smiling growl. "I always do."

Once again, Jess had the distinct feeling she was intruding on a private moment. Something primal, maybe a little dangerous. The two men reminded her of tigers circling a fire, preparing for battle. And Belinda, the fire between them, sat with a gratified smile on her face, eyes hidden under her pink visor and $200 sunglasses.

The tension broke when Parker's phone buzzed on the table. "I need to return this text. Would you all excuse me? Ladies, it was a pleasure. Belinda, I'll see you next week?"

"Yep," Orson said on his wife's behalf. "Take care, Parker."

"You, too, man."

With a winning smile for everyone, Parker sauntered off the patio toward the parking lot. Jess felt as if she'd been watching a soap opera, but the tennis pro's shoulders were relaxed, his pace unhurried.

"Should we go, babe?" Orson asked. "I figured we'd swing by the house…take a nice long shower, head over to the Lexus dealership."

But Belinda stared after Parker with a pout. "I can't believe you rescheduled my tennis lesson without asking. Now you want me to leave these girls? I invited them here."

"I am sorry, babe. I'll make it up to you." Orson didn't sound sorry. He sounded like a child angling for dessert. He took Belinda's hand and lifted her out of her seat, taking her face in his ruddy hands for an embarrassingly long kiss. Carras, Jess, and Delia exchanged furtive glances as the café's few other patrons visibly tried not to stare. When the kiss ended, Belinda's pricey sunglasses were askew and she was breathing heavily. Orson whispered something in her ear; if Jess had not been there herself, she would never have believed the way Belinda giggled in response.

"Like horny teenagers," Jess whispered to Delia.

Orson released his wife, who wobbled, ineffectually straightening her tennis dress. "Lunch is on me, ladies," he said. "Whatever you'd like, charge it to our club account. Just remind my wife that if she isn't naked in our bathroom in twenty minutes, the punishment will be severe." He patted Belinda firmly on the ass and walked away.

Jess sat with her mouth open. If Tom had talked to her like that, especially in front of people, she would've smacked him. And yet, there was something compelling about the interaction that sent a stab of envy through her chest.

Belinda sank into her chair and downed half a glass of sangria before speaking. "Sorry, girls. I wasn't expecting him to intrude on our meeting."

"Seems like things are going well for you two?" Delia said slowly.

"Things have been amazing for *weeks* now." Belinda leaned in confidentially. "And, if you want to know, they've been amazing on the couch and the kitchen table, too. And on my new $4,000 rug in front of the fireplace."

Carras looked up. "$4,000? For a rug?"

"On *sale*," Belinda stage-whispered. "Never thought I'd see the day Orson would let me spend that kind of money on something he didn't either get to shoot or drive." She toyed with a straw wrapper. "Though, I guess you could say he has done some driving on that rug."

"What's your secret?" Delia poured herself more sangria. "Did you do one of those thirty-day sex challenges? You know, Pure Indulgences sells a great kit for that challenge. I've had several customers say they love it."

There it was. In every conversation with Delia, it was a matter

of time before Pure Indulgences or VikingHome or Skin by Suzette came up. Delia had been selling every multilevel marketing
product available for at least a decade. She was good at it, probably
because it came naturally to her to mention products offhand in
conversations like this. Sometimes Jess thought Delia didn't notice
she was doing it. Her myriad product lines ran in the background
like music.

"Honey," Belinda said. "Of course I tried it. But Orson doesn't
like any challenge he doesn't set for himself. And we're not into...
toys and lotions and all that mess." She wrinkled her nose. "Too...
sticky. Unhygienic. No offense."

Glancing at Delia, Jess could see the internal war between her
ingrained need to defend Pure Indulgences' hypoallergenic massage oils and sensual creams, and the desire to win the approval of
the elusive Belinda Hayes-Currington.

"So, what did you do?" It was Carras, fiddling with her still-full
glass. "I mean, to spice things up with your husband?"

Belinda leaned over the iron table, and Jess found herself tilting
forward, intrigued in spite of herself. Belinda lowered her voice.
"Ladies, I'm going to tell you right now: the best investment I ever
made in my personal life was tennis lessons. I'm in the best shape
of my life and everyone is happier."

"Tennis lessons?"

Belinda considered Jess with unmitigated pity, as though it hurt
her that someone could be so slow. "Oh, girls. Do yourselves a
favor."

She reached into her tennis bag and pulled out three embossed
lime-green business cards, dropping them on the table as she stood.
"Now, if you'll excuse me, I have a date with my husband. You
heard Orrie—lunch is on him. Order whatever you like."

And with that, she scooted away, long tanned legs sashaying
beneath her tennis dress. The other three women were left to stare
at one another, and at "Parker Yung, Advanced Instruction" on the
cards she'd left behind.

Jess turned to Delia. "Did you know about this?"

Her neighbor's smile was slow and sweet. "I don't know what
you're talking about."

That evening, Jess had put the kids to bed and settled down to work when her phone buzzed on the desk next to her. She saw Delia's name light up the screen and let the call go to voicemail, hands perched over the keyboard. She stared at the document in front of her, re-reading the same sentence over and over.

She wasn't in the habit of ducking Delia's calls, but Jess knew this conversation would be about Belinda and Parker, and it would be a long one. Since Jess and Tom had moved in ten years ago, Delia had been a steady source of neighborhood gossip. The fact that Belinda Hayes-Currington seemed to have something going with the tennis pro—and had possibly suggested that the three of them should do the same—would be conversation fodder for weeks.

The phone lit up again, this time with a text.

Quit dodging my calls, Jess. I know you're there.

Tom's out of town, and the lights are off in the kids' rooms.

Jess rolled her eyes and called Delia back. "Sorry, I was in the bathroom."

"You were *not*," Delia said. "You're sitting at your desk. I can see the back of your head reflected in the mirror by your closet."

And *that* was the drawback of befriending the neighbor across the street. *So much for a peaceful evening.*

"So, what did you think?" It was the same tone of voice Delia used when Jess tried out a new VikingHome tool for her, or the new Skin by Suzette catalog was in.

"I think I'm getting curtains," Jess said drily. She glanced out the window at Delia's house and closed her blinds.

"Oh, come on. Belinda! And Orson, and Parker! Isn't it fascinating?"

"That's not the first word that comes to mind."

"Don't be judgmental, Jess. It's not becoming on you."

"I'm not being judgmental. I am..." Jess struggled for the words. "To each her own."

"I couldn't agree more. And I'm thinking we should get a little of Belinda's own for ourselves."

"What?" Jess froze. "Did you say... What?"

"I'm 100% serious. Did you see how happy she was today? And

Orson?"

"I saw." Jess had been trying all afternoon to remember the last time Tom told her to drop what she was doing and meet her in their bathroom naked. *Well, never.* The answer was never. "But she's playing with fire. Having an affair with some guy right under Orson's nose?"

"Come on, Jess. You can't be this naïve. It's not an *affair*, and he's not *some guy*. Tell me you know what he is."

Jess sighed. She knew, or thought she did. Some instinct had been explaining the situation to her throughout the whole surreal interaction this afternoon. It was why Parker hadn't been bothered at all by Orson, the way a regular lover might have been. And why Belinda had recommended him as though he were skin cream, or a workout video. "He's a...prostitute, right?"

"That's a crude way of putting it." *Delia, always proper.* "I'd call him an escort."

The confirmation took Jess aback. It's not that she found the idea of prostitution shocking—Jess wasn't naïve, despite Delia's teasing. She just always thought of it as something that happened in other places—not their sleepy, affluent suburb, where the biggest conflicts were about trim paint color and trees on the property line. "Whatever you call it, I can't believe the way she was acting in front of her husband. She's lucky he doesn't suspect something."

"She's lucky he *does*," Delia corrected. "At least, on some level he does. Did you see how attentive he was to her? And all those trips?"

Jess was fully aware Delia had pointed out the trips on purpose. Jess had complained about her travel yearnings over the past couple of years, missing the adventurous life she and Tom used to love. That wasn't even something she could blame on the kids, because they were old enough to join them now. But there was always something more pressing. Like the work Jess should be doing right now, instead of having the most insane conversation *ever* with Delia. "They seem happy. Good for them."

"That's exactly it," Delia said. "It should be *us* being that happy. When was the last time you had a high-quality, screeching orgasm? I mean, while your husband was in the room?"

Not counting the fabulous line of products from Pure Indulgences, *obviously*.

"That's beside the point. My marriage is fine. Just because every day isn't a Chris Isaak video doesn't mean Tom and I aren't happy. This is real life, Delia. I don't need to hire a prostitute for meaningless, awesome sex."

"Don't be crass. I'm not suggesting that anyone should have sex with a prostitute." Delia sounded offended. "None of us has to have sex with him."

"What are you saying, then? Because even if I could afford actual tennis lessons, they'd do nothing for my marriage." Jess paused. "What do you mean, 'none of us'?"

"I'm saying, what if our husbands had the same *impression* that Orson did today? What if we hire this guy—you, me, and Carras, I bet Belinda can get us like a group discount or something—and we pay him to make our husbands jealous? God, if Gage would look at me the way Orson devoured Belinda with his eyes today…"

Jess thought about the kiss at the table, tried to remember the last time Tom had done something embarrassingly affectionate in public. Or anywhere. "Where would I get the money, and how would I explain it to Tom?"

"Tennis lessons." Delia said. "Parker has a website and everything."

"You talked to him already?"

"I followed up with Belinda. A few feeling-out questions. He does some kind of monthly plan, apparently, and you get discounts for referring others."

"Geez. You and he really are in the same business, aren't you? Did Belinda get a hostess gift for today?" Jess choked back an absurd laugh. "An embroidered tennis bag and free cunnilingus?"

"Look, I thought the same thing when Belinda asked me to schedule today…"

"Wait. You *knew*?"

"Not exactly. I'd heard rumors about Parker over the last couple of months, and Belinda said she wanted to introduce us to her tennis coach. When he showed up at lunch, I put two and two together."

Jess stared at the blinking cursor on her screen. There was no chance she'd be able to concentrate on work now. "You mean, there's been a *hooker* teaching tennis lessons at the club for months? I had no idea."

"*Escort*," Delia corrected again. "Honestly, Jess. You sound like a 1980s cop show."

"And you're seriously considering hiring him?"

"I think we all should. There's a discount if we book more than one appointment."

"Have you lost your mind?"

"You said yourself that you and Tom have been missing a spark lately."

"Missing a spark, Delia. As in, we need to get a sitter and have a date night. Not a frigging male prostitute!" When her friend didn't respond, Jess went on. "I thought you and Gage had a…how do you put it…*flexible* arrangement? Why don't you go out and find some hot guy and have a normal affair? Why would you pay for sex?"

"It's not about *sex*, Jess. I said that already. Please try to keep up. It's about our husbands seeing us as *desirable*. Believing that another man wants us, to reinvigorate that feeling, you know, when they were pursuing us. Fighting for us. Remember that feeling?"

Unbidden, an image flashed into Jess's mind: Tom at twenty-two, half-drunk and tearful on the doorstep of her college apartment, the night she'd let another guy take her out on a date. The desperate longing and rare vulnerability on his face. How the light in the breezeway flickered behind him, the night air warm and sticky. How he held her that night as if he would never let her go, hot tears dripping onto her bare shoulders as he made love to her at dawn. "I remember."

"Of course you do. Every married woman does. I don't want this guy to *do* anything with us. I want to make our husbands *think* that he wants to. I want that feeling back."

Jess was quiet for a minute, thoughts swirling. It's not as though she were a prude or anything. She knew Delia and Gage had a marriage that was open, or at least unconventional, even though Delia was tight-lipped about it. It had never bothered Jess, as long as they were happy, the same way the idea of paying for sex didn't morally offend her. Jess was a live-and-let-live kind of girl. After all, she'd seen *The Wedding Date* at least a dozen times. She loved that movie.

And if she were being very honest, she wanted that feeling back, too. Tom had not looked at her as if he was crazy about her, terrified of losing her, in a very long time.

But like doing an angry-sexy tango with Dermot Mulroney in a flowing green dress, the idea of hiring an escort felt like something people did in the movies. It was the kind of thing you tittered about with girlfriends over cocktails at the beach, a funny exercise in "Would you ever…?" It wasn't something people *did*. You didn't call up the neighbor across the cul-de-sac and talk about group discounts and scheduling.

"At least say you'll think about it," Delia said. "Belinda is hoping to get him some new clients, so he doesn't have to take some job in Orlando…"

"Belinda, Belinda, Belinda…" Jess said irritably. "Can I ask why you're so desperate to have that woman's friendship? And don't say it's because you want her to throw one of your product parties and invite all her wealthy friends. There's more to it than that."

"This isn't about Belinda."

Jess could tell her friend was irritated. After almost a decade of friendship, sometimes Jess lost sight of how different she and Delia were. If they hadn't moved in across the street from each other all those years ago, she wasn't sure they would've become friends in other circumstances. Other than kids and location and husbands who traveled often, they didn't have much in common. The need to climb in the ranks of the Sugar Mills social structure was one major difference.

Still, she liked Delia, and didn't want to hurt her feelings. "I don't dislike Belinda. I don't think she's earned all the consideration you give her. That's all."

"This doesn't have to involve her. She made the connection, and I happen to think it's worth exploring."

"There are easier ways to make your husband jealous. Call up an old boyfriend and leave your phone out so he can see your dialing history."

"You're missing the point. That's the wrong *kind* of jealousy. What we want—"

"You, Delia. What *you* want."

"What we want is attention from a new guy, someone to make our husbands see us in a new way. Not bored wives desperate to rekindle an old flame. But confident, desirable women who can still attract a hot, young, half-Korean tennis pro with abs for miles. It's the American dream!"

Jess laughed. "Yes, I imagine this is exactly what our forefathers envisioned when they created our inalienable right to sexually objectify a twenty-something sports pro to manipulate our husbands. You should run for office."

"Laugh all you want. But when Tom comes home tomorrow night, you imagine that private cabana on the beach. Then tell me it's not worth it."

Jess didn't say that the exact thought had crossed her mind several times since lunch.

"All I'm asking is that you hear me out. Let's have coffee tomorrow, and if you still think I'm crazy, I'll never bring it up again."

"It will have to be Monday." Jess sighed. "Tom's back from the road tomorrow night and I have to get this project edited and out the door before he gets home."

"Perfect. Carras has Monday mornings free, too, doesn't she?"

"You can't seriously think Carras will be interested? Because I have to tell you, she's pretty conservative. I know you think I'm a goody-two-shoes, but I'm a wild child compared to Carras. Plus, she and Stuart are perfect. He fawns over her as it is."

"Don't be so sure about your perfect friend Carras. She didn't say much today, but she was paying very close attention, I can tell you." Delia paused. "Her eyes lit up when she saw Parker."

"That's because she recognized him, dingbat. They were in the same tennis league or whatever."

"All I'm saying is, every marriage has room for more excitement. I'll bet you twenty bucks Carras agrees with me."

"Not possible."

"Tell you what, I'll call Carras and explain. If she's open to it, you'll at least agree to discuss the idea."

Jess thought of sweet, intellectual Carras and unassuming Stuart. They loved comic books and zombies. They still sat on the couch together and held hands. They had cute little inside jokes that made Tom and Jess roll their eyes and gag. "You're on."

3

CARRAS

THAT NIGHT, CARRAS LAY AWAKE for a long time, thinking about signs from the universe. She had her knees propped up on a stack of pillows, her flat belly lifted at an incline so she could not see the TV that flashed beyond.

Her father didn't believe in signs; he had always relied on his work ethic and one-line platitudes from business books to guide him. Her mother had died too young for Carras to know her. But Carras had a distinct memory of her grandmother, a plump, dark woman in a vivid orange head wrap, pulling the meat from a conch with a paring knife and laughing with a smile so wide it seemed to split her face in half. Carras had been too young to participate in the conversations between her grandmother and the other "Belonger" women—the Islanders—or to understand what was said. But even though the memories were distant, she could hear the laughter to this day. And she had a suspicion her grandmother had believed in signs.

Stuart snored beside her, having done his manly duties for the night. These included fetching Carras water, covering her apparently fragile uterus with blankets, and asking about twelve times if she was comfortable, before drifting off to sleep. This hadn't taken long, because his duties tonight had also included pounding into her, sweating and panting like a man possessed, doing everything the books suggested to give them what they wanted most: a child.

Stuart didn't believe in signs, either.

He was facing away; his shoulder blades stuck out like the skinny kid he must once have been, the one place on his body that still held the hard lines and angles of adolescence. Was it weird that she loved the softness of him, the differences between their bodies? Stuart wasn't pale but his tawny, pink-beige skin was a stark contrast to her own dark, cool umber. And although her skin had been further tanned—and muscles honed—from years of sweat and sun on the tennis court, Stuart's had been subdued by bathing more often in the light of computer and television screens than he ever did in the sunlight.

Not that Stuart was flabby. He put in his time on the treadmill at the gym down the street, and sometimes lifted weights while they watched *Talking Dead* with Chris Hardwick. But unlike the hyper-ambitious athletes Carras had spent most of her adult life around, Stuart was not obsessed with his BMI or his bench weight or the comparison between protein bars and electrolyte gels. To her husband, staying fit was a practical necessity rather than a life's calling.

And Carras loved that about him. Stuart was beautiful to her, and deliciously, liberatingly normal. He never quizzed her about her protein regimen or gave her a funny look if she had a second slice of pizza. He never judged when she did her monthly head-first dive into a bowl of buttered popcorn, giant Toblerone, and a bottle of wine. Stuart would find her in those moments, on the couch, watching sappy movies in the dark, and join her—his own wineglass in hand. Wordless, innate acceptance. It was the best gift Carras had ever received.

She wanted to touch him now, to roll over and slide her hand between the rise of his hip and the relaxed arc of his elbow, to feel the tiny potbelly forming on her husband as they began the long, glorious process of growing old together.

But she couldn't, not yet. She was supposed to lie here in this awkward position for another seven minutes at least. Most of the books said ten minutes, but she and Stuart had agreed twenty would be better.

What could it hurt?

What could any of it hurt?

There was always some new wisdom, some new remedy to try. Eating yams. Chugging cough syrup. Coconut water mixed with green tea. Chiropractic adjustments. Oysters. Acupuncture. Blood tests, ovulation monitoring, and yet more tests, which all came back mystifyingly, infuriatingly *normal*. Two years of folk wisdom, internet remedies, injections, and very expensive failed IVF cycles. Theories were everywhere. Maybe all the hard years of training had taken a toll on Carras's body. Maybe there was something going on with Stuart that didn't show up in tests. Maybe it was stress. *Maybe, maybe, maybe…*

Three months ago, sitting in the doctor's office with her broken heart in her hands, Carras had suggested they consider adoption. But Stuart—normally rational and agreeable to a fault—pushed back. "You're still in your twenties."

"Twenty-eight. And you're thirty-six."

"Let's give it more time," he said. "I'm just…not ready to think about raising someone else's child."

"We would be raising *our* child," Carras corrected.

She saw the shame on Stuart's face as he realized what he'd said. "Right. Of course." He reached for her hand, pleading. "You know that's not what I meant, right? I've always pictured our child having your eyes, your strength…"

Exasperated, Carras took her hand away. "Even if we have a biological child, you know you won't be able to control those things, right? Nothing is going to be exactly what we pictured."

Across the desk, the doctor cleared her throat. "Listen. This is a heartbreaking time for every couple. You two have been through a lot—financially, emotionally, hormonally… Can I make a suggestion? Take six months off from treatments. Relax, let your body recover. Enjoy being a married couple for a while longer. Take a vacation. Come back, and we'll discuss the options again. Your husband is right, Mrs. Prather. Biologically speaking, you *do* still have plenty of time."

Wise enough advice. And as they shuffled out of the clinic to drown their disappointment in nachos and a matinee action movie, Carras did her best to accept it.

To be fair, they hadn't been married that long. Their courtship had been a whirlwind, the result of meeting at Comic-Con in San Diego five years ago. Stuart had made his annual pilgrimage with his gaming coworkers, and Carras was enjoying a much-needed break from pursuing her graduate degree in counseling and playing in endless tennis tournaments. Disappearing to Comic-Con for the weekend allowed her to hide out from her dad, her coach, and her thesis advisor simultaneously. Comic books and fantasy novels had been a lifeboat for her as a lonely, motherless child— moving to a new place once a year, living in the hotels that her immigrant father started out cleaning, and eventually owned and managed. Now her tennis career had her skipping from one hotel to the next, isolated in a sea of trainers, fans, and journalists. Carras loved immersing herself in a world where she was not the star, but just another rabid fan.

Stuart had hit on her, awkwardly, on the conference level of the San Diego Marriott Marquis. They were both dressed as characters from *The Walking Dead,* waiting in line to meet Andrew Lincoln; Stuart tapped her on the shoulder with some terrible joke about her character stealing a protein bar. He was cute, in a Bruce-Lee-meets-Clark-Kent-wearing-a-bandolier kind of way: with bulky glasses over his deep-set brown eyes that belied his rugged denim shirt and ripped khaki cargo pants.

She'd been ready to brush him off—like the countless guys who approached her at tennis tournaments—until it became obvious he had no idea who she was. Even when she told him, after they'd been talking in line for an hour, Stuart looked adorably blank and said, "I don't follow tennis, but that sounds pretty badass."

She had loved him ever since.

Their first "date" had been sitting in the lobby all night talking about zombies and superheroes. Their first, tentative kiss sometime between dawn and the overpriced hotel buffet breakfast. He was thirty, she was twenty-four; it was not until much later that it would occur to them they did not live in the same city, and it might be difficult to see each other again. Which they both desperately wanted to do.

So, she flew to Atlanta on her off-weeks from tennis, getting in her training runs and studying while he was at the office. She met him naked at the door when he came home, like an old-fashioned housewife. They would laugh, make love, laugh some more, forget to eat, and order late-night Chinese while Stuart complained unconvincingly that he had to be back at work in a few hours. Carras would shove him gently with her feet and tell him to go on to bed because nobody was forcing him to stay up with her, and soon they'd be making love again, on the couch, on the floor…

On weekends, Stuart did his best to fly to wherever Carras was playing. This was harder, because there was a high probability her father would be wherever Carras was. Since her mother's death, her father was all she had—her childhood spent following him as he chased success for them both. He lived in Waco now, where he'd finally settled when Carras got a full ride to Baylor, in the first house he'd owned since immigrating to the States. He still traveled to watch her compete, still quietly hovered in her life with his inspirational quotes at the ready.

Sebastian Lightbourne didn't disapprove of Stuart, but Carras sensed his desire to protect her from all potential risks, including distractions and heartbreak. So they all stayed in separate rooms when they traveled, and she and Stuart sneaked into each other's rooms, giggling like the teenagers Carras was learning to counsel.

After several months of this long-distance dance, Stuart got promoted, and proposed to Carras at a rooftop restaurant overlooking Atlanta. "What do you think?" He squeezed her hand and took in the skyline. "Could you be happy here?"

Carras didn't hesitate. "I can be happy wherever you are."

They were married a few months later. Carras graduated, got her counseling license, and retired from tennis over her father's objections that she still had several good years left. He stayed in Waco when Carras packed for Atlanta, the first time she had ever been permanently away from her father.

She and Stuart settled into their enormous house in Sugar Mills, near Stuart's college friends Tom and Jess, and their children Dash and Mina, who were still very young at the time. "Tom and Jess are built-in family," Stuart said. "Our kids can grow up together."

So began the business of getting to know each other. Their lovemaking that first year was much the same as it had been: seductive, unpretentious, endless. Carras had never done well on pills, so they used condoms, agreeing to start a family after a year, once they had settled in. Sometimes these days, Carras thought of all those condoms…the tense moments of frustrated digging in drawers, last-minute runs to the drugstore. Such wasted effort and emotion, avoiding the very thing they now wanted so badly.

As though pregnancy before they were ready was a thing to be avoided. As though they were in control.

Carras, who had never felt rooted anywhere, loved the promise of Stuart's fantasy. The stable family home, friends who would come and go. Maybe even a girlfriend to give her advice about raising young children, the sister Carras never had. They weren't quite like sisters, but Jess *was* lovely; Carras liked her and Tom. She didn't mind the quiet suburban life, or the sameness of the drive to her counseling practice in the afternoons. After a year, Stuart threw away his last box of condoms and they made love with joyful, giddy abandon, each time aware they could be changing their lives forever.

As each month passed without a positive pregnancy test, however, the purpose of sex grew larger in both their minds. The joyful abandon grew smaller, until there was very little abandon and Carras was clinging hard to joy.

At first they resolved to enjoy their time together before children. They were still new at married life. They had time. They loved their jobs. Carras was a natural with anxious teenagers; Stuart won awards for his innovative game designs. She had no student loans thanks to tennis scholarships, and with both of them working, they paid Stuart's off quickly. They socked away savings so she could stay home with the baby if she wanted.

"Trust me," Jess said, one morning over coffee. "One day you'll miss this time when it was just the two of you, and you could sleep in on weekends and watch grownup TV shows. You'll miss sex in the shower and vacations that don't involve the kids whining in the backseat of the car for hours."

So, they went to Turks and Caicos to visit Carras's relatives. They flew back to Comic-Con together. It was wonderful, but Carras couldn't help but notice how Stuart's gaze lingered on little boys weaving in and out of the crowds with foam light sabers, and little girls dressed as Wonder Woman or Princess Leia.

Back home, they tried out new restaurants in Atlanta as soon as they opened, and made a game of tabulating how much money they were saving by not having to pay a sitter. Carras dragged Stuart away for spa weekends and couples' massages, because she'd read that stress could impact fertility. They even spent a few months pretending they *weren't* trying, because Carras had read that many couples got pregnant after they gave up. But the game didn't fool her reproductive organs. Carras's ovaries knew as well as she did how badly they wanted a child.

Meanwhile, Jess and Tom's children grew. The likelihood of the Rodriguez children and their own being close friends decreased as the months and years went by. Dash was finishing first grade this year; Mina nearly done with third. How interested would they be in a newborn when the time came? At this rate, Mina was more likely to be a babysitter than playmate.

They weren't trying for children to match Tom and Jess's life. But as the Rodriguez children grew, it was a constant reminder of what Stuart had envisioned when he bought this huge house near his friends. He never said anything and Carras knew that he loved her, children or no children.

But they didn't make love on the couch anymore, or the floor after late-night Chinese. She never answered the door naked—in this neighborhood, that could go horribly wrong. Sex was a means to an end, with Carras feeling more like an empty flower pot than a desirable woman.

And now, her dad was sick.

Diagnosed with congestive heart failure six weeks ago, his prognosis ranged from three years to over a decade, depending on how well he cared for himself. For all his hard work, all his years supporting and pushing Carras, self-care was one thing at which Sebastian had never excelled. He downplayed his illness, refusing to allow Carras to come to Texas and take care of him. For all the years he'd critiqued every minute of her training, every bite of food she ate, Carras knew there was no way he'd tolerate the shoe being on the other foot.

But if he had a grandchild…

Carras checked the clock on her nightstand. Her fertilization time had been up for several minutes now. She was free to move around, free to reach out for her sleeping husband. *Maybe she would put a hand on his arm…* "Wake up," she would say. "Wake up and ravish me the way you used to. Like I was that girl in the Marriott dressed as Michonne, with my headband askew and dark circles under my eyes. Wake up and let's watch bad TV all night and call in sick tomorrow. Let's make love on the couch because there's no other way to get close enough, not because we're on a mission to create another human being."

But she didn't wake Stuart. Carras rolled off her mountain of baby-making pillows, flicked off the TV and went to the bathroom. She washed her face and brushed her teeth, examining her flat belly and curving hips in the mirror. Carras knew people thought of her as beautiful, and she liked the shape of her body. She knew she had a pleasant, friendly face. But she had never been obsessed with her appearance, never dieted except to stay in condition for tennis season. Her body had made itself useful: winning her college scholarships and occasional prize money at some of the smaller tournaments. Her body had given her pleasure, and Stuart, too. She traced the outline of her hips. Why couldn't her body do its job now?

She thought of Belinda Hayes-Currington. *Irritating woman.* Carras had never understood why Delia cared about fitting in with the country club snobs across the street. This hotel manager's daughter had enough of sitting around pools eating second-rate cafe food for one lifetime. And these days she only played tennis when Jess invited her, to be polite. Tennis was her old life. She liked her new one better.

Carras was intrigued, however, about the relationship between Belinda and Parker Yung. Belinda was rich and healthy and had those three towheaded children Carras had seen on Facebook. What would compel a woman with a perfect life to seek excitement with someone like Parker?

Carras did remember Parker from her tennis days, though they had never formally met. Several years younger than Carras, he was a cute, cocky kid, known as much for his charm as his epic backhand slice. She'd watched one or two of his matches and remembered he was fast and coordinated and competitive, and that his family was ever-present. "Tiger Mom," some of the other athletes had called Parker's mom, a diminutive but vocal Korean lady who yelled at her son from the stands and had been known to argue with officials after matches. Not that there was anything unusual about *that* in the world of competitive junior tennis.

Sometimes she had envied families like those, in which the parents pushed hard, but also cheered and celebrated with abandon. Her soft-spoken father never humiliated her on the court, never put her down or challenged her in front of others. She would know his approval or disapproval by the quality of the silence after each match, and by how long the silence went on. But he also never rejoiced too hard with her, never allowed celebration to overshadow quiet, resolute preparedness for the next day on the court. Occasionally she'd envied kids like Parker, who always knew where they stood. At least with his mother...

It struck her suddenly, what she'd been trying to remember. Parker's mother was Korean, but his dad had been a quiet white guy who always wore camouflage. Parker had been Parker *Davis* back then. Yung must have been his mother's name. Maybe his parents had divorced, and he'd changed his name in solidarity with his mother? Perhaps things weren't as perfect for him as Parker had made it seem. Carras returned to her sleeping husband and kissed the back of his shoulder; he did not stir. She turned off the light and lay awake for a long time, listening to the regular comforting sounds of Stuart's breath.

4

DELIA

Monday Morning

IT WASN'T THAT DELIA COULDN'T do this alone. She had access to money from Gage's substantial accounts, and he would support whatever hobbies she chose, including overpriced tennis lessons. He might hem and haw and pretend to complain, but he would never deny her. She'd learned that within a few months of marrying him.

And if she wanted to avoid a conversation with Gage at all, she had her "cookie jar" money, as he referred to the proceeds from her product lines and parties and the army of consultants working beneath her on each line. Little did he know the tiny account she kept at the local bank around the corner—where Gage did not have access—had nearly forty thousand dollars in it now. *Some cookie jar.*

She set her gourmet VikingHome pour-over coffeemaker to brew and wiped down the counter for the tenth time. Carras and Jess would be here soon, and Delia wasn't sure why it was so important to make things perfect.

Except that she didn't want to do this alone.

For one thing, Belinda had encouraged her to bring in other women. Parker would give them a discount, and apparently Belinda got some kind of referral bonus, which she had promised to share with Delia. Heaven knew she loved a good referral bonus. Jess had also been right—damn her—when she suggested Delia wanted an in with Belinda and the country club crowd, even though her friend could never understand why. For a girl who'd grown up in a dirt-floor house on the side of a hillbilly mountain in North Georgia, it was flattering to have Belinda Hayes-Currington seeking her out, choosing Delia to let in on the juiciest secret she'd heard for years. For once, she could share in something rather than withhold everything.

Delia couldn't explain things—her past, her marriage—even to Jess, the closest thing she'd had to a best friend since childhood. She'd learned long ago to limit her confidences with other women to the superficial, and to enjoy the private smugness she and Gage shared. People didn't understand. *How provincial they all were,* Gage would say, *with their religious fervor, their social mores.* "Wouldn't they all be shocked," he'd whispered to her once at a homeowner's association meeting, before their children were born, "to know what we did last night?"

He'd run a long, slender finger along her arm and she'd giggled with the familiar thrill of victory. She was an outsider in their midst, having her cake and eating it too, laughing at the people who'd been turning up their noses at Delia her whole life. She could play the suburban housewife she'd always admired by day, and still be the sex kitten Gage wanted by night, with no one the wiser. Until the babies came and life changed, and somehow their unconventional marriage had stopped being so unconventional. At least for Delia.

Gage was gone again (Belgium? France? She couldn't remember), and she'd spent the weekend running the kids from playdate to sleepover and back again. At ten, Lulu had reached the point in her preadolescent development during which she both hated and desperately needed Delia, often within the span of minutes. Sadie was four years older and had already been through this phase, but was still prone to lapse into it from time to time. On weekends like this one, when Gage was absent and the girls spent time in a cesspool of budding estrogen with their friends, emotions ran high. Delia sometimes envied Jess for her mix of boy and girl, and for her husband who—though he also traveled for work—seemed more frequently and deeply present at home. Tom never walked away from a fight with Jess, or from a teaching moment with his kids. Even when he was on the road, Jess could call Tom and put him on speakerphone with the children to say good-night or help resolve an argument.

Gage was a wonderful father. Delia would never have said otherwise. And he loved his girls. Doted on them—all three of them—like princesses. But he came from a stiff, upper-crust family, and was uncomfortable with interpersonal conflict that didn't involve stacks of black-and-white rules in law books. He could quote line for line from the Uniform Commercial Code, go toe-to-toe with an imports regulator, and then take the guy out for a beer when the case was resolved. But women's emotions baffled Gage, and on those rare occasions that he was alone with their daughters and some disagreement erupted, he would invariably call in Delia for help. Or buy both girls a present and call it a day.

Fine. Delia had known who Gage was when she married him. There had been no illusions between them. Given her history with impulsive, romanticized relationships, that was how Delia wanted it. She loved the comfortable practicality of knowing what to expect from her husband, and what he expected from her in return. She loved the security, the lifestyle, the gifts. The sweet surprises he always brought home for the three of them when he'd been traveling. Contentment was part of what she brought to their relationship. She was the force of beauty and stability that made their life exquisite. She couldn't afford unhappiness.

It was just that sometimes, she had the irritating sense that she needed more. From Gage. From herself.

But Gage had known when he married her, too. He had known—and very much appreciated—that Delia had a wild side. That she needed attention as much as affection. Maybe more, come to think of it. And he lavished her with it whenever they were together. One of the best things about Gage, what his clients loved and Delia loved too, was that when you were in the room with him, you felt like the only person in the world who mattered. When he took her out for dinner, he always chose a quiet table in the back, focused on her, asked about her day. He never interrupted with stories about himself or complaints about work. Never so much as glanced at the waitress or the hostess, other than to place their order. (Gage always ordered for her, and never got it wrong.) He did everything to make up for all the time he spent away, and how he spent that time.

Still, every once in a while, Delia craved more. Not sex, necessarily. But attention, admiration. Pursuit. Delia had always loved a chase.

After seventeen years, it was natural the chase wasn't what it used to be. She was forty-two, and even though Gage was three years her senior, he had always made it clear that he preferred younger women. *Needed* younger women, he'd said. Only for sex. Never love or emotional intimacy. Never a threat to their family life. It had felt so remote and irrelevant when she'd agreed to it: back when she was a struggling art school dropout, always two lap dances away from sleeping in her car. She loved Gage. But if she hadn't, she might have agreed to anything to get out. And, Delia realized now, part of her had been naïve enough to assume Gage's feelings would change as their relationship evolved.

This phase of their marriage—when she had become a porcelain doll, revered and cherished but seldom played with—had been as inevitable from the day Gage proposed to her as the ten-tiered wedding cake from his mother's world-renowned bakery. But that didn't mean Delia had to accept it without a fight. That had never been her style.

She meant what she told Jess; she had no interest in sleeping with other men, not even the irresistible Parker Yung. If that were what she'd wanted, she could have done it discreetly, years ago. But if a strapping young tennis pro could put the glitter back in Gage's stare across the dinner table—could bring back those nights when they would call his mother to babysit and have dirty sex in a hotel room after he pretended to pick her up at a bar—it might be worth it.

The doorbell rang, and Delia was disappointed to see Carras, rather than Jess, was the first to arrive. Carras was the wild card in this situation. She was nice enough, and Delia had grown used to having her around, because Jess dragged her along frequently for walks around the neighborhood or coffee. But she was even more different from Delia than Jess was, and much quieter, which Delia found disconcerting.

Carras had a sort of centered, calm confidence that most women envied because they lacked it. Delia was no exception. She related better to women who could expose their throats, confessing their insecurities and commiserating over the challenges of motherhood so that Delia could sweep in with a solution or advice. And if those solutions came from one of her product lines, so much the better.

It had irked Delia a little when Carras moved in a few years ago. Through her husband's friendship with Tom, Carras had an immediate in with Jess and by extension, Delia. There was no probation period, no good-natured gossip while they sized up the new girl. No opportunity to ensure Carras knew the place in the pecking order where a new neighbor without children ought to go. Maybe that was why Carras had never tried to impress Delia the way most new moms on the block did. Of course, in the end this made Delia respect Carras that much more. Hell, she liked the girl. But something about her cool confidence, her direct and guileless way of speaking, rattled Delia a little.

Carras brought an Entemann's raspberry coffee cake in a box—she did not bake—and even though they were a blatant violation of Delia's anti-preservative, whole food weekday diet, she appreciated the gesture. She wore tight jeans that accentuated her enviable curves, and an unbuttoned blue-and-white flannel over a white tank top. Delia experienced a reflexive pang of envy that even though Carras did not seem to understand dress code norms, she still looked better than Delia.

She settled Carras at the kitchen table and handed her a mug of fresh coffee. "Milk? Sugar?" They were almost never alone together. Delia wondered what the two of them would say to each other until Jess arrived.

"Both, please." Carras accepted the mug.

"No clients this morning?" Delia pulled out three kinds of milk from the fridge and began rummaging for her sugar bowl. "You see teenagers, correct?"

"I do have some adult clients who come during the day, but I take Monday mornings off."

"That must be nice." Delia put the milks and sugar on the table along with three spoons and settled herself in the chair opposite. "To be a private therapist, make your own hours."

"It is," Carras agreed. "Though my evenings are almost always booked solid. When people mention their favorite TV shows, I usually have no idea what they're talking about. Unless it's something Stuart records for us to watch together."

"It's sweet that y'all watch TV together," Delia said. "I don't think Gage and I ever do that, unless I'm willing to watch *Shark Tank* or *Mad Money* with him."

Carras looked at her, deep brown eyes wide open, head cocked to the side, but said nothing. Inexplicably, Delia's eyes filled with sudden tears. That was some kind of therapy voodoo, being able to stare at someone and make them cry for no reason. "It's fine," she heard herself explaining. "I've never been a big television person anyway. We have other shared interests, you know. Gage and I." *Sure you do,* she thought. *Which is why you're thinking of hiring a tennis pro to get his attention.*

Delia reached for a napkin and dabbed at her eyes. "Oh, these allergies! Doesn't Georgia drive you crazy in the spring?"

Carras shook her head. "I've never had allergies. But I've only lived here for a few years. People say it takes years to build up the irritation in your system."

Maybe it depends on the irritation, Delia thought.

There was a knock at the door, and Delia almost toppled her chair in the rush to let Jess in. "Have you recovered from the school play yet?" Delia asked as Jess followed her through to the kitchen with a container of strawberries. "I heard it was magnificent."

"It was great. But you know how it is, there's always the next thing," Jess said, helping herself to coffee. "I haven't even gotten stuff from the play put away yet, and already she needs paper cups for some project and they're asking for cookie decorating volunteers in Dash's class for the end-of-year party."

Delia washed the strawberries and cut them with her favorite VikingHome slicer and cutting board. "I miss those days, when the kids still wanted me to show up for stuff. But you're right, it's so stressful."

The plan was to start slowly. She knew Jess had a long-buried sense of unfulfilled adventure, and that although Jess adored Tom, their marriage had hit the lull of young child survival mode. Delia suspected there was a tiny kernel of interest in Jess's outrage about Parker.

A little venting about school and motherhood. A little gossip about the other neighbors: The rumors that the Wellingtons on the Annex Side were getting a divorce. That Sandy Patterson's daughter on the Club Side had become a lesbian at college, and how everyone couldn't stop talking about what a not-big-deal that was. A little fretting about Tom's road trip schedule for the summer and how Jess would manage getting the kids to camps and juggling her deadlines...

Normal, boring stressors. And then Delia would segue into the possibilities of Parker.

She cut a few razor-thin slices from Carras's store-bought pastry and served them onto little plates with the berries. Before she could even sit down, however, Carras spoke up.

"Have you talked to Belinda since lunch the other day?"

Delia paused in handing out the plates and saw her own surprised expression reflected on Jess's face. "Briefly. Why do you ask?"

A cloud passed over Carras's placid face, but she held Delia's gaze in that direct, unnerving way she had. "I was wondering if she was serious. About Parker and his...*lessons*."

"Carras!" Jess hissed, but Carras didn't meet her eye. She was holding Delia's gaze steady in her own.

Delia decided to meet directness with directness, no matter how surprised she might be. "She was serious. And I was planning to discuss the options with her. With Parker."

"You have to be kidding." Jess held her fork in midair. "Tell me neither one of you is considering this."

Carras gazed at her plate, but Delia had been waiting for this opening. "You two know each other through your husbands, right? Carras, did you know Jess and Tom when they were dating?"

Carras shook her head. "Stuart and I met after college; Jess and Tom were already married."

"Well. Maybe you don't know this one. Jess told me a story once. Remember, Jess? About the other guy on the newspaper, at the end of your senior year?"

"When did I tell you about Evan?"

"It was some party at your house. Maybe your anniversary? Tom's family was here from San Antonio."

"It was our tenth anniversary. We did a big party in the back-yard." Jess's brows knitted together in confusion. "I don't remember the conversation, though."

"Tequila," Delia said. "Your sister-in-law's margaritas, I believe. Anyway, you told me how there was a point in your relationship where things had kind of stalled out."

"Really?" Carras leaned in.

"It was weird," Jess said. "Because things had been going so well between us. In retrospect, I think he was getting cold feet. We got engaged a few months afterward."

"That's right," Delia said. "He was kind of freaking out on you, because he knew his job would have him traveling, and so would yours, right?"

"Yeah. Tom knew it was going to take work if we were going to stay together. All the flying, the buses, the girls hanging around after the games… I think he felt a little torn between our relation-ship and the chance to go sow his wild oats."

"Tom? Wild oats?" Carras laughed. "I can't imagine him giving another woman the time of day."

"Well, Tom at twenty-two was a different animal than he is today." Jess smiled.

Delia jumped on the analogy. "And do you remember telling me how you domesticated him?"

"I'm sure I didn't put it that way."

"Maybe not," Delia trilled, lifting a forkful of raspberry cof-fee cake, despite her better judgment. "But that's essentially what happened. You went out with this other dude because Tom was ignoring you."

"Evan." Jess smiled. "The features editor. A year younger than me. So driven."

"And *so* hot for you," Delia added. She loved this story. "Any-way, he solidified your relationship with Tom, didn't he?"

"That's overstating it. I would say, things with Evan…gave us a little nudge."

Carras goggled at Jess. "I've never heard you mention this guy."

"It's nothing," Jess said. "Delia thinks it's way more titillating than it was. Tom and I were having sort of a slow period, and Evan was this nice guy who liked me. He asked me out constantly, in weird ways. Little notes attached to wildflowers, or as comments to the pieces we were editing together. It would've been creepy, actually, if it hadn't been so sweet."

"Sounds like a recipe for rejection," Carras said.

"I know, right? But this one night, Tom bailed on me for like the third night in a row to hang out with the baseball team—it was after his knee injury so he wasn't playing anymore—and I decided on a whim to take Evan up on an invitation."

"You went out with the editor guy? While you were with Tom?"

"It wasn't a date. We were working late and he asked if I wanted to get something to eat."

"And you took him up on it." Delia grinned. "And Tom hit the fan. Didn't he show up drunk at your place?"

Delia loved the idea of easygoing, always-calm Tom getting so jealous that he banged on Jess's door in the middle of the night, annoying her roommates, staggering into Jess's crappy downtown Atlanta apartment. Gage would never have lowered himself to that kind of desperate behavior. *I don't play games*, he'd always told her. *We'll treat each other like adults, enjoy the mutual benefits.*

"He did." Jess was smiling now. "I'd never seen him like that."

"He was angry?" Carras looked concerned. "Tom has never seemed like the possessive type."

Delia felt a surge of annoyance. Carras was so serious all the time. Just because a man was passionate about the woman he loved, did it have to mean he was some kind of controlling a-hole?

But Jess laughed. "He was *pissed*, in every sense of the word, for about five minutes. Once we got to my room and started talking about it, how bad he felt about ditching me for the team so often, how hard it was for him not being part of something that had been such an integral part of his life..." She glanced up at Carras. "I'm sure you understand. If you'd been injured like Tom was, before you had the chance to get going in your career..."

"No sports talk." That wasn't why Delia was here, eating carbs. "Anyway. He came back to your room...and you talked."

"It was one of the best conversations we'd ever had," Jess said. "We'd been dating for two years by then, and things were pretty serious, but that night everything kind of clicked. He actually cried. Oh, God, don't tell him I told you that." She went pink, and busied herself by cutting a second slice of the cake. "And we… Um, things were, rather interesting in bed that night."

"Really?" Carras set down her fork.

"Let's say we explored some new territory, and leave it at that." Jess grinned. "Anyway, it put our relationship firmly on track. Tom proposed a few months later."

"All because you went out with this Evan guy."

"Not *all* because of Evan. I think Evan helped get Tom's attention. Made him realize that he couldn't take me for granted. That other guys were interested in me, too." Jess trailed off as she caught Delia's triumphant expression.

"*Exactly* the point with Parker," Delia said, pleased. "It's about reminding our men that we're still desirable. Getting the spark back. Can you imagine how great the sex would be *now*, with all your history, if you and Tom could re-create that night in your apartment?"

Jess shook her head, but her hand went reflexively to the necklace at her throat, and a tiny smile hovered at the corners of her mouth. "It wouldn't work the same way now. Things are…different. The stakes are higher, for one thing. We've been married fourteen years. We have the kids. Being interested in someone else now would be a betrayal."

"Which is why I'm saying that nothing is going to happen with this Parker guy. We're not going to betray our men, ladies." Delia sipped her coffee daintily. "But why not give them a teeny-tiny, harmless suggestion that we could if we wanted to? Remind them not to take us for granted. That's fair, right? Once a decade, give them a little nudge?"

Jess bit her lip. "I don't know…"

"So how would it work?" Carras said. "Did Belinda give you details?"

"You're not serious?" Jess said. "Stuart is incredibly devoted to you. Anyone can see the way he reacts when you walk in a room. I've felt a bit jealous from time to time, to be honest."

Delia was also interested in Carras's response. Stuart treated his wife more like a goddess who had come down from a mountain than a fellow lonely soul at a comic book convention.

"He is very devoted," Carras agreed. "It's just…well, you guys know how it is." She mustered a painful smile and even Delia could see that she was hiding something. "Every marriage has room for a little…something."

5

JESS

SHE'D PROMISED TO THINK ABOUT it. It was the best Jess could do, the only way Delia would let her leave. She plugged the kitchen sink and let the hot water run over the dishes, steaming up the dark window to the backyard. Every time she tried to make herself consider the possibility of it—hiring a man to *pretend* to be interested in her—she vacillated between appalled and pathetic.

It didn't shock her that Delia would come up with a scheme like this. Delia never said much explicitly, but Jess had picked up on her friend's moral flexibility over the years, and had some hints that she and Gage had been into some kinky stuff when they were younger. She was almost positive that Delia's husband had affairs while he was traveling, but could never get a sense of whether Delia was angry about it or not. Jess had been tempted to ask, once or twice, but something told her if Delia wanted to talk about it, she would.

Carras was another story. Jess had been floored by Carras's interest today in hiring Parker. She was a therapist, for heaven's sake; she worked with adolescents. She and Stuart seemed happy together: healthy and centered. It wasn't like Carras to be manipulative, especially not with something so...sketchy.

Sketchy. That was the word for this whole thing, and it made Jess feel like a prude every time she thought about it. In truth, she'd never had strong feelings about prostitution. She'd thought of it as more "icky" than "immoral." In her Poli-Sci 101 class in college, Jess had even been chosen to argue on the "for" side of,

"Should prostitution be legalized and regulated?" She'd had no qualms arguing to her classmates that the World's Oldest Profession would be safer for everyone involved, and provide a huge tax base to boot, if prostitution were legalized.

Doing it herself, though…

Well. Not doing *it*. The idea of sleeping with another man was abhorrent to her, and she had no plans to explore the weird territory Belinda was inhabiting. How could being with someone else make you happier being with your husband? It made zero sense.

She thought about Parker's deep, friendly eyes and spiky black hair that curled up in the front. Broad shoulders. Pecs she could see beneath the lime-green polo. He was someone she'd bump into in the protein powder aisle at Whole Foods. Not at all the image her mind conjured up for the word "prostitute."

"Stop using that word," Delia had said. "It sounds trashy. Call him an escort."

"Sex worker," Carras had corrected them both. "I believe that's the accepted term."

Now Jess stood over the kitchen sink after dinner, scrubbing and washing after homemade lasagna, spinach salad, and blueberry cobbler—all Tom's favorites. She wasn't big on cooking, but Tom had just returned from a ten-day road trip, and she'd known he would be sick of stadium food and hotel takeout. He'd taken the kids upstairs for baths and bedtime after dinner. They were wild; they always were, when he came home from a long trip. The last thundering steps overhead had quieted a few minutes ago.

She poured herself a second glass of red wine from the bottle on the counter—normally she stopped at one, especially when she was tired—and bypassed the piles of mail to read and bills to pay into the dark living room, plopping onto the fabric couch. She put her feet on the coffee table, nudging aside one of Dash's fidget spinners and a stack of Mina's books. She listened to the murmuring sounds of Tom reading upstairs.

She loved reading to the kids at bedtime; the ritual was so ingrained that she felt mildly guilty missing out. She could hear the rise and fall of Tom's inflection—he always added extra drama with his voice, picked up from all those years around sports announcers—and the occasional soft giggle from the kids. She considered joining them, but thought better of it.

It was his second night home, and last night had been swept up in the final showing of the school play and dinner afterward. The kids had missed him in ways even they didn't understand, expressed through whining, obstinance, and the ongoing, unspoken accusation that Jess alone was simply not enough. She could never explain this to Tom: how depleting his absences were, how hard it was to be the boring parent who was around all the time, eclipsed by the fun parent who swept in with stories and autographed baseballs and treasures from the airport gift shop. She knew he wrestled with enough guilt being gone; he didn't need her piling on. More than that, allowing herself to resent their roles would mean Jess had failed at her end of their life plan. *Unacceptable.*

Let him have his time with them. Jess could wait.

Jess reached for Mina's iPad on the coffee table and opened a radio app to stream a jazz station on low volume. She sank further into the couch, wineglass resting on her belly, allowing herself the rare luxury of inactivity.

She found herself thinking about Parker. Not the deep eyes and winning smile, but Parker as *potential.* Telling the story today about poor, sweet Evan from her college newspaper had left her spinning in memory. After the fight fifteen years ago, Tom had made love to her with tears rolling down his cheeks onto her naked body. It was the most vulnerable she'd ever seen him. They had not slept, she remembered, spending the whole night wordlessly exploring each other, committing themselves to each other months before Tom's grandmother's ring had made it official.

From that day on, they had no doubts. She'd accepted the management consulting job that allowed her to travel the world. He'd begun the arduous task of earning his chops in sports reporting, starting with his beloved baseball and working his way out to a wider audience. When they could travel together, they did. When they couldn't, they leaned on the infallible trust they had begun building that very night.

When Jess got pregnant with Mina, it seemed reasonable for her to be the one to give up the constant travel, despite her higher salary. She'd taken to contract work: editing proposals, and occasional short-term projects that were locally based. She'd watched from her home office as people she'd trained took promotions around her. She fielded editing assignments from brash new consultants who didn't remember her from the old days and treated her more like an assistant than a colleague. She sighed with envy when they forwarded their travel itineraries so she'd know when different assignments were due.

Of course, the joys of mothering Mina and Dash far outweighed the occasional longing to walk into a room and have everyone stop talking to hear what *she* had to say. Or to wake up in a strange city surrounded by the smells of unfamiliar cuisine and sound of another tongue. There was simply no comparison.

It wasn't as though she envied Tom's travel, either, which consisted of airport to ballpark to hotel business center to chain restaurant and back. Lather, rinse, repeat. She knew it was hard for him: Away from the kids, frequently bored. Living on nachos and cold chicken fingers and beer. Constantly worrying about deadlines and ad revenues and click rates. All while watching other athletes live out what had once been his dream.

Oddly, it had never occurred to her to worry there might be other women on the road. Logic and well-meaning friends told her Tom's job was high on the infidelity risk scale. Perhaps it was naïve, but if Tom accepted a drunken invitation at the hotel bar, Jess felt she would *know*. It was probably what all spouses told themselves, but even when she attempted—as an academic exercise—to imagine Tom being unfaithful, it simply didn't jive with the person she knew.

Still. It had been a long time since that night in her apartment. Since the last time they had explored each other's bodies for pure pleasure, for that inescapable connection they both desperately needed. It had been a long time since her husband cried in her arms and allowed her to hold him. Since their lives felt like a choice they were making together.

Her wineglass was empty, and the voices had stopped upstairs. Jess rolled herself up, grunting and stretching. She went up to the kids' rooms, turning off lights and lightly shaking her sleeping husband. He rolled blearily out of Dash's bed in sweats and a Hank Aaron T-shirt, put away the *Baseball Heroes* book he had been reading, and followed her down the stairs.

She connected the jazz radio to the kitchen speaker and topped off Tom's wineglass from dinner. He accepted it without comment, blinking in the light of the kitchen. His hair was a sexy mess, like Mark Ruffalo.

"The kids are glad you're home."

"I'm glad to be home."

He took a sip of the Pinot Noir and rested the glass on the counter. "Dinner was nice. What's with the music?" He froze. "Don't tell me you're pregnant?"

"What if I were?" Jess teased, raising her glass to remind him that she wasn't. She moved around the counter and put her hand on the small of his back. "I thought it would be nice to hang out without *SportsCenter* blaring in the background."

He shot her a quick look of reproach.

"Unless you need to work?" Normally when he got back from the road, he had a day or two before he needed to submit more pieces. She hoped she hadn't assumed wrong.

He slipped his arms around her waist, dropping a kiss lightly on her lips. "I do not need to work tonight. And if I did, I'd have to call in dead."

She ran a hand up his still-muscular arm. "Would a massage from your wife help resurrect you?"

"Oh, babe, you don't have to do that. I know you're exhausted, having the kids while I'm gone. Plus, you made this huge dinner…"

Jess leaned in close to his ear. "It would be my pleasure," she purred.

Needless to say, laughter was not the response she was trying to evoke.

"What?"

"Nothing, nothing." He was trying to pull himself together. "You sounded all sexy. You didn't sound like *you*."

Embarrassed, she pulled away, but Tom grabbed her waist. "Wait. That's not what I meant. You're very sexy." He pulled her against him and lowered his forehead to hers. "You're my beautiful wife, the sexiest woman I know."

"That's more like it."

"You caught me off guard, that's all." He kissed her on the nose.

"Let's take our wine upstairs. We can trade massages."

Tom nearly tripped over a remote-control car, which had somehow found its way into their room. He returned it to Dash's room, and then carried his half-emptied suitcase from their bed to the closet. Jess propped the iPad on her nightstand, still belting out jazz. She opened the bottom drawer and extracted a white-painted woven basket, with a cheerful gingham liner—the kind of thing Mina might have in her room to store doll shoes and accessories.

"Ah," Tom said behind her. "Grandma's Sex Basket."

"Shut up. You love it."

Jess had to admit it wasn't exactly a seductive black velvet box. But it fit in the back of the drawer inconspicuously, and it's not as if they kept anything super kinky in there, anyway. A pair of fuzzy handcuffs someone had given Jess at her bachelorette party, which they had used maybe twice in the first year of their marriage. A few Pure Indulgences products Delia had strong-armed Jess into buying over the years: a cream that supposedly mimicked human pheromones, which Tom said smelled like "the wrong end of an elephant." Special panties that vibrated via remote control (Jess had quite liked those, until the custom batteries died); and a mysterious string of beads she had ordered by accident and been too embarrassed to return. There was a weird dumbbell thing that Delia had insisted Jess needed for her Kegel muscles, but she kept forgetting to do it.

She put the basket on the bed, searching for the Pure Indulgences apple-flavored Forbidden Fruit massage oil. "Ugh. Seriously?"

"What's wrong?" Tom was shirtless, draped sideways across the bed, waiting for his masseuse.

She lifted the almost-empty, heart-shaped plastic bottle. They had only used it once, but apparently the top had leaked, bright-green apple oil soaking into the gingham basket liner and covering everything with a sticky, crusty coating. The fur on the handcuffs was matted and gooey; the synthetic fabric of the vibrating panties stuck to the side of the basket.

"It's a complete mess." She doubted the mechanical panties were machine washable.

Tom sat up and fished out the handcuffs, holding them up with one finger. "It smells like Jolly Ranchers and lube. Like Halloween in a whorehouse."

Jess glared at him. "Don't say 'whore.'"

"Sorry. *House of ill repute.*"

"This whole thing is ruined." The basket. The evening. Maybe both.

He tossed the handcuffs back and put a hand under her chin. "Don't sweat it, Gardner. We don't need this crap. Put it back and we'll clean it up later."

"Rodriguez," she corrected, smiling at his use of her maiden name.

"You better believe it, baby." He set the basket aside, pulling her close and kissing her neck. She put her hands on his bare shoulders, trying to ignore the scent of apple massage oil as she kneaded his tense muscles.

"Oh, God," he said into her shoulder. "You have no idea how much I need that. The hotel bed was miserable in Chicago, and the plane ride..."

"Poor baby," she cooed, working at the hard flesh around his neck with her knuckles. "Poor, poor thing."

He groaned in appreciation, and let his head sink against her belly as she pressed into his flesh. "Poor me," he slurred seductively. "I really need some TLC. It's hard being on the road with a bunch of idiots all the time."

Jess leaned over to kiss the top of his head, and Tom's hands slipped from her waist to cradle her ass. He squeezed appreciatively, as though juicing a couple of oranges; she felt the muscles in his back stiffen as he lifted her off the ground. She wrapped her legs around his waist and they tumbled onto the bed together, laughing. Tom braced his arms and rolled on top of her, grinning and toying with the buttons on her blouse.

"Look at that," Jess said, lying back. "You have some energy left after all."

"Look. At. That," he agreed. "What's up, buddy?"

It took her a confused moment to realize this question was not intended for her, but that Dash was standing in their doorway, a dark patch of moisture spreading across the front of his pajamas.

"I had an accident." His eyes took in their position on the bed with unaffected curiosity, perhaps wondering if they were playing some game they'd forgotten to include him in.

"I've got it," Jess said, re-buttoning her blouse with frustrated fingers. "It's okay, buddy. Go ahead to the bathroom and take your PJs off. I'll be right there to change your sheets."

When Dash had shuffled out, Tom said, "Are you sure he's okay? Mina never wet the bed at his age."

"He's *fine*. The pediatrician said boys take longer sometimes." She didn't mention that several of Dash's cohorts at school were still wearing overnight pull-ups, which Tom had vetoed over a year ago on the premise that Dash was "too old for diapers." Those kids' parents were probably having amazing sex right this minute.

Twenty minutes later, she had stripped and changed Dash's sheets and tucked him back in, with a couple of bonus lullabies to convince him to stay put. She padded back into the master bedroom, where Grandma's Sex Basket was still sitting on the nightstand (leaving a sticky outline on the wood, she would discover later). The jazz station and low lights had been turned off in favor of ESPN on their small bedroom television. And her husband was draped across the bed, snoring in the flickering light.

He was still shirtless, she noted, so A for effort there. But he'd changed into pajama bottoms while she was gone.

She pushed on his ribs to wake him. "Babe, get up and under the covers."

He barely stirred, murmuring against the pillow folded beneath him. "You're back. I missed you."

"I can see that. You could've at least cleaned up the oil."

"Going to," he said. "Right after."

"After?"

"Rock your world, baby. Love you so much. Sooo beautiful." This speech might have been more compelling if he hadn't been half-unconscious.

"I love you, too, you big lump." Jess sighed. "Go to bed."

He sat up, gave her a sleepy smile. "Tomorrow?"

"Yep." Or the next day. Or the day after that. She knew how this went. *Unless she changed something.* She picked up the sticky basket, and paused on her way to the trash. "Hey, Tom?"

"Hunhh?" He was already down again, pulling the covers over

his bare torso.

"I forgot to mention, I decided to start tennis lessons." She paused, heart pounding, a little dizzy with wine. "You don't mind, do you? They're a little pricey but I think they'll be worth it."

Jess chose to interpret the mumbling incoherence that followed as Tom giving the plan his unqualified approval.

6

MAIZY

MAIZY CALLAHAN HENRIKSSON WASN'T SURE what it was, but something was *up*.

The annual teacher appreciation breakfast was going swimmingly, as it always did. This was her favorite event of the year, and had been her initial entry point into volunteering at the school. Long before she'd risen through the ranks of the PTA, she'd been a tentative first-time kindergarten parent, too shy to take much of a role in the organizational side, but happy to bake endless Tupperware containers of brownies and cookies and muffins whenever the occasion demanded it.

Even now, when she was in charge of the whole PTA, she hadn't relinquished her original role as the baker of everyone's favorite sweets. She'd been baking for the past three weeks, late at night, and putting treats in the freezer each morning, on top of coordinating parent volunteers to take over the teachers' homeroom classes for an hour and handling all the end-of-year planning meetings. Technically, her successor should've been taking over some of these duties, because they were now in the final weeks of Maizy's last year as a parent at the school. But Judy Kirkpatrick was a rather uninspiring choice for PTA president, if you wanted Maizy's opinion about it, and although she had not gone out of her way, per se, to hand things off…well, Judy hadn't been killing herself to take things over, either.

So it wasn't a problem with the breakfast. They'd had good turnout and the teachers were happy. Everyone had shown up with what they were supposed to bring—even Delia Cargill, who was an hour late and a carton of orange juice short for everything.

In fact, it was Delia who had Maizy's attention today, along with Jess Rodriguez, whom Maizy actually liked. They both lived on the cul-de-sac at the end of Maizy's street, and frequently walked past her house engaged in conversation, impenetrable from the outside. Delia was always chatty and Jess was always smiling, but whenever Maizy casually stepped out the door in her walking shoes and waved hello, they would give her a wave and continue on. If she stopped either of them in the hallway at school or approached them at a PTA event like this one, Jess would say hello. Delia might smile, but she'd also keep talking as though Maizy weren't there. Maizy could never tell whether this was a signal that the conversation was important and private, or that Maizy should hang out and wait to be included. Eventually she would say, "Well, I've got to run," and slink away; or, if she stayed, the conversation would dissipate. They were never rude, exactly. It was just that Maizy invariably felt like the safety pin that had popped the balloon.

But today their conversation seemed even more closed-off than usual. And it wasn't even the usual peppy chatter that Maizy envied. All morning, the two of them had been standing off in a corner, murmuring in a way that called attention to itself by trying not to. They stopped talking any time another parent or even the teachers walked nearby, plastering on careful smiles that died as soon as the intruder walked away.

It was unlike Delia not to insist on being the center of attention at these events. Normally she'd be chatting up the teachers, taking credit for bringing in two jugs of orange juice as if she'd won the freaking Nobel Prize of Parent Involvement, trying to sell them her latest line of health shakes or essential oils or skin cream. Polite dismissal wasn't Delia Cargill's style, not when it came to potential customers or the people who could impact her children's golden path to Ivy League schools.

Delia had met her husband Gage while he was at Harvard Law. Maizy knew this because Delia mentioned it every fourth sentence. "When we were in Cambridge," she would say, or sometimes getting even bolder, "When *we* were at Harvard." As though cohabitation in Gage's apartment during his final year at law school—before they were even *married*—meant Delia had walked Harvard's hallowed halls herself. Delia conveniently never mentioned that she'd been in Boston with a previous boyfriend who dumped her as soon as they'd arrived, and that she met Gage while she was working at a bar. *When we were at Harvard.* Seriously.

But it wasn't Maizy's place to judge. She'd never said a word about the real story (told by Gage to Maizy's husband Anders, after a few too many beers at the last neighborhood pool party). She wasn't judging Delia and Jess's strange behavior now, either. Just… *observing.*

"Lovely job as always, Maizy." The principal, Nora Klein, was at her elbow. "I don't know how we'll survive without you next year."

"Oh, you'll be fine. Judy's fantastic."

She nodded to the other side of the room, where Judy Kirkpatrick stood vacantly next to an empty coffee carafe. *Come on, Judy.* Maizy sent frantic telepathy. *Make coffee. It's not rocket science.*

Mrs. Klein smiled. "We'll miss you. And Anders, too. The holiday auction won't be the same without his mountain bike lessons up for bid. They're a perennial favorite with the dads."

"I'm sure he'll continue to donate the lessons. We'll still be part of the community." Even as she said it, she knew Anders would be annoyed with her. He had already complained how amateur the guys were who bought his lessons; last year, one of the dads had flipped one of Anders's best bikes and bent the frame. "And, if not…" She trailed off, unsure how to gracefully back out.

Mrs. Klein, as patient and understanding with parents as she was with the kids in her charge, kept smiling fondly, as though she possessed the wisdom of experience far beyond Maizy's. Which was strange, because Mrs. Klein was only about a decade older. "We will miss you," she repeated, and patted Maizy's arm. "I'm going to snag another of your double-chocolate muffins before the fifth-grade teachers get over there. They have no shame by this time of year."

When Maizy turned to resume her study of Delia and Jess, she found they had disappeared. Of course, she thought with irritation. No one stays to clean up.

7

CARRAS

CARRAS PACED AROUND THE HOUSE, glancing at the clock every few minutes. Stuart was out of town, which was convenient, but it disconcerted Carras even more. She had woken early and taken a hot bath before donning an old tennis dress—careful not to choose one of her favorites, or the most flattering—and then wandered around the house she had frequently assured Stuart was too big, too rambling for her tastes.

Somehow, they had managed to fill the rooms. Stuart staked out the finished basement for his work and gaming (often interchangeable). It had come equipped with a wet bar and refrigerator from the previous owner, and they had moved in an ugly but supremely comfortable sectional sofa to accompany Stuart's gaming chairs and long tables covered in blinking black boxes. She knew visitors thought of it as a "man cave," but it was Carras's favorite part of the house. She loved the unpretentious couch and Stuart's giant television. They spent more weeknights curled up watching television and eating off paper plates downstairs than they ever did in their well-appointed kitchen.

Carras did not go down to the basement today. She couldn't invade that intimate, relaxed space with her thoughts this morning. Instead, she floated among the rooms and the furniture they had purchased together. She let her hand graze across spotless surfaces, maintained by a local maid service whose employees wore bright-blue uniforms and never seemed able to remember Carras's name.

Eventually, she wandered upstairs to the spare bedroom, where her tennis trophies and honors medals from college had been on display for far too long. She paused at the trophy shelf, seeing her own distorted image in the gold cups and three-dimensional plaques, and thought how quickly a person could turn into a different version of herself. She was proud of her tennis career, and had not objected when Stuart built the display shelves as a surprise. She knew Stuart adored her, almost to a fault, and making him proud made her happy. But it had been a comfort to know that the trophies would be consigned to the attic when this room was eventually converted into a nursery or playroom. The tokens of her former glory were just another reminder of how life was not moving forward in all the ways she had hoped. This thought piqued her curiosity about Parker Yung once again.

She sat down at the small desk by the window, where Carras's ancient laptop—the least sophisticated piece of electronics in the house—sat mostly dormant. Her initial search on "Parker Yung" yielded Parker's Instagram and Facebook profiles—which seemed to have identical pictures and captions where he auto-posted from one to the other—the home page for his tennis website, and Google's suggestion that perhaps she meant "Parker Young" instead? She tried "Parker Davis" and got back too many results to count—pictures of men and women, all shapes and colors.

Carras clicked back to the previous search and looked through Parker's public profiles, scouting for family photos, but found none. No sign of the "Tiger Mom" or Parker's dad. But something tickled at the back of her brain, but refused to come forward.

Her phone buzzed—her father's number in Waco—and Carras closed the browser. She'd do more thorough research later. "Hey, Pops. How are you feeling?"

"Oh, you know, Angel. Life gives us what we can handle. I always told you."

"Yes, you did." Her father loved these little sayings. Her childhood was woven together with them like a giant cross-stitch sampler. But now she had to wonder whether life had given her father congestive heart failure because he could handle it, or because life was cruel and random and sometimes wildly unfair. "Are you following the doctor's instructions? You're taking your medicine?"

"Eh... You know me. Only dead fish go with the flow."

"That's not an answer, Pops. You have to take care of yourself."

"Yes, yes. But I'm boring. There's nothing interesting about an old man with swollen ankles who can't climb the stairs without wheezing. I want to hear about you."

"What about me? Everything's fine. Stuart's great. We're fine."

He was quiet, and even halfway across the country, Carras knew he was expecting more from her. "What about my baby? When is that skinny husband of yours going to put down the video games and make me a grandfather?"

"I've told you, Pops. The games are his job. It's not like he's playing all day." She hadn't told her father that she and Stuart were trying their best to make him a grandfather. The last thing she needed was his constant coaching input on *that* process. And, what if they failed? She couldn't do that to him.

Her watch buzzed to indicate a text from Jess. *We're meeting 15 minutes early, right? Can we make it 20?*

"Pops, I need to go. Promise you'll take your medicine."

"Waste not, want not."

"How is that relevant?"

Before he answered, Jess texted again. *I might need some propping up.* And immediately after: *I might need a stiff drink.*

"Just making sure you were paying attention." Her dad laughed. "Now, I know that boy thinks you hung the moon, and I happen to agree, so I won't be too hard on him. He wants you all to himself. But time passes quickly when you're building a life. Like sand through the hourglass…"

"That's from a soap opera, Pops."

"Really? How about, triumph is 'umph' added to 'try.'"

"That's a new one. Bumper sticker?"

"Bye, Angel. Love you."

"Love you, too."

Carras hung up and texted Jess back *sure* with the laughing and crying emoji. Appropriate because Carras wasn't sure which one she felt like doing more.

She gathered her tennis bag, the familiar straps in her hand providing tactile comfort, and stepped out into the sunny April morning. She decided to walk—it was just over a mile from her house across Sweet River Road to the club. The sky was an unrealistic shade of blue, the morning cool but hinting of summer around the corner.

All told, it was a beautiful day for betraying your husband.

8

DELIA

DELIA PACED BESIDE THE COURT in her cutest tennis out-fit, waiting for Jess and Carras. She had reserved the court closest to the pagoda and picnic table—where Parker would meet them—for ten o'clock. Just in case.

She sat down at the picnic table, checked her phone, and stood back up again. No one had texted in the past few minutes, and not even 800+ Facebook friends offered anything to divert her attention. *Relax.* It was still half an hour until their meeting, and the other two were coming early so they could regroup one last time before meeting Parker.

So it was a surprise when she saw Parker at the other end of the court, walking toward her with a water bottle and racket. She felt an adolescent panic: he was even more attractive than when she'd met him at lunch the previous week. Delia froze, sat down, realized it was clear he had seen her, stood up again. She took out her phone and pretended to be reading something critically important as he approached.

Parker, impossibly normal and adorable, gave Delia a perfect, white-toothed smile. "Thanks for meeting me, Delia; I'm looking forward to hanging out with you."

One sentence, and already Delia felt naked and exposed. This was a mistake. Too late now.

"Are we going to play?" She nodded at the racket and water.

"Be ready for anything, I always say." He gave an awkward smile. "And I am a *pro,* I guess."

He was cute, and young, and seemed disarmingly nervous. Particularly after the bravado of his interaction with Orson at the cafe. "And you're early," Delia said. "Very professional."

Parker glanced around. "Your friends aren't here yet. Want to stretch it out while we wait?"

"Seriously?"

"Come on. It's better than whatever you're doing on that phone." He set the bottle and racket on the picnic table and offered her a hand. "Lie down in the grass and I'll take care of you right now."

She laughed and followed him to the grassy hill between the courts and the parking area. He gestured for her to lie on her back; as she did, Delia reminded herself she was too old and experienced to let this twenty-five-year-old rattle her. Parker lifted her feet expertly and leaned against them, stretching her hamstrings. It felt great, and even though there was nothing sexual in his manner, Delia felt strangely vulnerable, glad she'd worn shorts under her skirt.

"Starting without us?" Jess's voice, above her.

"Never." Parker grinned at Jess and Carras, but took the time to finish the stretch before helping Delia to her feet. He led the way back to the pagoda, picking up a discarded tennis ball and straddling the picnic bench. He passed the ball back and forth in his hands, smiling at the three of them.

Damn. He was effortlessly hot.

Parker seemed to be waiting for them to start, but Delia knew enough about business to know that whoever spoke first would have less power.

Jess cleared her throat. "Where do we start?"

Dammit, Jess.

Parker's smile widened. Delia saw immediately that he enjoyed this part of it. He reminded her of her younger self—eyes alight with the thrill of the chase. "Glad you asked, Jess. I'm sure Belinda explained that in addition to my regular tennis lessons, I also offer premium lessons, which are a more...flexible arrangement."

"You mean that you also offer sex?" Jess blurted.

Delia shot Jess a "be cool, for God's sake," look. It was Jess's style to be direct, especially when nervous, but there was something to be said for a little subtlety.

Parker didn't flinch. "You're the journalist, right? Not working on an article, are you?"

Jess blanched. "I'm not a journalist. My…husband is. But he doesn't write about this kind of stuff. He only does sports."

Parker's tone dipped into iciness. "In other words, he ruins lives in far more sanitized, commonplace ways."

The three women glanced between them. *Where had that come from?*

But Parker recovered his smile. "Now, I'll go over this since I don't know how much Belinda covered with you. The way premium lessons with a group discount work is that you pay cash in advance, ten hours each for the month. My usual rate is $350 an hour—"

Jess gasped.

Parker smiled. "But with the group rate, and the monthly minimum, it's $250 an hour, $2,500 each. You can pool your time—like if you wanted a whole day for some reason—or parcel it out into two-hour chunks. You can use it for tennis lessons, obviously, or…" He paused. "If you have other needs, the time can be spent there as well."

"Two and a half thousand dollars." Jess stared at the slats in the picnic table.

"What if our needs aren't…conventional?" Delia said, getting the conversation back on track.

Parker raised an eyebrow. "Well, I do have limits, but I think you'll find I'm open-minded."

Dammit. She'd been trying to be delicate, and instead she'd made him think they wanted something weird and kinky.

Jess rolled her eyes. "She means, the three of us don't want sex. We want your help making our husbands jealous, more affectionate. The way you've done with Belinda and Orson. That would be cheaper than sex, right?"

"You mean, flirt with you in front of your husbands?" Parker's brow furrowed. "Not trying to talk myself out of business, but you're all attractive women. Can't you find some random dudes and flirt with them?"

"Easy for you to say," Jess said. "You're twenty-whatever and hot as hell. Besides, we don't want our husbands to see us flirting with *random* guys. We want them to see a guy who *wants* us."

Parker gazed at Jess. "I can't imagine that would be a problem."

Jess flushed and turned away.

Delia took up the torch. "The point is, we want it to go exactly how we need it to go. Perfectly orchestrated."

"To intentionally put myself in the path of a jealous husband…" Parker whistled. "I don't know."

"None of our husbands are threatening types," Jess said. "Besides, you can help us with the man's perspective on things. Think of it like consulting work."

"Consulting, huh?" He hesitated.

Delia guessed that the challenge appealed to him, even if the fact they didn't want to sleep with him was a blow to his ego. She adopted her flirtiest expression. "Who knows? Maybe you'll even convince one of us to take full advantage of your services…"

Parker gave her a crooked grin. "You talked me into it."

"What about travel?" Carras said, ignoring the questioning glances from Delia and Jess.

"Sure," Parker said, back in his familiar territory. "I charge travel time and mileage for anything beyond a ten-mile radius, but if you booked, like, a full weekend or whatever, we can work up some kind of bulk rate. Which reminds me, I assume Belinda told you, it's five hundred each today for the deposit. The rest is payable once the schedules are confirmed."

There was a shuffling and rustling of bags as the women fished out bills and envelopes. Parker stood to collect the money, and Delia couldn't help but notice his muscular thighs as they pushed upright and he stepped back over the bench. "Now," he stashed the money in his tennis bag, "I think our court is ready."

9

JESS

"I NEED A PLAN," JESS SAID. "I cashed in my grandmother's stock and rented a human being for a month. So that's how long I have to make this work."

She accepted a glass of lemonade from Carras, who flopped down next to her on the couch. Tom was working from home and Delia's kitchen was being remodeled, so they had retreated to Carras's after tennis with Parker.

"It will work," Delia said. "And Tom will never know."

"But *I'll* know. Twenty-five hundred dollars. Hell. For that, Tom and I could hire a sitter and take a romantic vacation. At least for a weekend."

"You tried that," Delia reminded her. "Remember two years ago? You guys spent a weekend at that winery and Tom had food poisoning the whole time?"

"Don't remind me." Jess cringed. She'd been forced to go on all the tastings by herself while Tom lay in their dark hotel room, unable to get more than thirty feet from the toilet. "I *told* him not to eat ceviche from a gas station."

"That's disgusting," Carras said.

"I can't *begin* to tell you."

"My point is," Delia said. "Romantic getaways are hit-and-miss, aren't they? But to renew your husband's animal, possessive desire for you? That could get you through *years* of getaways. Not to mention average school-night sex."

"I get it, Delia, I do. And I want that so badly for my marriage. But I still don't know how this works without totally pissing our husbands off."

"Let's start simple. Take the tennis lessons like normal. First lesson, you tell Tom how awesome and friendly Parker is and ask if he's ever heard of him because he's so amazing. Before the second lesson, you ignore Tom and go to bed early to 'rest up' because it's so important you perform well the next day. That will ensure he's aware of what's happening because it will directly impact him. Afterward, you come home and emphasize how Parker complimented you on your swing, athleticism, etc."

Jess snorted. No one had ever complimented her athleticism.

"By the third lesson, you and Parker go shopping for something—a new racket, whatever—and conveniently stop off for lunch at a nearby cafe, where you post a selfie of you and your amazing new coach."

"Why can't I just hire a regular tennis coach for all that?"

Delia shrugged. "You could. And then you'd have to actually take lessons, and you'd have to find someone cute enough and available to have lunch and take a photo with you. *And* to not think you're a lonely stalker for asking…"

"Point taken," Jess said.

"I'm guessing the whole 'hot for teacher' thing will do it for Tom. He's so competitive. But if not, we'll have the end-of-year party coming up after that… You can slip Parker a little cash for some in-person attention."

"I don't like manipulating Tom. Great sex does me no good if he files for divorce." As soon as she said the words, Jess felt the superstitious need to undo them. "Not that he would. Especially since we're not actually going to…"

"Of course not," Delia said. "Parker is yummy, though, isn't he? I mean, if I *had* to be with someone…like, if my life depended on it…"

"You mean those situations that surely come up all the time in which your life depends on having hot animal sex with someone who isn't your spouse?"

"Shut up, Jess. You can seriously suck the fun out of anything. If you are so down on this idea, why are we here?" Delia gave Jess a devilish grin. "If you want to drop out, I can always find another third. I think Nancy McMurtry mentioned she is having problems with her marriage…"

"I'm not down on the idea, okay?" Jess felt sudden panic that Delia was going to cut her out of this deal, which—despite all the totally reasonable concerns she had about it—was the most interesting thing to happen in her life for years. "I'm trying to make sure we understand the risks. Don't you agree, Carras?"

"Hmmm?" Carras had been staring out into her backyard, which was starting to darken as heavy clouds gathered overhead. "Right."

Jess watched Carras for another moment before something registered. "Nancy McMurtry! Her husband has prostate cancer. I don't think a little jealousy is going to fix their sex life right now." She threw a pillow at Delia. "You're terrible."

"I wasn't serious," Delia said. "I took them a casserole, for heaven's sake."

Jess's phone buzzed with a new text message.

Tom: *Did the school call you?*

She was replying to ask what he meant when the phone vibrated in her hand, the Sugar Mills Elementary main line bright on the screen.

"Oh God." She rolled her eyes at Delia and Carras after the brief conversation with the nurse. "Dash barfed up his lunch again. It doesn't matter how many times I tell them he chokes on his food sometimes—they always treat it like the stomach flu."

It was only after she had climbed into her white SUV and began driving to the school that it occurred to Jess: Tom got the call first. He was listed first on the kids' school registration, and although the front office and clinic staff knew Jess was usually more available, today there had been a substitute nurse who called him first.

Tom was working from home today. So, theoretically, was Jess. Why was she the one driving to the school right now?

She dismissed the irritating thought. After all, she had been drinking lemonade with the girls, not pounding away on her laptop. Still, chances were good that Tom was home doing "research" by watching MLB videos. And after meeting all his recent deadlines…*he* should have a few minutes to run up to the school.

Not a big deal, but it was the principle. Tom's assumption—

maybe hers too—that even on a day they were both at home, the kids were still her responsibility first. Not that she minded.

Leaving the school with a rosy-cheeked, chatty Dash a few minutes later, Jess paused to let a pedestrian cross in front of her. Maizy Henriksson smiled perfunctorily and waved; then, seeing it was Jess, looked again. As she pulled up to the stop sign at the main road, Jess glanced in the rearview mirror to find that Maizy was still watching her from the sidewalk.

10

MAIZY

"THERE'S SOMETHING HAPPENING ON OUR street," Maizy said, as Anders brought her a stack of dirty dishes from the table. The girls had already fled from the table and decamped to the bonus room upstairs, where she would find them watching *Vampire Diaries*, side by side, each glued to her own phone screen.

"Like, with the home values? I checked last month and the value of our house was up by a little bit. About three thousand dollars."

"No, with the neighbors. Jess, Delia, and that Carras woman."

Anders appeared disappointed they weren't going to talk about real estate, but gamely tried to engage anyway. "Who is Carras?"

"You know, Stuart's wife. Jess and Tom's friend. They live between our house and the cul-de-sac. No kids."

He was blank.

"She was some kind of tennis phenom, back in the day? A little taller than me? Strong legs, very pretty. Anyway, the three of them have been walking together every night lately. All of a sudden."

This seemed to trigger something for Anders. "Oh! Carras is the black one?"

"You can't say 'black one.'"

"Why not?"

"I don't know. It just sounds wrong."

"She's black, right? African-American?"

"Yes. Well, no. She's from the Caribbean, I think. Is that African?"

"Nope. Why didn't you say she was black, when you were de-scribing her?"

Maizy sighed, exasperated. "I don't know. That's not the point."

"There are maybe four black families in this whole neigh-borhood." Anders plowed on, eyes lighting with the intellectual pleasure of outsmarting her. "It certainly would've been a helpful descriptor. I would've known immediately who you were talking about."

"I don't know," she repeated, flustered. "I didn't think it was important."

"It's not *important*—it's *descriptive*. You were afraid that if you described her as black, you'd sound racist. That's *so* American. Do you think this Carras person doesn't already know she's black?"

Now Maizy regretted bringing up the topic at all. His argu-ment sounded logical, but it irked her that he was homing in on the tiny, irrelevant detail of how she'd approached the conversa-tion, rather than listening to what she was trying to say. "You're as American as I am," she said, playing his game of technicalities. "You were born in Seattle."

"Ah, but I have dual citizenship," he reminded her. "And in Norway, when someone is black or white or brown, we simply say so. It's not racist. In fact, you could argue that American reluctance to speak frankly about race is what allows racism to fester here."

Maizy felt him watching her as she rinsed the dinner plates and put them in the dishwasher. He was probably right; Anders gener-ally was. But as he should know by now, Maizy found it difficult to speak frankly about most things. It wasn't her style. She closed the dishwasher. "I'm going to have a scoop of ice cream. Want some?"

"No, thanks." He patted his tight belly. Anders watched what he ate religiously, and Maizy admired him for it. But sometimes she wished he would indulge with her a little.

In the quiet, he seemed to pick up on her irritation and soften. "So, these three women. They're walking a lot?"

"I know it sounds silly, but it feels like there's a *purpose* to it. Like every time I've seen them go by lately, they're in this su-per-serious conversation."

"Maybe they're trying to lose weight," he said.

"I think it's more than that." Telepathically, she begged her husband not to suggest that Maizy should join them in their quest for weight loss. It was a sore point between them and she didn't have the energy for it tonight. Always pear-shaped, Maizy had grown a little plumper in the past few years. Normally it didn't bother her that Anders encouraged her to eat healthier and exercise—he certainly took care of himself and it wasn't unreasonable for them to be on the same page. But sometimes it felt a bit critical.

Anders must have gotten the message, because he stepped forward and put his arms around her, pressing her against his strong, lean body. "You feel left out," he guessed. "They're walking without you?"

"No. Yes. I'm not sure. It's weird, right? I have plenty on my plate—the end of the school year, handing things off to useless Judy Kirkpatrick..."

He shrugged. "Maybe it's time for you to get out of the house more. Now that Agatha is heading to middle school, you could go back to work."

This again. "Anders, I don't know..."

"I'm just saying, you've got an accounting degree and you're a smart woman. I think it's safe to say you've done your time with the little bake sales and being around for the kids while they were young. They're getting big now; they don't need Mommy all the time. You should get back to the real world, make friends there. Quit worrying about the housewives and their drama."

Anders closed the ice cream carton, which she'd abandoned when he hugged her, and returned it to the freezer. He seemed unaware that he'd stabbed her multiple times in the heart.

It was like being little again herself, with her mother pushing her toward the playground on a summer day. *Go make friends. Be nice to the other kids and they will be nice to you.* Maizy looked at the bowl, where she'd only managed to get a half-scoop of Moose Tracks before Anders intervened. She wanted at least twice that much, but it would be piggish to open the freezer again now. Maybe she'd come back down while he was asleep.

"We don't need the money," she reminded him. This was the third or fourth time in the last couple of years he had broached the subject of Maizy returning to her job as a CPA. To be fair, that had been the original plan when Elise was born. She would stay home until they were done having children and the youngest went off to kindergarten, and then search for a job. No pressure, no rush. Wait for the perfect fit: something close to home, maybe part-time.

But when Agatha reached kindergarten, they were still trying to figure out how to manage her asthma effectively, and Maizy didn't like being more than a few miles from the school until she was certain it was well-controlled. Two years later, Maizy's mother had moved in with them and Maizy had attempted to care for her, until the Alzheimer's was too much and she needed elevated care. She still visited the assisted living home once a week, even though her mother hadn't recognized her for more than a year now.

In the meantime, she'd become so involved at the school. The volunteering that began as a way to stay close to Agatha had turned into an unpaid job, and to be honest, Maizy enjoyed it. The school needed her: in the media center, at the PTA meetings, for fundraisers and special events. The teachers devoured her baked goods with appreciative gusto. No one complained about fat or calories, suggested she was wasting her time by helping out, or put away the fucking ice cream before she even had a whole bowl.

"Of *course* we don't need the money," Anders said. "But you used to enjoy working. You were so *driven* when we first met. I thought you might want to get back into it, have something that's just for you."

Maizy couldn't help thinking that if she were going to do something just for herself, other people's taxes wouldn't exactly top the list. She tried to steer the subject in a more pleasant direction, spooning a bit of ice cream playfully into her mouth and letting the spoon linger there. "Was that what attracted you to me? My *drive?*"

He smiled and took the bowl from her, putting it in the sink despite a lump of ice cream still remaining. "Well. There's more than one kind of drive," he said seductively, his slight over-annunciation—an endearing side effect of being raised by Norwegian immigrants—bringing her back to the days when she'd worked in the university library and they started up a flirtation at the return desk. Maizy stood on tiptoe to kiss him, and felt the familiar thrill as he bent his long neck to reach her mouth with his.

Anders grasped her waist and lifted her onto the counter. Maizy ignored his slight grunt of effort, continuing to kiss him until they were both lost in it. Like the old days.

"Let's go upstairs," he whispered.

Maizy gave him a playful smirk. "Why not here on the counter?"

"Not sanitary." He pulled her down. "Besides, I wouldn't want the kids to walk in."

Fair enough. Maizy followed him upstairs, flipping off lights. It was all business by the time they got to the bedroom. Anders locked the door, turned out the lights and shed his clothes in what seemed like a single fluid motion. He draped his clothes carefully on a chair. Maizy followed suit, thinking that a weeknight lovemaking session was gift enough without needing a long seduction.

Almost before she had settled herself on the bed, Anders was pushing into her, thrusting and groaning and whispering her name in a soft, pleading monotone. When he was done, he rolled to one side and reached a practiced hand between her legs, stroking and rubbing in the familiar way that resulted from years of marriage. She was very aroused—it had been awhile, and unexpected sex was always thrilling—and the deft movements of his hand brought her heightened pleasure. Waves of tension mounted inside as she frantically whispered his name.

Until. He sighed.

It wasn't a big, dramatic sigh or an intentional sound. It was just audible enough for Maizy to notice, breaking her concentration as she searched the dark for his face, wondering whether he was bored or tired or both. "Anders?"

"Yes, baby, yes." The way he said it, with forced enthusiasm, coupled with an increase in both the speed and firmness with which he touched her, sapped the romance from the moment like Ron Weasley with a deluminator. His movements against her flesh became painful and rough as her arousal decreased. Rather than noticing and slowing down, Anders moved harder and faster, his *oh, babys* sounding more like a religious recitation than an impassioned plea for pleasure.

Well, that was it.

Maizy put a hand on his wrist to stop him.

"You okay?"

"Yes, it's …" She knew that mentioning his lack of enthusiasm would start a fight, and she wanted him to be glad he'd initiated weeknight sex. Maybe it could happen again sometime. "I'm just…tired. I didn't realize until now, but it was such a long day."

"Sugar." He kissed her temple and pat her belly.

Confused that her devoutly European husband was calling her by such a Southern endearment, she responded, "Beg your pardon?"

"It's sugar. Making you tired. All those processed foods and sweets you eat when you're too busy to cook lunch. We should do another cleanse soon. That will help. I'll go online and order some of the shakes."

Anders rolled away from her and off the bed in a single athletic motion. He pulled his phone from the pants draped over a chair. Maizy watched his face light up blue in the darkness.

"You don't have to order it right this minute, do you?"

"No time like the present. You liked the chocolate best, right?"

"Sure."

Truthfully, Maizy hated all the protein shakes Anders made her drink, hated more that he insisted they follow the crazy cleanse to the letter for two whole weeks. She wouldn't have minded doing these healthy kicks with him if he weren't so rigid about it. Like, if he would cheat with her on day seven instead of sanctimoniously sticking with the program so that she had to eat potato chips in her car and throw the bag away in a public trash can to hide the evidence.

Potato chips. Now *that* sounded good right now…

"Done. They'll be here next week and we'll start May first. It will be the perfect way to get ready for summer, right?"

"Right." Maizy's body ached with unfulfilled desire, and she wanted to ask Anders to come back to bed, kiss her on the neck, touch her—more slowly this time, not like he was racing to the finish line.

He tossed the phone on his nightstand. "Mind if I shower first?"

When he had closed the bathroom door, Maizy pulled the sheets over her naked body. She ran her hands over her soft belly and the love handles at her sides, trying to feel herself from Anders's point of view. Everything was a bit wobblier than it had been when they started dating, but she'd always had a bit of extra stuffing, as her dad would've said. It had never bothered Anders, and in fact he'd often commented in the early days that there was more of her to love. More to hold.

She heard the toilet flush and shower door swing open as Anders got in. He would be at least ten minutes, and their door was still locked. She reached tentatively between her legs to pick up where her husband had left off. But after a couple of minutes picturing Chris Pratt in a Speedo serving her a frosty poolside drink, she found herself more focused on the contents of the glass than on the guy holding it. Summer would be here soon, time for margaritas and piña coladas and...ice cream. She wondered whether the bowl downstairs had fully melted.

Then Anders was back, slipping under the sheets while he was still damp. She rolled over to kiss him.

But before it could progress, he said, "Shower's all yours."

By the time she emerged, steaming, her skin pink from the hot water and a headband holding back her short, damp curls, Anders was fast asleep. Snoring like a big, healthy Scandinavian bear. Maizy crawled in next to him, turned on her reading lamp, and focused hard on not going downstairs to bake and eat her feelings. It took a long time to fall asleep, and when she did, Maizy dreamed of Chris Pratt and Moose Tracks.

11

JESS

JESS WAITED AT THE PICNIC table by the tennis courts, the same spot where Parker had given them the spiel the previous week. She was clutching her tennis bag, which she'd meticulously packed the night before. Spray-on deodorant, a change of socks, a travel first-aid kit (what did she think was going to happen?) and a wad of cash, rolled up tight in an interior pocket. Proceeds from the sale of her grandmother's GE stock certificate.

She unzipped the bag for the fiftieth time and fingered the roll of bills. Their financial advisor hadn't questioned it, when she'd asked for half the proceeds in cash and the other half to be deposited into the kids' college funds. If Tom ever decided to look into things, he would figure out that some of the money had gone missing. But he probably didn't even remember the stock from Nana Gardner, and the details of their financial life were never Tom's favorite topic of discussion anyway. Besides, it was *her* stock, from long before their marriage, and she could use the proceeds for whatever purpose she wanted. Or at least, that's what Jess was telling herself.

When Parker's yellow Jeep pulled into the lot up the hill, Jess fought the panicked temptation to run. He hoisted himself over the door and strode toward her, smiling. How was she supposed to greet him? A hug? High-five? Air kisses, like Belinda and Delia?

"Hello," she said, when he got close enough, and thrust the wad of bills into his outstretched hand. "It's all there."

She could see this was the wrong move, because he glanced around to make sure no one was around, half-chuckling. "Relax."

He put the bills into the side pocket of his own tennis bag. "It's just lessons."

"Did Delia, um, brief you? I mean, about what we were planning." After a long conversation and much whining, Jess had conceded that Delia's plan of getting to Tom by sparking his sense of sportsmanlike competition was the best option available.

Parker nodded. "She said your husband used to be a jock, relates best to athletics, and might get irritated if your tennis coach seemed too invested in you. Trust me, I know the type."

"Tom isn't a *type*," she corrected. Then, worried that she sounded defensive, added, "He travels a lot for work, and we don't socialize outside the house much. There aren't many natural opportunities for him to see me interact with other men."

"Can't say I blame him," Parker said. "If I were married to someone like you, I wouldn't want to share with the world, either."

It was a line, and Jess knew it. He was almost fifteen years her junior and women paid him to say what they wanted to hear. Still, she felt the blood pooling in her cheeks and across her throat. "So, how does this work? I mean, what now?"

"Why don't we start with your serve? Unless there's something else you want to work on?"

"You mean… Like a regular lesson?" Jess wasn't sure what she'd been expecting. Tennis lessons were part of the plan. But for $250 an hour, they should come with something special. Like a physics lecture. Poetry reading. Or maybe a super-hot millennial telling her over and over that if she belonged to him, he wouldn't want to share her with the world.

"Relax, Jess. It's a place to start. The more organic this feels to you, the more authentic it will seem to your husband."

Parker shouldered his bag and led her through the back gate of the court and tossed his stuff on the bench next to the court. "Are you ready to serve?"

"Sure. I have to warn you; my serve is pretty awful. Carras has tried to help me a few times, but I haven't gotten very far."

He studied her, sizing her up. "It's your shoulders. You're holding a lot of tension there. I can see it from here. Come on."

He led her to the well-worn spot behind the serving line, where the green surface was brown with use. "Show me."

Jess felt shy and exposed. Odd, considering this was the most innocuous part of the whole scheme. Of all the things she'd worried about over the last few days—humiliation, divorce, her mug shot on the local news—having her tennis serve scrutinized wasn't one of them.

No sooner had she extended her arm with the ball in her hand than Parker stopped her, hands on her shoulders. "Yep. It's all this tension. Your arms should be in a straight plane when you start, to create a fluid motion. But you look like a lowercase *M* with these hunching shoulders. No wonder you can't get any momentum."

Without warning, he pressed his thumb into a surprisingly tender muscle between her shoulder blade and neck. Jess winced. Parker kept continual pressure on the spot while she whistled through her teeth.

"Tell me about your husband."

"I beg your pardon? Ouch."

"I'm giving you something else to think about. Breathe in through your nose; picture the oxygen going to the spot where my thumb is. So, what's the deal? He travels a lot?"

"Yes. Mostly during baseball season, but he does some feature work, too. Local barbecue scene, music, that kind of thing."

"No other sports?"

"Sometimes he reports on other teams, but usually it's a human-interest angle. He played baseball himself; that's what he loves. He feels his knowledge of the other sports isn't deep enough to add anything."

Parker shifted the location of his thumb to the other side of her spine and began the process again. The place where he had been pressing felt tingly and sore, but looser.

"How often do you do this?" she asked, going with his theory of getting her mind off the pain.

"All the time. The deep tissue work on the pressure points really makes a difference."

"No, I mean, the…premium lessons. I had never heard of this until Delia explained it to me, but apparently it happens all the time, right under our noses." When he didn't answer, she added, "If you don't mind my asking."

He pressed harder. "It's okay to be curious. Breathe, Jess. Send oxygen to the spot. Give the muscles permission to let go."

She tried to do as he asked, envisioning little oxygen molecules floating in her bloodstream to the spot above her shoulder blade. She closed her eyes and inhaled deeply.

"Every client is different," Parker said. "But you'd be surprised how many people are living the American dream in abject loneliness."

Jess snorted and opened her eyes. "Abject loneliness?"

"Are you surprised that's the case, or surprised a big dumb athlete has the vocabulary to describe it?"

She contained her reaction immediately, helped along by the sharp increase in pressure against a nerve in her back. "Neither," she said. "Just an unexpected turn of phrase."

Parker's hand dropped and he came around to face her. He was so young, so confident. There was something familiar about his bearing, the casual wisdom of someone too young to know how little he knew. It reminded her, Jess realized with a start, of herself at that age.

"I'm going to put my hand on your shoulder, right above your chest. Is that okay?" All calm professionalism.

"Sure."

He put the heel of his palm against her pectoral muscle, between her breast and collarbone. With the other hand, he lifted her arm and pulled it toward him, stretching. It felt amazing. Maybe this *was* worth $250 an hour.

"To answer your question. On any given week, about half my clients are doing standard tennis lessons, and half are doing the more flexible premium sessions. For those clients, I show up when they need me. I listen. If they want to play tennis, we play tennis. If they want to have coffee and talk about the challenges of marriage and raising families, we do that. If they need something physical…" He made a tiny circle against her collarbone with his thumb and Jess felt an involuntary thrill. "I can do that too. I think people—women especially—like to have someone in their life who will consistently do things on their terms."

"Basically, you're a really hot therapist."

He laughed and switched hands, to stretch her other side. "How many therapists do you know who will unknot your shoulders for you?"

"Fair point." She sighed with the pleasant burn of her muscles.

"A therapist is a much more formal relationship, right? You have to go to their office and sit and be vulnerable each week, whether you want to or not. Therapists have medical treatment plans, and books that label people and put them in boxes. My clients don't need that. Or at least, they don't need it from me."

He released her arm and let it float down to her side. "I'm here to help you, Jess, with whatever you need. You're in the driver's seat. I am here to do whatever makes you comfortable."

Was it Jess's imagination, or had he stepped closer? She felt warm and relaxed, a little heady. "I think what I need right now is some water."

His smile was slow and sexy as it lit up his features, his voice deep when he answered, "That can absolutely be arranged."

She turned on wobbly knees, feeling his presence behind her like a flame. No wonder women were lining up and pawning their jewelry for this guy.

They sat on the bench, Jess pounding water as though she'd actually been playing tennis for the last fifteen minutes, rather than letting a hot twenty-something massage her tense muscles. Parker sat amiably next to her, unhurried, companionable. She couldn't figure out what to make of this guy, or how to take the next steps toward what she really wanted: for *Tom* to look at her with that same confident innocence as this virtual stranger.

Parker stood and stretched next to her; over his shoulder, Jess saw Maizy Henriksson standing on the café patio up the hill, staring at them.

"Oh, crap."

"What? Your husband already?" Parker took a step closer and put a hand on her shoulder.

"No, almost as bad. It's Maizy Henriksson. Our resident busybody."

He turned and waved exuberantly up at Maizy, a huge smile on his face. "Oh, hello dear," he said in a mock-little old lady voice. "Nothing going on in your own life? Spying on everyone else?"

A startled Maizy waved back, tentatively.

Jess did the same, and turned to pick up her racket. "Guess it's time to get back out there."

"Your wish is my command." Parker grinned.

"You serve." She tossed a ball at him, more confident than she'd felt twenty minutes ago. "Show me how it's done."

As they rallied the ball back and forth, Parker paused to serve each time, explaining the correct form. But Jess had a hard time listening. In some ways, Maizy seeing them here was as dangerous as Tom would've been. The PTA president and mother extraordinaire—with her super-hot Scandinavian husband and adorable, well-mannered children who probably never choked on their food and threw up all over the lunch table—seemed to know everything that went on in their community.

Maizy and Delia had both lived in the subdivision longer than Jess, and their daughters were close in age, which might have made them natural friends. But they had never seemed to click. Delia didn't talk about it other than to roll her eyes and say, "That woman, I swear."

Jess didn't mind Maizy, particularly. The woman was awkward sometimes, and her excellence at all things kid- and school-related was annoying. It probably didn't help, Jess thought as she swiped at and missed Parker's next serve, that Maizy was the picture of everything Jess had failed to become as a parent.

While Jess would career into the school on two wheels, simultaneously shoving a half-eaten bagel into Dash's mouth while trying to de-knot Mina's ponytail, wishing she'd accepted the reality that they were going to be tardy sooner so she could have at least changed out of her pajama pants before walking into the school…Maizy would be standing by the front desk in full makeup, wearing a beatific smile as though she'd been placed in that spot specifically to welcome tardy, disorganized mothers. It was completely unfair for Jess to resent Maizy's genetic predisposition for super-parenting and school involvement. And to be fair, she had always been nice to Jess. But there was something perfect and smug about Maizy Henriksson. And her perfect, smug brownies.

As she and Parker played, Jess discreetly watched Maizy on the patio. She was hovering at one of the bistro tables closest to the tennis courts, looking at her phone, perhaps waiting for someone. But as Jess's first hour with Parker came to an end—with him

standing behind her, moving her arms in a perfect serve motion—
Maizy seemed to tire of waiting, and left by the side stairs to the
parking lot. Something about this made Jess feel guilty and uneasy, even though she'd done nothing wrong. (Unless you counted
drastically overpaying for tennis lessons.)

The rest of her time with Parker went by quickly. He was funny, a natural teacher. He had a way about him that put Jess at
ease, made her forget the weird situation. They worked on several
strokes; the session ended with Parker directing her to sit in front
of him while he rolled his knuckles back and forth across her tense
shoulders.

Eyes closed in bliss, Jess wondered whether she would have the
courage to use this man—*boy, really*—the way she planned. *There
had to be another way to revitalize her marriage…* Parker changed his
grip, opening his hands to massage her shoulders. The way a lover would. The way Tom used to. Jess sat up straighter, the change
making her nervous.

"Relax. Enjoy your time." Parker's voice was husky. "That's all
any of us can do, right?"

Time with Parker? Or time on the planet? Solid advice either way.
She tried to obey, letting herself lean into his strong hands. As he
worked the muscles on either side of her neck, Jess let out a small,
involuntary groan.

"Atta girl," he coaxed.

"You're amazing," she said. *Two minutes left.*

"You deserve amazing." He worked back down her neck,
around her collarbone, and the pectoral muscles he'd helped her
stretch earlier. His touch was perfect, slow, gentle circles of light
pressure. It was not specifically sexual, and yet she felt her body
responding to the touch, nipples hardening. She flushed with pleasure and a hint of embarrassment; they were still very much in
public. *One minute.*

He pulled her gently back against his knees, hands resting firmly on her shoulders. His voice in her ear was deep, seductive. "As a
therapist would say, I'm afraid our time is up." She moved to stand,
but he stilled her with his hands. "Don't get up. Give yourself a
minute to relax."

She did, feeling the loss of his presence behind her as he stood to get his bag. She fought the urge to jump up and follow him out, to let all the day's stressors back in. But he was right; she needed to relax more, and sitting here for three minutes wouldn't hurt anyone. Besides, with the way he just made her feel, Jess wasn't sure she could face him.

Behind her, he leaned down. "By the way, relaxation becomes you. You make the sexiest noises, just having your shoulders rubbed. Your husband is a damn lucky guy."

Even after hearing his footfalls, the gate open and close, after the sounds of his Jeep starting up and the rub of tires on pavement…she could still feel his breath on her neck, hear his compliment echo through her. It was like the reverberation of speakers after a loud concert, staying with her long after the source of the sensation was gone.

It was an old feeling, this sense of heading into uncharted waters. The terrifying thrill of something new and scary, of taking a risk. She had not felt it in so long: the gleeful stomach drop each time she held a positive pregnancy test; the sense on her wedding night that her whole life had been wonderfully and irrevocably changed; the feeling she used to get entering a new country—a new stamp on her passport. It had been awhile, but she recognized the intake of breath on the precipice of adventure.

This was going to be trouble.

12

DELIA

GAGE CAME HOME FROM BELGIUM at almost eleven that night. Delia was sitting at the kitchen table with a glass of wine, staring at a magazine open to the same page for almost half an hour.

The girls were in bed; it had been a long afternoon of shuffling between Girl Scouts, cheerleading, and soccer. They'd been forced to get dinner from the Chick-fil-A drive-through at 8:30, and still both girls had homework afterward.

Delia had floated through the evening, unable to keep her focus trained for very long. She'd forgotten she was snack mom at Lulu's soccer game and had to make an emergency run to the nearest gas station, dropping fifty dollars on individual Nutri-Grain bars and bottles of PowerAde. She'd had to wipe the dust from the bars and peel off the individual price tags before distributing them to the team. Later, she let Sadie skip half her English outline and promised to write a note of excuse the next morning.

It wasn't like Delia. She wasn't one of those moms—what were they called? Helicopter parents?—who constantly made excuses for her children and bargained with teachers to make life easier. But she loved that at fourteen, Sadie was still into both cheerleading and Girl Scouts, so Delia was willing to accommodate both schedules. Eventually, middle school social pressure would force Sadie to choose between them. There wasn't much overlap between the girls who cheered and chattered and wore bows in their hair, and the girls who still wanted to sell cookies and go camping. If it had been Delia, she already would've dropped scouting, to be honest. The hideous uniforms alone…

Still, there was something lovely and little-girl about her eighth-grader who worked her tail off for every badge, as hard as she worked on herkies and splits. She could catch up on English later.

"Hello, gorgeous." Gage dropped his oversized suitcase at the doorway to the kitchen and hung a garment bag on the hinge. "Any wine left in that bottle? I'm beat."

He took the seat across from her as Delia rose to fetch another wine glass. She kissed the top of his head as she set it down in front of him. "Hungry? Or did they feed you on the flight?"

"I'm fine. How are the girls?"

"Same as always. Sadie's still Overachiever of the Year. Lulu is going to need a soccer scholarship to get to college. Assuming she doesn't fail out of fourth grade."

Gage set down his glass. "She's not having problems with that teacher again?"

"I'm not sure the problem is entirely with the teacher. She's doing poorly in math now, too, and she goes to a different teacher for that." Delia crossed to the pantry for a sleeve of crackers, and began arranging them on a plate with some cheese and olives. He'd said he wasn't hungry, but Gage generally wanted something when he got off the plane. Besides, she needed an excuse to break eye contact. "They're saying she doesn't listen. She's very bright…"

"Of course, she's bright," he said.

"But she's missing key directions because she's talking in class."

"Well, at least she's developing socially. So many kids these days don't know how to interact. They spend too much time on screens and online."

Delia thought of sweet Lulu, with her auburn braids and freckles, laughing with her teammates on the soccer field. Technology or not, he was right about their youngest daughter's social skills. That said, Delia thought there was more to the story.

"True… But the feedback I got from Mrs. Marsh today was that Lulu is becoming increasingly defiant when they call her on being too chatty. She talks back, questions the rules, gets snotty about their authority. She does it with me, too."

"Leadership. Questioning authority is a mark of genius. You've said it yourself—well-behaved women rarely make history. Right?"

"I agree. And the teachers all seem to really like Lu…" She set the plate of hors d'oeuvres in front of him, trying to think how to diplomatically word what Mrs. Marsh had said.

"What's not to like?" Gage gave Delia's round bottom a squeeze. "She's beautiful and charming, and knows her own mind. Like her mother."

Delia smiled. It was nice—after several days of worrisome feedback about Lulu's behavior—to hear her so unequivocally defended. Gage was saying, in large part, what Delia had been thinking. But she also sensed he was less concerned about the repercussions of Lulu's "leadership skills" than she was.

It was true, Delia had gotten by on 30% competence and 70% charm for most of her short-lived academic career. But things were different now, and she wanted both her girls to have a more substantial education than Delia had, wanted them to have marketable skills so they would never have to rely on anyone. Hard skills that no one could question, on top of charm and the ability to sell, which they were likely to inherit from both their parents.

Was it okay that Lulu was already showing signs of defiance at school? That hadn't been Delia's style, even during her "troubled" teenage years. Gage talked a big game now, with the cavalier attitude of a successful man, mid-success. But something told her he would not have been so bold as to question a teacher's authority in fourth grade. Hell, Gage had been—as his mother never failed to remind her— a straight-A student, even at the very competitive prep school he attended almost from birth.

On the other hand, kids were different now. When either of the girls had friends over to visit, for example, no one called her Mrs. Cargill, or treated her with the half-terrified reverence with which she was taught to view all adults. She was "Miss Delia" to most, "Delia" to some, and "Excuse me? Can I have a snack?" to a few others.

Delia didn't mind. She liked that things weren't as formal these days. She liked the idea that her daughters and their friends might see her as more of a peer, rather than a Maizy Henriksson type: chubby, aproned, decidedly uncool. Maybe if Delia made amazing cookies and volunteered at the school every week, she could walk down the hall with Starbucks for Mrs. Marsh and solve the whole thing in minutes. But long-term, there was only so much cookies could do. And if it came down to being cool, fun, approachable… Delia was willing to bet that as they navigated the teen years, her daughters would be more likely to confide their crushes and heartbreaks in Delia than Maizy's would. Not that it was a competition. Or anything.

Maizy's daughters were adored by all the teachers. Probably because, like their mother, they were sort of vanilla. Rule followers, teacher's pets. Nice enough, but could you really expect kids like that to be exceptional?

No, Gage was right. She watched him pick up his phone and thumb across the screen. Better to have the challenges of parenting high-spirited girls now, and watch them exceed expectations later. Delia certainly had. No one thought that Delia, growing up in a two-room house in the rural mountains of Gilmer County, would have a life like this one. A house like this one. A handsome, successful husband, who could've walked off the pages of GQ to eat crackers at her table. She had remade herself from nothing. That same strength was in her girls, whether they knew it or not.

"What?" Gage said. He was typing; Delia had been staring.

"Nothing. I'm glad you're home."

"I'm glad to be home. I still would rather you didn't lurk."

Embarrassed, she stood. "You must be thirsty. Would you like some water?"

"Sure." He didn't look up.

"Work stuff?" She tried to sound lighthearted, casual. As any wife would when her husband was texting at nearly midnight.

"It's Alana," he said. "Letting me know she made it home safely."

"Alana was traveling with you this week? Did you mention that?"

"Considering she's the lead on this project, it makes sense, don't you think?" There was a warning edge to his voice.

"Of course. You usually tell me who is on your trips. That's all."

"Delia."

"Forget it, Gage. I wasn't asking anything. Let's move on."

"We've been over this."

"I know. I'm just tired. Let's go to bed, okay?"

He smiled then, but he was typing on his phone again, so it was hard to tell who the smile was for. "Go ahead. I'll be up in a minute. I'm going to finish my wine."

She knew better. She honestly did. But something inside her wouldn't let sleeping dogs lie. Especially when the sleeping dog had been sleeping elsewhere for more than a week, while Delia settled for the cold, firm touch of her Pure Indulgences vibrator collection. All excellent, quality devices—hypoallergenic, and some of them waterproof for bathtub enjoyment. But after a long day holding everything together, negotiating with a tween and a fourth grader to get ready for bed, waiting for them to be soundly enough asleep that they wouldn't hear the buzzing noises…battery-powered lovers were limited consolation.

She moved toward him, careful not to look at the phone, and picked up his wineglass. "I'll be happy to help you finish," she purred, the way he used to love. She took a sip of his wine and, gracefully as possible, straddled his lap so that he was forced to move the phone aside. "And if you're very well-behaved, I might even finish *you*."

"Babe. I've been up for twenty-four hours."

"Then come to bed and let your wife take care of you. Work will be here in the morning."

"It's not that simple. You know how it is with my trips… There's always something I have to take care of right when I get home."

Just like that, her attempt at seduction turned to humiliation. Delia realized too late that there was no graceful, kitten-like way to slide off your husband's lap with a full glass of red wine and a kitchen table pressing into your back.

It didn't help that Gage was looking at her with a mixture of annoyance and pity. He put his free hand lightly on her hip, patting her like a horse. "Tomorrow night. Promise."

This made it worse. Made her angry. To not want her now was bad enough; to offer her a consolation prize, to commit to loving her with the same enthusiasm he might resolve to go to the gym in the morning… It was infuriating. It was insulting. As if she were an unpleasant chore.

What made her angriest, however, was that she found herself

clinging to that promise of tomorrow, even as her pride rejected the very idea.

"It's all right, darling," she mustered as she disentangled herself from his lap. "To be honest, I'm exhausted myself. I just thought you might appreciate a warm welcome. From *home*." She glanced significantly at his phone, refilled her wineglass, and made her way upstairs to run a hot bath.

13

MAIZY

MAIZY HELD THE PLASTIC CONTAINER against her chest, staring down at the straw "Ramblin' Wreck" welcome mat at her feet. The right half of the words were worn off where people had gone in and out, so that it said "Ram Wre." Maizy resisted the temptation to remove a twig embedded in the mat at an awkward angle. *Someone could trip.* With Maizy's luck, it would be her—falling on her face as she left Jess's today would be the perfect ending to this misadventure.

The thought struck her: *did the Rodriguez kids have nut allergies?* She'd read a story online about a girl who died after eating off a plate that had once had a peanut butter sandwich on it. Why had Maizy chosen peanut butter chip brownies at the last minute? She should have played it safe. She shouldn't be here at all. These women didn't like her. Jess was the friendliest of the three, but with Delia Cargill in the mix, there was no way Maizy would break in to their girls' club.

But she had already rung the damn doorbell.

Just as she was contemplating high-tailing it back to her car ("ding-dong ditch," the neighborhood boys still called it), Jess Rodriguez came to the door in faded Georgia Tech athletic shorts and a white T-shirt with a coffee stain, brow furrowed in confusion. "Hi, Maizy. Everything okay?"

She thrust the Tupperware forward. "I baked you some brownies. They have peanut butter chips in them, though." She pulled the brownies back, giving the comical appearance that she was teasing Jess with brownies. Like the weirdest bully ever. "Your kids don't have allergies, do they?"

Jess shook her head, not reaching for the container. "This is… kind of you, Maizy."

Better to get to it. "Can I come in? Are you busy?"

Jess stood aside, one hand reaching unconsciously for a necklace she wasn't wearing. "Is everything all right?"

Maizy didn't answer, but followed Jess to the kitchen. She opened the brownies and set them on the table, next to a pile of papers—kids' artwork, bills, flyers about school events. Maizy recognized some of these, having printed them herself: The familiar scalloped borders on lavender paper advertising the spring fling at the end of the year. The bright-orange reminder that all library books had to be returned to the media center by May 15.

Jess turned on the Keurig. "Coffee?"

"Please. Thanks for offering."

Neither of them spoke as they waited for the motorized sound of the coffee brewing. Jess leaned against the counter, waiting for Maizy to speak.

"I don't know exactly what's going on," Maizy said, as Jess set the cup down in front of her. She steeled herself and the words came out in a rush. "I know you and Delia and Carras are up to something."

"Beg your pardon?"

"I think it has something to do with that tennis coach. That Parker kid."

The color drained from Jess's face, even though her neighbor didn't so much as twitch.

"I've heard rumors about him," Maizy went on. It turned out that being president of the PTA and overseeing had its benefits, as did being the quiet kind of person people often dismissed. Maizy often found herself sitting in the corner of a booth at some chi-chi cafe, typing up meeting minutes while three or five other women forgot she was there and began gossiping indiscriminately.

"I don't know what you're talking about." The tremor in Jess's voice, however, said otherwise.

Maizy allowed herself to enjoy it, for a split second. The fear in Jess's eyes, the giddy power she felt putting it there. "Don't worry. I have no intention of telling anyone what you're up to."

"I'm not…*up* to anything, Maizy." Jess straightened, the initial shock fading.

Maizy's window was closing—the last thing she wanted was for Jess to feel defensive. She leaned forward, put a hand on Jess's arm. "I don't want to cause problems. I…" She hesitated. Once she said it, there would be no going back. "I want in."

"What?"

"I want you to introduce me, or whatever, to Parker."

There was a long silence as the two women eyed each other across the table. Finally, Jess sighed and reached for the biggest brownie. "Peanut butter chip, you said?" Then, taking a generous, gooey bite: "This is going to be the end of me."

14

CARRAS

CARRAS WAS SITTING ON HER back deck in the dark when Jess called that evening. She'd gone out to put the cover over Stuart's grill—rain was forecast for tomorrow—and ended up sitting in one of the cushioned chairs facing the grove of trees at the back of their fence line, listening to the sounds of evening falling around her. The crickets and cicadas began softly in the woods beyond their yard and the sound slowly rolled forward until the cacophony enveloped her. Stuart claimed he didn't even notice the noises of Georgia's nocturnal insects anymore, but Carras never tired of them. They sounded like an imaginary childhood to her, one in which both her parents were alive and they took vacations: camping, or to the beach.

When the phone buzzed on the chair beside her and Jess's name lit up the screen, it was full dark. She hadn't turned on the lights inside, and the stars were blocked by the cloud cover of tomorrow's impending rain.

"Hey, Jess." It took Carras a beat to adjust to the intrusion on her solitude. "What's up?"

"Can Delia and I come over? Are you busy?"

Carras checked the time. Eight o'clock. "Sure. Is everything okay?"

"Have you eaten? I have leftover mac and cheese I can bring. It's homemade."

On cue, Carras's stomach roiled with hunger at the mention of food. "Are you sure Tom won't mind? I know he loves your mac and cheese for lunch."

"He's leaving again in the morning. We'll be there in ten minutes."

The three of them sat at Carras's table once more, this time in the dim light of the recessed lighting in the kitchen, while Carras ate forkfuls of Jess's goopy, stringy macaroni with cut up sausages, and Delia tried hard not to look disgusted. Delia had been trying to adopt a vegan diet ever since Belinda Hayes-Currington had made her read *Skinny Bitch*, and of course she looked great. But Delia had always looked great, as far as Carras could tell, and she sure as hell didn't seem any happier for the effort.

"I'm thinking this could be a good thing," Jess said, as she finished relaying her conversation with Maizy that afternoon. "Maybe Parker would increase our discount or even lower the minimum hours he's charging us. It could take some pressure off."

"I don't trust her," Delia said. "She might be trying to get information to lord over us."

Not having a child at the school, Carras had scarcely interacted with Maizy Henriksson beyond waving hello as their cars passed going in and out of the neighborhood. But she knew Delia didn't like Maizy, though it wasn't clear why.

"I don't think so," Jess said. "I know she's not your favorite person, but she seemed sincere. It sounds like she and Anders have been growing apart, and when I explained our plan…"

Delia glared at Jess. "I still can't believe you told her everything."

"I couldn't help it. She already had a pretty good idea. And…" Jess paused, biting her lip. "Honestly, she seemed a little desperate."

"She's always fucking desperate," Delia said, a rare instance of cursing from her sweet magnolia mouth. It was like your house cat bursting into song. "Sorry, y'all. But that's who Maizy is. She wants to be a part of whatever she's not part of."

"Why are you so hard on her?" Jess said. "She's not that bad. A little awkward, maybe. But nice."

"That's just it. She's so perfectly nice, all the time. So…I don't know. Old-school maternal."

"Old-school maternal?" Jess laughed. "What does that even mean?"

"It's not enough for her to be a great mom to her kids; we all have to *see* her being a great mom. All the time. Why else do you think she got involved up to her elbows in the PTA? She couldn't stand to not be the center of attention."

Jess gave Delia a quizzical look. "You won't even have to spend time with her. We all have our separate time with Parker. Besides, now that she knows, I think we'd better help her out, or she might…."

Carras's chest tightened. "Would she report us to the police?"

"For what?" Delia snapped. "None of us are doing anything illegal with Parker. Prostitution is only illegal if you actually have *sex*."

Carras's heart thudded in her chest, and she had the sudden, intense fear that both women could read her thoughts. As if everything were written on her face.

But Jess was focused on Delia. "Did you look that up? In a law book?"

"Not technically," Delia admitted.

"We should help Maizy out." Jess switched to the singsong voice of a mother bribing a child with a treat. "I'll bet she would buy something from you at every Pure Indulgences party for the rest of time."

"That would be nice," Delia conceded. "I'm so close to being a Level Three Consultant… But it's not just being around Maizy that concerns me. It's the fact that she'll be *in*. She'll have power over us, and she'll be able to insert herself into our lives. Can you imagine her coming outside the next time we're on a walk? Or asking us to join the fifth-grade graduation committee? How the hell can we say no if she can ruin us with a few words to our husbands?"

"It sounds like she already knows that much," Carras offered. "I don't see that we have much choice."

With uncharacteristic disregard for the state of her hair and makeup, Delia lowered her head to the table for several beats, saying nothing. Carras exchanged a look with Jess. Delia seemed more upset about their venture including someone she didn't like than she was about the risk of contracting with a sex worker in the first place. Trust, Carras supposed, was a hard-won thing in Delia's life. She wasn't sure what she had done to earn it herself, or whether she was still riding on Jess's recommendation.

"I'll text Maizy and tell her to join us." Jess pat Delia's head, like a child who'd been teased on the playground. "It's our only option. This will all be worth it when we're comparing stories about how fantastic our sex lives are."

"Carras," Delia said into the table. "Do you have any hard liquor? I'm going to need it."

15

JESS

JESS STOOD IN FRONT OF her full-length mirror in the short black tennis dress with hot-pink piping down the sides (the cute, expensive kind no one seemed to wear to actually play tennis). She'd applied, removed, and reapplied her makeup three times. Pretty, but not too much.

She'd braided her long dark hair down either side, the way Tom liked, even though he always called her Pippi Longstocking. He never got tired of that joke, the same way he never got tired of saying, "I don't know, can you?" when the kids asked him if they could do something without using the proper phrase "May I." She smiled as she lifted her braids out to the side the way he always did. Funny how the things that irritated her the most about Tom were the things she missed when he wasn't here.

Despite the costume, she was not going to the tennis courts today. Parker was coming to pick her up in an hour, like a date. They were driving to some specialty tennis store he knew about, half an hour away in another of Atlanta's outer-ring suburbs. The premise of their trip was to get her a proper, top-end tennis racket. Then they'd happen to stop in a cafe, where he would take a selfie of the two of them having a great time, post it on Instagram and Facebook, and tag her. Tom, who was scheduled to come home tomorrow, would see it pop up in his feed and wonder...

"Delia, you have to come with me." Jess blurted out the words as soon as her friend had picked up the phone.

"For the last time, Parker is not a serial killer, Jess. If he wanted to murder you, he would've done it last week when he had his hands on your neck for that amazing massage I'm so jealous of. Quit worrying."

"I'm not worried about being murdered," Jess said. "Much."

Delia snorted.

"This needs to be subtler. It's out of character for me to go off with a man I barely know and let him post a picture of me. I want Tom to think I'm desirable, not desperate." There was more to it. Even after the shoulder massage on the tennis court, Jess had come away feeling guilty, as though she'd cheated on Tom simply by being there. And maybe, on some level Jess knew Delia wouldn't understand, she *had*.

"Jess, we've been over this…"

"I think it would be more realistic if the three of us were together and Parker leans too close to me in the picture or something. And…" she considered, "Tom would totally believe that I'd have cocktails at lunch if I were with you."

Delia was quiet.

Jess could tell she had her on the hook with the mention of cocktails. "I'll buy lunch. It's the least I can do after Maizy…"

Her friend snorted again. Jess knew Delia was still irritated with her about Maizy, even though it wasn't Jess's fault. Still, she'd take the fall if it meant not having to get in a car with this guy alone.

"I have to be home by two," Delia said finally. "Lulu has soccer practice after school."

"Thank you, thank you, thank you," Jess gushed. "You won't regret it. You're so much better at this stuff than I am."

"Quit buttering me up. I've already agreed to it."

When Parker arrived, Jess noted with a surge of satisfaction that he looked confused (and perhaps a bit disappointed) to see Delia emerge behind her. "I brought reinforcements!" Jess called cheerily. "I know you're the tennis expert, but Delia can spot a bargain from a mile off. And I might need some clothes, too."

"Great." Parker smiled. He held open the door to his bright-yellow Jeep with gallantry that made him look both older and younger than he was. "My lady."

When Jess slid into the front seat and he'd closed the door behind her, he assisted Delia into the backseat from the driver's side. He did not, Jess noticed, call Delia "my lady."

"What's this?" Delia looked down at the backseat. She pulled up a long-stemmed rose, blood red and luscious. "This must be for you, Lady Jessica."

Jess glanced at Parker, whose jaw was clenched as he stared past Delia to back out of the driveway. "No big deal," he said. "A little token."

"Thank you."

"Well, I look forward to whatever token you have in store for me next week," Delia said, with a slight edge to her voice. "I'm not a rose girl, though, so you know. I prefer calla lilies."

"Every woman is different," Parker said. "You never know what you'll get."

He drove them out to the main road, then turned north until he found a long two-lane highway that ran east-west. "No one goes this way," he explained. "It takes a couple of extra minutes, but it beats sitting at red lights for half the time. Especially with the top open."

Wind whipped through the car as he drove, and Jess was glad she'd braided her hair. Delia had left hers down; it blew around and into her face as they progressed. Soon the sleek, blonde curtain Jess envied had become a rat's nest of multi-tonal chaos. When they stopped at a red light and Delia shifted to see the results in the mirror, she gasped. Jess had to restrain a giggle, followed by a mouthed apology.

Parker grinned. "In a Jeep, you can tell the indoor girls from the outdoor girls pretty quick." He put a hand on Jess's knee. "Outdoor girls aren't fussy about their hair; they're always ready for anything."

"I am not an 'indoor girl,'" Delia objected. "I just didn't realize a wind tunnel was on the agenda today."

Parker laughed. "I'm teasing, Delia. You look great." He lowered his gaze to Jess. "You both do."

Parker pulled into a small strip mall and parked in front of It's A Racquet! He assisted Delia out of the back while Jess hurried out on her own. She wasn't sure why she didn't want her door opened for her. She never minded when Tom did it.

The store was smaller than she'd imagined: not a warehouse like the golf outlets and sporting goods retailers she'd visited with

Tom. It was more like a gift boutique. Once her eyes adjusted, she saw it was packed with, not just shiny rackets and artful pyramids of balls, but high-priced tennis outfits in every color of the rainbow and accessories Jess had never imagined. Quilted racket covers and patterned tennis backpacks pricier than any purse Jess had ever owned. There were purses, too: in bold block colors, paired with tennis outfits on mannequins as though to demonstrate that you could go straight from the court to lunch with the girls or out to the mall.

"I hate to go anywhere straight from tennis," she said. "I always smell terrible."

"What's that?" Parker stood by the wall of rackets, hands behind his back like a general inspecting the troops.

"Nothing," Jess said hurriedly. "Verbal diarrhea."

Delia rolled her eyes.

"Parker!" The shop girl, a petite redhead with dark freckles everywhere, perhaps twenty-two, hustled up to them, hugging Parker and shaking hands with the two women. "Where have you been? We've missed you!"

Her name was Maddie, they learned as Parker explained the reason for their visit. Maddie had a new shipment of rackets in she wanted Parker to see. "They're in the stockroom, not even out yet. Otherwise, I'd invite you all back…"

"Sorry," he mouthed over his shoulder as Maddie led him away.

"It's fine," Jess mouthed back. It was funny, actually, watching self-assured Parker turn docile in the hands of such a tiny woman. She wondered whether they'd had a thing.

"Oh my God," Delia said, when the twenty-somethings were out of earshot. "He *likes* you."

Jess's face went warm. "He's being nice. I'm sure he's that way with all his clients."

"Bullshit," Delia said, her graceful Southern lilt elevating the word. "I'm his client, too, and I'm chopped liver next to you right now."

Jess couldn't tell whether Delia was impressed or offended. Maybe both.

"It's because this is my time," Jess assured her, picking up a pink and black racket from one of the many hooks on the wall. It looked as if someone had designed it as an accessory for the dress she was wearing. "I'm paying big bucks to have his full attention today. He'll fawn all over you next time."

Delia looked dubious but said nothing else. Parker emerged a few minutes later, grinning like a Cheshire cat, with Maddie beaming behind him.

"Okay, ladies. You have to promise to keep this a secret. Take it to your graves, okay?"

Jess and Delia glanced at each other and nodded.

"This is the new PowerForce Titanium 4000." He held up a sleek, slate-gray racket with almost no ornamentation. It was like one of those matte black credit cards for people who were so rich they'd left all the precious metal cards behind. Belinda Hayes-Currington was a matte black credit card kind of girl. "It's got a carbonite shaft, special alloy grip. It's not on the market for another, what…?"

"Next month," Maddie said. "Which is why you seriously can't tell anyone I sold it to you. The manufacturer will have my ass." She gave Parker a nervous look.

He elbowed her. "I told you, Maddie, these ladies are cool. Right, girls?"

Jess nodded dumbly. *We're cool. We can totally be cool.*

"They're good to keep secrets," he added, and Jess felt his eyes on her. That same delicious, dangerous feeling crept over her—the way she'd felt with Parker's hands on her neck.

"We are," Delia said flirtatiously. "Secrets are totally in our realm."

Our realm? What was she, queen of the fairies?

"Feel this." Parker handed Jess the racket. "See how ergonomic the handle is? It's designed to conform to your grip."

He moved behind Jess and positioned his hands over hers, putting her fingers in the proper position. His face was almost next to hers; his voice thrummed in her ear. "Just like that. Feel how it moves with you? Can't you imagine holding that all day and never getting tired?"

Delia coughed.

Maddie looked confused.

Jess ignored them both. "I can't even imagine how expensive

this is."

"It will be $299 when it goes on sale next month," Maddie said.

Jess released the racket from her grip. "Well, then, I hope the new owners enjoy it!"

Parker made a pouting face, which Jess had to admit was pretty endearing, even if it did remind her a little of Dash when he wanted something.

"I can't spend that kind of money on…" Jess trailed off. Finances were not the most comfortable topic at the moment.

Maddie reached for the racket. "Honestly, I shouldn't sell it early anyway," she said. "I thought since we've known each other so long…"

"I'll buy it," Delia said, and all three turned to look at her.

"It's the least I can do." Delia handed Maddie her credit card—platinum, not black, but still. "We'll take two of them."

Maddie took the card. Parker grinned at Delia. "Nicely done."

"Sometimes an indoor girl can be useful," Delia teased.

"I never said indoor girls weren't useful."

"Just wait." Delia arched a pretty eyebrow at him. "You have no idea."

She flounced off to the cash register, and Parker gestured for Jess to go before him. She couldn't help but notice, however, that he was now watching Delia. And even though she hadn't wanted extra attention from him—had wanted desperately to deny it—now that it was no longer on her, she felt a twinge of jealousy. An irrational desire to win back the light in Parker's eyes.

16

JESS

B Y THE TIME THEY REACHED the cafe, with $600 worth of sure-to-be-underused rackets in a bag in the back of Parker's Jeep, Jess had hold of her senses again. While Delia and Parker chattered about tennis form and equipment, Jess let herself zone out. She laid her head back against the seat and let the sun shine on her face as they drove, feeling the pleasant sensation of the breeze beating against her face.

A memory flooded back, swift and fleeting. She needed to name it before it disappeared. "Have I ever told you that I once worked as a waitress in a nightclub on Santorini?"

There was stunned silence from her two companions. Jess wondered whether she'd interrupted their conversation without realizing it.

"Um, no," Delia said. "I don't think you have. Was that while you were hitchhiking through Europe?"

"I didn't hitchhike." Jess opened her eyes and turned to Parker, who looked interested. "At least not most of the way. It was the summer before my junior year in college. I worked at this nightclub—it was a pub, I guess—they served food all day and in the evening they turned down the lights and put on techno music. It was owned by these two brothers... Oh, God, what were their names?"

"Anyway," Delia prompted.

"Anyway. I got there after hiking through Italy, almost out of money, so I stayed in this super-cheap hostel next door to the nightclub. But someone stole my traveler's checks—I had like

$200 left at that point—so I had to find a job to pay for my lodging and the ferry ride back."

Delia wrinkled her nose. "You were stranded in a foreign country and became a waitress at a nightclub? Isn't that dangerous?"

Jess laughed. "You're making it sound so seedy. Santorini is mostly tourists. It's a beautiful island with beaches and those cool buildings with the blue domes."

"I've seen those!" Parker said.

"Right? The customers were mostly kids like me, traveling, partying, hoping to meet other people who spoke English to hang out with for a while. I served drinks and made people comfortable and got huge tips from American guys who couldn't do the currency conversions right. It was a fun job."

"I still can't believe you started working for some random Greek dudes to pay your bills. It's like washing dishes in a restaurant because you can't pay for your meal."

"It was either that or call my parents for money, cut my trip short, or both. My dad would've made me pay him back if he'd had to wire money anyway." Jess sighed, remembering how free she'd felt then, the whole world open to any possibility her heart could imagine.

"Sounds like an adventure," Parker said. "And now for another. We're here."

There was not much special about Toro's, the Mexican place Parker had chosen, other than its proximity to the tennis store and its rooftop bar on what was turning out to be a lovely day. Still, it held the promise of tacos, tequila, and a perfect setting for Instagram glory.

They settled themselves at a shiny metal table in the corner, Parker in the middle and Jess and Delia at his flanks. He ordered chips, salsa, and guacamole for the table, plus a light beer for himself. When Jess said she'd stick with water, Delia rolled her eyes. "I thought the whole idea was to let Tom know you're capable of having a life without him. How are you going to do that if you're drinking water with your collar buttoned up to your chin?"

Jess reached for the collar of her tennis dress reflexively, where two of the three buttons were fastened. Maybe Delia had a point. "I am not trying to let Tom know I can have a life without him.

I'm trying to remind him how fun our life is *together*."

"Two skinny margaritas," Delia told the waiter. "No salt." She pushed back her chair. "I'm going to the girls' room. You two figure out what we're doing." And she sashayed away, slender hips swinging to the beat of her own soundtrack, as always.

Parker watched her go. "Your friend sure has personality."

"She does," Jess agreed. "It's rare that she doesn't get her way."

"I could see that. I've known a lot of women like her...like you guys, in my time. And she's one of the spunkiest."

"Really?" Jess was surprised. "What about Belinda?" She thought of Belinda's unquestioning confidence, the nonchalance with which she allowed her husband and lover to meet over sangria at the club.

Parker gave her a look. "You know I'm not going to talk about other clients. I *will* say that most women call me because they don't have that spunk anymore, or the confidence to show it off the way they used to." He leaned closer. "They need someone to remind them how amazing they are."

Jess couldn't help shifting toward him. "They do?"

He touched her chin, expression too wise and knowing for his young face. Jess had the terrible urge to giggle.

"And you know what else? Delia is right about one thing."

"She is?"

He let his hand drift down her throat. Jess swallowed and felt goose bumps prickle her skin at the touch. Parker reached for the middle button on her open collar and unbuttoned it, never breaking eye contact. "Better."

The clearing of a throat brought their attention to the waiter, who held a tray with drinks and a basket of chips and salsa. Delia stood a few feet behind him, smirking. Jess reeled backward and Parker laughed. "Relax, J-Rod. You didn't do anything...untoward."

J-Rod. Like A-Rod. Why did he have to make a baseball reference? It brought her mind right back to Tom, despite that she was still flushed from someone else's touch. *Ugh.* A guy who could almost be her son... *Double ugh.*

"So how are we doing this?" Delia seated herself delicately. She'd managed to get her hair back to perfect order.

"I don't…" Jess started to explain that she and Parker hadn't talked about the plan while Delia was gone, because they'd been… what *had* they been talking about?

"If I can make a suggestion?" Parker said. "Let's ask our server to take a picture of us when he comes back; I'll post it to all my social media accounts, and tag you, Jess? We'll all be in the picture, but I'll be sure to lean your way." He grinned. "I'll pretend I like you."

Jess felt herself go red again. *He liked her.* Delia was right. Why did that matter? It didn't matter. But he liked her. *Oh, damn, damn, damn.*

Like all the best spur-of-the-moment candid photos, it took several minutes to set up. Delia stood in the waiter's position with Parker's phone and coached the other two on arranging the chips, beer bottle, and margarita glasses so that they appeared to best effect. She insisted that Parker keep his arm around Jess's shoulders ("for composition purposes"). Jess tried very hard to neither lean too hard into him, or flinch from his touch.

Before the waiter could capture this perfectly orchestrated scenario, however, he emerged with their food order and they had to start the process over to accommodate plates of tacos and enchiladas. Finally, the waiter returned and agreed to take the picture with Parker's phone. "Can you take three or four, please?" Parker said.

One, two, three… Jess smiled, and he squeezed her shoulders so tight that she thought she might fold in on herself. "Lean forward," Delia hissed. "Show off your cleavage."

One, two, three… big cheesy grin, this time with Parker's hand relaxing closer to her neck. Less strenuous, but more intimate.

One, two, three… as Jess gave her best "having a blast with friends" smile, Parker kissed her on the cheek. Surprised, Jess pulled back to face him, and *one, two, three…* Parker, rat bastard, kissed her on the mouth.

It wasn't long or passionate, and later Jess would rationalize that she hadn't had time to pull away. When she put her hand on his chest to push back, she heard Delia saying "Well," over and over. *Well, well, well…*

Jess stared at Parker, but he turned away, collecting his phone from the waiter with casual gratitude. He grinned when he felt her looking at him. "What? Too much?"

"I should think so," Jess said, not sure why she sounded like an eighty-year-old schoolteacher all of a sudden.

He looked sheepish. "Guess I got carried away." He pulled up the photo; both Jess and Delia leaned in to get a closer look. Jess couldn't remember the last time she'd seen herself in a kissing picture. *Her wedding?* She hated her profile, but other than that it wasn't the worst picture of herself she'd ever seen: the braids framing her face and black dress against her light-olive skin. And that was the totally, exact wrong thing to be thinking while looking at a picture of yourself kissing another man.

"You look good," Delia said.

"I won't post this one," Parker said. "If you don't want."

"No, I don't *want*." Jess fumed. "The idea is a hint of jealousy, not grounds for divorce."

"So, I'll delete it?" His finger hovered over the trash can in the corner.

Jess stared at the picture. There was a little thrill of excitement in her belly seeing herself like that—ogling her own image the way she would a celebrity in the tabloids. *God, Parker was photogenic.* Nothing wrong with *his* profile. "Yes. Delete. Please."

Parker tapped the screen. "Shame," he said. "It's a great picture."

The screen filled with the previous shot, in which Parker was kissing Jess on the cheek. It might have been cute—still a little edgy for Jess's tastes—except that one of her eyelids was half-lowered so that she looked drunk, even though less than an inch had disappeared from her margarita. "Delete," she said, and Parker clicked obediently.

The picture before that one turned out to be pretty perfect. They were all three looking at the camera, smiling over their festive frozen drinks and plates of delicious-looking food. Parker's hand was on Jess's shoulder, somewhere between the friendly drape of a casual acquaintance and a more intimate touch. Intriguing, yet defensible.

"Nope," said Delia. "I look pasty."

"You look *fine*." Jess was trying not to sound exasperated.

"Let's check out the first one," Delia said.

Parker swiped to the first picture. Jess could see little difference in Delia's skin tone, but the interaction between herself and Parker looked more stilted. His hand was farther out on her shoulder, his smile glossier. *The more organic this feels to you, the more authentic it will seem to your husband.*

As if on cue, her phone buzzed with a text from Tom. *Change of plans. Have to stay another couple days in Cleveland.* He was supposed to be returning now, had promised to pick up the kids on his way home. *Can u get kids or should I text your mom?*

He had waited until he was supposed to be well on his way to let her know. Surely, he'd been notified before this moment—otherwise he'd have gone to the Cleveland airport three hours ago and be in the air now. She was annoyed, but not enough to have her mother buzzing around, cleaning up Jess's kitchen as though a few pieces of the kids' artwork and permission slips lying around were proof that she was the most disorganized mother on the planet.

I'll get them, she texted back, pushing away her barely touched margarita.

You're the best. You can have the day off Thursday. ☺

Thursday did her no damn good. Jess hadn't paid $750-plus for professional company and margaritas on Thursday. Not that Tom knew this. And if he did, he'd be rightfully pissed. But knowing she was in the wrong didn't entirely cancel out Jess's irritation.

Fine.

Love ya, Gardner.

U 2.

She turned back to Parker and Delia, who were bent over the phone, swiping back and forth, zooming in and out.

"This one." Jess pointed to the second picture, the one that looked most authentically flirty. "Sorry, D, but it's my day, and I need this."

Delia sat back and tossed her hair. "I suppose I can be pasty online for the sake of your marriage."

They ate, discussing the caption Parker would use to post the picture to Instagram and Facebook. He typed it and the three of them discussed how to word it just right—flirty and innocent, but ripe with possibility. It reminded Jess of being with her girlfriends in high school, rehearsing what she was going to say to the cute boy in her geometry class the next day.

In the end, they decided on: *Best part of the job: hanging out with lovely ladies like these two!* Parker added a series of emojis that included cocktails, tennis rackets, and something that Jess assumed was supposed to be a relaxed smiley, white-gloved hands splayed out behind its head.

As they ate, she watched the icy margarita melt and separate, until the frost had run off the glass and it was nothing but lime-green liquid with a layer of salty foam on top. She wondered when Tom would check Instagram or Facebook and see that she'd been tagged, and what his reaction would be. Angry? Curious? Aroused?

Jess checked several times, but there was no further communication from Tom during lunch. Even as they paid their bill and descended to the main floor exit, she wasn't sure which response she was hoping for.

17

JESS

IT TURNED OUT THAT TOM'S reaction was irritatingly neutral. He saw the picture later that evening and "liked" it on
Facebook. Jess discovered this after she'd put the kids to bed and
sat alone in their bedroom, refreshing her phone and thinking of
all the other ways she could've spent $800.

Now, she was watching reruns of *The Big Bang Theory* and
drinking herbal tea, as close to self-indulgence as she was going to
come tonight. She checked her phone constantly, waiting for Tom
to expound on his "like" of the picture, or at least text her.

It was eleven thirty when he called. "Sorry, babe. Long day. Joe
decided he wants some kind of retrospective on franchises who
are beloved losers, so I had to put in a couple of extra days here to
get interviews."

"That's fine." Jess yawned.

"I hope I didn't ruin your day."

"It's fine." She flipped the channel on the muted TV. Her irritation with Tom and fascination with Parker were both being
overshadowed by the need for sleep.

"I, uh…saw on Facebook that you were out with friends this
afternoon," he said cautiously.

Jess sat up. *Here it was.* She had to be careful, like reeling in a fish
the way her grandfather had taught her years ago.

"It was a last-minute thing. I had a tennis lesson; Parker said
Delia and I both needed new rackets. We ended up shopping and
running out for lunch afterward." It all came out in a rush. Jess
cringed; she sounded too rehearsed. "No biggie."

No biggie?

"Parker said you needed a new racket?"

She tried to sound dispassionate. "Yeah, something about the titanium frame and an ergonomic handle. He said it would improve my game."

"There's nothing wrong with your tennis game, is there?"

"Well…" This was not the part of her afternoon she'd been prepared to defend. "I figured since I'm taking the lessons, I should go ahead and invest in the equipment, too. Right?" She decided not to mention that Delia had purchased the racket for her. Keep it simple.

"I thought you were just playing socially. Last year you said you were getting tired of tennis." Tom sounded more alert than he had in their conversations for the last several days. He hadn't asked this many questions about either of the kids' school days.

"I'm getting back into it, I guess. Maybe after playing with Carras the other day, or meeting Parker…" She trailed off, waiting.

"Did you change your mind about that tournament next season?"

"I haven't decided." She wanted to redirect the conversation back to the picture. Who cared about *tennis*? "I'll see what Parker thinks after we work on my ground strokes."

Tom was quiet.

Jess went in for the kill. "Parker has been super helpful. Did I already ask if you've heard of him?"

"Yeah. I hadn't."

"He thinks I could play at a higher level. Maybe even join ALTA at B or A level."

"I told you that years ago; I thought you didn't want to play organized tennis."

She tried to sound casual. "You did? I don't remember."

It was working. She couldn't believe it. It was like that moment in high school physics when they hooked the alarm clock up to the potato, knowing exactly what was going to happen, and still feeling flabbergasted that it worked.

"What kind of fancy racket did you get?"

Shit. She couldn't even remember. "The something-something Titanium 4000?"

"The new PowerForce? Are you serious? Aren't those things like crazy expensive?"

"They're not even out yet. Parker has an in with someone at the tennis store, so he worked it out for us."

She waited for his reaction. *Come on, Tom. Ask me about Parker. Tell me you're coming home tomorrow instead of Thursday. Tell me you love me, miss me. Ask me why a twenty-something tennis pro has his arm on my shoulder.*

"I guess I'm a little surprised."

Yes. Here it comes. Fight for me. Fight for us.

She made her voice nonchalant. "Oh?"

"You bought a new racket without me. And you didn't go to Doug's Sporting Goods. He's a fan of my work; he gives us a great discount."

Jess flopped back on the bed in frustration. As usual, Tom was missing the point. "I went with Parker and Delia, babe. I was going on his recommendation. He's kind of the expert."

"You could've told Parker about Doug's. He's better than those overpriced boutique stores and you know damn well he's fighting to stay in business."

Jess had no idea what to say. It had not once occurred to her that *where* she bought the overpriced racket before going to lunch with the cute guy would figure in to the jealousy scenario. And Tom didn't sound jealous at all. He sounded disappointed.

"I told you I was taking lessons, Tom. I went with what my coach recommended."

"It's not a big deal, I guess. I'm just surprised you forgot about Doug. It's not like you to follow these country club people to the trendy places."

"Country club people? It was *Delia*."

"You know what I mean. Doug is a friend. And you're the one who's always complaining about the extravagant lifestyle and the one-upmanship."

He had her there. Jess sighed. "I'm sorry."

She loved Doug; she loved supporting businesses that meant something to the community. She hated being trendy. And she'd violated all those rules today. Not to mention a few others.

She decided to give it one more shot, to redirect Tom's attention and not feel as if she'd wasted the day. "Did you at least like the picture? Did you see the braids?" She pitched her voice to sound cute and flirty. "Did I look okay?"

Tom's response was automatic. "You always look great," he said. "I keep telling you that you're too worried about how you look on Facebook. People spend too much time curating their online images instead of having real relationships."

"True." He was right, but it wasn't what Jess wanted to hear right now. Especially considering she'd curated an image specifically for him, to no effect.

"Listen, babe, I gotta get some sleep. They've set up an early interview tomorrow at this old lady's house. She's been to every Indians home game since 1966."

"That's interesting." No longer sleepy, Jess did not want the conversation to end, leaving her alone in a house with a muted TV and two sleeping kids.

"Hoping so." Clearly Tom had no interest in keeping the conversation alive.

"Well, okay. Call me tomorrow?"

"I'll try. There's a game tomorrow night and I'm supposed to be in the owner's box. I *will* pick up the kids Thursday afternoon, though. Promise."

"Tom?"

"Yeah?"

"I love you."

"You too. Goodnight, Gardner."

"Goodnight."

18

CARRAS

"WELL, THAT WAS A BIG, fat *nothing.*" Jess plopped down at her kitchen table. "Not only did it never *once* occur to my husband that he might have some kind of sexual rival, he shamed me for not supporting our friend's store. I'm going to have to go to Doug's next week and stock up on athletic socks and running shorts."

They were sitting in the Rodriguezes' kitchen, two days after Jess's ill-fated Instagram-Facebook project, around the coffeepot and pastry that was becoming their routine. Except this time the pastry was homemade, and even Delia was allowing herself to eat a normal human serving. Maizy Henriksson had joined them.

"Tom trusts you, Jess," Maizy said. "That has to be a good thing."

Jess looked sick. "Now I feel *worse*," she whined. "I can't do this anymore. I'm going to pay Parker for my five remaining hours and be done."

"Maizy, please." Delia's voice dripped with irritation.

Carras helped herself to a second slice of the pastry: some layered, buttery, iced thing Maizy had called "Scandinavian Kringler."

"Don't give up yet," Delia continued. "We'll think of something. In the meantime, I want to hear about Carras's plan. You've been so secretive."

Carras felt three pairs of eyes turn to stare at her, as she bit off a piece of the Kringler, the hard icing dangling from her lips. "Oomph," she said, trying to coax it gracefully into her mouth. "There's a conference in San Antonio next weekend I've been planning to attend, using sports in interventions with adolescents.

I realized that if Parker could come with me, we could—"

She stopped, feeling blood rush to her cheeks. "I think that would get Stuart's attention."

"Won't a whole weekend be expensive?" Jess asked. "Not that it's any of my business."

Carras nodded, thinking of her conversation with Parker when she'd called him the day before. "Yeah. But he's giving me a bulk rate—four thousand plus travel expenses. And that would be instead of my ten hours, so…it's still less than twice the minimum for the month."

"But… Why would Parker go with you?" Delia asked. "I mean, ostensibly?"

"We're going to say he's developing a tennis camp for kids with emotional issues, and I'm—consulting with him or something."

"That is such a good idea," Maizy said. "We should offer that through the school somehow." She sat up. "Wait. Maybe I can tie into that? Like maybe he and I will have meetings to talk about running it at the school through the PTA."

"But you're leaving the school," Delia said flatly. "You won't be the PTA president anymore."

Maizy shrugged. "So? I can still champion an idea, right? I still have influence."

Delia rolled her eyes.

Jess groaned. "I don't think we need to be sticklers about the PTA, Delia, since the tennis camp is *fake*. It's a pretense for everyone to hang around Parker so that their husbands notice, remember? There's not actually going to be any camp."

Delia looked abashed for the first time since Carras had known her. "I'm playing devil's advocate. Anders might ask the same question, you know."

"I'll figure that out," Maizy said. "Anyway, it's perfect because I was trying to think of a reason Parker would know me. I'm going to set it up so that we just happen to run into each other while I'm out with Anders for dinner one night."

"That's like, fifteen minutes of Parker's time," Delia said. "How are you going to meet the ten-hour minimum?"

Her tone indicated that she'd known all along Maizy was going to fail to live up to the requirements. Carras felt a little sorry for

Maizy, but she was glad the attention had turned from her.

"I'm going to do my ten hours all in one day," Maizy said. "I get nervous around new people; I think I should spend some time with Parker first. So it feels authentic when we bump into each other."

Delia looked as though she wanted to say something, but stopped herself. Carras took another sip of her coffee, feeling Jess's gaze on her.

"So, Delia," Maizy said after a brief silence. "I'm sure you have something spectacular and dramatic planned for your time with Parker?"

"She's having him text her." Jess smiled. "It's a texting affair."

"Gage is more likely to be upset by someone intruding on my time with him than..." Delia hesitated. "More conventional jealousy."

"Are you saying he wouldn't be upset if you sleep with someone else, as long as you do it on your own time?" Maizy asked. "I thought *my* marriage was messed up."

Delia's eyes blazed with anger. "Our marriage isn't *messed up*. It's just not something we ordered from a Pottery Barn catalog. We respect each other. Gage would never want me to stay home and bake pastries all day." She waved a hand over the Kringler pan.

Carras shifted in her seat. She had never been one for conflict—it was why she'd chosen adolescent therapy instead of marriage therapy—and it was clear something was brewing here.

"Delia," Jess said, cutting through the tension. "Maybe you should use some of your Parker hours and join Carras's trip. You could save her some money."

Carras looked at Jess, disbelieving.

"I couldn't do that," Delia said, even as her face lit up. "I've never left Gage with the girls for more than an evening. Besides, I wouldn't want to intrude on Carras's time."

Yes, Carras thought. *This is going to be hard enough without an audience.*

"Why not?" Jess was uncharacteristically pushy. "It's time Gage had some quality time with his daughters instead of leaving you at home. And Carras, you're going to this conference, right? Delia could keep Parker company while you're in sessions."

What could Carras say? *I don't feel as close to Delia as you do and don't want to turn this into a party? I'd rather have Parker to myself?* "I'm...not sure Stuart will get jealous if it's a group trip."

"Oh, come on. Stuart is even more oblivious than Tom. He's not going to get jealous from the trip alone, no matter who goes with you. You're going to have to hit him over the head with it. Delia might even be able to help."

On the one hand, Jess was right: Stuart was unlikely to be alarmed by much of anything Carras could do. On the other, she couldn't say that—unlike the other women—upsetting her husband wasn't part of Carras's plan. She had her own reasons for wanting to be alone with Parker Yung, and she was never planning to discuss those with anyone.

"It would be nice to get away," Delia said. "And Parker's texts would drive Gage crazier if he knew we'd been away together... Would you mind, Carras? I'll split Parker's fee with you, and I can help with Stuart..."

They were all looking at her, waiting. "Sure," Carras said, trying to sound upbeat. "That will be fun."

19

CARRAS

ONCE THE IDEA SUNK IN, Carras realized that Delia joining the trip solved many problems at once. They could consolidate their separate time with Parker for the month into one long weekend, sparing Carras some of the added expense. It gave the trip extra legitimacy, with Delia pretending to lend her planning skills to the tennis camp venture.

It also gave Delia direction on her quest to get Gage's attention, because so far she'd come up with nothing that would irritate him enough to matter. Privately, Carras thought Gage must be pretty damn patient if Delia was having such a hard time irritating him, but she never said so.

From there, it was simple enough to arrange. Carras registered for the conference, and booked plane tickets for herself and Parker—hers on the credit card she shared with Stuart, Parker's from the separate account with her tennis winnings. For his part, Stuart loved the idea of Carras using her background to help kids with special needs, which added to her shame. Maybe when all this was resolved, she would start a real camp like the fake one they'd created.

Carras chose a quiet hotel down the street from the conference, with an indoor pool and views of the Riverwalk. She reserved three rooms, requesting different floors for each of them: herself, Delia, and Parker.

Now, she stood alone in her room, having changed outfits three times, waiting for Delia to knock at the door. She'd booked Parker's flight a couple of hours behind theirs, partly to save money, and partly to avoid having to sit on a plane making conversation. This gave the women time to settle in and make last-minute preparations. The three of them were going to dinner tonight; the conference started tomorrow. Carras would attend all day, so Delia and Parker had the day to do their own thing; they'd meet back up in the evening.

Now that it was here, Carras found it oddly reassuring to know that Delia would be here with her this weekend. She was the least likely person Carras would've chosen as a friend: they had absolutely nothing in common. But Carras admired her savvy, and the way she thought quickly on her feet. Delia had a way of keeping her head above a situation. It reminded her, Carras realized with a start, of her father.

Technically, Carras had more in common with Parker—tennis careers, immigrant parents—but something about him unnerved her. In her "Parker Davis" research, she'd managed to find that he'd lost his scholarship at Vanderbilt for accepting money and gifts from boosters. It hadn't been a big enough scandal to get national attention, because the school had cooperated with the NCAA investigation and it was found that only Parker and a couple of individual boosters were involved. According to the news articles, he'd been offered the opportunity to stay enrolled at the school without his athletic scholarship, but declined. He played in a few tournaments independently but never made it very far. It explained why the tennis pro option was the logical next career move, but how he'd made the leap from there to high-end sex worker was less clear.

His story tugged at her heart, perhaps because it could so easily have been her own. Competitive athletics wasn't as glamorous as people believed. Yes, you got your picture taken and fans cheered for you and sometimes kids even asked for your autograph. You got shoes and clothes with a sponsor's logo if you were lucky, a fair bit of prize money or cash sponsorships if you were even luckier. But one twist of the knee, one wrong step…and it could all be over. At one point in her life, high stakes added to the excitement. Now, they terrified her. Now, she had far more to lose.

The knock at the door startled her, and it was a relief to hear Delia's voice call, "Knock, knock! I hope you're not already smashed because I have bourbon!"

Delia not only had a bottle of Four Roses, but two Old Fashioned glasses filled with ice. "I went down to the bar," she explained. "The ones in the rooms are never clean."

Carras rolled her eyes, but accepted the glass of strong amber liquid.

"I think I've figured out my plan," Delia explained. "I'm going to text Gage an amazing picture of me and Parker on the Riverwalk tomorrow, having a blast. And then, when he responds, wondering, I'll say I meant to text Parker, play it off like it was an accident. And when he calls me, I'll make sure Parker is there in the background."

"Geez, Delia, that sounds kind of…" Carras searched for words. "I don't know, like something you would do when you're trying to get a guy to ask you out, not when you're already married."

Delia shrugged. "The same principles apply, at least when it comes to Gage. Besides, he's not on social media. It's not like I can post it there."

Carras glanced at Delia's ten-pound engagement and wedding rings, still sparkly on her slim hand after a decade and a half of marriage. She sensed there was more to the story about her and Gage and their marriage than plain old marital humdrums.

"What about you?" Delia tipped back her glass. "What's your plan? You've been pretty evasive. Technically, you could have all evening tomorrow if you wanted, since I have Parker to myself during the day."

Carras hesitated. "My plan is just…being here. Stuart was already asking lots of probing questions before I left."

This wasn't true, and she had a feeling Delia knew it. Stuart had paused a video game he was beta testing long enough to walk Carras out the door, still wearing the headset he used to talk to his development team as he loaded her suitcase into the car and kissed her. The closest thing to a probing question had been, "Do you have your sweater? I know you get cold on airplanes."

"Carras," Delia said after a while. "I know we're not close or anything, but if you wanted to tell me something… I mean, Jess is married to your husband's best friend, and her loyalties might be divided…"

It was so tempting. The bourbon was warm and inviting in her chest. Carras had no one to talk to—her father had been it, and she couldn't burden him with this. She'd never had close girl-friends, always moving around, always on the court... What would it feel like to spill her heart over bourbon in San Antonio and hope for the best?

To explain that even though she'd made all these plans and spent all this money, Carras wasn't sure she could go through with it. That she had loved two men in her life: the husband who gave her more joy than she could've dreamed, and the father she was watching slip away. That she knew a baby wouldn't fix everything, but she longed to see that light in both men's eyes before it was too late. That her thighs still ached from making love to her husband last night, and there was an ovulation kit in her suitcase. Something told her Delia, of all people, might understand.

The phone between them lit up with a text. *I'm in the lobby. You lovely ladies ready for a night out?*

They both stared at the screen.

Delia smiled. "Well. Are we?" She poured another splash of bourbon into their glasses and they clinked, before heading down to the lobby, both hoping for things they could not articulate.

20

DELIA

DINNER WITH PARKER AND CARRAS turned out to be more fun than Delia had imagined. They found a steakhouse that also specialized in cocktails and had a hilarious and attentive waiter who seemed to be on a mission to keep them laughing, while showcasing the skills of the bartender, who seemed to be his boyfriend. Or maybe he wanted it that way.

Without planning it, the perfect moment to send Gage a picture of her and Parker came up naturally: a boozy selfie with gorgeous colorful cocktails in the background and a bone-in ribeye in the front. Parker looked yummier than usual in a lavender Oxford and perfect spiky hair, and Delia looked fetching in a low-cut fuchsia top, if she did say so herself. She texted the picture to Gage without comment at first, thinking that when he questioned her, she'd pull the "oops, did I send that to you?" thing.

But when her husband hadn't responded after several minutes, she abandoned the "accidental text" angle. Instead she wrote: *See? Photographic evidence your wife can still be fun.*

She was pleased with this, actually. A more direct, Jess-and-Tom-like approach. Simply telling him what she wanted him to know. But Gage didn't respond until they were halfway through dessert. *You're gorgeous. Any idea where Lulu's retainer would be?*

Ugh. She typed out a hasty response, and asked whether the girls wanted to talk to her, the way they did when they were younger. A pause.

They're good. Eating pizza and watching some unbearable teen movie.

She sent a smiley face, and was trying to decide whether to

send him something flirty, or call him from the restaurant so he could hear Parker's voice having the best time in the background.

But Gage beat her to it: *Headed upstairs to work. Love you, goodnight.*

Across the table, Parker and Carras were laughing like old friends. Delia tuned back in to find they were talking about some tennis coach they'd had in common who always spit when he yelled.

"Coach Spittleton!" Carras shrieked, her face lit with uncharacteristic delight.

"Yeah," Parker agreed. "But we called him the Soakmaster."

"You always had to stand back from him," Carras explained, bringing Delia into the conversation. "One time he spit in this girl's eye, and when she wiped it away, he started yelling louder at her for crying."

"Yeah," Parker agreed. "The guy was such an asshole on top of it. If he figured out you were dodging the spit, it made him angrier."

Delia tried to laugh along, an outsider trying to get an inside joke.

"He did," Carras assured her through peals of laughter, as though Delia had questioned the truth of Parker's words. "He really did."

"Whatever happened to that jerk wad? Is he still torturing kids somewhere?"

Carras wiped her eyes. "I think he passed away. Colon cancer or something."

With obvious effort, Parker reined in his laughter and transformed it into solemnity. "Jesus. Well, that's a downer. Thanks, Carras."

"Sorry," she said, straight-faced. "I didn't *give* him the cancer, though."

For a moment, the table was silent in the wake of inappropriate humor, and then all three burst out laughing again, just as the waiter brought a tray of mini-cocktails to sample.

"Geez," Parker said, in awe of the multi-colored shot glasses before them. "Glad we're taking Uber."

A couple of hours later, the three of them staggered amiably into the lobby of the hotel, pleasantly tipsy and companionable. As they reached the elevator bank, Delia realized she'd briefly forgotten that she and Carras were paying Parker an absurd hourly rate to be here. It felt like three friends out for an evening. She couldn't remember feeling this way, and in fact wasn't sure she ever had. Delia wasn't good at relaxing around people. Not for real.

She pressed 16 for her own floor and 18 for Carras. Parker was on another floor, but she wasn't sure which one and he didn't press any buttons himself. When the doors closed, he said, "I was thinking of a late swim. You ladies interested?"

Carras shook her head. "I shouldn't. I actually have to do this class tomorrow. But you two go ahead."

"Delia?" Parker raised an eyebrow. "You can't be tired yet, can you?"

It sounded lovely. Late night in the hot tub with a handsome young guy. No strings, no regrets. It was the kind of scenario that would present most married women with a true moral quandary, and confusing feelings about betraying their husbands. But Gage would not feel betrayed. She was *allowed* this. It was part of their understanding that if he had needs, so could she. Gage was nothing if not egalitarian. *Damn him.*

"No, thanks. I really shouldn't." The words were out before she had made the decision to say them. And the elevator door slid open to her floor.

"Are you sure?" Parker said. "I can grab my suit and be down in eight minutes."

"I don't have a suit."

"Wear a T-shirt. There won't be anyone around."

"I can't, really." She touched his arm, watched the muscle ripple beneath the fabric of his shirt. "Thank you, Parker. It's been a nice night. Carras, I'll text you in the morning."

And then the doors were closed behind her and she was walking, a little unsteadily, toward her room, wondering what the hell she was thinking. *Note to self,* she thought as she fished for her room key. *Next time you agree to be in an open marriage, make sure you actually want to sleep with someone besides your asshole husband.*

In the next fifteen minutes, Delia changed her mind seven

times. She didn't want to go to bed alone, again. She *did* want—for the first time in years—to stumble down to the pool and feel silly and carefree and a little dangerous. She put on silky pajamas and got ready for bed, and then put the hotel bathrobe on and off three times. The problem was, she wanted those things with *Gage*. And he wanted them with Alana. Or whichever other younger, perkier version of Delia he was spending time with these days.

It was only a hot tub. She didn't have to do anything she didn't want to. When would she have a chance like this again? She and Gage never did this kind of thing anymore, even on the rare occasions they spent a night or two away from the kids. If he did, he didn't tell her about it. There was no classy way to say: *Hey babe, I'm in a hot tub with another woman, but we agreed to an open marriage, so no whining now.*

Of course Gage never told her those things. Discretion was part of their promise. Fine. She wouldn't tell him either.

But wasn't telling him the whole point?

Delia flopped back onto the bed. Was there a way to let Gage know, so he could get jealous, without breaking their agreement not to rub each other's nose in it? And then, the truth: she *wanted* to rub his nose in it. She wanted him to hurt the way she did, so he would know what he'd been doing to her.

Or, maybe she'd simply take back a little of her own. Have a little fun.

Damn, Parker was cute.

She was paying him anyway.

It was just the hot tub.

She didn't have to decide now. She could get down there and let it happen naturally.

Before she could spin for another fifteen minutes, she forced herself to text Parker. *Still thinking of a swim? I may be changing my mind.*

He didn't respond.

He might be asleep. Or already in the water. She slipped on her sandals, tucked her phone and room key into the pocket of the robe, and grabbed a bath towel. *Heading down now, hope to see you.*

A man in a suit eyed her up and down as she got on the elevator. Delia wished she knew Parker's room number so she could swing by and pick him up in person. Carras would know, but she was probably asleep.

She got off on the second floor and made her way to the rooftop pool, enclosed in glass and surrounded by city lights. The lights were on; wet spots on the pavement and a discarded beer can near the hot tub told her it had been recently vacated. That couldn't have been Parker. Maybe he was changing to come down? Or had stopped by the restroom? She looked around the empty space, head spinning, nose filled with the smell of chlorine, and sat in a side chair to wait.

She texted Carras. *Awake? Know Parker's room number?* She started to add some plausible excuse for needing this information at two in the morning, but ended up sending a sheepish emoji instead.

No response.

She waited a few more minutes, getting increasingly sleepy and irritable. A tall, clean-cut man in athletic shorts and a T-shirt entered the pool area and stripped down unceremoniously to a black Speedo. He dived into the pool, barely glancing at her, and began swimming laps with perfect form. European businessman, perhaps? Keeping up his fitness routine despite the odd hours? It was obscene. Didn't he know people were busy having drunken personal crises here right now?

It was exactly the obnoxious sort of thing Gage would've done.

Delia watched the man complete three seamless laps, then strolled out to the front desk. The uniformed attendant was kind, but insisted she couldn't give out another guest's room number, even to a member of his party. "Have you tried texting him?" the woman offered.

"Great idea!" Delia said. "I hadn't thought of that."

Rather than be offended by the blatant sarcasm, the clerk handed Delia a complimentary bottle of water, possibly implying that her custom-created cocktails were showing. It was more out of stubborn frustration than real desire that Delia took the elevator to Carras's floor rather than her own. She wouldn't *wake* Carras, of course, because that would be inconsiderate. But if her friend responded to a light knock, she might know Parker's room number, right?

And if not, at least Delia could reclaim the bourbon.

When she got to Carras's door, she paused, checked the number, and walked down the hallway again. That couldn't be right, could it? She pulled up the text message where Carras had sent her the number earlier, and double-checked it against the door where she stood.

It was right.

And Delia could hardly believe it, because she heard two low murmuring voices on the other side. It wasn't the TV, she decided. That was *definitely* Carras. Maybe on the phone with Stuart, with the TV in the background? Delia held her breath and waited, mind racing with what on earth she would say if someone opened the door right now. But she had to be sure, and she didn't leave until she was, that the other voice absolutely belonged to Parker Yung.

21

CARRAS

"I DON'T UNDERSTAND," PARKER SAID FOR the third time, and Carras began to get frustrated.

"Yes. You do, Parker." She pushed the paper across the bedspread to him, struggling to maintain whatever minuscule sense of seduction had not already been sucked out of the situation. "Sign it, and the money is yours."

His eyes flicked to the stack of bills resting next to the paper. "So this is…"

"Ten thousand dollars. It's about what I used to win at some of the regional tournaments." She smiled ruefully. "Not bad for a night's work."

He grimaced, and Carras wondered whether she'd miscalculated by comparing the payoff to tennis prize money. Parker probably resented that she'd made it as a semipro athlete for so much longer than he had.

But as he feathered the bills across his thumb, his signature grin returned. "I have to say, I don't consider it work. You're a beautiful woman, Carras."

She fought off the repulsion his flattery made her feel. "The money isn't for the work," she said evenly. "It's for your signature on that page."

He looked at the paper, which she'd drawn up by copying the verbiage from several forms she'd found online. "So I'm signing away my parental rights? This is a new one, I gotta say."

"*If* a child were to result from…" She swallowed. "Anything that happens tonight, this document says that you agree not to sue for any parental rights, and I agree the same. I won't come after you for child support, and you promise to disappear from my life completely."

"It still feels weird," Parker said. "I've never even thought of having a kid before."

"This won't be your kid," she said firmly. "It will be mine and Stuart's. Period, end of story. Think of it like donating to a sperm bank. Even I won't know which night he or she was conceived."

If I can even conceive, she thought. *If not, I'm risking everything for nothing.*

"But I'm... Is your husband...? Is it going to be a problem if this kid looks a quarter Korean?"

Carras laughed—whether at Parker's directness, or out of nervous tension, she wasn't sure. But she was ready for this question, had asked it of herself repeatedly. "I don't think so. My husband's mother is from the Philippines, and his father's family are all either Italian or dark-haired Irish. I know it's not the same as being Korean..."

Parker nodded and stared at the paper she'd given him, allowing Carras to examine his features up close. The concern had crossed her mind too, of course, but she had been so busy trying to muster her courage that she couldn't focus on it. Now, she compared the arch of Parker's brow, the deep-set brown eyes, and the wide, flat line of his nose—slightly off-center in a way that made him both imperfect and decidedly more attractive—to the image of Stuart's face burned into her memory.

Stuart's jaw was squarer, perhaps. Parker's skin had more of a pinkish hue, while Stuart's was a shade more olive. Other than that, their features weren't so different. Similar enough, she hoped, to keep her secret from Stuart forever.

But they would never be similar enough to fool Carras's heart. Not for one night. Not for one second.

"Are you sure about this?" Parker looked at her, hotel pen poised over the waiver. "Obviously I'm not an expert on marriage, but this seems like the kind of thing that could haunt you for a long time."

Nope. She wasn't going down this road again, not now. Her dad was dying. Soon he would leave behind his only daughter and a dream of the grandchildren he'd worked so hard to make a life for. There was no telling if or when she and Stuart would have a child, no knowing why it hadn't happened so far. Maybe the problem was with Carras, and none of this would matter. But if not…if their infertility was on Stuart's side, and she had been given this opportunity at the moment she needed it most… It *had* to be a sign. It was a gift, and as much as it shamed her to accept it, she couldn't bring herself to pass it up.

But she wouldn't let him see her vulnerability. "Is it going to haunt *you*, Parker?" She tried to channel Jess's directness, Delia's salesmanship. "Because that's all you need to decide right now."

He gave her his slow, seductive grin—the one she was sure made women crazy—and scrawled his signature on the paper. "Regrets aren't my style."

She took the paper, sealed it in an envelope she had addressed to herself and tucked it into her suitcase in the small closet. When she returned, Parker was already sprawled out, shirtless, hands tucked behind his head. "Looks like I'm all yours," he said, offering up his half-naked body like a feast. He was incredibly, inhumanly attractive; Carras could count his rippling ab muscles all the way to the seductive V-shape leading down to his loose-fitting jeans. But he didn't look like a feast to her. He looked like two hundred well-muscled pounds of so-not-Stuart. She poured a healthy slug of Delia's bourbon into two glasses and brought them over, downing hers in one gulp as she sat next to him on the edge of the bed.

Parker sat up effortlessly, stomach muscles rippling. His lips were inches from hers, and she could smell the whiskey on his breath. "I used to see you on the court when I was young, and later, in the magazines." His voice was deep and husky; he grazed a hand across her cheek and behind her ear. "You were one of my heroes, because I knew your family was different. Like mine. I always thought you were so beautiful."

He leaned in to kiss her and Carras jerked her head toward the ceiling in a dodge. Parker kissed her neck instead, sending an involuntary thrill down her throat to her belly. "Now that I know you in person," he tugged on her earlobe with his teeth, "I can see you're more than beautiful. You're captivating."

Carras let out a breath, which unintentionally emerged like a groan of pleasure. Parker responded by running a hand down her neck to her collarbone, and deftly unbuttoned her blouse with one hand while pulling her closer by the waist with the other. Her stomach clenched in an excruciating combination of arousal, shame, and panic.

"Does he appreciate you?" Parker said smoothly between kisses against her collarbone. Carras could tell it was a line he said often. He didn't sound rehearsed, but...automated. The way some people always said "Oh, baby," or "Oh, yeah."

"I love you." Stuart always said, "I love you." Over and over. Until she was embarrassed by the intensity of it, and then enveloped by it. Until the words entered her at every place where his body touched hers and she felt it spreading inside her like warm gin, from her core to her fingers and toes. Until she believed it. Until she heard her own voice saying it back. Over and over.

"Does he know how lucky he is?" Parker was murmuring now, tugging her blouse off her shoulders in practiced seduction.

You've got it wrong, she thought. *It's the other way around.*

"Don't talk about my husband." Her voice came out like ice, trembling. "*Ever.*"

Parker paused with his hands on her shoulders, where he'd been running them beneath the straps of her bra. He looked at her face, as though he might be about to say something—reassure her, make a joke, maybe—but his playful grin faded, and he nodded.

"Would you like me to take this off?" He tugged at the straps. They were stark white against her dark skin—she'd intentionally chosen something basic and unsexy. She shook her head and his hands relaxed, motionless.

He was waiting for her to make the move.

Carras stood, slowly, and unbuttoned her jeans, hands shaking.

Parker helped her, covering her trembling hands with his own, sliding the jeans over her hips and down her body. "Relax," he whispered, putting a light kiss over her navel that gave her chills. "Put your hands on my shoulders."

She did as he said, and felt the smooth, taut muscles there. So different from Stuart's regular, slightly hunched, computer-guy shoulders. Stuart had a mole on his left shoulder near his neck. She missed it desperately. She wanted to kiss every mole and freckle, lose herself in the moment and make love to her husband. Make a baby with him, a baby like him.

Parker kissed the hollow of her throat, and slid expert fingers beneath the elastic of her panties. Carras looked at the ceiling and tried not to shake, to remain standing strong. He splayed his hands against her round hips, so that her underwear pulled arousingly tight against her, and then slid his hands down her body in a sleek, fluid motion. This done, his hands reversed track back up her legs and settled on her waist, where he pulled her gently toward him.

"You'll have to be on top," she said to a sprinkler in the ceiling above. "It's better for conception."

"I can live with that." Parker tugged her down toward the bed so that she was forced to look at him. "But I think this is going to go better for both of us if you relax and enjoy yourself."

He was right. Conception was more likely when a woman was aroused. She'd read it in all the books. And when she had an orgasm, too, but Carras didn't see *that* happening. She sat on the bed and let Parker coax her back against the pillows. She pulled a pillow from the other side of the bed and positioned it under her hips. "I'll try."

Parker laughed. "You're lucky I'm a professional," he said lightly. "Because a regular dude would be down in the bar right now, nursing his bruised ego."

When she didn't respond, he clicked off the bedside lamp, plunging them into darkness. Carras was glad she'd kept the blackout curtains closed: dark was better. He didn't throw himself on top of her immediately, or even try to kiss her again, but sat next to her on the edge of the bed and pulled her hand into his lap. He laid it against the hard muscle of his thigh and rubbed a big, slow circle in her palm with his thumb. Carras wanted to tell him to stop seducing her and get this over with already, but she knew it wouldn't help. He'd mentioned his bruised ego as a joke, but even a confident professional like Parker probably wouldn't perform well under that kind of pressure.

One at a time, Parker massaged her palms and rolled her hands around on the wrists, the way a manicurist might, forcing the tension to loosen. Next, he ran his hands up and down her arms, gently kneading her clenched arm and chest muscles until she was forced deeper into the pillows and felt her nipples harden with his proximity to her breasts. Then he stepped away, and she heard him shimmy out of his boxers before moving to the foot of the bed to begin expertly kneading her feet with his knuckles.

Admittedly, it felt amazing. She began to envision herself at a secluded spa, maybe with some of those lavender aromatherapy candles. When she listened to her body, Carras found that her breathing and heartrate had slowed. In the dark, she could almost sink entirely into the bed, almost disconnect from where she was, whose hands were on her skin.

When Parker moved to her calves, however, his motion became slower and firmer, more sensual. Her breathing quickened again as he worked up to and rounded her knees, pushing them gently apart as he continued to knead along the front of her thighs. He was moving more quickly now, purposefully, and the illusion that she could be in a therapeutic spa dissipated as her body came alive without her. Strong thumbs traced rhythmic circles along the inside of her thighs, moving up, up… She felt her own, equally strong muscles resist and relax, her body growing slick and tremulous under his touch. With each rotation of his thumbs, he pushed her legs a little farther apart, until she could feel the warmth of him radiating between them, and knew he was on his knees in front of her.

"Ready?" Parker offered softly, grazing his thumb against her warmth in the darkness, making her shiver with anticipation. They were at the point of no return. He was offering her himself, and the last out. Her last chance to *not* become the woman who'd done this thing.

But she had already become that woman, Carras knew. Ever since the idea had occurred to her a few weeks ago, she had known deep down that she would do this. And now, there was a pleasant heavy feeling in her limbs, a buzzing in her ears, a tight thrumming in her abdomen. The primal desires of her body screaming over the last whispers of reservation.

"Yes," she croaked, arching her back to move her hips toward this man she did not love, for the sake of the ones she did. "I'm ready."

22

DELIA

DELIA SAT AT THE PATIO table on the San Antonio Riverwalk in her favorite sunglasses and floral dress, the barely touched hotel breakfast in front of her, watching the river sparkle in the Friday morning sunlight.

Carras was gone to the seminar for the day. She'd texted Delia this morning and apologized for: *passing out on you guys—so exhausted and I never drink!* Delia had resisted the temptation to reply with, *Yeah, right.* Carras also said she'd be done at four and hoped Delia and Parker had a fun day.

Parker, however, still hadn't replied at all, and smart money was on him still sleeping it off. *Was he in his own room, or still in Carras's?* Not that it was any of her business.

Delia picked up her phone again, re-reading texts from her daughters this morning and checking all their social media accounts to see if anything new had been posted. Of course not, because Lulu had soccer practice and Sadie was at cheerleading. But other than a perfunctory *good-morning-how's-it-going-fine-how-are-you-where-do-we-keep-the-sunscreen* exchange with Gage, she had nothing else to go on about how her family was doing.

Damn Parker, she thought acidly as she tossed the phone back on the table and watched the slow trickle of tourists beginning to flow past her on the wide concrete pathway beside the river. The feeling surprised her. Why should she care if Parker spent the night with Carras, or if he brought Jess a rose when he picked her up? He wasn't her boyfriend, or her husband. She didn't have feelings for the guy; she barely knew him. He was an escort, and she hadn't spent any of her paid time with him yet. Why should it bother her if he ended up in Carras's room last night? That was his job, right?

She picked up her fork and moved the *chilaquiles con chorizo* around on her plate, considering another bite. They were delicious, with fresh tomatoes and cilantro topping the tostadas and eggs—*Tom and Jess would like these,* she thought, remembering his family was from this area—but Delia had no appetite. She glanced at her phone again. Almost nine. Was it okay to text Parker this early, remind him that her time was starting?

No. Too business-like, too pathetic. She wasn't going to beg.

Maybe he and Carras had only been talking last night. That is what she'd heard, after all. Perhaps there was some connection between them, from their tennis days, that Carras was downplaying for some reason. She'd said she barely remembered crossing paths with Parker, but all those jokes last night about the spitting dude... Had she known him better than she was letting on? It was possible they'd just been catching up, talking about racket strings or whatever tennis people did in their spare time.

Delia was beginning to regret tagging along on this trip. It was stupid, really. She'd never been the type to invite herself along to anything—she'd never had to—and it made no sense for her to spend her hard-earned money on time with Parker on a trip he was taking with someone else. This whole thing was a business deal that *Delia* had arranged, and now she felt like a third wheel.

Damn. *A third wheel.* Just like she felt around Jess and Tom with their companionable ribbing, while Gage was out of town or in the other room on business calls that never ended. Like she felt more and more often with her girls—now old enough to enjoy each other's company more than hers, at least when they weren't trying to murder each other. Just like how she felt in her marriage.

Before she could follow this depressing line of thought too far down the rabbit hole, Delia's attention was caught by a jogger a few blocks down the Riverwalk. He had dark hair, broad shoulders, and strong, masculine legs pumping hard in navy-blue athletic shorts. His skin glistened beneath a white muscle shirt that clung to him in all the right places. She hated muscle shirts on men—they didn't look good on *anyone.* But as he got close enough that she could make out his features, she saw that Parker

Yung was clearly an exception.

He pulled up to a walk a few steps from her table, grinning, and plopped into the seat across from hers. "Morning," he panted, then gestured at her full ice-water, which had gathered condensation from sitting untouched. "Do you mind?"

"Help yourself." Delia watched as he drained the cold water without the ice hitting his face and splashing all over him, which is what would have happened to a normal human. *He really was godlike*, she mused, as she watched his throat working above his smooth, sweaty chest. "I'm surprised you had the energy for a run this morning."

"Why wouldn't I?" He set down the glass and peered at her with the most genuine, guileless expression. She could say it now, his expression said. She could ask him about Carras, and he might even tell her the truth. Or he might remind her that he kept his client's confidences. But she would know by how he reacted.

"All those cocktails last night." She chickened out. "I know I couldn't run to save my life right now."

"You look like you're holding up okay." He eyed her appreciatively. "That's a very pretty dress."

Bastard. How did he disarm her? She immediately forgot her wounded, jealous feelings when he flashed that smile and tossed her a basic compliment.

"So what are we doing today?" he asked. "I'm all yours, as soon as I shower."

Delia let one tiny, flirty pout creep into her voice. "Shower? I assumed my time with you started at nine, like Carras's conference…"

He glanced at his watch. "Damn. You're right. I'm seven minutes behind." He stood and offered her a sweaty hand. "I guess you'll have to join me in the shower, then."

Delia laughed. "No way. I've already done my face regimen and hair this morning. I'm not showering again with *anyone*."

"I see where I fall in the pecking order," he said. "Under makeup and hair. That's harsh."

"To be fair, it's very expensive makeup. I know because I sell it."

"Whew. Still. I'll have to see if I can earn my way up the list today." Parker leaned over and kissed her on the cheek, his sweaty skin brushing hers and making her heart race. "Give me twelve minutes to shower and get back down. I'll make it up to you, I promise."

"Fine," Delia said, trying to sound annoyed.

He grinned, forked a mouthful of her chilaquiles, and sauntered back into the hotel building. As the glass door closed behind him, Delia saw in the reflection a table full of women in their twenties, watching him go with undisguised appreciation. She sat up a little straighter, showing them she was the kind of woman that a guy like Parker would hurry back to.

He was back in eleven minutes, not that Delia was counting, looking fresh and smelling amazing. He wore a tight-fitting gray T-shirt and loose jeans, with his black hair artfully sculpted into a spiky wave to one side. Like a one-man boy band.

"Won't you be hot?" Delia asked, looking at the jeans. It was already getting warm, even with the cooling effect of the river nearby.

"I'll never be hotter than you in that dress," he retorted, nodding at her cleavage. "But I guess it depends on what we're doing today."

She didn't know how a guy so young managed to be so relentlessly charming. Parker could make anything sound a little dirty, a little seductive…and yet, his unassuming brown eyes and open, youthful expression always looked sincere. It was as if he'd been waiting his whole life to say these things to some cute girl, and now he had his chance. She had to remind herself that the lines *weren't* just for her. Far from it.

"I hadn't thought that far ahead, to be honest." Delia rose from the now-cleared table. "Maybe we'll go for a walk?"

Parker's brow furrowed as he extended his elbow for her to take, like in a ballroom. "You didn't plan ahead? That doesn't sound like you, at least from what I know so far."

Delia laughed. "You have me pegged already. But maybe that's what I'm paying you for: permission to be spontaneous."

"Somehow I don't think you need anyone's permission for anything," he said, and they set out along the river.

They didn't talk at first. Parker seemed to enjoy the quiet stroll along the river as much as Delia did. It was a beautiful day, with an impossibly blue sky reflected in the water, banked on both sides by colorful umbrellas and boats waiting for their cargo of tourists.

They came to a pedestrian bridge, a beautiful concrete arch over the water, sheathed in greenery and shaded by trees hanging lazily over the water. Parker took her hand and walked to the center of the bridge, where he leaned on the wall with his elbows. Delia did the same, and for several minutes they were looking over the water in an easy silence.

"So," Parker said, after the relative excitement of waving to a small boat of twenty or so elderly tourists as it passed beneath them, "are you going to tell me, or do you want me to ask?"

"Ask what?" Delia said, startled.

"Why we're here," he said. "Not in San Antonio, but in general. You don't want to sleep with me, and your husband is five states away, not being jealous. So what is this about?"

"How do you know I don't want to sleep with you?" she challenged. "I texted you last night, didn't I?"

Parker shook his head. "You wouldn't have gone through with it. If you wanted me, you would have made it happen within a week of us meeting. That's the kind of woman you are." He laughed. "There's a chance I wouldn't even have charged you."

"I do love a bargain," Delia joked, but her voice fell flat.

Parker looked up the river as a second boat made its slow way toward them. This one had high sides with lacy cutouts, as though its occupants were floating down the river in a basket. He watched it approach lazily, as though he had nowhere else to be and all the time in the world to wait for her response. Delia found this feeling both unfamiliar and a little disconcerting.

"My husband and I have...an arrangement." She heard herself saying the words.

Parker shifted to face her, leaning against the wall with his left side and putting his right hand in the pocket of his jeans.

Damn. He was like a living, breathing page from *Men's Health.*

"You mean an open marriage."

She nodded. Of course, he wouldn't be surprised. Parker would've heard it all in his line of work.

"So if you and Gage have an open marriage, why are we here, sneaking around?" Parker reached up to brush a wind-blown lock of hair back behind her shoulder. "I have the feeling Mrs. Delia Cargill can attract any kind of guy she wants, and if Gage doesn't care who you sleep with…"

She cringed to hear it put in such bald terms. Delia was used to niceties, even between herself and her husband. Polite euphemisms and side-stepping, when they couldn't avoid confronting the subject altogether. "I wouldn't say that he doesn't *care*," she said. "But yes. I am free to…partake in experiences with other people, as long as I'm discreet and it doesn't interfere with parenting the girls."

"But that's not what we're doing?"

"No. I never have."

"Really?" He looked surprised. "You mean to say you've never taken advantage of the open-door policy?"

"Not once. In seventeen years. I've been completely faithful. Pathetic, isn't it?"

Parker was quiet, then put a hand on Delia's chin. His voice was soft. "You've been loyal to your husband. What's pathetic about that?"

"Because it isn't mutual." Then, she thought better of it. "I mean, the loyalty is mutual. I truly believe Gage would do anything for me or our girls. But this was our agreement when we got married. He didn't want to—get married, I mean—but I wanted a family and I couldn't stand the idea of doing it with anyone else. Also, naïve. I was basically trailer trash back then—"

"No way," Parker said. "You?"

She laughed. "Believe it or not, I was waiting tables in a gentleman's club, living in a ratty apartment with six other girls in Boston, after my boyfriend…well, he wasn't very nice. Anyway, Gage picked me up out of nowhere. He loved me. *Loves* me." She wasn't sure why she needed Parker to understand this. "Gage wanted the American dream, and the reputation that comes with being a family man. But he knew he didn't want a traditional marriage. He's not built for it. He said he would never get married unless he found someone who felt the same way."

"And you felt the same way?"

"I did. Sort of." Delia shrugged. "Honestly, at that point in my life, I was happy to have some stability. Gage was rich and handsome and everything different than where I'd come from, the guys I'd been with. He still is. And given that my 'true love' had dumped me on my ass, alone in a strange city with no money to get home to Georgia…well, the idea that marriage could be honest and respectful, and everyone could get what they need, with no fairy-tale illusions…"

She looked up at Parker's brown eyes, wide with concern. She should have stopped this several minutes ago, but there was something calming about telling her story to this strange guy who had no stake in it. Besides, she was paying him. "This is all covered under your hooker-client privilege, right?" She laughed weakly. "Like a therapist?"

"If anyone can understand the need for affection without fairy tales, it's me." Parker pushed off the wall, putting both hands in his pockets as they set off across the bridge. "But you still haven't explained what we're doing here. If you and Gage have an open relationship, why do you need to be here with me?"

She sighed. It was stupid. She knew it without even hearing it aloud. No point in holding back now. "For the first several years of our marriage, Gage didn't…take advantage of our agreement. At least, not that I knew of, and he was always adamant that he'd be honest about it. He turned out to love being a dad, and he didn't mind my body during pregnancy, even when I thought I looked disgusting. When the girls were little, I worked super hard to make sure he had no reason to look elsewhere. I used moisturizer and face cream religiously, did these workout DVDs six or seven times a week, drank protein shakes for breakfast and lunch—that was my first home business, actually—I refused to let myself go the way some mothers do. I never wore a shirt all day with spit up on it, never wore a ponytail unless I was working out… And it *worked*. When Gage traveled, he called me every night and we'd talk forever. When he got home, we'd put the girls to bed and stay up half the night making love. Not as wild as we had once been together, but steady. Solid. Like a normal family."

"Sounds awesome," Parker said, and they turned up the Riverwalk back in the direction they'd come. "Not that I know anything about marriage. Or normal families."

"It was," Delia agreed. "And I know I shouldn't have, but I let myself believe that I'd managed to transcend our original agreement. For years, Gage didn't mention wanting to be with other women or suggest that I should seek out other men. I thought maybe we'd settled into a normal life together."

"But you hadn't?"

She shook her head. "Gage hadn't. I...I think I did. I love him. I don't need anyone else. But a couple of years ago, he came home from a long trip, and when we got into bed..."

"No fireworks?"

"It wasn't even that. I reached for him, and he...pushed me away..." There was a lump in Delia's throat. "Very gentle. Very polite. He said, 'I'm good, sweetheart. There's a girl in the Brussels office. She's very discreet.' Like I offered him dinner and he was letting me know he ate on the plane."

"Jesus Christ." Parker was appalled, and this made Delia even more ashamed. She was so pathetic that she'd shocked the *prostitute*. "That was it? You never had sex again?"

She shrugged. "We did. We do. Once in a while, especially if he's been home for a long stretch. But it's all conventional now. No more kinky positions and ripping each other's clothes off. Quiet, missionary style, with the lights off."

"Like...a normal marriage?" Parker offered.

Delia laughed. "Probably. But I never wanted a normal marriage. I loved that Gage made me feel exceptional."

They slowed as a crowd filled the path in front of them, gathering to watch traditional Mexican dancers in impossibly bright dresses spin and twirl in the walkway. Delia watched as the women in their garish but beautiful yellows, oranges, and pinks turned and danced to music from a nearby stereo, held by a bored-looking teenage boy in a traditional mariachi costume. Five dancers, ranging from early twenties to late forties. Their dark hair was slicked back into identical buns, each with a large flower that matched her dress. It was like something from an old movie poster. As she watched the women move in coordinated, stylized grace, Delia thought how beautiful it must be to be a part of something like that. To know exactly who you are.

The dance ended, the crowd applauded, and Delia fished a dollar out of her purse to put in the sombrero carried by the bored boy. As Delia dropped the tip in the hat, one of the women shouted something in Spanish and he rolled his eyes dramatically—like Sadie would have.

"Your situation is unique," Parker said when the crowd cleared. "But parts of it sound really normal, you know? Things aren't as exciting as they once were. Vanilla sex, wandering attention…"

Delia thought about that. "If it were normal humdrums, maybe I could handle it. But these last few months, Gage has been more and more disconnected." She hesitated, then continued. "There's this one woman. Alana."

"Ah," Parker said. "Alana."

"He texts her constantly, and I know he's with her more than he ever was the other girls. I think she spends the night in his hotel room, which used to be where he drew the line." She laughed bitterly. "Like there was ever a line."

"You're hoping Gage will think you and I are in a real relationship."

"Not exactly. But if he gets a taste of his own medicine, if someone is texting me constantly, takes my attention away from him, makes his life harder…maybe he'll realize…"

"That he's hurting you," Parker finished softly.

Delia swiped at her eyes. She *never* cried. It was a rule. "How are you only twenty-five? You're like Dr. Fucking Phil, but hotter."

"Way hotter, I hope," he said. "Let's go shopping. I'll buy you something beautiful to wear around your neck."

"You've got to be kidding," she said. "*You'll* buy?"

"Consider it a kickback." He grinned. "You can tell Gage I saw it and insisted on getting it for you."

"That *would* piss him off," Delia conceded. Sparkly gifts were the one thing Gage did consistently, and it always mattered that she wore what he bought.

"Perfect. First, let's find something to eat. All I've had was a protein bar and that one bite off your plate. We're going to spend the day making up inside jokes I can text you later while your husband is at home."

He took her hand, and as they wound their way through the

picturesque, seemingly disconnected world of the Riverwalk, De-lia felt her mood lightening with every step. She had never told anyone about her marriage in such frank terms, and to have some-one accept it so easily…

This was Parker's true gift. He could do this even though you knew the game. *You knew* there were other women who felt the same way around him. You'd spoken to these women. You'd seen him do it. Yet there was something mesmerizing in his frank assess-ment. He could look at you and see—not a mother, or chauffeur, or tutor; not a wife or business partner or the person who'd mis-placed your favorite socks—but a woman. Beautiful, in her own way and own right. This guy was wasted on the tennis courts.

He bought her a *concha* from a Mexican bakery, and, later, a mar-bled turquoise pendant on a thick silver chain. Its teardrop shape hung heavily against her chest, stopping just above her cleavage in a way that was both beautiful and suggestive. She let him put it on her and wore it for the rest of the trip. But his listening ear, and the way he'd heard her story without judgment, were the best gifts anyone had given Delia in a long time.

23

MAIZY

THE DOORBELL RANG JUST AFTER noon the following Friday. Maizy checked her hair in three different mirrors before answering. Having Parker come over early had seemed like a great idea when she'd thought of it, and even when Carras and Delia returned from their trip last weekend. Both reported enjoying Parker's company, and that it wasn't awkward at all.

She wanted that. Good company, not awkward, not one of the kids' teachers or the parents who hung around so they'd have their pick of the PTA volunteer opportunities. More importantly, she didn't think she could flirt convincingly with someone she'd met once for fifteen minutes. At least, not well enough to convince Anders.

Now that Maizy had to open the door to this ridiculously hot guy and let him into her empty house, however... She was beginning to feel panicky, the way she did on rare occasions that boys had asked her out in high school. Maizy was better with the friend zone.

"Hi." Parker was freshly showered, wearing cargo shorts, a powder-blue polo, and what appeared to be an expensive watch. It was strange seeing him in anything other than athletic shorts, but Maizy had decided the premise of her taking high-level tennis lessons—after years of limiting her exercise to walking the dog and the occasional yoga DVD—was not something Anders would believe, much less support.

"Hi," Maizy repeated. After an awkward pause, she gestured him in, touching the collar of the oversized white linen shirt she wore with her favorite stretchy black capris. She had tried on several outfits this morning after Anders and the girls left.

"What a great house," Parker said. "Who's the mountain biker?"

He was looking at the mantel, where Anders's trophies were lined up, like the girls' cheerleading and soccer trophies upstairs. "My husband."

"Sweet." Parker nodded approval, then turned to face Maizy, looking down from a few inches above her. "Should we finalize the plan for tonight?"

"Of course. Would you like some coffee?"

"Have any green tea?"

She rummaged in the cabinets and found a box of peppermint green tea. While Maizy put the kettle on, Parker leaned against the marble countertop. "Delia tells me you're the head of the PTA?"

Maizy smiled. "It's a miserable, unpaid job, but somebody has to do it."

He laughed. "I'm thinking when I bump into you guys tonight, we'll pretend that we had a meeting today about the tennis program thing at the school? We can be all, 'hey, long time no see,' like it's a funny coincidence. And then I'll make it obvious that I enjoyed hanging out with you, maybe linger a little too long. Nothing overt."

"That's actually…a perfect plan," Maizy said.

He smirked. "Well, actually…thanks."

"I didn't mean—"

"It's fine, Maizy. I'm used to people underestimating me. I've always used it as a competitive advantage."

"I'm sure you have." Maizy found herself staring at his muscled arms and chest. He pulled his phone out of his pocket and Maizy gave him the name of the restaurant where she and Anders would be.

"Your reservation is at seven? I'll stop by at eight. We want to make sure your meal is well under way." He gave her a wry grin. "That way, if the whole jealousy thing works on your husband, you'll be able to go straight home and reap the benefits."

"Should we nail down information about this program you're doing at the school?"

Parker shrugged, pushing himself off the counter and crossing to her island, where the teakettle was beginning to hiss. "Be vague. The whole point is that Anders will focus on how excited I am to see you."

"I think we need details," Maizy fretted. She poured the boiling water into two mugs, even though she hated tea. Anders drank hot tea occasionally, and one of his brothers' wives always wanted it at Christmas. Which was why Maizy had it, and why it was dusty. "I've always heard when you tell a lie it's important to get the details right."

He tilted his head, accepting the mug. Hers was too hot to touch, but his hands—calloused from tennis—didn't seem bothered. "You don't lie much, Maizy, do you?"

"Never. I'm terrible at it."

Parker slid a hand across the surface of the island and touched hers. *Electric.* "It will be fine. Anders won't be interested in some little event at school, will he?"

"He never is." Maizy was forced to agree. "I'm so nervous. I've never done anything like this before."

He curled his fingers around her hand. "Of course you haven't. What kind of lunatic would be married to someone like you and not pay attention to what he has?"

It was a lie, Maizy knew. She had a mirror; she knew she was a good thirty pounds heavier than she had been on their wedding day. She'd heard the whispers among Anders's health-conscious family when they thought she couldn't hear them. *She eats so many carbs. All those baked goods... No wonder. If I could stay home like she does, I'd be at the gym every day for hours.*

But it was a nice lie. And even though she had no illusions about why Parker was telling it, she enjoyed it just the same. It had been such a long time since anyone had complimented anything about her, other than her baking or her organizational skills.

Parker checked the pricey-looking watch. "It's almost one; sounds like we've settled things for tonight. What do you want to do now?" Parker took a step closer and Maizy had to resist taking a half-step back. "You have me all day."

"Don't you have...somewhere you'd rather be?"

"Nope."

Maizy looked in despair around her tidy kitchen, which was

about two decades behind the style of the time. The kids wouldn't be home for another three hours. The middle school bus dropped Elise off after four o'clock, and Agatha had play practice until five. Did Parker expect to be entertained? Today was laundry day, and she was supposed to be working on a spreadsheet to hand off to Judy Kirkpatrick next week. Did Parker expect…? She shook her head. "I don't know."

He lifted the steaming mug and gestured at the screened-in porch beyond the kitchen windows. "That looks nice. Why don't we sit out there?"

It had been one of Maizy's favorite features of the house when they moved in. She'd spent weeks decorating it, with a cozy porch swing and rattan chairs with bright colored cushions. But now she never made time to go out there, unless Anders's family was here and she was hosting, bringing out beers for his brothers and the skinny cocktails favored by their wives. "You want to sit on the porch?"

"Why not?" Parker tossed his teabag in the kitchen trash and strode toward the door. "It's a nice day out. I bet you never just sit, do you?"

He settled himself on the swing and patted the seat next to him. Maizy hesitated, an awkward voice inside questioning whether she were too heavy to sit with him. But Parker took her hand and tugged her. Maizy sat on the edge of the swing, straight-backed and holding her mug of tea out from her body.

She was afraid to touch him, afraid to seem like she didn't want to touch him. What were other women like with this man? Was there some universe Maizy had never visited in which this was normal? Where the wives and mothers she saw in the carpool lane felt comfortable sitting next to a guy like this, on a sunny day, on a swing, far from prying eyes and children and husbands?

"Maizy. Relax. I'm not going to do anything that makes you uncomfortable."

Too late for that. Maizy tried to shift back a couple of inches, but her shorts caught on the edge of the swing, causing hot tea to spill over her hands and splatter on the red striped indoor-outdoor rug, which Maizy had loved until Anders referred to it as "redneck chic."

Parker hurriedly set down his own mug and took Maizy's from her hands. "Are you okay?"

Without waiting, he pulled her back into the house and ran her hands under cool water from the kitchen tap. "People always think ice, but water is better," he said, looking into her eyes.

Maizy felt warm from more than her reddened hands, which Parker was cradling in his own as the cool water ran over them.

"I'm fine, really."

"Are you sure? Your hands seem pretty red."

She pulled her hands away and dried them on a flour sack towel. The rough fabric stung a little, but she'd burned herself enough in the kitchen to know this wasn't serious. She led Parker back out to the porch and sat more confidently on the swing, this time relaxing back against the wood frame and holding it still with her feet while Parker got settled. He reached for her hand but she waved it away. "Honestly, I don't even like tea."

"Then why were you drinking it?"

Maizy shrugged. "Sometimes it's easier to do for myself what I'm already doing for others. You know, eating mac and cheese with the kids, pretending to like Lutefisk—"

"What's Lutefisk?"

"This disgusting fish dish that Anders's mom brings over at Christmas. Anyway, it's a habit, I guess."

"I would never pretend to like something disgusting for my mother-in-law."

Maizy laughed. "Spoken like a man who's never had a mother-in-law."

"Fair enough," he conceded. "But don't you think it's okay for you to like what you like, be who you are, and still expect Anders and his family to appreciate you?"

Maizy sighed. *Be yourself.* It was the message of every children's show she'd been forced to watch over the years, the message she gave her girls every chance she got. "Sure. It's just not always that simple."

Parker looked at her with curiosity. "It's not?"

He was so sweet. So oddly innocent. How could she explain?

How do you tell someone in their early twenties, especially someone as attractive and confident as Parker, that life is a series of compromises with yourself and others? How could she explain what it was like to be the quiet, nerdy girl who worked in the library all through college—not because she needed the money, though she had, but because she felt safe there? To always be a little on the outside of the group, a little awkward, a little less than... And then to have someone like Anders—tall, blond, beautiful—to have him not only notice her, but find something lovable in her...

Maizy had heard the whispers when they were dating, or imagined she had. She felt the unspoken question when Anders introduced her to his family, his ageless parents and three godlike brothers, who all shared his height, good looks, and a capacity for long-distance running that seemed unnatural to Maizy. And their three stunning wives, who all looked different enough at the outset...until Maizy realized on the first family beach trip that she was the only Mrs. Henriksson, including Anders's *mother*, who did not pack a tiny bikini and/or tight black running shorts with pricey tennis shoes for the family walk.

Parker would never understand what it was like to huff along in knee-length jean shorts and leather sandals, sweating through a seven-dollar Target T-shirt and the only bra she'd brought on the trip, trying not to sound like she was in the throes of an asthma attack, keeping pace with her mother- and sisters-in-law along a boardwalk that went on forever.

"I've always had a hard time fitting in with my husband's family. I guess if I can make them more comfortable in my home by politely eating what they bring, or serving foods they like, that has to be a good thing. Maybe it's hard to understand at your age." She realized, as soon as it came out of her mouth, how condescending "at your age" must sound. "I mean, being a single guy, and...popular." *Great. Seventh grade, all over again.*

"Maybe I understand more than you think." Parker swirled the tea in his half-empty cup. Little bits of sediment floated up and settled again at the bottom. "My mom is from Korea. She moved here with her family in the sixties. My dad is white, and I mean white-white. Like rural South Georgia redneck white. They met at a small agricultural college near where my dad grew up. He was there to be a farmer like his family; she was there because it was the second-cheapest college in the United States, and they were too proud to send her to the cheapest one. They wanted her to get a degree—they didn't care in what."

"Fascinating." Maizy hadn't known there was an agricultural college in Georgia. Her own family had moved down from Boston when Maizy was in middle school, and she'd never been south of Atlanta except to drive to Florida.

Parker took a long swig of his tea. "Yeah. My mom's family hated my dad. My aunts and uncles all married good Korean spouses; my sister and I were the only half-white cousins. My grandmother refused to learn English; she always complained that we weren't Korean enough. That we had lost who we were."

"That's so sad."

"My dad's family were worse. They treated my sister and me like half-breeds. Our cousins would call us all kinds of racial slurs, and when our parents objected, Dad's family said we needed to develop thick skin. Like they were doing us a favor. My grandparents would give my white cousins all these amazing toys for Christmas: you know, motorized cars, videogame systems, new bikes… My sister and I always got some kind of hand-me-down clothes or toys they'd bought at Goodwill."

"Your parents let them get away with that?" If someone treated Maizy's girls that way, she would've knocked them into next week, family or no family.

"I think they objected in private, at least at first. And Mom and Dad always bought us something awesome to balance it out. But we weren't allowed to complain. Dad said we shouldn't give them the satisfaction. He told us to smile and say thank you, and pretend it was the best thing we'd ever gotten. He said, 'never reward somebody being cruel to you, or you'll be their prisoner forever.'"

"How awful." Maizy put her hand on Parker's arm. Suddenly she was seeing him not as an abstract, intimidating adventure or even the man in front of her, but as a little boy he must once have been.

Parker stood, collecting both mugs. "It was a long time ago. And an important lesson. I wanted you to know that I understand, at least a little."

"I would say so." Maizy stood, but he gently pressed her back onto the swing.

"You sit. I'm going to bring what you want to drink. Coffee?"

"I'll get it. You won't know where anything is."

"It's in the kitchen, right? I'll figure it out. Cream and sugar?"

"Just cream."

"I'm going to bring you some coffee, and one of those cinnamon buns on the counter that look homemade. Are they?"

"They are, but I don't…"

"I'll bring us both one. And we'll sit here and talk about whatever you want. Me, you, your husband's asshole family. Whatever. And then, we'll do whatever you want." He paused in the doorway. "What would you be doing today if I weren't here?"

She smiled, sheepish. Maizy desperately wanted to have a more interesting answer, but her brain couldn't find anything on short notice. Besides, Parker had been so honest and vulnerable with her. "Honestly? Laundry."

"Perfect," he said, leaving her alone on her porch for the first time in recent memory. "I am excellent at folding."

24

MAIZY

A FEW HOURS LATER, MAIZY SAT in La Bella Ristorante Italiano, staring at her husband over one empty glass of red wine, one full one, and a single flickering candle. Anders was on his phone, thumbing out an email in response to some last-minute Friday night work crisis. "I hate to do this," he'd said ten minutes ago when some alert had popped up on his phone. "Banks are still open on the West Coast. I know it's our anniversary."

"Of course," Maizy had said cheerfully. Her cheer had now evaporated, along with her Merlot. It was Friday night; their anniversary was next week. It annoyed Maizy that he couldn't step back from work for a couple of hours.

But she was distracted herself, to be honest. While Anders fretted about work, Maizy's mind was on a handsome tennis player who had accepted subpar, racist Christmas presents with grace, and by contrast, had given her the best few hours she'd had in a long time.

She checked her watch, the silvery bangle she only wore on special occasions, refusing to follow Anders's lead by pulling out her phone to check the time. It was 7:55, two minutes later than last time she checked. It felt like an eternity since Parker had left her house in time for her to go pick up Agatha at play practice. And the five minutes before she'd see him again felt like an eternity of equivalent size.

She was excited, but also dreading it, the same way she dreaded speaking at the schoolwide PTA meetings. This was a performance, on which she would be evaluated and judged. And in this case, her judge would be—not the 500-plus parents who attended PTA meetings—but her own husband. Funny how that was so much harder.

It was terrifying. And she couldn't wait. She flicked her wrist again: 7:56. When Anders glanced up with a raised eyebrow, Maizy pretended she'd been reaching for her wineglass. Which was stupid. Because it was empty.

"Sorry about this," he said. "I'll be done in a second."

"No problem." She let out a nervous breath. Maizy had no idea what to say to her husband right now anyway.

Anders furrowed his brow. "Don't be a martyr, Maizy. Next time schedule this for a Saturday night when I can get free."

She started to object, but the waiter stopped by with a basket of bread for the table and a fresh glass of wine. Maizy thanked him; Anders didn't even glance up. No point in pulling him out of his train of thought to argue with him. It would just delay whatever he was doing and make him grouchy.

She picked up a slice of the crusty bread, still hot in the center, and spread butter luxuriously across its surface. Biting into it, she lost herself in the events of this afternoon. Parker had been true to his word: he was excellent at folding laundry.

At first, Maizy had resisted letting him help. The piles of kids' clothes, towels, and socks would all be around tomorrow. "Let's do something fun instead," she told Parker.

"Like what?"

"We could…" Maizy ran through several ideas, none of which seemed right. She didn't want to be seen in public with Parker, because that would detract from her plan of running into him randomly tonight. Plus, being as recognizable as she was by other parents at the school, there was no way Maizy could be seen with the handsome young tennis pro and not start gossip ablaze. That ruled out everything that popped into her mind.

Sensing her hesitation, Parker put an end to it. "Come on. This will be fun, if we make it that way. I love laundry."

He was so sincere, Maizy couldn't resist.

For the first time since she'd married Anders at twenty-three, Maizy Callahan Henriksson led a man who wasn't her husband into her bedroom. She was glad she'd managed to make the bed this morning. There were three baskets of laundry already clean and waiting, and Parker began folding the girls' leggings and T-shirts with minimal direction, while Maizy sorted the next load to put in the wash down the hall. He knew which items to hang, and which to fold in neat rows on Anders's side of the bed—after all, he'd had a younger sister and a mother who didn't allow him to cut corners. And to Maizy's surprise, he shared her addiction to *Jane the Virgin*. Not only did he not roll his eyes when she told him that's what she watched on laundry day, but he was a few episodes ahead of her and seemed to enjoy watching Maizy's reaction to the twists and turns of the plot. Laundry day had never gone by so fast.

"Those idiots." Anders put down his phone on the candlelit table at last. "They couldn't manage their way out of a paper bag without me to hold their hands and change their diapers."

He reached for the last piece of bread, raising an eyebrow at Maizy. "Thanks for saving me a slice?"

Shame crept up her skin like poison ivy as she realized she'd eaten three pieces of bread without noticing. "Sorry."

Anders must have noticed her expression then, because he softened. "It's fine. I was working during our anniversary celebration. That's on me."

That's on me was the closest to an apology she could expect from him. She lifted her glass. "To us."

"To us." He drank. "So. What kind of trouble did you get up to today?"

She nearly spat out her wine, and covered with a coughing fit that drew the attention of nearby tables. Behind Anders, Parker Yung had walked in with a gorgeous, thirty-ish blonde in a short black cocktail dress with a plunging neckline. Not so much a neckline as two strips of fabric covering her nipples. Parker wore a tailored charcoal-gray blazer over a T-shirt and jeans, hair spiked with shiny gel. He looked amazing.

"Are you all right?" Anders smiled apologetically at the other diners.

"Fine," Maizy croaked, looking away from Parker and his date, biting down hard on irrational jealousy rising in her throat. He hadn't mentioned he was bringing a date. Of course, it didn't matter; he was free to do as he liked. But their afternoon folding laundry had felt so intimate, and they'd talked nonstop. It was surprising he hadn't mentioned he'd be bringing someone.

"You should look into that gluten-free diet Marisol is always talking about," Anders said, mentioning—as he so often did—the most perfect and accomplished of his perfect sisters-in-law. Marisol was nice enough, but it was hard to get her talking about anything except health and fitness. Maizy often felt that Marisol was looking at her like a project to be improved, rather than a person. "She said it cut down on all that phlegm and congestion."

"I choked, honey. It's not phlegm. It's Merlot."

Maizy took a breath to re-center. This wasn't the mood she wanted to be in when Parker stopped by the table for their "coincidental" meeting. She wanted to be graceful, full of aplomb, with that light-honeyed laughter Delia always seemed to have in social situations. She wanted people to look at her the way she was looking at the blonde in the almost-dress. The way she looked at people like Belinda Hayes-Currington and Delia and Jess Rodriguez. But now she was defensive and irritable. Not what the moment called for at all.

Fortunately, Anders's focus was redirected by the waiter, who brought their salads and asked if they wanted more bread. "No thanks," Anders said.

"I'd love more bread." Maizy touched the waiter's arm. She wasn't sure what possessed her to do it. Anders was probably right about the gluten or carbs or whatever. There was a reason her pear shape had grown more pronounced in her forties, and she suspected her love of baked goods had more than a little to do with it. Plus, she'd ordered baked ziti with meat sauce and melted mozzarella. The last thing she needed was more bread.

Still, the surprised look on his face was worth it.

"That's okay, isn't it?"

Anders looked mortified. He couldn't deny his wife all the bread she wanted on their anniversary. What kind of asshole would that make him? "Sure." He smiled. "It's a special night. Get whatever you like."

"I agree." She held Anders's gaze with a smile so content, it couldn't possibly be a challenge. But she knew that's exactly what she was doing. Maybe this was all part of the game they would play. Take back a little control, make him a little jealous. She would force this man to look at her the way he once had. The only question was whether he would still love the person he saw when he did.

"Maizy Henriksson?" Parker's voice interrupted before the conversation could progress.

She looked up, feigning surprise and hoping like hell it didn't look too rehearsed.

As Parker strode toward their table, the little blonde in tow, he looked even more spectacular than when he had walked in. "It's Parker," he said, as though anyone would not recognize him. "From the tennis camp at Sugar Mills?"

"Parker! Of course." Maizy's heart sped up.

He dropped the blonde's hand and opened his arms as he leaned toward Maizy, and she stood to hug him just as he leaned down. There was an awkward moment when his arms encircled Maizy while she was still half-crouching, but Parker steadied her as she rose. The cloth napkin tumbled from her lap; Parker bent to retrieve it while Maizy smoothed her dress.

He grinned as he handed it to her. "Sorry. Kind of threw myself at you there." He extended a hand to Anders. "Parker Yung. I've been working with Maizy on the tennis programs at the elementary school."

"Anders Henriksson."

She didn't look at Anders, but she could tell from Parker's end of the interaction that her husband had elected to remain seated. Instead, she let her gaze land on the woman, who was fidgeting with the hem of her dress. "Hi, I'm Maizy."

Parker seemed to remember his date. "Oh! This is my friend Clarissa. Remember me telling you about Maizy? She runs everything at that school where I've been helping out—she's a total organizational genius. And she makes the best goddamned brownies I've ever tasted."

"Pleasure." The girl shook Maizy's hand, bangle bracelets rattling. Her hand was slim and cold, her expression not much warmer.

"I'm glad we ran into you," Parker said expansively. "I had some ideas about the camp and I realized I didn't have your number. Give me one second." He pulled out his phone, then glanced at Maizy and Anders in turn. "If I'm not interrupting a special evening?"

"Actually…" Anders started.

"It's no problem," Maizy said at the same time.

"Awesome. I love it when stuff works out like this." Parker was playing it up, brown eyes shining at Maizy as if she were his favorite person on earth. "Hit me with it."

Maizy recited her number, and out of habit, spelled her first name for him.

"I know how to spell it, Maizy." His voice was low, a tone of playful annoyance. Parker was as good an actor as he was a tennis player.

She wondered whether Anders was picking up on this.

"Okay if I text you Monday? I'm really excited about a couple of these ideas."

"Sure."

He grasped her hand in both of his, holding it for a long beat, smiling. "Great running into you. Really cool."

He didn't let go until Anders cleared his throat. Parker dropped her hand, then, laughing at himself like he had not realized how long he'd been touching her and now felt awkward. As though Parker ever could be awkward. "I'll let you guys get back to your night."

It was so simple. Maizy watched Parker and the girl walk away to their own table. The simplest of exchanges, the kind of thing she might have done on any given day with another of the moms at the school, or one of the teachers, if they'd bumped into one another. It had taken under two minutes, but somehow Parker had filled that with implications so subtle she couldn't have explained them.

Anders was staring at her. "Well, he seems interesting."

She affected casualness. "Parker? He's a nice guy."

"Nice kid," Anders corrected. "He looks about twelve."

Maizy laughed. "He's twenty-five or twenty-six, I think. He's really dedicated to the kids."

"What is a guy that age doing hanging around the school? He

doesn't have kids there, does he?"

"He's not even married yet." She thought of the slim, unhappy woman with the bangle bracelets. "As far as I know."

Anders forked a tomato. "It's weird. Why would someone that age want to hang around a bunch of soccer moms and kids? It's not natural."

"Oh, stop. You make it sound smarmy."

"I'm just saying, when I was that age, no way in hell I'd be donating my time at the local elementary school. I was too busy trying to get my career off the ground." His sandy eyebrows arched. "Or get laid."

"Not everyone is like you, Anders. Maybe he doesn't want to wear a suit and work at the bank from nine to five. Maybe he has a different passion in life. Maybe he wants to give back to the community." *And give, and give, and give…*

It was absurd, and she knew it. Despite the fact that the conversation was heading in the right direction—Anders was clearly irritated—Maizy felt defensive of Parker. And she felt something else odd, something she hadn't felt in a long time: Confident. Beautiful. Desirable.

Even though she knew the light in Parker's eye was an act, it was still having an effect on her. Her mind knew the truth, but her body and spirit were responding anyway. She was holding her head higher, letting her fingers toy with the necklace at her throat, remembering what it was like to feel sexy and wanted, rather than matronly and chubby. Maybe this was why movie actors sometimes fell for their costars.

The waiter brought their dishes: Maizy's bubbly, cheesy pasta and Anders's grilled chicken with steamed vegetables. Anders asked the waiter to bring to-go boxes right away, so they could set aside half their meals for later, a portion control trick he'd read in some health magazine. It did help, Maizy supposed, and she certainly didn't need all the carbs and fat in the steaming dish before her, but she still hated the way it made her feel—like a child who needed her meat cut for her. Also, she noticed with irritation, he seemed to be putting more than half her dish in the box. Two bites in, and she already felt robbed. Well. She was ordering dessert, damn him.

"It's all the cheese," he said, catching her stare. "Dairy is so bad for you. You know humans are the only species who feed their young milk after they're old enough for solid food? All other mammals stop breastfeeding as soon as their kids are old enough to find their own food, and yet we consume the milk of another species for our entire lifetimes. It's not natural."

"Neither is wearing spandex and riding a steel frame with two rubber wheels around the woods for no reason," she said irritably. "But you seem comfortable doing that every weekend."

Anders's mouth hung open. It had been a long time since she'd challenged him openly. When they were young and dating, they'd had long, thrilling debates—science and politics and books— sometimes until the wee hours of the morning. Friendly arguments that ended with sex or sleep or both, only to resume the following evening or a few days later, morphing into a new debate on a new topic. She'd been able to hold her own with him back then: Maizy was well-read and clever, and although her thoughts didn't form as quickly as his did, they were usually cogent and well-considered. Lately, Maizy didn't have time to be as well-read as Anders seemed to, and she didn't have the energy to dive into a debate when there were dishes to wash, lunches to prepare, and costumes to sew for the school play. Letting Anders make his pronouncements with her quiet support had become a marital expedient.

Still. He was attacking *cheese* now. Every woman had her limits.

"Are you going to start this again? Tonight? We agreed it was good for us both to have hobbies. I have the mountain biking and landscaping the yard. And you have..."

Parenting our children. The thought surprised her, and Maizy felt a sweet, vicious stab of gratification followed by relief that she hadn't said it out loud. Anders was a great father, and a hard worker. It was a gift that she got more time with their children, and the stress relief he felt after a day at work on the bike was worth it to all of them in the tension it took out of their household. Sometimes, however, she wondered why she didn't deserve a similar release.

Was this what she wanted to do tonight? Fight about fair division of labor and who had more fun?

No. Maizy wanted to get *laid*. She wanted her husband to want her the way he once had. To skip a day on the bike because he wanted to be home with her and the girls, not because she'd nagged him into it. She knew couples who treated their marriages like transactions—keeping score and counting hours and trading off their children like a burden to be managed, rather than a joy to be embraced. That wasn't Maizy's style, and it wasn't (from what she could tell) the road to happiness, either.

"I have my baking and crafting," she said, putting a conciliatory hand on his. "And you're very supportive. I was teasing about the dairy thing."

He gave her the same "I'm listening, convince me" look both girls did when they were little and she tried to coax them out of a tantrum. Maizy nearly laughed at the similarity but managed to keep control. "You have to admit, it is kind of a silly idea that we drive around in cars and work in tall buildings and fly planes and run on treadmills, but we're supposed to eat like Neanderthals for some reason. I mean, you know I love Marisol, but her ideas are a little out there sometimes."

The mention of Marisol gave Anders the out he was looking for, someone for them to align against so he didn't have to feel his wife was making fun of his ideas. "You make a good point," he said. "Lars did mention she gets a little intense about it. He had to sneak out the other night for a bacon cheeseburger. Told her he was going to the gym."

They both laughed, and Maizy took a liberal sip of her wine, basking. They relaxed after that, talking more like normal, but with Anders occasionally looking as though he were trying to figure her out. To remember something, maybe. He did not pull out his phone for the remainder of the evening.

She didn't see Parker again before they left the restaurant, but she felt his presence like a talisman. And although Anders didn't mention him again either, Maizy knew he had not forgotten the interaction.

They made love that night with the lights on, after both girls were tucked in and the leftovers refrigerated. They even knocked over one of the piles of laundry that Parker had meticulously folded that afternoon and left on the foot of her bed. Maizy didn't mind. Not one little bit.

25

JESS

JESS WAS GOING TO END things with Parker. In the two weeks since the Mexican restaurant, she had privately decided that while she wanted the spark back in her marriage, she didn't want it on these terms.

Fine. She'd like to have sex more often. What married person wouldn't? Maybe Tom didn't fawn over her the way he had in college; maybe she didn't wake up every morning feeling like a sex goddess. But there was plenty she no longer did for Tom either, probably without realizing. When was the last time she'd left a love note in his suitcase when he left town? Or gotten a Brazilian wax for their anniversary? (She knew the answer to that one: post-Mina, pre-Dash.)

Yes, things had changed. But on the whole, their life together was pretty damn good.

She was trying to decide what to do with the five hours that remained with Parker this month—*book real tennis lessons, maybe, or take the loss?*—when Parker texted.

Hey. You around?

She stared at the screen. She was around, Tom was in St. Louis, the kids were at school. Was there any reason not to tell Parker that? She thought of all the stories she'd heard, spouses divorcing after one of them found incriminating text messages on the other's phone. Parker was supposed to be discreet. As she typed what she hoped was an innocuous reply, she imagined Tom reading over her shoulder. *I'm around. What's up?*

Can we talk? In person?

Panic set in as Jess watched the three little dots bounce at the bottom of her chat screen, Parker still typing. This was *not* the innocent exchange she would want Tom to see. The next message made it worse: *I need to see you.*

What could she do? Ignore him? Pretend she didn't understand? Sorry, wrong number?

Is everything okay?

The pause before his reply stretched for what felt like hours, with Jess perched anxiously at her breakfast bar, unable to walk away from the phone.

Yes. Just need to see your face.

She was trying to figure out how to tell him (a) no way in hell he could come to her house right now and (b) he couldn't text her things like that, when her phone buzzed again.

10:00? Tennis court?

Ok. That was an hour from now, and she hoped her short reply would shut down the texts in the meantime. At least the tennis courts were public, and she could tell Parker in person not to text her anymore. And—she was sure of this now—that she wanted out. End of story, keep the change, have a nice day.

With a creeping sense of shame, Jess deleted the conversation and Parker's number, and cleared her phone's chat history. She was a person who did this now. She hid money from her husband and covered her digital tracks. *Could she ever go back?*

Parker's car wasn't there when she arrived, so Jess waited in her car with the air conditioning on, listening to the radio. Terrible for the environment, but in the Georgia humidity, even mid-mornings were stifling these days. It was not Parker, however, who arrived a couple of minutes later and ambled to the picnic table.

Delia seemed not to see Jess, striding toward the court with her bazillion dollar tennis racket, twin to the one in Jess's passenger seat. She paused at the picnic table, paced back and forth, then noticed Jess and waved, confused. Jess got out as Maizy pulled into the space next to her, almost taking off her door.

"What are you doing here?" Delia called. "I thought you needed to switch days?"

Maizy was stepping out of her car, wearing the same confused expression. She glanced in the backseat of Jess's car. "How's Mina? Is she with you?"

"No, she's at school."

Maizy made a face. "You know you're not supposed to send her within twenty-four hours after vomiting, right?"

"Vomiting?"

"For once, I agree with Maizy," Delia said, coming up on them. "Next week is the last week of school. You can't get everyone sick."

"I'm *not* getting everyone sick," Jess said irritably. "Mina is fine."

"Then why did you need to cancel an appointment with Parker? Not that I mind." Delia smoothed her hair, pulled into a neat ponytail under a Sugar Mills tennis visor. She was also wearing the big turquoise pendant she'd had on constantly since her trip to San Antonio. Not the most practical choice for tennis.

"I thought I was taking Jess's time?" Maizy said, her skin mottled pink. "Parker said…"

She trailed off as the yellow Jeep careened into the lot, pulling to a confident stop a few spaces down. Parker hopped out, grabbing his racket from the backseat and flinging it over his shoulder in one fluid motion. "Morning, ladies!" He headed for the covered picnic table. "Let's talk, okay?"

The three women looked at one another in consternation and followed. Parker perched on the bench facing the parking lot, knees spread wide and fingers interlaced in front of him. Delia sat across from him, legs crossed primly. Her face held a strange resolution, like a defiant child awaiting a punishment that she would endure, but not give her parents the satisfaction of hating.

Jess felt no such confidence. Even though she knew Parker had lied to get them here, part of her was irrationally expecting a phone call from the school that Mina was puking. At least it would be a change of pace from Dash, who had a frequent flyer card in the nurse's office.

Jess sat next to Delia, and Maizy hesitated, glancing nervously at the space on the bench beside them. Maizy wasn't obese, but she certainly had a wider backside than either of the other women. Jess could tell it made her self-conscious, and tried to shift toward

Delia, but Parker slid down the bench.

"Please, Maizy." He patted the seat next to him and addressed them like a committee. "Thanks for coming, ladies. You look ravishing, as always."

Ravishing? What twenty-something dude said *ravishing*?

"Sorry for being shady to get you here. I thought it would be easier than trying to explain over the phone."

"Where's Carras?" Delia asked, eyes steady on Parker.

"Carras couldn't make it," he said. "She had to work. I'll loop around with her later."

Delia sat expressionless and stiff, not blinking.

"Parker, what's going on?" Maizy's question was so genuine, her hand on his arm so motherly, that Jess felt a little sorry for her.

"Don't worry, everything is fine." Parker was smooth and confident as ever, but he was not meeting their eyes. "It's time to take things to the next level."

"What level is that?" Despite the sweetness in her Southern drawl, Delia's directness came through. Jess began to get worried.

"Thanks for asking, Delia. Now, I want to start by saying that my affection for each one of you is genuine. You are all beautiful women: smart, talented..." He put a hand on Maizy's, where she was still touching his arm. "Sexy. The fact that your husbands don't realize this is criminal, as far as I'm concerned."

Jess felt a twang of familiar guilt and defensiveness on Tom's behalf. Had she made her husband out to be so uncaring? Maizy looked ready to melt into the bench.

"Thanks, Parker. We think you're real sweet too." Delia spoke through her most sugary smile. "Do get to the point."

Parker grinned at her. "Anyway, I hope you have all found this helpful so far. And that your husbands have begun to treasure you as they should. I think we can all agree that is priceless."

The alarm bells Jess had heard in the distance when Parker texted this morning were now clanging hard in her head.

"As I explained at our first meeting, premium lessons are a unique service, and obviously I incur a good bit of risk to provide them. It's my pleasure, of course. I love making women feel valued, like the goddesses you are. But," here Parker spread his hands in a gesture of resignation, "love doesn't pay the bills, as you all know."

Jess's stomach knotted, the protein bar she'd scarfed down earlier a concrete block in her belly.

"I've been able to offer you guys a big discount, and I hope you'll agree that I've been accommodating about how you used your time." He glanced at Jess. "Here's the deal. The more premium clients I have, the more flexible and reasonable I can be with everyone. It's like any other premium membership." He waved a hand at the brick clubhouse with its dome and columns. "I've heard the club here requires six months' notice if you leave, to give them time to fill your slot."

"They never enforce that," Delia said. "It's designed to prevent a mass exodus if the board has to make an unpopular decision. The unspoken requirement is thirty days."

Parker shrugged. "Fair enough. Considering the risks and additional effort involved in providing premium services, it's important that I have a continuous clientele. If you guys were to back out now, for example, if none of you renew next month..." Now he looked at Jess. "I couldn't recoup that income from regular lessons on short notice."

The three women exchanged looks. Jess wondered whether Maizy and Delia had been planning to end their time with him, too.

"I sincerely hope you're not all leaving me." Parker gave them his Instagram smile. "I dig hanging out with you."

Jess's head was spinning, unable to keep up. The way Parker seamlessly floated between flattery, flirtation, business... And something else. Something she couldn't quite put her finger on. *Menacing* wasn't the right word, but...

Delia cut through the noise. "What do you want, Parker? Why are we here?"

Parker didn't flinch. "If you ladies feel you no longer want my services after this month, all I need is help finding my next premium clients."

"You mean," Delia said, "you expect us to either continue paying you $2500 a month or we have to find people who will?"

"You just have to share—discreetly, of course—the information about my premium services. Let other women know how it's helped your marriage. Then you introduce us. I'll offer them the same deal I've offered you, if you find three or four."

"What if we can't find anyone?" Maizy asked, panicked. "I wouldn't know where to start…" She trailed off, face cloudy, and stared at the ground under the picnic table.

"You shouldn't have a problem. These affluent suburbs are crawling with women like you. Women whose husbands travel, work all the time to maintain the lifestyle you enjoy. You're all wonderful people, doing all the right stuff. Raising your kids, supporting your school, making brownies. But your spouses don't appreciate you…" His voice went an octave lower. "Don't satisfy you the way they should. I'm asking, if I've helped you with that, you show your appreciation by recommending me to someone else. It's basically a referral program."

Delia snorted.

Parker glanced at her but kept going. "In fact, if you decide to continue using my premium services, I'll give you 10% off for every referral that lasts at least two months. I have women on my client list who've been receiving tennis lessons—or whatever recreation their heart desires—for free, for months."

"It's a pyramid scheme," Jess said.

"I prefer multilevel marketing," Parker said, with a wry look at Delia. "I'm not a scheming kind of guy. Just a former almost-pro athlete, with a shit-ton of student loans and a dream of bringing pleasure to beautiful women."

Jess wasn't going to be distracted by the "beautiful women" bullshit. "You did this to Belinda, too," she said. "She recruited us, and now we're supposed to recruit others. So… What? If I can find ten friends who need extra attention from their husbands, I could become like, the best tennis player in the neighborhood for free?"

She'd meant it as a rhetorical question, but Parker responded in earnest. "Probably not, with Carras around. But you do have some natural athletic ability. We could develop that, get you into the best shape of your life. I'm sure Tom would find you irresistible then. And if that's not your thing, we can still have lunch and margaritas, keep your Instagram feed lively. As I've said, I'm very flexible, as the three of you already know."

Jess asked the question she suspected they were all thinking.

"And if we can't do either? Find anyone to replace us, or pay you every month? I couldn't afford it even if I wanted to."

Parker took a deep, exaggerated breath. "Well, that's hard, isn't it? You have marriages to protect. And there's only so long these things can stay under the radar." He pulled out his phone and turned it so the three of them could see the screen. "I have copies of all these on a secure server, of course." Casually, as though he were talking about balls and rackets he kept in storage. It took Jess a surreal moment to process that she was looking at a picture of herself on the rooftop patio of the Mexican restaurant.

The shot was shocking in its familiarity and its foreignness. Delia had been cropped out and a filter applied so that it looked like a romantic evening rather than sunny lunchtime. In the center, Jess and Parker were kissing, margaritas arranged carefully in front of them. An instant after this was taken, she had pulled back from Parker in surprise. He had gone too far. They discussed it. He'd deleted it.

But here it was, far more incriminating than the real moment had been.

"I back up my deleted photos before they permanently disappear," Parker said. "I'm always afraid I'll lose something important."

Lose something important. Jess's head spun. Parker had this picture. She was kissing Parker in the picture. Parker was showing her the picture, which meant he could also show Tom the picture. With sudden horror, she tried to imagine Tom seeing this. She saw the hurt shatter him, a mirror splintering into thousands of irreparable pieces.

Delia spoke. "You bastard. This is blackmail."

Parker didn't answer, but swiped the screen to the left. The next image was black-and-white, artsy-looking, like something from a professional model shoot. It featured Parker lying alone on his side on a bed Jess didn't recognize. There were crisp white linen and pillows surrounding him, against a headboard of dark mahogany. He was shirtless, with his elbow cocked behind his head, showing off amazing biceps and forearms. The way the bedspread languished teasingly at the bottom of his torso implied that he was naked under the covers. At the bottom right corner of the photo, near the junction of his body in the bedspread, half of a black lacy bra was visible. As though it had been tossed aside in a moment of passion.

"What is this?" Jess's mind was trying to work out why a half-naked picture of Parker was relevant.

When he didn't respond, she followed his gaze to Maizy, whose face had drained completely of color. She was staring at the screen, her throat working as though she were trying to swallow cardboard. "It's my bedroom."

Delia snatched the phone. Parker did not resist, holding Maizy's gaze without flinching. His expression was neither angry nor spiteful. A guileless, open connection, as though he'd told them a painful truth and was simply waiting for them to process it.

"Holy shit." Delia showed the phone to Jess, where she had zoomed in on the nightstand behind Parker. There, on the nightstand, glinted a metal frame. Jess recognized the picture, even through the grainy resolution: four smiling people holding hands in a meadow. It had been Maizy's profile picture on Facebook for at least a couple of years now. The girls in matching white dresses and red bows, Maizy and Anders sporting jeans and white button-downs. The Henriksson family portrait was unmistakable, as was the seemingly naked tennis pro lounging in front of it.

"When did you take this, Parker?" Maizy's skin was blotchy with outrage. "When I was in the bathroom?"

"I don't remember," Parker said. "It was such an eventful afternoon; the sequencing is kind of a blur."

Delia turned on Maizy. "You slept with him? We agreed none of us would. I can't believe I let them talk me into you being a part of this."

"I. Didn't." Maizy's expression hardened, and it was like a different person addressing Delia. "Not that you would have any room to judge me if I had."

"Excuse me?"

"Oh, you know *exactly* what I mean. I don't think someone who met her husband while working in a strip club should be judging anyone."

Delia gasped, horrified. "I can't imagine why you would think..."

Maizy did not relent. "Oh, don't give me that blue-blood, refined Southern Belle garbage, because I don't buy it. You think I'm some pathetic, middle-class housewife. And maybe I am. But I'm part of this community, and I know more than you think I do about people around here. Unlike you, I choose not to judge."

For a moment, Jess thought Delia was going to go across the table at the PTA president. Parker, bright eyes shifting back and forth between the women like an excited child, seemed to have the same idea. He also seemed pretty damn psyched about it.

"Okay." Jess put her hand on Delia's arm. "We're a little off track here. Can we take for granted, Parker, that you have similar pictures of Carras and Delia?"

Parker pocketed his phone. A fleeting disappointment that there wouldn't be a fight in front of him faded as he resumed his professional air. "Similar evidence, yes. Pictures." He glanced at Delia. "Recordings. But I can assure you, I'm the soul of discretion."

"You sound like a bad detective movie," Jess said. "Don't say things like that."

"Whatever. If I couldn't keep a secret, I wouldn't have been in this business for so long."

Maizy snorted.

"You help me, I'll help you."

"It's blackmail," Jess repeated unnecessarily. She fidgeted with her wedding ring, sour panic rising in the back of her throat.

Parker shrugged. "Call it whatever you like."

"We could report you," she said, already sensing this was not a viable option.

"You could," he agreed. "But I will caution you, Jess, that even though you have not engaged in anything technically illegal, it's possible," he looked at Delia and Maizy in turn, "that at least one of your friends took things a bit farther."

Delia's expression melted from outrage into understanding; her gaze dropped to stare at the table.

Parker smiled. "In case you still think reporting me is a good idea, know that records and mementos from my clients are stored securely in a place that only I know how to find. If anything happens—if I were to, say, get arrested—my mom has a key to a safe deposit box. It contains a list of my clients and instructions for how to find everything. Just in case."

"Your *mom* knows?" Maizy's anger gave way to horror.

Parker laughed. "Not the details. But I've told her the safe deposit box is the first place she should go in any emergency."

Jess's brain was finally catching up. Parker had set it up so that his arrest would mean the immediate humiliation and downfall of all his clients.

"I've got a lesson in twenty minutes, ladies." He stood and slung his tennis bag over his shoulder. "It's been a pleasure."

26

ᴅELIA

DELIA CARGILL WAS *PISSED*. IT was not an emotion she was accustomed to. She often felt irritated or frustrated, or even so stressed that she got snappy with her kids. She was a mom; her husband was gone a lot; it happened. But she handled things the classy way her affluent neighbors would expect.

In this moment, however, she was full-on, country-girl, shit-kicking pissed off. She paced back and forth in front of the picnic table, swinging her racket back and forth like a saber, while Jess and Maizy watched in numb amazement.

"I can't believe that mother-fucking mother fucker is black-mailing us!" Delia said, aware that this was not only unladylike speech, but unoriginal as well. She pulled out her phone. "I have to tell Belinda!"

Jess sighed. "Don't you think Belinda already knows?"

Delia stopped.

"She sent us to him, right? He's probably blackmailing her with the same deal," Jess said, her voice disconnected. "And now he expects us to throw somebody else under the bus. I can't do that."

"But he ate my cinnamon rolls," Maizy said, in a similar tone of disbelief. "He folded laundry with me. We sat on the porch swing and talked. I thought we were…"

"Friends?" Jess offered. "Me, too. We're idiots."

"Why would he do that, though?" Maizy said. "If he was pulling a scheme like this the whole time, why bother being nice to us? Why try to develop a bond? It feels…unnecessary. He already had our money. He…"

"He needed us to trust him enough to get the evidence." Delia thought of the conversation on the bridge, all the taboo things she'd revealed about her marriage that would certainly endanger her standing in the community, and Gage's standing at work. "He got me talking about…private things. And I didn't think anything of it at the time, but he kept his hand in his pocket. I think he was recording on his phone."

"You have embarrassing secrets?" Maizy asked.

Delia could see how desperate she was to bring her down, to gloat over Delia's humanity.

"I think maybe you should worry about the naked man in your bed with your family's portrait behind him," she fired back. "Your own secrets are enough without adding mine to your burden."

Jess put her head between her knees, staring down at the pine straw. "I was coming here to end it with him. I didn't even want this. Not anymore. I was going to pay him off and walk away."

"At least you got some of what you came for," Delia said. "Parker only texted me a couple of times after the trip and Gage wasn't around either time. I even left my phone out later on and he didn't notice."

"Maybe, but the stupid picture didn't work on Tom, either. I think we're in a similar position."

Maizy looked between them, thoughtful. "I still say there's something going on we don't understand. This is odd behavior for Parker."

"What? You know him so well?" Delia challenged. "If he's willing to have sex with desperate women for money, as you may have experienced, he's capable of other forms of lying and deceit."

"As I may have experienced?" Maizy echoed. "What are you saying?"

Delia wasn't sure what she was saying. But something was off. And unlike Maizy, she wasn't so sure the problem wasn't within their group. "Just that it's naïve to think he would be above this kind of behavior. He's clearly demonstrating otherwise."

Maizy stared at her, but didn't argue.

"I think Maizy has a point," Jess said. "Parker has always struck me as mischievous, not conniving. He's the type to break the rules to get what he wants, not to intentionally hurt people."

"I don't think psychoanalyzing the guy who's trying to ruin us is super helpful at this point. Speaking of that, where the hell is Carras?"

"She had to work, remember?" Jess said.

Delia thought of Carras and Parker in the hotel room, deep in conversation. "Or maybe...she has a different relationship with Parker than the rest of us. She *did* know him from their semipro days, didn't she? Maybe she downplayed how well..."

"No," Jess interrupted. "I know Carras isn't as chatty and open as some people, but I've gotten to know her pretty well. I don't think she would lie about this."

"Fine," Delia conceded. "In any case, I think we underestimated Parker Yung."

"You think?" Jess put her head back in her hands. "I never should have done this. Tom is going to leave me. I was coming here to end it..."

Delia's anger was beginning to dissipate. She put a hand on Jess's shoulder. "We'll figure it out. It will all be okay."

"How?"

"I have absolutely no idea."

Their phones all buzzed simultaneously; Maizy got to hers first. "It's Carras. Parker stopped by her office."

"Oh, geez," Jess said. "Couldn't he have called her, or at least waited until she wasn't busy with her depressed teens?"

"He probably wanted to make sure he could find her," Delia said. "Somewhere she couldn't dodge the conversation."

She was calmer now, thinking more clearly. She was still pissed; there was a certain twisted genius to the idea that an escort service would push its clients to find other clients. It probably led to safer, better-paying situations for him. And the blackmail was distasteful, but probably effective at keeping people quiet, and making sure they were selective about whom they recruited. The way Belinda had chosen her. After so many years in multilevel marketing, she understood—not Parker's ethics, obviously, and she still wanted to punch him in the face—but at least his business model.

Of course, Delia had never blackmailed her customers, or forced anyone to buy something they didn't want. But still. There were aggressive incentive systems and peer pressure, and the little speech she gave at each gathering, about how her businesses had given her the extra income her family needed. Those speeches were useful for recruiting other representatives ("kitchen mavens," "organizational specialists," "pleasure consultants"). But they also presented an unspoken polite demand on the party guests: Here we are, and I've taken all this time to share these wonderful products with you. I've validated your irritations with everyday inconveniences and offered you solutions. I've understood your loneliness and poor body image and sexual dissatisfaction, and most importantly, your need to know that others feel the same. At the end, I've offered you validation and connection and a little something to make your life better. The *least* you can do is buy something. Better yet, start your own business and push all this stuff on your friends, too.

It wasn't as manipulative or horrible as what Parker was doing. People very often did not buy anything from Delia, and she never threatened to send incriminating pictures to their spouses. But did she, on occasion, treat a non-buyer with a little bit of frostiness at the grocery store or the next PTA event? Delia couldn't deny it.

Even if she could see parallels between herself and Parker, there was nothing fun about being duped. Especially when the duper had used your greatest vulnerability against you: the desire for love and affection from your spouse.

27

JESS

THE SUGAR MILLS COUNTRY CLUB Summer Kickoff Party was open to all the families in both the country club and the annex across the street. It was a combination annual meeting, neighborhood barbecue, and sports banquet for the club's swim and tennis teams. It was run—naturally—by Belinda Hayes-Currington.

It was a hot day, a week after their horrid conversation with Parker, and despite hours of walking side by side through the neighborhood and staring at one another over endless cups of coffee, none of them had thought of a way out. The last thing Jess wanted to do was volunteer to help the woman who'd roped them into this mess. But she'd committed to Belinda—and more importantly, promised the kids—weeks ago, and couldn't think of a good reason to back out.

"Mommy, can we get a hot dog?" Dash ran up to her, dripping as he tugged on her shirt. He had that beautiful little boy look about him, ribs and collarbone pronounced beneath his smooth bronze skin, slick with water from the pool.

Mina was on his heels in her flowery swimsuit. "Mom, tell Dash he can't have a hot dog until he apologizes for punching my pony float. He hurt Mrs. Pinkwhistle's feelings."

"Mrs. Pinkwhistle hurt more than Daddy's feelings," Tom said with a grimace, one hand guarding his crotch. "It's a good thing we weren't planning on giving you guys any more siblings."

Jess smiled, despite her foul mood, but Mina was less than sympathetic. "That wasn't my fault, Daddy. You're the one who told us to get off the float."

"I meant one at a time, because she's not big enough to hold both of you. Which is why she was underwater." He looked mournfully at Jess. "Which is *also* why, when they bailed, she went flying up, straight into my junk."

Jess laughed, then covered her mouth when she saw Tom's irritated expression. "Go get hot dogs, babies," she said through her fingers. "Let's let Daddy recover."

She retrieved two icy beers from the small bar at the far end of the pool. The bartender was the same waiter who had served them white wine sangria the first time they'd met with Belinda here. Jess may have been imagining it, but she felt that he gave her an extra-long look as he put the beers on beverage napkins and took her club member number for the check. Even as she made her way back to Tom and he put a beer discreetly between his legs, she imagined she felt the bartender's eyes on her. But when she dared to glance up a few seconds later, he was serving cherry Cokes with extra cherries to three giggling teenage girls.

This whole thing was making her *completely* paranoid.

"Aren't you supposed to be helping with something?" Tom looked at the clubhouse, where Belinda was flitting in and out of the banquet room doors with her ironed khaki shorts and clipboard.

"But you're injured," Jess protested. "What if the kids need something?"

"They're eating hot dogs. I'll be recovered in a minute." Tom shifted on the pool chair and cringed. "Though I wouldn't be devastated if that damn pony float meets with an accident this afternoon."

Jess made her way to the large banquet room on the lower level of the clubhouse, which opened out onto the pool area. She spotted Delia inside, carrying an aluminum pan toward the clubhouse kitchen. Before she could make her way to her friend, however, Belinda stepped into her path.

"Oh, Jess, I am so glad you're here. We could use another pair of hands."

"Oh, could you?" Jess said, unable to keep the sarcasm out of her voice. "Anything I can do to make your life easier, Belinda. Say the word."

Confusion flickered across Belinda's pretty face, gone in an instant. Her voice was controlled and even. "I appreciate that. We all have to do our part, don't we?"

Jess wanted to smack her. Enough of the polite pretending that everything was normal, and that Belinda hadn't put everything dear to Jess at risk…even if Parker was blackmailing her, too. She opened her mouth to speak, but Delia drew up beside her and squeezed her hand.

"Thanks, Belinda. We've got it. Jess can help me clear these tables and set up the trophies."

Delia steered her away from Belinda, who gave Jess another long look before she turned her attention to something outside. "You can't say anything to her," she hissed. "Not here."

"Don't tell me after all this you are still sucking up to that awful woman?"

"Absolutely not. But I know that making a scene in front of all these people—including our *husbands*—would be a bad idea."

Jess glanced through the wall of windows at Tom, still sitting in the same chair, but now enjoying a hot dog with Dash. "I hope he reminds Dash to chew slowly," she said. What a nightmare to have the summer kickoff party disrupted by puked-up hot dog. As she watched, though, Tom put a hand on Dash's shoulders and demonstrated slow, exaggerated chewing. He was such a good dad. What if she'd ruined it already?

"Point taken. What are we supposed to do?"

Their task was to clear the barbecue supplies from the folding tables in the lower room—the tile-floored one that accommodated wet feet and casual parties, in contrast to the luxuriously carpeted banquet hall upstairs—and to set up the trophy area for the awards later in the afternoon. She and Delia worked in silence, putting away leftovers, wadding up plastic tablecloths, and wiping down tables for swim and tennis trophies.

They were about to start arranging the trophy tables, when Delia was called upstairs to help Belinda with something. Jess was relieved not to be dragged along—she couldn't face Belinda again—and she wanted to finish her duties quickly and return to her family. Thinking back to past years, she began to arrange the tables around herself, pulling one end at a time.

"You know they have staff for this stuff, right?"

The table she'd been moving slipped off her fingers in surprise. It was Parker Yung.

Jess tried not to let him see that his presence rattled her. "I'm fine. The staff are busy with the party, and Belinda says they don't know where everything goes anyway." She focused hard on getting the table in front of her parallel with the wall. Anything but look at him. "What are you doing here?"

"I'm always invited to these things, since I help with the tennis program. But I don't usually bother." Parker glanced out to the pool. "Isn't your husband missing you?"

Jess bristled and moved to a table at the other end of the room, talking over her shoulder. "He's with our children. And he knows they need my help in here. Tom trusts me." She turned to find that Parker had positioned himself at the other end of the table, ready to help her. "Even though he probably shouldn't."

"Of course he should. You didn't do anything wrong," Parker said. "Though to be honest, sometimes I wish you had."

A thrill of anger and flattered arousal ran through her traitorous body. *The snide little shit.* She wanted so badly to undo what she had done. To take back the awful, weak moments when she'd thought her marriage wasn't enough. When she'd been thinking that Tom wasn't allowed to be human. That he owed her, not just the consistent love and loyalty and affection that he'd always provided, but also a steady, uninterrupted stream of limitless passion and attraction. She'd expected more from him than she could from herself.

"What do you want, Parker?"

"Nothing. I just…"

Her irritation and fear turned to icy anger in her belly. "Look. You're going to get your money. I don't know how, but we will pay you. We'll get you what you want."

In truth, she *really* didn't know how they were going to do that. She sure as hell didn't have it to spare; it's not like her grandmother was going to die again and leave her more stock she could secretly cash in. And in the week since Parker had dropped his bombshell, Jess had not thought of a single person she felt comfortable roping into the stupid scheme. But he didn't need to know that right now. "My family is outside. I'm going out to join them as soon as I'm done here. I'd like you to leave me alone. You owe me that much."

Parker looked cowed. "I wasn't trying to…I mean…"

They lifted the next table as he fumbled with his words. *He was a great actor*, Jess thought.

"Jess. I wanted to see you alone for a minute. Nothing shady, I promise. I wanted to say, I mean, in case you were wondering…"

She let go of her end of the table, dropping it from six inches up so that it made a gratifying clatter. She spun on her heel and went for the next table.

"I wanted you to know that I did like you. *Do* like you. As a friend. I know that sounds ridiculous—"

"You know what, Parker? It does sound ridiculous. Friends don't blackmail each other. They don't fleece money from people they claim to like, or threaten to destroy each other's marriages. That's not the basis of a friendship. That's not the basis of anything."

"Jess, I wish I could make you understand. There's stuff I can't tell you. And I know it wouldn't change anything if I could. But I wanted you to know you're different. If things weren't like they are, I would—"

"You'd what? Hang out? Play tennis and swap recipes?" Hot anger and humiliation rose in her cheeks. *What the hell was this conversation?*

Parker dropped his head and shuffled his feet, the way Dash did when he was in trouble. It was comical how this grown man looked so much like her first-grader. Would have been comical, at least, if her husband had not walked in. Jess's stomach dropped, throat tightened.

"Hey, Gardner. The kids are with Stuart and Carras, eating ice cream. Dash charmed his way to an extra scoop…" Tom trailed off as the tension in the room seemed to block his progress. The smile he'd been wearing hardened in place. "What's going on?"

"Nothing," Jess said brightly, fighting off rising panic. "Parker was helping me move these tables for Delia. She's upstairs. Parker, this is my husband Tom."

The two men shook hands. She could no longer see Parker's

expression, but Tom's was full of consternation, despite a polite half-smile.

"I've been helping your wife with her serve," Parker said. "She's a natural athlete."

"I've always told her that."

"And you're *the* Tom Rodriguez, right? The Braves beat writer? I love your blog."

It was a big, fat lie and Jess knew it. Parker was playing Tom the same way he played everyone. This infuriated her almost as much as the blackmail.

"Thanks, man." Tom circled the table and put his hand on Jess's waist, something he rarely did in public. Whether he was claiming or supporting her, she wasn't sure.

Parker appeared unfazed. "I remember you played at Georgia Tech in the late 1990s. I had an older cousin who went there, took me to a couple of games. Didn't you play for the Braves for a little while, too?"

Jess turned to stare at him. *Had he only pretended not to know who Tom was originally? Or had he been researching?* Both possibilities gave her chills.

"Just a season in the minors," Tom was saying. "Tore my ACL sliding into second and that was it." He pulled Jess closer and kissed her on the temple. He *never* did that. "Can I help?"

Here we go, she thought as the two men—the baby-faced tennis pro and her almost middle-aged but still handsome husband—took stations at opposite ends of the table and looked to her for direction.

Tom lifted his end of the table higher than necessary, and Parker followed suit to keep it level. Tom raised his side again, almost to chest level, arm muscles flexing at an awkward angle that showed off their strength. Parker did the same, until she had directed them to the right spot, when Tom dropped the table from several inches up, leaving it to reverberate in Parker's hands.

So *this* was the reaction she'd paid twenty-five hundred dollars for. This was how her husband responded when it finally occurred to him to be jealous.

Jess watched with bemused awe as the two men shuffled around the room—which might as well have been a wrestling ring, the way they were circling it—sizing each other up. Neither looked at her, except to verify that they were putting the tables in the right places. If Parker dropped his end first, Tom would nudge the table half an inch one way or the other, making a show of squaring it up. If Parker held on to his end longer, Tom jumped to the next table and began moving it with little self-satisfied grunts of effort.

For his part, the tennis pro seemed to have lost his signature nonchalance, treating the arrangement of tables like a life-or-death scenario. Either there was a kernel of truth in what Parker had said about liking her, or he was excellent at playing the role of romantic rival.

When the tables were done, Tom returned to Jess's side and put a hand on her shoulder. "Thanks for the help, Peter."

"It's Parker."

"What's that? Oh. Ha! Peter Parker." He grinned at Jess. "See what my brain did there? Funny. You a Spiderman fan, Parker?"

"I don't have a lot of time for movies."

"Good for you. And here I thought all millennials were super-glued to their screens. Well, thanks again for helping Jess." Tom released her and stuck out his hand. "I know she appreciates it."

"It's my pleasure." To her astonishment, the two men were gripping each other's hands like sworn enemies. It was Evan the features guy all over again. Except terrifying.

"See you soon, Jess," Parker said. "Nice to meet you, Tom."

When the tennis pro exited, Jess braced herself. *Was Tom going to confront her? Kiss her? Demand to know the exact nature of her relationship with this kid?* Her hands were hot and itchy; she clenched and stretched them at her sides.

But when the sunlit door closed, Tom only said, "Everything okay, Gardner?"

"Sure," she croaked. "Why?"

He shrugged. "No reason. I'm going to go check on the kids. Want me to save you some ice cream, or is Delia keeping you trapped all afternoon?"

Jess realized she'd forgotten Delia hustling around upstairs with Belinda, probably pissed Jess hadn't come up to help. "Save me some. Chocolate if they have it."

"Will do." Tom mock-saluted her, his expression showing none of the tension she had felt moments ago. God, had all that puffed-up chest bumping with Parker been about Jess at all? Or was Tom naturally competitive with any dude who encroached on his territory? She could've been a bowling trophy or a disputed length of fence along the property line. Once he'd staked his claim, Tom was going right back to taking her for granted. *Biggest waste of money since the weekend of food poisoning at the winery.*

Jess was still standing alone among the perfectly parallel tables when Delia came down with a load of plastic trophies in a cardboard box. "You *have* to come upstairs and help me. I've been trying to get information about Parker out of Belinda for an hour and she keeps dodging. She spent ten whole minutes having a fake conversation on her cell phone to avoid...What happened to you? You look awful."

Jess looked at her friend, filled with despair and frustration and the sense that she'd just been on a rollercoaster. "I have no fucking idea."

28

DELIA

IT WAS AFTER THE AWARDS ceremonies were over, as dusk was settling over the pool and the parents with the youngest children had gone home. Delia roamed the club area, restless, helping out in fits and spurts. Trying to figure out how to corner Belinda.

She'd had a week, but Delia was still having trouble reconciling the Belinda Hayes-Currington she admired and emulated with the woman who would knowingly set them up for extortion. They all assumed Belinda was also being blackmailed. But if so, Delia wondered how she'd managed to make it look as though she enjoyed Parker's company at their first meeting. The two of them had been practically dripping in sex, even in front of Orson.

Delia knew she should be as pissed at Belinda as she was at Parker—the other three women had said as much—but she'd been so flattered by Belinda's sudden outreach of friendship, it was hard to accept that none of it was real. There had to be more to the story, but she needed Belinda to explain.

As Delia removed soggy streamers from the diving board railing—which decorating genius had thought *this* was a good idea?—she spotted Belinda across the pool with Orson, pressing a cup into his hand as he chatted with another middle-aged white guy in a golf visor. He accepted the drink, handing Belinda an empty cup in return. Within seconds, he began gesturing so clumsily that the other guy took a covert step backward to avoid getting drenched. Belinda put a hand on Orson's arm and guided the drink toward him. Delia couldn't hear what she said, but whatever it was made him grin at his wife and chug the drink.

How mortifying. *For all the faults in her marriage with Gage*, Delia thought, *at least he didn't require a nursemaid…* She watched Belinda insert herself under Orson's arm, encouraging him to lean on her. *Was it possible Orson Currington IV was an alcoholic? Was that why Belinda sought solace with Parker?*

She couldn't approach Belinda now, so Delia continued her walk around the party area, picking up bits of trash and keeping an eye out for Parker. He'd been around earlier—Jess had reported on the uncomfortable interaction between him and Tom—but so far, Delia had managed to avoid him. She was still too pissed off to talk to him without her redneck side clawing its way out to do some serious damage. There was a time in her life when Delia would've solved the Parker problem by sending one of her brothers after him with a tire iron, or commissioning her favorite bouncer to give him a friendly reminder.

But she wasn't that redneck girl with the seedy past any more. She was Mrs. Gage Cargill: refined, respectable, and flawless. Besides, she hadn't seen Parker in a couple of hours, which made her both hopeful that he'd gone home for the night, and nervous that he could be lurking around any corner.

The happy chatter and splashing of the older children and a few adults went on long after sunset. Gage, who had flown home from Belgium this morning, had put in a quick appearance and taken the girls home before sunset. He had some kind of crazy Skype call to be on with one of his Asian clients, and Lulu had accepted an invitation to sleep over at a friend's. Sadie wanted to wash her hair and text her friends. Delia had tried briefly to get her to stay, but was overpowered by eye rolling and the long-suffering sighs of a budding teen.

Delia had hung around, hoping to catch Belinda, and—truthfully—avoiding going home. She and Gage had scarcely had a chance to speak today; Delia thought it might be for the best. Parker's extortion had made her edgy and cranky all week, and Gage *hated* moodiness. Now that their daughters were beginning to express their own hormonal outrage, nothing seemed to piss Gage off more than added emotional vulnerability on Delia's part.

So rather than try to control her frustration at home, it was easier to hang out at the pool, playing the role of officious neighborhood volunteer. She chatted with Jess and Tom until they left (holding hands, no less) and said a brief hello to Carras and Stuart, who had taken advantage of the kids clearing out to get in the pool together.

Delia ordered a margarita in a plastic cup from the bar and made her way beyond the pool gate out to the tennis courts. She had intended to take a break from the crowd, to be alone with her thoughts. As she neared the little picnic pavilion, however, she slowed at the sound of voices. Arguing.

She took a few steps farther along the path, moving quietly now, curiosity pulling her forward. Two figures were silhouetted by the lights of the parking lot beyond. A man, sitting hunched over, facing away from the table: elbows on his knees, face in his hands. In front of him, a pear-shaped woman with hands on hips, her hair an unmistakable frizzy halo even in the dark. *Maizy.*

Delia should turn and go back to the party, mind her own business. Maizy could be talking with Anders, having a perfectly normal conversation. Kissing. Confessing. But something about Maizy's posture, and the slumped figure of the man, made Delia curious beyond resisting. Besides, weren't they in this together? If something was happening with Maizy and Parker, didn't Delia have an obligation to assist her? Or, at least find out what was going on for her own sake?

She moved off the path and away from the emergency lighting on the tennis courts, so she could approach without being seen. She was about twenty yards away when she was sure: the man *was* Parker. She stopped in her tracks, because his body language was so very un-Parker. Humble. Penitent, even.

She held her breath to listen.

"I don't think you're a bad man, Parker. That's not what I'm saying." Maizy's voice was firm and reassuring. "I'm saying you could do better than this. You could be better."

Parker mumbled something Delia couldn't hear, despite straining against the dark.

"I refuse to believe that. I refuse to accept that the man who stood in my kitchen, who sat on my porch…" A motor revved at the far end of the parking lot and blocked the sound temporarily. But Delia thought she heard, "bedroom."

Even from this distance, Delia could feel the emotion in Maizy's voice. Although she couldn't make out Parker's words, the mumbling tone was different from that of the cocky, self-assured tennis pro she had walked with in San Antonio. As Delia watched, he reached for Maizy's ample hips and pulled her toward him, so that his head rested against her belly. Her hands went awkwardly up in the air as though she didn't know what to do with them; then her shoulders relaxed and she put both hands on the sides of Parker's head, soothing.

Delia felt uncomfortable, as though she'd walked up on people having sex on the picnic table in the dark. Quiet as possible, Delia made her way back through the dark, resisting the temptation to pull out her phone and text Jess until she was back at the clubhouse.

29

JESS

"I DON'T UNDERSTAND WHAT YOU'RE SAYING. Like, were they kissing, or…what?"

Jess cradled the phone on her shoulder as she stepped into the garage and closed the door. Tom was upstairs putting the kids to bed, but she wasn't taking any chances. They'd come home sunburned and boozy; Tom had soldiered through two rounds of Monopoly Junior with the kids while the two of them spoke in double entendres that went over Dash and Mina's heads. *You totally get to pass Go, if you know what I mean.* Not a world-class seduction, but she was doing her damnedest.

"It was more than that. Not even that. They didn't kiss, that I saw."

"So, was he…pleasuring her or something?" Jess shuddered. The idea of Maizy sprawled out on the picnic table by the tennis courts, Parker's face between her thighs, was too much.

"Ew. No!"

"Come on, Delia, you're never shy about sexual terminology at your Pure Indulgences parties. Why are you being coy now?"

"That's what I'm trying to say. There wasn't anything overtly sexual. It was…intimate."

"They were sitting at a table."

"He was sitting. She was standing in front of him. And they were arguing."

"Not surprising, considering our situation." She thought of her own run-in with Parker earlier. "Can we finish this? I'm trying to get upstairs before my husband falls asleep and I miss my sex window."

"They were arguing, and I couldn't hear everything, but…he seemed sad and sorry that she was angry. He held her. Not in a sexy way, but the way you hold someone you love but you can't bear to face."

"And you could tell all of this from…how far away?"

Delia sighed. "They seemed close. I'm wondering if she was in on all this with him."

"Maizy Henriksson, a criminal mastermind? She's like, what, Parker's pimp?"

"No. Maybe. I don't know. He's just…never been that way with the rest of us. He was all apologetic, like a dog who's gotten into the trash."

Jess wanted to tell Delia he'd given her the same line in the clubhouse earlier, but she didn't think this was the moment. "Look, I know Maizy isn't your favorite person, but you might be reading too much into this. Is it possible, sweetie, that given how you dislike her, that maybe Parker being emotional with Maizy is making you…jealous?"

"No," Delia said. "It's not possible."

The door to the house opened. "Don't tell me you're searching for torture devices out here."

Jess whirled.

When Tom saw she was on the phone, he mouthed, "Sorry!"

"It's fine," Jess said. "I was taking the recycling out and talking to Delia."

"I'll let you go," Delia said.

"No, it's okay. I'll just be a minute."

"The recycling bucket's right here," Tom said. "You'll need that."

Jess gave him a sheepish look. "Hang on, Delia, don't go."

"If you're thinking rope tonight, grab the synthetic kind that's hanging over the toolbox. That natural stuff is too itchy." Tom rubbed his wrists with a devilish grin and closed the door behind him.

Delia's voice was dismissive. "I have to run anyway."

"Wait—"

But the phone was silent, the screen lighting up with a picture of Tom and the kids in their Braves gear in front of SunTrust Park. After a flurry of activity, Jess was standing alone in the garage with her phone and the recycling bin, which smelled like fermenting apple juice.

Meanwhile, Tom was heading upstairs, tipsy and making jokes about being tied up. Tom didn't do suave or flattering or smoldering. Jokes were his romantic currency, and he was offering Jess an evening they hadn't had in a long time. If she went up now, she might get to the bedroom before he turned on ESPN and went from a heady, playful drunk to an exhausted dad.

She put the phone on the garage shelf, where tomorrow she'd pretend to be surprised to find it. Her husband and kids were safe upstairs. Anything else could wait.

Jess woke at six the next morning to the sound of knocking on her bedroom door. She and Tom were curled together, naked and pleasantly sticky from the night before. They *never* did that any-more—no matter how sleepy she was, Jess pulled her pajamas back on at night, in case the kids needed them or the house caught fire. But last night had been different. Long, slow kisses and making love in that awed, fascinated way they had in college. Twice.

She tried to sit up, but Tom's arm across her breasts held her in place. "No," he whispered. "Stay." Louder, he called toward the door. "What's up, buddy?"

It was Dash. "I'm hungry. Why is your door locked?"

"He's upset," Jess said, trying again to reach for her robe. "I don't want him to feel locked out."

"Shh… He can handle this. If he cries, I'll let you up." Tom kissed the back of her neck, sending reverberations and pleasant memories through her body. "Buddy? Mommy and I need privacy for a few minutes. There's cereal in the pantry. Go downstairs and watch cartoons for a little while."

"But I don't want to watch PBS," Dash whined. "We always have to."

"You can watch any cartoons you want, champ. They don't even have to be educational." Jess started to protest, but Tom squeezed her nipple, making her yelp. "He'll survive, I promise," he said huskily.

"But I can't pour the milk," Dash whined.

"Aha!" Jess said, rolling to face her husband in triumph. "The milk!"

She wasn't sure why she was pushing back, letting herself get anxious about the kids needing her when Tom was trying to keep her in bed with him. This was the intimacy she'd been looking to recapture, after all, and a big part of her would've liked nothing better than to stay in bed with her husband all Sunday. But the intensity of their passion was as foreign as it was coveted, and some part of her felt the pull of their comfortable routine. It was some twisted psychology of modern motherhood, Jess thought; as soon as she began to enjoy herself or put her own needs first, a fountain of mommy guilt welled up inside, and lists of all the ways her family needed her materialized in her vision. Maybe this—as much as natural marital atrophy—had contributed to their slowing sex life.

But today, Tom wasn't having it.

"Okay, dude. Here's what you do," he said to the closed door, running a rough hand between Jess's bare breasts. "Go wake up your sister and tell her I asked her to please go downstairs with you, and help you pour milk on your cereal. You can watch any cartoons you want, as long as I don't hear fighting."

"Mina never helps me. I want to watch *Paw Patrol* and she hates that."

"Tell Mina that if you guys can go downstairs and eat breakfast and watch TV quietly until 8:00, I'll give you both five dollars."

"Five dollars!" Jess smacked him on the arm, as they heard Dash's footsteps retreat down the hall and into Mina's room. "You can't bribe them like that."

"I sure as hell can." Tom slid his hand down the length of her body, stroked her hip and thigh. "It's the cheapest date we've ever had."

"But now they'll expect to be paid whenever I want them to do anything." Her voice lost strength as he grazed the inside of her thigh. She'd been about to say, "And you won't be here to handle it," when Tom's hand tangled itself in the thicket of her hair and he kissed the hollow of her throat.

"I'll make it up to you," he said thickly, as he spread her legs with two fingers and began to stroke her, recalling the previous night's sensations with raw intensity. She squirmed, and he pressed firmly, grinning. "But you have to promise to be quiet until 8:00."

Jess relaxed into his touch, into the deliciousness of making love on a Sunday morning. For a few sweet moments, Jess enjoyed the gasping, giggling state of perfection she'd worked so imperfectly to achieve.

It was almost nine when Jess stepped out into the garage to retrieve her abandoned phone. She was wearing her favorite old pajama bottoms and Tom's T-shirt from the night before, her rat's-nest hair piled on her head with a clip. The kids had finished their cereal and sat slack-jawed in front of the cartoons. The kitchen table was strewn with sticky crumbs and milk and—for some reason—*four* boxes of cereal.

Normally she would have seen a parenting fail. But today she saw the signs of a messy, normal contentment. Her anxiety about Parker had taken a backseat to the triple-orgasm glow of realizing she was still in love with her goofball husband.

She'd known when she put the phone down, there was a decent chance of missing a text or two from Delia. They'd been friends for almost a decade, and rarely had a difference of opinion, much less the stilted exchange from last night. Part of Jess felt guilty that she hadn't called her friend back. But that part of her had been bound, gagged, and silenced by the part of her that desperately needed a decent orgasm and wanted to ride her husband like a racehorse. Her friendship with Delia mattered, of course, but she knew it would all be smoothed over once they had a chance to talk. Maybe they'd even go for a walk this evening while Tom was packing to go back on the road.

As it turned out, however, she'd missed more than a couple of texts from Delia. She had seven missed calls and sixty-four unread text messages. Her heart felt immediate, nameless panic. Her frantic brain went down the checklist: the kids were inside; Tom was upstairs taking a shower. *Could it be one of her parents? Tom's parents?*

As she fumbled to enter her password—messing it up three times—she tried to remember the last time she'd spoken to Tom's mother. Her own mom had called just yesterday and everything sounded fine. Not that that meant anything.

As soon as the screen loaded, a low battery warning sign appeared; she swiped it away. A quick scan of the missed calls revealed Delia (five calls) and Carras (two calls). There was a red "3" badge over her voicemail icon. Instead of dialing voicemail, however, she went to the texts, hoping for more information faster.

There were four new conversations in her feed: one each from Delia, Maizy, and Carras. And a group conversation at the top that included all four of them. She touched this one to bring it up, scanning quickly.

The police are saying it happened while the party was still going.
A diversion?
I'm sure Orson is livid.
Poor Belinda. Never thought I'd say that.
Do you think she was in on it?
So they have no idea where P went?
No way she was in on it. Why would she do that to her own house?
I heard he broke some Belle Époque lamp of hers. $8000.
No, no one knows. The police think he left the country.
Where did you hear that? None of this is on the news.
I talked to Sandy Patterson. Next door to the Curringtons.
Where the hell is Jess?
IDK. Her car is in the driveway, and so is Tom's truck.
Oh God. It's on the news again.
What channel?
They're showing the front of their house. Police lights flashing. Channel 2.
God, it looks so seedy from that angle. Like one of those places in town.
Anders is already complaining that our property values are going down. If people think this is a robbery area.

The low battery reminder popped up again, warning Jess that her phone would shut down if not plugged into power. She went back inside and pivoted away from the living room, where her children were watching cartoons. Upstairs, she ducked into the guest bedroom that doubled as her office. She plugged in her phone and settled on the carpet by the outlet. The phone lit up and buzzed almost out of her hands. *Delia.*

"Hey. What's going on?"

"What do you mean, what's going on? Where the hell are you?"

"I'm home. My phone died." *Close enough.* "I saw messages from you guys. What happened?"

"Oh my God, Jess. I can't believe you don't know." Delia hesitated. "Parker's *gone*. He broke into Belinda's house last night after the party, broke some stuff, rifled through Belinda's underwear drawer..."

"He couldn't have," Jess said, bewildered. "I mean, they were home, right? We saw everyone at the party."

"I guess they were still at the clubhouse, cleaning up or something. Apparently, the kids stayed with their grandmother."

"How do they know it was Parker?" Jess's brain refused to wrap itself around the information. *It couldn't be.* "He wouldn't..." But she stopped herself, thinking of the ice in his dark eyes when he'd informed them he was going to be extorting money from them. *Maybe he would.*

"Well, Sandy Patterson lives next door, and she saw his Jeep in front of their house at some point during the party. She didn't go, you know; she wouldn't be caught dead at a pool party. But she's a good customer for my skincare line. Huge pores. And when they got home, the place was trashed, some jewelry missing..."

"That doesn't sound like Parker."

"It gets worse," Delia said. "Apparently he managed to get hold of some of their banking information and passwords. He stole a couple million dollars from their retirement account."

Jess gasped. "I can't believe it."

"I know," Delia said. For once she didn't sound like the person with the answer to everything. "I heard Orson went ballistic, called the police *and* the press. It's all over the news now, and everyone knows Orson... They'll be investigating. Which means..."

"Oh, God." Jess let her head fall back against the wall.

The silence stretched between them, sickly and unbearable. *The picture. The kiss that hadn't even been a real kiss. If Tom saw...* Jess felt sick. *He was whistling in the shower. They'd had the best sex in a decade.*

"Try not to panic..." But the panic was clear in Delia's voice. "Let's all just be normal and wait for information."

"Just be normal?" Jess squeaked. "Okay, that's easy. Sure."

Delia said something else, but Jess didn't hear because Tom had appeared in the doorway, looking down at her. "You know you can charge your phone in the bedroom? I don't bite…unless you want me to." He grinned, looked refreshed in shorts and a T-shirt, with his dark, thinning hair wet and spikey. He was heartbreaking-ly cute, even all these years later. "You okay, Gardner?"

"I'm fine," she said, trying to mirror his smile. She covered the phone. "Delia and Gage are having a spat, that's all."

He frowned, and the genuine concern on his expression was a knife to her heart. Tom bent down and kissed her on the forehead. "Shower is all yours. Unless you want company? I don't mind going twice."

Jess squeezed his hand, and her chest constricted. "Thanks. I'll be out in a minute." It was in her voice already, whatever this thing was going to do to her. To them.

Tom's smile faded, but he didn't say anything else as he closed the door behind him.

30

CARRAS

THE FOUR OF THEM MET at Jess's house the next day, after the kids had been packed off to school and Tom had caught his rideshare to the airport. The mood was more solemn than last time they'd met, and the coffee was way too strong.

"Sorry. It's road tar." Jess waved a tired hand at it. There were bags under her eyes, as Carras knew were under her own. Even Maizy had failed at her usual habit of bringing baked goods. She shuffled in with a box of fast-food donuts and put them on Jess's table, where they sat untouched.

They had the local news on in the background, but there had been little new information this morning: a replay of the police car in front of the Curringtons' house in the early hours yesterday, and some shaky shots of Parker's yellow Jeep, which had been found in an economy parking lot at the airport last night. The footage was accompanied by a red banner across the bottom of the screen: "Scandal in the Suburbs?"

Great, Carras thought. That was going to be the hashtag for this thing. *#ScandalintheSuburbs*. And when they figured out Carras was involved, the story would skyrocket, and every picture of her in a short tennis dress from a weird angle would be splashed all over the news. Her dad was going to see it. *#RuinMyLife*.

A few minutes ago, the programming had switched to a perky talk show, where for some reason a woman from the audience was dancing awkwardly in a rainstorm of confetti.

"Maybe the fact that he went with economy parking means he's planning to come back?" Maizy said, with hope in her voice.

"Or that he's innocent? This could all still be a misunderstanding."

"Right," Delia said. "He *accidentally* wandered into Orson and Belinda's house, tripped over a bunch of valuable items, and landed in Belinda's underwear drawer. Upstairs. Then three-point-four million dollars fell into his pockets on accident."

"Delia," Jess said.

"Oh, wait, sorry. Not his pockets. An offshore bank account. I hear that happens by accident all the time."

"You made your point," Maizy said. "You don't have to be such a bitch about it."

They all turned to Maizy in surprise.

"Sorry. I'm testy." Maizy reached for a chocolate frosted donut and took an unhappy bite. "I can't believe he did this."

"You can't?" Delia glared at Maizy. "After what he did to us? Sounds like he just upped his game from extortion to outright theft."

"It is weird, though," Jess agreed. "I mean, I talked to him Saturday. And he seemed…normal. I mean, considering the situation. It's like he was trying to make me less angry with him. And, I don't know…if he knew he'd be leaving the country the next day, would he be concerned about my feelings?"

"Maybe that's *why* he was concerned," Carras said. Even she had noticed that Parker seemed to have a special affection for Jess. "Maybe he didn't want to leave on a bad note."

"It's hard to tell." Jess bit her lip. "He did say he wanted to tell me something. But Tom interrupted us, and they got all weird. Competitive."

Maizy's head snapped up. "You mean it worked? Tom got jealous when he saw you with Parker?"

Jess gave her a grim smile. "It worked. Tom finally responded the way I'd been hoping he would…" She trailed off, reddening.

It was funny to Carras how much Tom's jealousy surprised Jess. She had been a close observer of their marriage for a few years, and although she didn't find it hard to believe that they might have problems in the bedroom (who didn't?), she didn't understand how Jess could fail to see that Tom was crazy about her. Jess talked often about Stuart's devotion to Carras, and she was right. But it wasn't news to Carras. She *knew* her husband loved her. That had never been the problem. Maybe it was a special brand of insecurity that made otherwise confident and beautiful women doubt the affection of their devoted husbands.

"It's okay," Carras said. "That you got something good out of this situation. No matter what happens, we have to feel that way, for our own sanity. Whatever Parker did to Belinda and Orson had nothing to do with any of us, or our arrangements with him."

"Unfortunately," Delia said, "I'm not sure the police are going to see it that way. And if they find the evidence he kept on us…"

"But why would he lead them to us?" Maizy's brow wrinkled. "We kept our end of the deal."

"It doesn't matter." Jess pushed herself away from the table and crossed to the coffeepot, unceremoniously pouring the brown sludge down the drain. "It doesn't matter what we did, or even what Parker intended. If the police are investigating him, it's a matter of time before they find everything and come asking questions."

Delia's phone buzzed on the table and she picked it up, swiping at the screen. Jess was leaning against the counter, pressing the palms of her hands into her forehead.

"Sit down." Carras got up to help, despite the queasy feeling in her own belly. "Let me do this."

Jess didn't object, so Carras rinsed the coffeepot and located the filters in Jess's cabinet, glad to have a use for her restless body, and to not have to face this conversation head-on.

"Text from Sandy Patterson," Delia said. "She took a casserole over to Belinda's house, and it sounds like the police think Parker had an accomplice. Someone who helped him get access to her accounts. They grilled the Curringtons most of the day yesterday about who else knows enough about them to have their passwords."

Carras heard Jess plop back down in her seat. "I wonder why they think that. Couldn't he have stolen her passwords during one of their…sessions?"

"Maybe." Delia was still staring at her phone. "Sandy says Belinda thinks they're going to be interviewing everyone at the party as witnesses. They're talking to their household staff and a bunch of people in Orson's company."

"Oh God." Maizy put her hand to her chest. "What if someone saw him talking to Jess? Or any of us?"

"You mean, like at the tennis pavilion?" Delia said without inflection. "Like, after dark?"

Carras had started the coffeemaker and was heading back to the table, but something in Delia's tone made her pause.

Maizy's face went pale first, then splotchy pink and white. "What are you talking about?"

"You know what I'm talking about. I saw you."

"What? When?"

Delia's tone was steady and neutral. She didn't take her eyes from Maizy. "After the pool party, when most people had gone. I was taking a break before helping with cleanup. I walked down between the tennis courts."

Maizy's head hit the table. "Oh God. Oh God, oh God, oh God," she said into her lap.

Carras resumed her seat and reached for a donut. She'd been smelling them all morning and finally felt up to eating one.

"You'd better tell us about it." Delia made no move to comfort the pitiful woman. "Like it or not, we're on the same team now."

Maizy sat up in exasperation. "It wasn't what you think. We weren't…doing anything untoward. We were talking."

"About what?"

"You know. Probably the same thing all of you would want to talk to him about. This whole blackmail situation. I thought I could talk Parker out of it, get him to delete the pictures." She laughed bitterly. "You guys don't know Anders. His view of the world is…rigid. Black-and-white. He would never understand what happened with Parker."

Jess spoke up. "I think it's fair to say none of our husbands would be thrilled about this. Or the money that should be in our kids' college funds. At least you and Anders can afford it."

Maizy looked agonized. "That's not what I meant. It's not… Jess, I understand your financial situation. I wish I could help."

"Don't do me any favors."

"Please don't get angry. It's not about the money. I mean, I know money is a big piece of it. But, Anders…" Maizy reached for the donut box as though she were going to get a second one, then her hand recoiled. "He seriously won't understand this. And his family..."

"Yeah, Anders and his family. You talked about that last time," Delia said. "But Anders is also in banking, isn't he?"

Maizy looked up at Delia. "What are you saying?"

"I'm saying that I'm not a lawyer, but being married to one means I could find my way around the Uniform Commercial Code if I needed to. Maybe someone who's been married to a banker for two decades would know how to create an offshore account."

Maizy straightened. "Are you accusing me of something?"

"Of course not, Maizy dear," Delia said with mock sweetness. "I'm saying that it was a pretty intense conversation the two of you were having the other night."

"Ladies," Carras said, trying to defuse the tension. "Let's not—"

Maizy ignored her. "If we're looking for Parker's accomplice in this room, I think you need to look for a mirror," she spat at Delia. "Because you and Carras have both been secretive about what happened in San Antonio. And why you needed Parker in the first place."

Carras felt her stomach turn with anxiety. The donut on the napkin in front of her smelled oily and foul; she pushed it away. She needed to say something, to change the direction of the conversation. "I don't think we should be turning on each other..." she started, with no idea what she could say next to rein in the emotions. This was why she didn't do couples' therapy. She hated yelling, hated having to wrest back a conversation that had gone off the rails.

"Maizy." Jess stood to step into the next room. "Come on."

But Maizy faced Delia, the two of them looking like lionesses about to pounce. "Anyway, I think understanding *international law* would point to an accomplice as much as a husband who works at the bank."

"Girls!" The voice came oddly distorted, reverberating through the kitchen. They all turned to see Jess holding a child's purple megaphone with buttons on the side for different voices.

"Sorry." Jess looked at the toy. "It was the only thing I had handy."

"Well, that's useful," Delia said.

"The point is, Carras is right. No matter what our connections to Parker have been in the last few weeks, we have to separate ourselves from whatever else he's done. We need to stick together. Right, Carras?"

But Carras didn't feel gratified. She felt miserable. She stood, backing away from the table and its smells of food and acrimony. Jess's eyes were wide with trust, counting on Carras to bring sanity to the situation. She felt that trust like a weight pressing on her chest; it made her dizzy.

"Would you excuse me for a minute, please?" Carras heard herself say, and she dashed to Jess's powder room just in time to vomit up three sips of coffee and half a donut. *Two more things to cross off the list of foods she could eat.* Carras knew, no matter what happened next, things were never going to be the same.

31

MAIZY

PARKER'S BETRAYAL OF THE CURRINGTONS hit the Sugar Mills community in waves, starting fresh each day as more information emerged. Everyone knew the Curringtons; even those who had a passing or frosty acquaintance with them couldn't say often enough what a sweet family they were and how horrible it all was. Many passwords were changed, many urgent calls made to install, update, or check on security systems on both sides of Sweet River Road.

Most people who played tennis had known Parker, too, or at least seen him around. He seemed like such a nice kid, they all said, and so *handsome*. It struck Maizy as funny that people seemed to consider this a particularly bitter irony. Not just that someone in their community had committed a crime, or that their neighbors had been victimized, but that someone so *attractive* had done it. It violated the Sugar Mills concept of what made a good person.

But there were a few residents, women specifically, whom Maizy noticed were visibly quieter now that Parker had disappeared. She would see them at the grocery store or bringing their kids to the pool; they avoided eye contact, or stared at their phones as if they had something important going on.

The more salacious rumors began circulating mid-week, even before the news broke that police were investigating a possible "prostitution ring" in the affluent suburb. Supposedly, there were dozens of women, in Sugar Mills and elsewhere. People could not wait to speculate about the likely candidates for scandal. *Could you ever? Right here in our neighborhood?* It was all so distasteful. It was all so delicious.

Maybe it was her reputation as the PTA president, or perhaps her less-than-sexy demeanor, but people simply assumed Maizy had no part in it. As a result, they felt free to share their theories and gossip with her, and to hope Maizy would have something to share in return. She never did. She listened.

Today, Maizy sent her girls to the basement to watch a movie because Carras, Delia, and Jess were coming over. Maizy pulled cinnamon rolls—the ones Parker liked—out of the oven to cool and put a pitcher of lemonade on the table. She'd made coffee, too, but it was warm outside, and Maizy had noticed that Carras had not been drinking it lately.

The four of them were now meeting daily to discuss what little news was being released publicly and the gossip they each picked up from others. It came out that Parker had flown to Miami and on to Havana the night of the swim party. His parents had both been brought in for questioning but had not commented. His younger sister worked for a tech company in California (the press were always careful to note that this didn't *necessarily* mean she was involved with the electronic theft of the funds).

Delia arrived first with her youngest daughter. Maizy was careful to keep her face neutral when she opened the door. "My girls are downstairs, Lulu. Do you want some lemonade?"

Lulu declined with a polite, freckled smile and Maizy watched her descend to the basement. She knew from her own girls that Lulu was smart and usually kind, but could be a force to be reckoned with. Not unlike her mother.

"Am I first?" Delia said.

Maizy nodded and led her through to the kitchen. She and Delia rarely spoke directly; an unspoken truce had developed between them since the confrontation at Jess's table. But she wasn't sure how long it would last, and she had the distinct sense Delia still didn't trust her. The feeling was mutual.

Still, Maizy didn't want to rock the boat. "Cinnamon roll?"

"No, thanks." Delia wrinkled her nose. "Swimsuit weather—no carbs."

"Right," Maizy said, pretending she knew all about quitting carbs for swimsuit weather. As though swimsuit weather meant anything to Maizy besides biker shorts and bulky T-shirts over an industrial strength, Kevlar bathing suit she hoped to hell no one would ever see. "I thought the kids might enjoy them."

She sat across from Delia, and decided to focus on the issue at hand. "Have you heard anything from Belinda?"

"A little. Maybe we should wait for the others? I can go over all of it at once."

"Sure." They sat in silence for several excruciating moments.

When the doorbell rang, Maizy bolted out of her seat so fast that she nearly knocked the chair over. Jess and Carras stood together on the front steps. *Thank God.*

"I finally talked to Belinda last night," Delia said, when they had settled themselves at the table and shipped the kids down to the basement. "She's a wreck, poor girl. I can't even imagine what she and Orson have been through."

"I'm sure," Jess said. "Losing a fraction of their millions, and an eight-thousand-dollar lamp. Which I'm sure was insured."

"It was a bigger percentage of their wealth than everyone thought. I guess Orson had some financial issues a couple years ago, and apparently he sold off stock in his family's company to cover some debts. And since he and Belinda have been spending more than usual lately—"

"Eight-thousand-dollar lamp," Jess said, with an eyebrow cocked. "And nude beach vacations."

"And the sex rug." Carras smirked. "Remember? That was like four thousand."

"*Anyway,*" Delia said, glaring.

Maizy bit back a smile. Maybe she couldn't rock the boat with Delia, but it was fun to watch her get irritated with other people.

"Belinda told me the police brought her and Orson in again this week, separately. They told her the IP address the transfer was made from matches their home wireless network. Either Parker hacked in using a laptop—which there's nothing in his background to indicate he was capable of doing—or he had help from a far more tech savvy person, like a cybercriminal."

"Ooooor," Jess drawled. "He was schtooping Belinda for money and used their computer while she was in the shower."

Delia nodded. "Belinda didn't say it directly, but it sounds like that might be what happened. Maybe she had her passwords written down somewhere and Parker found them."

"Oh, God," Maizy said. "My passwords are all in a little notebook next to the computer. It's too complicated—I can never remember them all."

"Obviously something you should change," Delia said, as if Maizy were a six-year-old. "Anyone who broke into your house, or came in during a party, could get access to all your accounts."

Maizy thought of Parker, half-naked (at least) on her bed, next to her family picture, with her own black lacy bra draped seductively nearby. If he'd managed to pull that off while she was in the bathroom, what else could he have managed? He'd been here for hours, helping her fold laundry, building her confidence, making her feel... She glanced at the screened porch on the other side of the kitchen. The minute everyone left, she was going to check her accounts. The panic made her wish everyone would leave now. But it had been more than a week since Parker skipped town. Surely, if he were going to steal from her and Anders, he'd have done it already?

"Has Orson figured out yet that Parker spent time in their house?" Carras asked. "Did Belinda say?"

Delia shook her head. "He'd have hit the fan. Belinda would have mentioned it."

Jess gave her a skeptical look. "Are you sure? It's not like the two of you are close. She pushed us into this scheme, knowing Parker would end up blackmailing us. Do you think she's going to tell you everything she knows?"

"I don't know if we should trust Belinda," Maizy agreed, careful not to look at Delia.

"I'm not *trusting* her," Delia said through clenched teeth. "I'm trying to milk her for whatever information she can give us. She said she would text me if she hears anything from the cops today; that's more than any of you have managed to find."

"Cheese on bread," Carras murmured. "Delia the spy."

Carras didn't seem to have noticed what she'd said. Maizy was struck with the sudden urge to laugh, a lump in her chest that pressed upward and forced itself out as a weird braying sound. Once she heard the sound, she lost control, and it turned into a terrible case of the giggles.

Carras looked confused at first, then broke into a smile. Jess, biting back her own laugh, erupted in a snort. Which was universally regarded as hilarious.

"What in holy hell is going on with you people?" Delia scowled. "This isn't funny."

And that, as everyone with kids should know, was the *worst* thing you could say to someone who couldn't stop laughing. But Maizy couldn't say this, because now she was laughing uncontrollably, gripping the side of the table as tears streaked down her cheeks, sucking hard for breath. "Sorry, sorry... I'm sorry... I don't know why I can't..."

It was absurd, but it felt good. As though something Maizy had kept locked inside was forcing its way out. As if her muscles had been clenched for so long that once they let go, she had to pee. "Excuse me," she managed, and grabbed a napkin to wipe her eyes as she headed toward the powder room.

"What the actual hell?" Delia stared at her phone, and Maizy paused in the doorway, sobering to listen.

"What?" Jess asked.

"It's Belinda. The police called her and Orson in again this morning. They claim to know how Parker made his money, and to have a list of his clients."

The laughter in Maizy's chest evaporated as quickly as it had come. "But," she said, stupidly, obviously. "That's us."

32

JESS

JESS WASN'T SURE HOW LONG they all stared at one another in silence. Delia typed furiously on her phone, asking Belinda for more information. Soon, however, she dropped the phone in her lap and leaned back against the chair in resignation.

Maizy, who was shifting from one foot to the other, excused herself to the bathroom. None of them spoke or moved. Jess couldn't get her head around what was happening.

Jess saw it now: the path behind her was littered with opportunities to come clean with her husband and face the consequences. Before the blackmail. When Parker threatened blackmail. After Tom's standoff with Parker at the clubhouse. She could imagine Tom's disappointed face, what he would say. "You put our family's savings at risk with this guy, all because you couldn't talk to me?"

She had no excuse. She had been putting off telling him until it felt like the right time. *And now…* She stared at her phone, face up on the table in front of her. She should pick up the phone right this minute and tell her husband what was going on. He was the only person whose opinion mattered to her, the only person she trusted with everything. The fact that these women knew the most sordid thing about her, and not Tom, deepened her sense of shame.

She was willing her hand to reach for the phone, gathering her courage to face—not Tom's anger, though of course he would be—but her own shame. And then, as though it sensed her connection to it, the phone lit up and vibrated. They all four jumped.

The caller ID read, "Sugar Mills Government Exchange." Jess's stomach sank. She glanced at the other three, but their faces were as blank and terrified as her own.

"Hello?"

"May I speak with Jessica Ann Gardner Rodriguez?"

The use of her full legal name did nothing to allay her fears. "This is her. She. This is she."

"Mrs. Rodriguez, this is Officer Cynthia Baskins, with the Sugar Mills Police Department. Can you confirm that you live at 785 Sugar St.?"

"I do. Is everything okay?"

"Yes, ma'am. I'm sure you are aware that there is a grand larceny investigation going on in your area. We are reaching out to determine if you can provide additional information."

"Well, Parker Yung was my tennis instructor, but I don't think I have any insights."

The woman cut her off. "Yes, ma'am. That's understandable. We're asking everyone to come in and talk with us anyway. Sometimes people know more than they realize. We have a schedule set up with hour-long windows, starting tomorrow morning. The next available appointment is 10:00 a.m. Would that work for you?"

Tomorrow morning. "Well, my husband travels for work and I don't think I'd have time to find a sitter. Next week, I—"

"We have arranged for supervised childcare in our community education room. We have multiple interview rooms open to accommodate the long list of witnesses, so your children may be with others, supervised by two of our school safety officers."

"School safety officers," Jess repeated.

"Yes, ma'am. There will be two officers at all times, at least one of them female." The woman paused. "I believe they will be watching *Finding Nemo.* They also have playing cards and age-appropriate board games."

Jess almost laughed. As though this was what she'd be worried about when called in for questioning. One of the other moms must have asked for details about the arrangements. Only in Sugar Mills.

"Can I put you down for the 10:00 slot tomorrow? You'll be with Officer Reed in interview Room B. There is free parking in the surface lot up the hill from the police station. Please arrive at least fifteen minutes before your scheduled time. We have a questionnaire for you to fill out and we'll need to get a copy of your driver's license."

Like the doctor's office, Jess thought grimly.

"Mrs. Rodriguez? Can I put you down for 10:00 tomorrow?"

"Um. Yes. I guess so. Do I…" Jess hesitated. Every crime show she'd ever seen was colliding in her head at once. Interrogation rooms, bad coffee, confrontations, Vincent D'Onofrio pretending to befriend her and then turning on her with a scathing impeachment of her psychological flaws. And there were *so* many flaws. "Do I need a lawyer? Or anything?"

The woman's tone changed from administrative to hard and serious. "I don't know, Mrs. Rodriguez. You are not under arrest, but you are entitled to an attorney if you feel you need one. Do you feel you need one?"

"No. I just… I've never done this before."

The woman's tone softened again. "Most people haven't, Mrs. Rodriguez. But we're gathering information here. You are welcome to consult an attorney before coming in. Just notify me as soon as possible so that I can fill your slot with someone else."

And, Jess thought, *notify the lead investigator that she was being uncooperative.* "Lawyered up," they called it on TV.

"No, it's fine. The whole situation is so unnerving. You understand."

"I do, Mrs. Rodriguez." It sounded as if the call might be over, but then the woman said, "Did you say your husband is going out of town tomorrow? Is he Tomás Carlos Rodriguez?"

A chill ran down Jess's back. "Yes?"

"Do you have any indication when he'll be returning? He is on my list as well."

"Tom? He wouldn't know anything about—I mean, he was not involved, he never dealt with the tennis lessons. Tom doesn't play tennis." She was babbling, but she couldn't stop.

"Yes, ma'am. We're trying to be thorough. When will he be back?"

"Sometime next week. He travels a lot. He's a sports reporter. Maybe Tuesday? I could check his schedule and call you back."

"Make a note of it for Officer Reed tomorrow. He'll update the file. Do you have any other questions?"

Jess had about a thousand, but none of them were appropriate. "No, ma'am. I'll be in tomorrow at ten."

When Jess hung up, Maizy was pacing back and forth in the living room on her phone. No sooner had Jess replaced her own phone on the table than Delia's buzzed in her lap. They exchanged a look and Delia answered. For the first time since she'd met her indomitable neighbor years ago, Jess heard Delia's voice waver.

"I wonder," Carras said, as her own phone began to buzz in the bag hanging off the back of her chair, "when this is over, if we'll decide it was worth it."

33

JESS

WHEN JESS GOT HOME, TOM was not working in his usual spot, but watching cartoons on the couch with Dash on one side and Mina on the other. He wore gray sweatpants that she'd seen him in a million times and white athletic socks with a hole in one toe.

Jess felt a tiny surge of irritation—he was supposed to be working. And if he didn't need to work, there was unfolded laundry in the dryer and a pile of dirty dishes in the sink. Jess *never* got to snuggle with the kids and watch cartoons when she was working from home. And she was *always* working from home.

She immediately felt ashamed of these thoughts, and the irritation was replaced by a swell of affection for her family, snuggled up innocently on the couch. Jess was not a terribly sentimental person, but she wanted to snap a picture of them right then, to remember this ordinary summer day. Before their whole lives would turn upside down.

"Hey, Gardner. I didn't realize you'd come in." Tom extracted himself from beneath Dash's reclining form and followed Jess to the kitchen. "I was taking a quick break before I got started on the dishes."

"I just came from Maizy's." *She had to tell him.* "I got a call from the police department."

"God. Is everything okay?"

He looked so worried, hot shame flowed through her once again. "Everything's fine. They are interviewing everybody about Parker. All his tennis clients."

Tom cocked his head to one side. "Why?"

"I guess…in case any of us saw something suspicious. During tennis."

Tom opened the refrigerator, pulled out a bag of grapes and popped one into his mouth. "What on earth would a tennis client know about this asshole stealing money from people?"

"You should wash those before you eat them. And I don't know, maybe it's one of those things where they're hoping you saw something that didn't seem significant at the time…"

Tom popped another unwashed grape into his mouth, grinning, and then took the rest over to the sink to wash them. "That doesn't sound right."

"It doesn't?" Jess was panicked. How was she going to explain? *Tell him, you idiot. Tell him now.*

Tom set the dripping grapes straight onto the counter. Without comment, Jess handed him a paper towel to put underneath them. He pulled out the bread, and with a glance at the clock, Jess realized he was making lunch for the kids.

"Tom…I have to tell you. I mean, how would you feel if…"

"What, babe?" He set down the peanut butter jar and looked at her. "Oh, Jesus. Don't tell me you gave that little asshole your credit card or something? Shit. How did you pay for lessons?"

She recoiled. "That's not it. I paid cash."

"Good," he said, looking relieved for about two seconds, before his expression changed to confusion. "Why?"

Jess shrugged. "Parker said that was better."

Tom seemed to be trying to make up his mind about something. "Right. Of course, he's probably not paying taxes on his fees. Little asshole."

Jess had to laugh. "I guess in the scheme of things, that isn't the worst thing he's done."

"I was talking to Frank, the local news guy, and he thinks the police are looking for a girlfriend. Based on Parker's age and profession, Frank thinks it's unlikely he concocted this scheme by himself. Like maybe he was stealing a little bit from his clients here and there, overcharging them or whatever, but the girlfriend was probably the one who pushed him to go big and steal from the Curringtons. She may be in Cuba already, waiting."

"Why would Frank assume it's a woman? Why not a business partner or something?"

Tom grinned. "Only a man in love would take that kind of risk out of nowhere. Why would he suddenly become a master criminal, unless he was trying to buy some hot woman Jimmy Choos?"

"It's weird that's where your mind goes," Jess said. "Considering I've never owned a pair of shoes that cost more than sixty dollars."

"Well, it was Frank's theory—sixty dollars!" Tom whistled. "What'd you do, visit the White House?"

Jess threw a grape at him, and he ducked, laughing. She had an involuntary image in her mind of Parker, lying naked on the floor while a dominatrix—who in her imagination looked like Sharon Stone from the early nineties—walked on his chest wearing sky-high stilettos.

"I'm glad you aren't into that kind of stuff," Tom said. "I couldn't handle it."

Jess coughed. "What?"

"You know, the fashionista stuff. Prada bags and shoes that cost more than my truck."

"Oh. Right."

"I told Frank that the other day in the staffroom. I'm like, you should have married a sweatpants and flannel girl like I did." He kissed her on the cheek. "Low maintenance is the way to go."

"I'm not totally low maintenance," she defended. "I require some maintaining. And I almost never wear sweatpants anymore."

Tom glanced at Jess's bottom half, which happened to be adorned in the tight black yoga capris she wore for walking in the summer. "Close enough." He carried the sandwiches into the living room for the kids.

It shouldn't have hurt her feelings. Jess had never been a fashion person, never understood the women who were. He was right; she did choose comfort and practicality most of the time. And from Tom, "low maintenance" was a compliment. He'd always told her that he preferred women who were natural beauties, who didn't wear a ton of makeup or slow everything down navigating in absurdly tall shoes. Jess had always been proud of being that kind of woman: unpretentious, desirable just as she was.

But now that forty was around the corner, sometimes it was

hard to see the natural beauty he'd fallen in love with before she'd put on concealer and mascara. And maybe, once in a while, she wanted to try out some beautiful shoes or treat herself to a bag that wasn't from Target. It seemed unfair that she had to continue to fit Tom's vision of her from their college days in order for her husband to see her as beautiful.

She pulled out four additional slices of bread, searched the fridge for sliced ham, and began a second set of sandwiches for Tom and herself. She couldn't dissect the imperfections of her marriage now. She had to focus on Parker and the investigation. She had to tell Tom he'd be called in to talk to the police. She needed to come clean about what had happened (and what hadn't) before things got any worse.

He returned while she was spreading the mustard. "Dash wants chips. Do we have any?"

"I'll bring them out in a minute. If we do it now, he won't eat the sandwich."

Tom swiped a slice of ham from the package. "I still don't understand why they'd be talking to Parker's tennis clients. Like, are they thinking you would have seen something significant while he was helping you with your serve? Was there ever a woman with him?"

Jess thought about the blonde woman Maizy had mentioned seeing at the restaurant. Had she been waiting for Parker in Cuba with a rum drink and a disguise? Had Jess been watching too many movies? "No, he never brought a woman to our lessons."

"I guess they have to be thorough, but it's kind of strange, bringing everyone in to the station like that. Not that I'm an expert, but that doesn't sound normal for a theft investigation." For the first time, it looked like it was occurring to Tom to worry.

Jess's heart squeezed.

"I don't know." Jess bit her lip, putting the mustard knife in the sink. "I think…Parker's business… He did things a little differently than most tennis coaches." There. She'd started. Baby steps.

"What do you mean?"

Oh God. The next step was huge. "Tom, I need to tell you something. And you might get angry, but I need you to listen."

His face turned to confusion and worry. "What is it, babe?"

"Can we sit down?"

"Sure."

"Mommy!" Mina called from the other room.

"I'll go," Tom said, turning.

"Moooooommmy!"

"No." Jess stopped him. "They need to learn to be self-sufficient. When you cater to their every whim, they end up treating me like a servant when you're gone. Mina! Please come here if you need us. Mommy and Daddy are making their own lunch in the kitchen."

There was a shuffling sound in the little hallway between the living room and kitchen as Mina emerged, face red with tears, and covered in what Jess quickly deduced were chunks of partially digested peanut butter sandwich. "Dash threw up on me!"

Ten hours later, they lay freshly showered and exhausted in bed. The couch, the carpet, and the kids had been sanitized. Tom had been sent to the store for more disinfectant cleaner while Jess took Dash to urgent care to confirm that, yes, there was still nothing wrong with him other than the fact that he wasn't chewing his food very well.

There was a rerun of *The Big Bang Theory* on in the background. Jess slid her arm across Tom's waist. He was leaving in the morning, and there was no way she could tell him this over the phone while he was in a hotel room in a strange city.

"You still awake?" A toe in the water.

"Mmm-hmm." He put his arm around her shoulder. "Your hair is wet."

"I'll go dry it in a minute. There's just…something I want to say."

He yawned and shifted toward her. "What's up?"

"Well, first I want to say you know how much I love you, right?"

"Enough that you're still around," he said.

"Yeah, but in every marriage, don't you think it's normal after a certain number of years, to start drifting apart?"

"It is?" He sat up, facing her.

"I mean, not drifting, but… Cooling off. You know." She looked around, letting her eyes settle on the television across the room. "Romance wise."

The crinkle between Tom's eyebrows, from years of squinting at ballgames, deepened in confusion. "Okay…"

"I mean, don't you think it's normal? After a couple of decades, a couple of kids…the passion is bound to wane a little. You start taking each other for granted, not noticing each other." She wanted him to understand how she'd been feeling, to explain why the thing with Parker had seemed like a good idea at the time.

"If you're saying that we don't fuck like bunnies six times a week like we did in college, yeah. I'd say that's normal. But I hope I don't take you for granted. Do I?"

He looked so worried that it almost broke Jess's heart. "No." Her throat clogged with shame and tenderness. Could it have been this easy all along? A frank conversation with wet hair after a day dealing with kid puke?

"I totally notice you." Tom touched an errant curl lying across her forehead, and let his hand graze the side of her face to her chin, fingering the tiny raised spot on her jawline. "For example, I remember when you got this scar."

Jess smiled. "Snow day, my senior year."

"You insisted on walking to the library even though the sidewalk was a sheet of ice."

"And *you* insisted on coming with me. If you hadn't been dragging me forward like an idiot, I would've fallen on my ass like a normal person, instead of on my face."

"I was helping you up the hill, like a generous boyfriend. I should have been throwing snowballs in the quad with everybody else." He kissed her. "But I couldn't stand the idea of you walking through the blizzard alone."

Jess felt a prickle of goose bumps across her skin, as though she were back on North Avenue on that clear, frozen day. "It was four inches. Hardly a blizzard."

"We didn't get a lot of snow in San Antonio." He kissed the scar. "Maybe that's why I'd never seen anyone do a face plant on the ice like that. You looked like a drunk moose."

She pinched him, hard, on the fleshy spot under his ribs. "You laughed at me, while I was bleeding. How did you ever talk me into marrying you after that?"

"I made sure you were okay first." He pushed her backward, rolling on top of her, and kissed her hard. "Besides, I have a few other compelling qualities."

As Tom kissed her, Jess's confession dissipated in her throat, evaporating into thin air. Tom made love to her, lights and TV on and everything, as though he had something to prove. It was like the night of the pool party, except the furious urgency was replaced by a slow admiration of every part of her body. He kissed every inch of her, peeling off her old Ramblin' Wreck T-shirt and ripped cotton panties, as though both were exquisite lingerie. He buried his face between her thighs and thrust his tongue into her, lapping against her skin until she melted against him. As his tongue circled excruciatingly, Jess bucked and rocked, putting a pillow over her face to avoid crying out. But Tom held her in place, strong hands pressing into the flesh of her hips, groaning into her with desire. The vibrations of his deep voice against her, and the knowledge that he was enjoying this as much as she was, sent her over the edge and beyond reason.

Soon his mouth and hands released her, and she felt the weight of him on top of her, the thick pleasure of him inside her. He rose up on his elbows. "I. Always. Notice. You." And then they were lost in their private world, the place she'd thought she'd been missing.

Later, she lay with Tom's fingers tangled in her wet hair and the TV still chattering in the background, her mind foggy with pleasure.

"I'm glad we talked," Tom murmured. "You know you can always come to me, right?"

That was her final chance, to rouse him again and let him know there had been more to it. But curled in his arms like that, in the safety of their regained intimacy, unpleasant realities seemed very far away.

Maybe she would never have to tell him. Maybe by the time Tom got home next week, the situation would be resolved. Parker might be caught, or his girlfriend. Maybe Tom would never be interviewed by a police officer who would explain that his wife had hired a male escort to make him jealous. It was a remote possibility.

But as Tom's breathing became regular, she let herself focus on it like a light in the darkness.

Jess hoped the light in the darkness wasn't an oncoming train.

34

MAIZY

MAIZY'S INTERVIEW WAS AT NINE o'clock. She'd chosen the first slot of the day so that she could leave Agatha home with Elise for an hour or so, and they would be too sleepy to get into much trouble before she got home. At 8:30, she pulled into the parking lot at the police precinct at City Hall. They'd said to arrive fifteen minutes early, but Maizy had been up for hours already, too twitchy to sit in the house. She checked her makeup, reapplied lipstick, and fiddled with her bag before resigning herself to walking in.

She'd never been to the police station, and had only been to City Hall once or twice over the years—to pay a tax bill, to file for a permit when Anders built the gazebo behind their house. She felt nervous in her old suit and heels and a string of pearls to try to make a good impression. Did it look like she was taking this seriously? As if she were trying to compensate for something? Too late to go home now. She'd try to exude the confidence she did not feel.

Maizy had not mentioned the interview to Anders, after debating for a while. It was an audit week at the bank; he was super busy and preoccupied. This would make things worse.

Best to leave Anders out of it until there was a reason to bring him in. She was buzzed in through the heavy door, which clanged closed behind her. Maizy wasn't sure what she'd been expecting, but the police station looked more like a low-rent doctor's waiting room than anything else. There was dated linoleum on the floor, and standard plastic waiting room chairs surrounding a muted television, tuned to CNN. A woman in civilian clothes with her graying hair pulled into a tight bun handed Maizy a clipboard with three pages of forms on it. "Print your legal name and residence information. I'll need a copy of your driver's license, and don't sign the sworn statement on the next page until you're with the interviewing officer."

The forms took less than five minutes to fill out, so Maizy sat in one of the plastic chairs, crossing and uncrossing her legs. The next time the entry door opened, she saw a familiar face. Officer Will, who often directed the traffic in and out of the elementary school's carpool line during her girls' tenure at Sugar Mills Elementary. He didn't do it often these days—Maizy suspected he'd been promoted or moved to a different part of the district— but she remembered him as the most attractive and friendly of the safety officers. Many early mornings with her girls fighting or whining in the backseat had been brightened by the sight of Officer Will and his compact, lean form and calm demeanor. Some of the traffic cops got worked up about carpool, whistling nonstop or yelling at the drivers; others had no sense of flow, leaving traffic to build up in one part of the system while impatient drivers stuttered on their brakes in the other. Officer Will, however, never let the stress of commuting parents get to him. It didn't hurt that he looked amazing in those motorcycle boots.

He was wearing them now, ten feet away, along with the motorcycle jacket with the reflector strips all over it. The shiny, dark skin of his closely shaven head shone beneath the fluorescent lights, as he swiped an entry badge at the next set of doors. Judging by the return smile from the woman in the bun, he had the same effect on his coworkers as he did on Maizy in carpool. She set up a little straighter in the chair.

It wasn't Officer Will, however, who called Maizy back for her interview. She got Officer Hutchins, an older white man, serious and perfunctory. No adorable smile. No motorcycle boots. He called her name at five till nine, just as Delia was being buzzed in the front door, in towering heels and skinny jeans with a long flowing tank top. She waved at Maizy as if they were passing in the grocery store.

Officer Hutchins led her to interview Room B. On the way,

they passed Officer Will in Room A. He was sitting back in a swivel chair behind the desk, laughing at something another policeman was saying. He caught Maizy's eye as she passed, and she waved before considering that it might not be appropriate. Before she could see whether Officer Will reacted, they had passed the doorway and she was sitting across from Officer Hutchins in a very bland small room, with cinderblock walls thick with glossy white paint.

"I'm going to record this interview, Mrs. Henriksson." He placed a pocket-size recorder on the desk between them. He reconfirmed her name and details, reminded her that she was not under arrest, not required to speak to him, and free to contact an attorney if she felt it necessary at any point. Maizy agreed that she understood.

"As I'm sure you are aware, Mrs. Henriksson, we've called you in today to get information about the activities of Parker Davis, also known as Parker Yung. I believe you know the young man?"

"Um. Yes. He's a tennis instructor." *Davis?* It shouldn't have surprised her that Parker used an alias, but she felt another piece of the ground beneath her feet disappear nonetheless. "We were working on putting together a special program for the kids at the elementary school." She hated lying to the police, but Anders would remember that from the restaurant if he was interviewed.

Officer Hutchins produced a file from a stack on the chair next to him. It was a slim manila folder with brackets at the top on both sides. As he talked, he put the forms Maizy had signed on top of a few other papers and closed the brackets. "That would be Sugar Mills Elementary?"

Maizy nodded, then realized she needed to speak for the recorder. "Yes. Both my daughters went there."

"Not there anymore?" Officer Hutchins flipped up the pages in her file, scanning.

"Well, no. My youngest, Agatha, just graduated fifth grade."

"But you were working on a program with Mr. Davis? Mr. Yung? When was the program intended to start?"

Maizy's stomach sank. "We hadn't gotten that far. He just said he wanted to do something, maybe a summer camp or something after school. I'm not sure."

"Why do you think he came to you?" Officer Hutchins's voice was level. "Were you already acquainted?"

"I was the PTA president at Sugar Mills. He thought I would be able to garner support for his ideas." She was starting to panic now, positive that Officer Hutchins could tell she was making this up as she went along.

"But you're not the president anymore?"

"Not technically, now that summer has started. But I was still president when he and I were discussing a possible program."

He made a noncommittal humming noise in his throat. "When he reached out to you about the camp, was that before or after you signed up for tennis lessons with him?"

Um... Crap. Maizy was no good at duplicity. She hadn't mentioned tennis lessons because she hadn't taken tennis lessons. What if they had financial records? If she denied taking lessons, there was no way to explain her paying Parker. If she said she took lessons, the lies were getting deeper...

"Mrs. Henriksson? Are you alright? Did you need me to repeat the question?"

Maizy smiled, attempting her best Delia impression. "I was trying to remember. We had such a busy spring this year. I have one daughter in dance and the other does drama, plus the PTA. It's easy to get things mixed up."

"Take your time," Officer Hutchins said. "I will say I'm surprised, as busy as you are, that you had time for tennis lessons."

"Well, I am trying to take care of myself. And I've always been interested in tennis."

He regarded her unapologetically, eyes roving over her straining suit jacket and ample chest. "I would think so, since you sprang for the premium lessons. Tell you what, if my wife came home and told me she bought $1200 worth of tennis lessons, I'da fallen out of my chair. Of course, my wife wouldn't know which end of the tennis racket to use."

He was trying to disarm her, but the jab at his wife irked Maizy. "Well, Officer, maybe you'd be surprised what your wife is capable of, given the chance."

For the first time, he smiled. "I do know that's right, Mrs. Henriksson. I hope you got your money's worth. How far in advance were your lessons booked? For over $1000, it must've been the whole summer, right?"

"How do you know how much I paid him?"

The officer didn't respond except to raise a graying eyebrow.

Maizy wasn't sure what he was fishing for, but she didn't have a good answer, and instinct told her to be careful. "I paid for several hours of coaching in advance. He gave me a discount."

Officer Hutchins looked at her for a long time, waiting for her to elaborate. When she didn't, he sighed and flipped over a new page on his notepad. "Are you aware, Mrs. Henriksson, that Parker Yung-Davis is not just a tennis coach, but also a high-end male escort?"

She'd imagined, dreaded, and rehearsed this question in her head for the last week but Officer Hutchins still managed to shock her with it. Trying to keep her face composed, yet surprised, she said the words she'd practiced. "I have no idea what you mean."

"A male escort. A prostitute, Mrs. Henriksson." He pulled out a second folder, thicker, and opened it to face her. It was like an employment portfolio for a criminal. There were three sets of black-and-white mug shots—Parker at various ages, looking bedraggled or scared or defiant. Behind these were clipped papers that Maizy could only assume were Parker's rap sheets. There were fingerprint arrays and forms filled in by typewriters.

"Mr. Davis has been arrested three times that we know of, including in his home state of California. Soliciting, prostitution, even possession with intent to distribute when he was nineteen. He began using Yung, his mother's maiden name, when he moved to the area a couple of years ago. We believe he targeted affluent housewives, especially lonely, insecure types." He glanced at Maizy. "No offense. He preyed on their need for attention, their desperation, and then threatened to out them to their husbands or employers if they didn't pay up. We believe most of them did. Until the alleged incident with Mr. and Mrs. Currington, he was charging small enough amounts that his victims felt it was a small price to pay for his silence."

Maizy felt disoriented. Here she was, in her quiet suburban town, the cute school traffic cop in the room next door. Her daughters' dance school was a block away. Her favorite restaurant across the street.

"Myself, I can see how this would happen," Officer Hutchins said. "See it all the time with football stars around here. They grow up believing they've got one exceptional talent, build their whole world around being the captain of the team, getting that scholarship, impressing the girls. Then they go off to college, and maybe they're not as good compared to the competition at the next level, or maybe they get injured, which is what happened to your Mr. Yung. Anyway, suddenly the one thing we've all been praising them for doing, they can't do anymore. Some of those kids adjust and do fine. Others don't know how to work hard at anything else. Sad, don't you think?"

"Very sad," she agreed. "But I'm not sure what this has to do with me."

He took another meaningful pause before continuing. "The FBI believes Mr. Yung had an accomplice in the theft perpetrated on Mr. and Mrs. Currington, and that person might have been one of his current or former clients. We're still going through all of Mr. Yung's records and notes. He left behind a good bit of information. Notes, pictures…that kind of thing."

At "pictures," Maizy stilled.

"Some of his clients have come forward already, to explain the nature of their relationship. Hoping the DA will look favorably on those who came forward early. I'm guessing you're the type who made a mistake, maybe had a vulnerable moment. I can see the appeal: a younger man, somebody with no expectations, who doesn't care if you put on a pound or two." He leaned forward sympathetically. "But you're not the type who would obstruct an investigation."

That was it. If she'd been unsure how to handle this moment, Officer Condescension had made up her mind. "I'm not sure you know what type I am at all, Officer. Of course, this is all a terrible shock to me, and I had no idea this sort of thing was going on with Parker. If I hear anything, I will let you know." Anger made her braver than she'd thought possible. "Is that all? My children need me at home."

Officer Hutchins closed the folders and pushed back from the table. "Yes, ma'am. That's all for now." He shuffled around the table and reached for the door. "Is your husband in town, Mrs. Henriksson?"

"He is. Why do you ask?"

"We'll need you both to stay in town for now, until everything is cleared up."

She kept her composure, and her righteous anger, all the way out to her car, which was already heating up from the summer day. Maizy pulled out of the lot using the ticket validated by the police clerk, and drove almost a mile toward home before she pulled off on the side of the road and cried. Big, ugly sobs with her head in her hands and her hazard lights on.

What in God's name had she been thinking, pushing back like that against a police officer questioning her about a crime? This wasn't some sideways criticism from her in-laws about the calories in her chicken cacciatore. This was a criminal investigation. And they were going to talk to Anders. He worked for a bank, and he would be questioned about a financial crime. *God, if he had to explain to his bosses...* He would never forgive her. All of this would have been not simply wasted effort, but self-sabotage.

She started the car to head home only when she had sweated through her dated, ugly suit, and realized that the longer she sat here with her hazards on, the more likely a police car would pull up behind her. She couldn't think what could be worse than that right now. Except for everything else.

35

DELIA

OFFICER WILLIAM REED, OR OFFICER Will as he was fondly known at the elementary school, had been nice and genuine and straightforward. The police knew about Parker's side business; he had a record and was using an alias. If Officer Will was correct, however, the department wasn't especially interested in going after the clients of his escort business. Their priority was helping the FBI with the theft.

"I'll be honest," the cute cop had said. "I'm not a detective; just helping with these initial interviews. But it seems to me there's no reason to go after this dude's escort clients. It would be hard to prove anything, and the push around here is all about the missing money. The FBI is investigating the theft, and we have to show the Currington family we're doing everything we can to identify his accomplice."

Delia revealed nothing, of course. She'd expressed—if Delia did say so herself—the perfect balance between visceral shock about Parker, and being worldly enough to know that such unsavory things might go on. It was important not to seem too naïve. Or too knowledgeable. Sort of like a first date.

At home, she sent both girls to play at a friend's—a new family on the other side of the neighborhood who had every Barbie toy known to woman—and planted herself at the kitchen table with her laptop. Gage was in his office upstairs, so she pulled up some innocuous sites about swim lessons and fifth-grade math worksheets, and then opened a private browser window to begin searching. Things like, "is prostitution illegal if you don't have sex?"

And, "are paid escorts illegal without sexual contact?"

The answers were vague, and after a cursory investigation, she found herself roving into the unpleasant territory of sexual slavery and street crime. None of that applied to her situation with Parker. This would be reassuring if she felt more certain the police would see it that way. And Gage.

She heard him moving around upstairs, and closed the search window before he could come down. But the footsteps tracked to their bedroom, and she heard the shower, strange for mid-af-ternoon. Maybe he wanted to go out? They could all go to their favorite restaurant tonight, and out for ice cream. A treat to relieve some of the stress. Delia needed to remind herself what she'd done this for.

But when Gage came downstairs a few minutes later, he was not only clean and dressed, but packed as well. "Are the girls back?"

"I was about to go get them." She looked at his bag.

"Yeah. Sorry. Belgium. I can't get out of it."

"Since when?" Delia tried to hide her annoyance. Travel was part of his existence, she knew, but this was last minute, even for him.

"Just now. I had to book a six o'clock flight or wait till tomor-row. And it can't wait. Can you get the girls so I can say goodbye?"

"Why don't you come with me? We can all take you to the airport. Eat at Waffle House on the way, like we did when they were little."

He let out an exasperated breath. "Delia. I would love to, you know that. But I still have details to wrap up and I'll be in a rush."

"Is it...her?" She hated herself, hated the words as soon as they came out of her mouth.

Gage's face clouded with anger. "God dammit, Delia. Do we have to do this every fucking time?"

"No. It's fine. I'm caught off guard, that's all." She reached for her keys and purse to go get their children.

Gage softened. "I shouldn't have yelled. I'm under a lot of pres-sure right now and I need my wife to be supportive."

"I shouldn't have questioned you." She put on a grim smile. "I do know the drill."

As she turned for the door, he caught Delia's wrist to stop her.

"It's not her. Honestly. I doubt she'll even be there, if that helps."

It should have made her feel better. The fact that Gage was leaving abruptly for his work, not his lover, should have made things easier. But acknowledging Alana (and the others) never became less painful, despite their marital arrangement. And, today, Delia needed Gage here. She wanted to be able to say, "Please don't go. I need you. I'm scared. And I'm jealous of the other women, and I wish we didn't have this stupid arrangement anymore."

But she couldn't say any of that. If Gage knew about her deal with Parker, he'd be furious. Not jealous, but outraged that she'd spent money and taken such a big risk on something he would've allowed her for free. A little discretion, that was their deal. If she told him what she'd done, he'd be pissed that she'd exposed him and their family to a police investigation and possible bad publicity. It could undermine his career, which was worse than undermining their marriage.

So, she fetched the girls, and Gage had left in a flurry of kisses and tickles and hugs on the couch, with promises to bring back gifts and chocolates for all three of his favorite women. Afterward, the girls had been sulky as they always were when he left, and Delia had found herself pouring a sizable glass of white wine at 4:30.

And for the first time in her adult life, she found herself needing her girlfriends. *Can we talk?* Delia texted, once her daughters were tucked upstairs with a marathon of some idiotic teenage show they loved.

Carras was the first to respond: *Sure. Where?*

Tom is out of town. Have kids, Jess texted.

Can you bring them here? Delia asked. *My girls can watch them.*

I can come there, Maizy chimed in.

Pizza? Half an hour?

After three affirmative responses, Delia called her favorite pizza place, poured a second glass and went upstairs to put on something more comfortable than the outfit from this morning's interview. She felt buzzy and light, ready to vent her frustrations to the few women who could understand. Before meeting Jess, Delia had never had close girlfriends. And even Jess she'd kept at a distance for a long time, preferring large, purposeful parties (and the safe small talk that came with pitching her many product lines) to intense, close-knit friendships. But now—even though she didn't love being vulnerable around Maizy—she found herself enjoying their little group, and looking forward to the daily crisis updates that brought them together.

Maybe instead of trying to win her husband's attention, Delia would have been as happy learning to play bridge on Thursday nights...

The doorbell rang as she was upstairs, pulling on her baggy sweatpants. She still had on the dressy top she'd worn for her police interview, so she called downstairs. "Sadie! Can you get the pizza? The money is by the door!"

No answer. The girls were too absorbed in whatever they were watching. Delia left her bedroom and leaned over the banister. "Lulu! Can you get the door?"

The doorbell rang again. Apparently, the pizza boy had somewhere to be.

Delia took a woeful glance in the mirror at her mismatched outfit. She should finish changing, but then the guy might give up and leave. She went downstairs and opened the door, the pizza guy's tip shrinking with each step.

It wasn't the pizza. "Mrs. Cargill?" A petite redheaded woman in a blue police uniform. "I'm Officer Nancy Hicks from the Sugar Mills PD. I'm afraid we have more questions for you concerning your relationship with Mr. Parker Yung."

"That's fine," Delia said. "I'll be happy to come back in tomorrow morning."

"I'm sorry, ma'am. I'm afraid it can't wait. I'm going to have to ask you to come with me. I understand you have young children. Is there someone home who can keep them?"

"Their dad just left for the airport. But if it's a short interview, I can leave them here alone. My oldest is fourteen."

The woman gave her a thoughtful look. "I'm afraid this will be more involved than the voluntary interviews this morning. You may want to make overnight arrangements."

In her pocket, Delia's phone rattled with incoming texts. Probably because her friends could see the police car outside her house.

"I can come in, if you like, while you call someone to come be with them. If not, we can always get someone from social services."

Social services. Jesus H. Christ. "You mean foster care?"

The woman didn't appear offended or irritated. "It's an option we can offer until you can reach someone to be with them."

"No." Delia sighed, suddenly tired from wine and inevitability. "Come in. Let me call my mother-in-law."

36

CARRAS

A S CARRAS LOOKED AROUND THE small holding cell, all she could think was how glad she was that her father couldn't see her now. The room itself was not all that different from the interview room where she'd met with Officer Hutchins earlier in the day: the same institutional cinderblock walls coated with glossy white paint. Instead of a desk in the center, however, this room had a low metal shelf bench mounted on three of the four walls. Above it was a strange shadow of grime, where countless drunk drivers, petty thieves, and small-time drug runners had sat leaning against the walls. On the fourth wall was a squat metal toilet and sink, and the single door in and out. There was a weird smell of sulfur and disinfectant and stale alcohol fumes. She felt nauseated.

Her three neighbors had already been in the cell when the officer led her in, along with an elderly woman wearing many layers of clothes despite the warm weather, snoring on the bench seat in one corner. Across from Carras, Jess sat with her head in her hands, muttering to herself. Delia, who was wearing the odd combination of gray sweats, pink flip-flops, and a flowing, lacy top, was about a foot away from Jess. She'd taken the opposite posture: spine straight, shoulders back, chin held high. She had one leg crossed over the other as though she were waiting to be called for a job interview.

Maizy was leaning against the back wall, with her feet pulled up and crossed under her. She'd been wearing athletic shoes with laces that they had confiscated on arrival, so she sat in her sock feet and leggings as if she were hanging out in a freshman dorm, catnapping before study group.

None of them had said much since Carras had arrived—she'd been the last—half an hour ago. She felt disconnected from her body, and the situation. From a distance, she diagnosed herself with shock but there was nothing she could do about it.

The arrest had been strange. Some of it was like TV, with the Miranda rights and the pat-down the female officer had given her before putting handcuffs on Carras and helping her into the back of the car. But there had also been a level of graciousness she hadn't expected. The woman had asked politely whether she could come in and had complimented Stuart's vintage *Night of the Living Dead* poster, before explaining that new evidence had come to light during the course of the investigation and Carras was one of a handful of people they were arresting for solicitation of prostitution. "I'm surprised, frankly," the woman had said. "I was under the impression they were primarily interested in finding the accomplice to the theft."

Carras said nothing. *Was the officer baiting her? Trying to trick her into saying something?* The petite redheaded woman seemed harmless enough, with her open, moon face. The officer was bubbly, chatting as though arresting Carras was just another mildly interesting thing she had to do today. She'd waited while Carras shakily turned off the television and looked for her keys. In the process of searching for them, she realized Stuart had left his own keys behind when the Uber picked him up for the airport that morning.

Carras held them up. "My husband will need these. He won't be able to get in."

"If you take them to the station, they'll put them in a locker until you make bail. I'd hide them outside somewhere if I were you, or leave them with a neighbor."

But my neighbors are all in jail, too. Carras had seen the frantic texts, the patrol cars going back and forth. "Can I bring my phone?"

"You can, but they'll take it. I can't let you use it now, but the deputies will look up contact information for you if you don't know the numbers by heart. And, you might want it if you are released tonight. Now, if they send y'all to County later, you'll need someone to pick it up for you."

If she was released. *If* they went to County. *Where the hell was County?*

In the end, Carras had left her phone at home, and called her husband on the courtesy phone hanging outside the cell she was in now. He had a big presentation at a gaming convention today; she hated that she was ruining it. She'd left him a voicemail that went something along the lines of, "Hey, sorry to bother you at the thing. Hope it's going well. When you get out, would you be able to call Tom and wire him some money from our savings? I'll pay us back from my own account later. I just... Um, I've been arrested. It's a big misunderstanding about this thing with Parker. I'm sure they are arresting everyone he had contact with, trying to flush someone out..."

At that point, the tall male officer standing next to her, the cute black guy Maizy had mentioned directed traffic by the school, cleared his throat. When Carras glanced at him, he stared at the ceiling.

"Anyway, please call Tom. He's out of town, too, but I am sure he is working on sending someone to get us. I love you."

That was half an hour ago, and now Carras was staring at the top of Jess's head. Her friend had not moved from the folded-over position she'd assumed as soon as Carras had entered the room. The silence enveloping them added to her anxiety, interrupted only by the ticking of a classroom-style clock bolted behind a metal cage, and occasional snores and burps from the sleeping lady.

"Where is Tom, again?" Carras knew the answer, but couldn't stand the silence.

"Boston," Jess said, not looking up. "I left a voicemail, but who knows if he'll even get it until after tonight's game."

"But you left the kids with your parents? Surely they'll try to reach him?"

Jess sighed and pushed up on her knees. "I told my parents I had the stomach flu. They won't call him. For once I wish his parents lived in Atlanta, because they would be in touch with him constantly if they had the kids. They've never understood that his job actually requires him to concentrate on the games."

She grimaced as she finished the sentence, as though her temporary foray into the minutiae of family life had made her forget where she was.

"I had to tell Gage's mom," Delia said miserably. "That woman is an absolute wolfhound. It was so humiliating, having to talk her into it in front of the police officer. I had to have it on speaker, you know? The woman looked like she felt sorry for me."

"Did you have the redheaded officer? She seemed…nice."

Delia nodded. They both looked at the door.

"I'm glad it wasn't Officer Will," Maizy said. "I saw him when we came in to interview this morning. It would be mortifying to have him be the one to put you in handcuffs."

When she realized what she'd said, Maizy turned crimson. Officer Will was attractive, Carras thought. And he seemed as kind as he could be, considering the circumstances. But Maizy seemed to have a special affinity for him.

"What in the ever-loving fuck are you guys even *talking* about?" Jess stood. "This isn't some Caribbean cruise we're on, trying to decide who the best cabin steward is. We're in jail, you guys. *Jail.* Whatever happens, our kids are going to find out. Our parents and in-laws and the whole fucking community is going to find out. My husband is going to divorce me. And y'all are talking about the different cops who handcuffed us, like they're the fucking entertainment staff?"

"Whoa, Jess," Delia said. "Take it easy."

When she looked up at Jess, the walls behind her angry friend shifted in Carras's vision. She looked back at the floor and tried to remember the last time she'd eaten. *Lunch, maybe?*

"Sorry," Jess said. "I just think we need to be discussing our next move, not ogling the cute cop."

"I wasn't *ogling* him," Maizy said, puffing up. "And I resent the implication that somehow I'm not taking this *seriously* enough. I have as much to lose as you do. At least you three all have parents to be on your team. Mine are… not around. And Anders's family is going to *love* this when they find out. I bet his brothers will prepare the divorce filing themselves."

Carras opened her mouth to say that she didn't have parents on her team, not really, but she didn't have the energy. Her dad's condition was an issue for another day, and the last thing she could handle in this moment was a sudden outpouring of sympathy.

"Jess is right," Delia said. "We need to quit sniping at each other and try to figure out our next move."

"Easy for you to say," Maizy said. "You have an international lawyer for a husband, and almost unlimited resources. Who wants to bet that you end up doing some kind of light community service, while the rest of us serve hard time?"

"Hard time?" Delia echoed with a smirk. "Who are you, Al Capone?"

"Make fun of me all you want. Everyone knows these situations are easier with money. Some of us won't be able to afford a massive defense fund like I'm sure you will have."

"Maybe you can have a bake sale," Delia said. "Better yet, maybe you should have thought of that before you pushed your way in on *our* arrangement. No one twisted your arm for this, Maizy. In fact, I recommended strongly against letting you in, for exactly this reason."

"Great," Maizy said, looking uncharacteristically smug. "Tell that to the officer outside. Maybe they'll let me go."

"Guys." Jess had resumed her station on the bench and looked even more exhausted than before her outburst. "Stop fighting. They're probably listening to everything that's said in here."

"I don't care," Delia said. "I did nothing wrong. There's nothing illegal about anything *I* did."

Carras might have been imagining it, still focused on the floor and taking deep breaths. But she thought Delia glanced her way when she said this.

"Look. Parker had lots of clients, right?" Delia went on. "There were a ton of people being interviewed over the last couple of days. But the four of us are the only ones here. Why us?"

"What are you saying?" Jess said. "You think one of us was Parker's accomplice?"

"No. Well, maybe." Delia looked at Maizy, who snorted. "Probably not. But we must all be connected in Parker's records, and the police must have some reason to think at least one of us is a viable suspect."

"Or all of us," Carras said, trying to slow her beating heart. She wasn't his accomplice, at least not in the theft of Belinda's money. Parker was *her* accomplice. He had never needed to threaten her, never showed her the evidence he would have against her, because they both knew it already. *The signed contract. Ten thousand dollars, cash.* She'd done nothing to help him steal anything, or to get away. Selfishly, however, her life was better with him gone. *The farther away, the better...*

"Someone slept with him," Delia said. "And obviously the police have evidence of that. They're using the solicitation and prostitution charges to build a case against Parker and whoever might have helped him. So whoever it is should tell the truth. Let's clear this up and go home. It's only fair. We agreed from the very beginning that none of us would do that." She looked at the ceiling near the door, where a small security camera was mounted, and annunciated, "Because that would be *illegal* and *wrong.*"

Jess snorted. "You don't seriously think that is helping us, do you?"

"I didn't know we agreed that," Maizy said. "I wasn't with you guys at the beginning."

"Ha! You *did* sleep with him. I *knew* it." Delia was triumphant.

"I did *not.*" Maizy went pink again. "I am trying to understand why you guys talked about that and didn't tell me. It...never occurred to me that there would be such a big legal distinction. I guess I figured it was all, you know. Wrong."

"Ugh." Jess moaned. "What the hell were we thinking?"

Delia looked irritated. "You didn't seem to think it was so wrong after the pool party."

Maizy blanched. "What the hell is that supposed to mean?"

"It means I *saw* you, remember? You're going to tell me that was innocent, the way Parker leaned his head into you, that night by the tennis courts? How do we know you weren't helping him plan to rob Belinda? You do know your way around the banking system."

"Now you're being ridiculous," Maizy said.

"Am I?" Delia whirled on her. "This whole thing could be a setup. You pushed your way in to this arrangement with us, and then you appear to be one of the last people who saw Parker before he took off. I watched you two that night; you certainly seemed chummy."

"That's *right!*" Maizy growled and her eyes filled with tears of rage. "And it pisses you off, doesn't it, Delia? You can't stand the thought that the chubby lady who bakes cookies and serves on the PTA might have something to offer a guy like Parker in a way that you can't, no matter how many stupid fitness DVDs and disgusting, chalky nutrition shakes you buy!"

"How. Dare. You!" Delia lunged, and it took both Jess and Carras to keep her from taking out Maizy's eyeballs. "Those shakes are *not* chalky! They have phytonutrients!"

"I'll go confess to helping him right now if you can even *spell* phytonutrients!"

"Stop! Girls, stop it!" Jess was pushing the women apart like a wrestling referee, and Carras tried to help by putting herself between them, planting her feet on the industrial tile floor. "We can't turn on each other."

Carras wasn't sure what might've happened next—Maizy taunting, Delia apoplectic with rage—but the sleeping lady began to groan. It started as a low constant moan, as though someone were starting up an old machine. But as the four women turned to look at their cell companion, the noise grew louder, a series of *ohs* punctuating through the air. This ended with the woman rolling onto her back and beginning to vomit straight up in the air, splattering the walls and bench—not to mention her stringy, graying hair—and choking herself so that the process started again.

Carras heard Jess say, "Oh my God."

Delia said, "That's disgusting."

"We need to roll her over," Maizy said. "Jess, help me move her. Carras… Oh. Never mind. Delia, go to the buzzer and call for help."

Carras did not look back at Maizy, because she was too busy hunching over the disgusting metal toilet, hurling up what little was left of her lunch. The pungent smell of vomit behind her and the disinfectant in the toilet beneath her made Carras's insides roil and heave again, though this time there was not much to bring up.

She pressed the button on the wall to flush and pulled herself onto the bench nearby, tucking her knees up in front of her and burying her face in her arms to avoid looking up at the poor woman on the other side of the cell. Carras had always been a bit squeamish about these things. She'd seen one of her teammates break his leg sliding into a stadium wall once, and the memory of it still gave her nightmares. It was one of many reasons she worried about becoming a mother. How useful would she be if when her own child vomited, Carras went running for the bathroom herself?

She heard the buzzer sound, and several people entered the room. "Okay, ladies. Thank you for alerting us. You can be seated, please, with your hands in your lap, if you don't mind." Carras recognized the voice of the little redheaded officer who had been at her house earlier. "Ma'am? Are you all right?"

"She got sick, too," she heard Jess explain. "Right after."

Carras turned her head so she could see the officer. There were two other female officers, both wearing latex gloves, helping the woman sit up. The much-discussed cute traffic cop stood at the doorway with one hand lightly touching his holster. In case they all decided to gang up on him, Carras supposed. "I'm fine. Just a little squeamish about smells."

"I understand." The redheaded officer turned to the lady. "All right, Gladys. Let's get you cleaned up while we wait for the paramedics. Looks like you'll be in the hospital tonight instead of with us."

"Food's better there anyway," Gladys slurred irritably as the female officers led her out. As she passed Officer Will at the door, she added with a slur, "Not better company, though. That dadgum hospital ain't got no sexy brown sugar like you, honey."

Carras was appalled, and embarrassed for him, but Officer Will smiled. "Take care of yourself, Gladys. Save me some Jell-O."

He stood guard as she left with her escorts, and a custodian in a tan jumpsuit entered with a cleaning cart. Carras felt a stab of nostalgia and longing for her father, remembering all the early years that he'd greeted her wearing something similar, smelling of sweat and cleaner and the sweet clove cigarettes he smoked in the car when she wasn't with him. She wanted out of this room, wanted to go call him right now, to see how he was feeling. The whole point of this was for her father to enjoy whatever time he had left knowing his daughter was happy, and that her family would go on and live out the dream he'd worked so hard to create. Now she'd lost the simple ability to call and talk to him, just when it mattered most.

"Are you okay?" Jess said.

"Maybe you do have the stomach flu," Delia said with a weak smile.

"I'm fine," Carras said. "I feel much better." This was true. The brick she'd been carrying in her stomach since she'd been arrested seemed to have purged itself from her body.

"Sounds more like food poisoning than the stomach flu," Maizy offered.

"Thank you, Dr. Henriksson," Delia said archly. She didn't look at Maizy, though, but kept an eye on Carras as though trying to solve a puzzle.

"You're a doctor?" Officer Will said from the doorway.

Carras could see the flush rise from Maizy's chest up her neck to her cheeks. The poor woman really was an open book. "She's kidding." Maizy gave Delia a look. "I'm just a stay-at-home mom."

"Never say that," Officer Will said. "Being a mom is the most important job there is."

"Thank you," Maizy said. "I was president of the PTA at Sugar Mills Elementary for the last few years. You were one of our safety officers, weren't you?"

"I *thought* you looked familiar." Officer Will beamed. "You're the one who makes those amazing cherry chocolate chip cookies, right? You gave them to all of us at the holidays in those little tins."

Carras thought Maizy might explode with pride.

"I do! I make them every year. I'm glad to know you like them. I always wonder if anyone eats them. I'm sure you get so many goodies that time of year."

"We do, and of course we're grateful for all of them." Officer Will leaned in. "But those cherry chocolate things, man. People fight over those. Last year when I picked them up at the school, I tried to pretend we didn't get any. Stuck them on the floorboard of the squad car to take home, but somebody ratted me out."

Maizy laughed, and put her hand to her throat in a dainty gesture. "Well, if I'd known that, I would've made you your very own batch."

My God, Carras thought. *She's flirting.* She wanted to look away—poor Maizy was embarrassing herself—but there was nowhere to look besides the mess on the floor the custodian was cleaning. The last thing she wanted was to make herself sick again.

She glanced at Jess to see whether her friend was noticing this weird phenomenon, but Jess had gone back to staring thoughtfully at the floor. *Good*, Carras thought; *maybe she's coming up with some sort of plan.*

37

JESS

JESS HAD ABSOLUTELY NO IDEA what to do.

She'd never been to jail before. She'd never been in trouble before, except for a speeding ticket her sophomore year of college and the time she'd been caught sneaking Tom out of her all-girls dorm at sunrise on a Sunday. He thought it was hilarious and sexy back then. Somehow, Jess didn't think he was going to feel the same way about this.

After Officer Will and the custodian left, it was just the four of them. At first, the women were quiet as the caged clock over the door ticked away the time in silence. Her kids were safe; her parents loved Dash and Mina. But there was something primal and frustrating about not being able to reach her children. Being withheld from them by force felt very different than being away from them by choice. She couldn't imagine what it must be like for incarcerated mothers.

It had been more than five hours since her arrest, and her back and tailbone ached from sitting on the cold, hard bench. A couple of hours earlier, someone had brought them sub sandwiches with turkey on stale bread with little packets of mayonnaise and mustard. They had accepted the sandwiches in silence, but none of them could eat more than a couple of bites.

She'd heard once that an innocent man will stay up all night after being arrested, fretting and panicking and worrying. But a guilty man will go to sleep in his cell, knowing that he's been caught and relieved of the pressures of being on the run. She'd never given this a bit of wisdom much thought, but now she felt the untruth of it deeply. Because Jess *was* guilty, and the thought of sleeping on these cold, hard benches was the last thing on her mind.

She hadn't helped Parker steal anything, of course. Not that she was devastated for Belinda Hayes-Currington or anything, but Jess wouldn't have been a part of that even if she'd had skills to offer. And she hadn't slept with him, hadn't actually paid him for sex.

But she *was* guilty. Marriage had gotten hard, and instead of reinvesting herself with her whole heart, Jess had tried an easy, unfair solution: to manipulate her husband back into the passion they had once known. Telling herself that she was talked into it, as though Delia or Carras or anyone else could have made Jess do something that she didn't want to do, was a cop-out.

"I'm sorry I said you couldn't spell phytonutrients," Maizy said. "That was unfair."

"I baited you into it." Delia bit her thumbnail and lowered her voice. "And I *can* spell it. It's on every package of shakes I sell."

Maizy laughed. "I've always looked up to you, Delia, ever since we both moved into the neighborhood. We both have two girls, the exact same age, both have husbands who travel, both stay home… I could never understand why you didn't want me around."

"It was for all those reasons," Delia said. "We had too much in common. There were…so many expectations when I met you. I know it sounds terrible, but you called me twice a week for play-dates, constantly invited me to hang out."

"Wow, that *is* terrible," Jess said. "Couldn't you have had her arrested sooner?"

"You're saying I came on too strong," Maizy said. "I get it."

"No. Well, yes. A little," Delia said. "But mostly it was me. I grew up with my dad and brothers and it was horrible. I had terrible relationships with men afterward, but I had nothing at all with girls. I've never been able to do close friendships with women."

"Me either," Carras said. "Until now."

Maizy looked at them each in turn, smiling. Then she took in a deep breath. "I am not Parker's accomplice."

"Well, that's a relief," Delia said.

"But I did meet with him that night and I did…try to talk him out of, whatever it was." She glanced at the security camera over the door. "I didn't know what he was planning, or with whom. I had no details I could've acted on to stop him. But I got the feeling from the way he was talking that he was planning to do something big, something stupid. I was trying to help him talk through it…in sort of a maternal way."

Her face dropped into her hands; her shoulders shook. Jess looked at the other two, wondering whether to comfort her or wait. But then Maizy raised her head and gasped for air, tears of laughter streaming down her pink cheeks. "It's funny, right? I think I'm the only person on earth who could hire a prostitute and end up trying to mother him."

"Shh…" Delia said. "The camera."

Maizy shrugged. "I'll take my medicine. It's all coming out at home tonight anyway."

It was 10:45 when the buzzer sounded and the door opened. It was neither Officer Will nor the redheaded woman, but a tall guy Jess didn't recognize with a bushy brown mustache. He looked perfunctorily around the room, consulting a clipboard. "Rodriguez, Jessica Ann Gardner?"

Jess stood. "That's me. Sir."

The man glared at her. "Prather, Carras Evangeline Lightbourne." He pronounced Carras like *car-ass*. Carras stood, but didn't say anything.

"Cargill, Delia Rae Rutledge."

Delia stood slowly, looking surprised. The officer looked at Maizy, then back at his clipboard. "If I have called your name, follow me please."

"Are we being released?" Delia asked.

The man didn't answer, but led them toward a small room near the front of the police station. Behind a counter in the middle were three walls of bookshelves containing files and labeled boxes. The officer lifted a hinge door on the counter and walked through, locating three baskets with each of their last names scrawled on index cards in the front. He put the baskets unceremoniously on the counter, and thrust three bright-orange forms across at them. "Verify that all your belongings are present before signing. The department cannot be responsible for losses that are not reported immediately." He looked at Jess. "That means, before you leave the building."

"Yes sir." Jess wondered whether theft was a huge problem at the police station.

Her own belongings, however, seemed to be all present and accounted for. Delia and Carras must've found the same thing, because they both signed the orange forms. "Wait here, please." The officer took the forms and disappeared.

"Why are they letting us go?" Carras said. "And why not Maizy?"

Jess looked back toward the holding cell, concerned. "I wonder if she wants us to call Anders for her."

"She called him earlier, didn't she?" Delia said. "I don't remember—did she say if she got through?"

Before they could discuss it further, the officer returned with copies of the orange sheets, and a packet of paperwork for each of them. "This is your bond agreement. Your court date is printed at the bottom. You are not permitted to leave the State of Georgia before that date without permission from Sugar County Court. If you have travel plans, I suggest you change them. If you can't, I recommend you call the number at the bottom first thing tomorrow. Sometimes it takes awhile to get the request processed."

They all signed in the myriad places he indicated. Jess didn't bother to read what she was signing. At this point, she didn't care what it took to get on the other side of that door. When they walked through, however, and she saw Tom, she almost wanted to turn and go back to the holding cell. He looked weary from travel and worry, his hands in the pockets of an old sweatshirt he kept in his car. His brown eyes were rimmed in red, and his tired expression held none of the lovable goofball he'd been the other night.

Stuart was with him, still wearing a business suit from his presentation earlier that day in Las Vegas. If Tom looked tired, Stuart looked terrified. As soon as they'd cleared the door, he rushed to put his arms around Carras. "My God, baby. Are you all right?"

Carras extracted herself from his embrace, but held his hands.

"I'm fine. I'm sure it's all a misunderstanding."

"Of course it is," Delia said brightly. "It will all get sorted out."

But Tom didn't join in the chorus of optimism. He simply raised his eyebrows at Jess. "You okay?"

All she could do was nod.

38

JESS

IT TURNED OUT THAT JESS'S parents' instincts about their daughter were intact. They'd known that Jess didn't have the stomach flu, and Dash—bless him—had spoken excitedly about seeing more than one police car on the street tonight. They'd called and texted Tom until he left Fenway Park for the first flight home.

They didn't ask what was going on, Tom said, as he and Jess drove the half block home from Carras and Stuart's. They wanted her to know they loved her, and they could keep the kids for a couple of days if needed. "Your mom said something about having them help her organize the basement. So I figure they'll be scratching at the door first thing tomorrow." It was a joke, but his tone was mirthless.

Up until now, the conversation in the car had been stilted and awkward, but at least buoyed by the presence of Delia, Carras, and Stuart. Tom had explained how he'd been able to meet Stuart's flight at the gate, and the two of them had managed to wake up a friend from college who worked at a bank so they could figure out how to get cash for bail. They had tried Anders first, of course, but it had taken him awhile to get back to them. He had, however, assured them he would be able to retrieve his own wife shortly.

"Did you get hold of Gage?" Delia asked. "Sometimes he checks emails on those long flights."

Stuart shook his head. "We couldn't reach him, but we knew he would want us to bail you out." With that, he had pulled Carras closer to him and rubbed her shoulders. "I know if the situation were reversed, I would want someone to get you out of that place as quickly as possible."

She couldn't be sure, in the dark, but Jess thought Tom rolled his eyes. Usually Stuart and Carras's over-sappiness was a shared joke between them, but tonight Tom's cynicism irked her. Not that she had any right to be irked. If anything, Jess was the irker in this situation.

Now they were alone. Tom pulled the car into the driveway and turned it off. The house was dark—it was after midnight—but when Jess unbuckled her seat belt and moved to open the door, Tom did not follow. She closed the door and waited in silence, watching her husband's inscrutable expression in profile while the yellow dome light of her sensible, maternal SUV faded to black.

It was a long time before Tom spoke. "I think you'd better tell me what we're into." When she didn't respond, he added, "Come on, Gardner. I'm not *fucking* Stuart. I know something is going on, and I think maybe you tried to tell me. Maybe you chickened out, or maybe I'm an asshole and didn't listen, but either way I think now's the time."

His voice was like ice. She wanted to touch him, but something told her it was a bad idea.

"I don't know where to start," she began.

"Okay. How about we start with, did you know fucking Parker was a fucking prostitute?"

She swallowed. "It's not that simple. I mean, you're making it sound so dirty."

"Well, Jess, explain to me how my wife being arrested for solicitation of prostitution with a twenty-five-year-old dude is, like, not dirty. Oh, and by the way, that dude stole a shitload of money from one of his other clients and you saw fit not to even mention that we were at risk."

"First, I had nothing to do with the missing money. I didn't know he was going to do that. Also, I didn't sleep with him."

He made a *psssh* sound with his lips. "I know that, you idiot. I may not be as starry-eyed as Stuart Prather, but I still know who I married. At least I think I do."

Jess fidgeted in the seat. Her back was sore from hours in that stupid cell, and she imagined her clothes still smelled like vomit from poor Gladys. She wanted a shower, pajamas, a warm bed. She wanted the husband she knew and loved to hold her, tease her and tell her everything would be all right. "Can we go inside and talk about this?"

"I'd rather not," he said curtly. "If you have something devastating to tell me, I don't want to hear it in our house. I don't want to taint our home with whatever this is." He slammed a fist on the steering wheel and she jumped. "The fucking car can always be replaced."

A knife twisted in her chest. Jess hated herself so hard for what she had done to him. *Was* doing to him. She let her face fall into her hands. "I know you're not going to believe this, but I did this for you. For us."

Tom's voice was even and cold. "I'm not even going to pretend I understand what that means."

"We hired Parker—I did—to make you jealous. He had this service, he called it premium lessons… The details aren't important. Anyway, I knew he was an escort, but we all told him we didn't want anything sexual. We just—I. *I* wanted you to notice him liking me. To…wonder."

"Why?" Without seeing him clearly, Jess could still picture his incredulous expression. "Jesus Christ, Jessica. People have affairs all the time, and they take pains to hide them from their spouses. Why would you *pretend* you were having an affair?"

"I didn't want you to think I was having an affair. I wanted to remind you that it was, you know, possible. That another man could be attracted to me. I thought that would give us our spark back. Kind of like when I went on the date with Evan in college. It made you jealous, and our relationship intensified."

Tom turned toward her now. "You mean that skinny gay dude who worked on the paper? I would never have been jealous of that guy."

"You were. I remember. And Evan is not gay."

"I have seen some extremely descriptive Facebook posts to the contrary," Tom said. "He works for the Associated Press now. Nice guy. I've run into him a couple of times."

"You have? Why didn't you tell me?"

"We're getting a little off track with the accusations, don't you think? There's a stack of bail paperwork on the center console here, and a decent chunk of my salary for the year just went to a bail bondsman."

"Sorry. Really, Tom. I am sorry."

"You did this to make me jealous?"

She nodded. "It's stupid, I know. It was a crazy idea, and a huge waste of money, but I never thought I would get arrested... I wanted you to see the picture on Instagram or Facebook, and be reminded that somebody else might find me attractive."

"Instagram... Wait. How huge was the waste of money?"

"That's hardly the point."

She could feel him staring her down.

"Two thousand dollars." She cringed. "Give or take."

"What? Are you serious? Where did you get this money?"

She told him about her grandmother's GE stock. "I put what was left over into the kids' college accounts."

"Oh, you did? Well, that makes everything better." He got out of the car, slammed the driver's door and stormed into the house, leaving the front door wide open behind him.

Jess followed, wary.

He hadn't turned on any lights, but she could hear him moving around. "Not that it matters," she called into the echoing darkness. "But that was my own money. My grandmother left me that stock when I was a kid."

He froze. No further sound indicated where he was or what he was doing.

For a moment, Jess began to feel creeped out. She flipped on the foyer light. "I guess I was hoping you'd be flattered that I spent that kind of money trying to get your attention. Or at least find it endearing, or something. It sounds pathetic now that I say it out loud."

"*Your* money," he said softly from the dark living room beyond her. "I didn't think we were keeping things separate."

"Ugh. I never should've said that. It's not what I meant. Just..." She squinted into the blackness of the living room, walking in the direction of his voice. The words faded and died in her throat, because none of the rationalizations she'd told herself at the time were even worth mentioning now.

"Do you have any idea," Tom said, a disembodied voice in the dark, "how many strip clubs I have the opportunity to go to every week while I'm on the road?"

"I don't know. Lots. But you hate strip clubs."

"Yes, I do. And I hate cheap girls in hotel bars who throw themselves at me thinking I'll get them in with the team somehow. I don't want any of that. I turn it down, every time, Jess. The lap dances, the hotel keys, the propositions in elevators."

"In elevators? Seriously?"

"Swear to God."

"You never told me."

"Why would I tell you? I never wanted you to worry. I never wanted to set foot on that airplane, bound for some city that's not home, and know that you'd be sitting here with our kids, picturing me fighting off women. Wondering if tonight would be the night that I would cave, or have too much to drink, or maybe even be as pissed at you as I am right now."

She heard his voice break in the darkness, and as she stepped beyond the light of the foyer, she could make out the outline of Tom sitting in the armchair in the far corner of the room.

His voice gritted through the next words. "I never wanted you to feel for a *second* the way I feel right now."

It was a blow. She sank to her knees in front of him.

"God, Tom, I never wanted you to feel hurt like this. I only wanted you to feel the tiniest bit of jealousy. To help us reconnect. I've never wanted anyone else."

He was quiet. She touched his knee.

"And... Not that I'm defending myself, or that I would do it again, but...it did work. The day of the pool party, you were jealous of Parker, you have to admit. And that night we connected. For the first time in a while."

"Don't you understand? That makes it worse." He pushed her hand away. "It doesn't make me feel better, Jessica, that your little scheme worked on me. I feel manipulated. I feel like the best sex we've had in a while wasn't really ours. It was something you orchestrated. And now... I don't know. It's hard to imagine feeling comfortable with you again."

"Please don't say that." Her throat closed around a sob.

"It's not about the money, or even the fact that you got arrest-ed—which, by the way, could jeopardize both our careers, not to mention our family life—I can deal with all of that. I could, if you had been arrested...I don't know, protesting for something you believe in, or standing up for someone. I told you before we got married that I would follow you through fire; maybe you've forgotten that. I meant it. But this? I don't know."

He stood, removing her hand from his leg.

Her chest and throat constricted as though around shards of glass, and she reached for him. "Tom, please. Let's talk."

He moved aside. "I think we'd better not say anything else to-night."

He went to the doorway of the foyer, where he stood silhou-etted by the sole light on in their home. He turned back when she stood to follow him. "Tell me this, because the next time I sleep might be a long time from now, but when I do, I want to know that there's nothing I don't know."

"Okay." Her voice trembled.

"You said you never wanted anyone else. Are you saying you never felt any attraction for this guy? He never touched you at all?"

Jess swallowed hard. Every fiber of her being wanted to say no. Clear and unequivocal. She wanted to give Tom what he need-ed, so they could heal. Over the next several days, she would re-play this moment, this decision, and wonder whether she'd done the right thing. But it was Tom, and she owed him honesty. "He rubbed my shoulders once. On the tennis court. It was completely innocent, and nothing happened. But it had been so long since someone new touched me like that..." She stopped herself before launching into a rationalization that would only be self-serving.

"It turned you on." His voice was flat.

Her response was barely a whisper. "Yes."

"And you continued to spend time with him after that. You were drinking margaritas, in that picture. That was after this mas-sage thing?"

She nodded, so slowly that she could feel the weight of her skull grind against the bones of her neck. "And he kissed me that day. I didn't want him to; I didn't kiss him back. Delia was there—

she can tell you. But he took a picture. Now I realize that's why he kissed me, so he'd have the picture to hold over my head if I didn't keep paying, or find him a new client."

A pause. "This kid was a piece of work, wasn't he?"

She nodded again, still staring at the floor.

"Okay," Tom said, after a long moment. "I'm done for tonight. I'll get blankets and a pillow out of the linen closet."

"Babe. Please don't sleep on the couch."

"I'm not," he said. "You are."

39

DELIA

THE WHOLE CAR RIDE HOME with the Rodríguezes and Prathers, Delia tried to stay perky while dreading coming home to her dark, empty house. The girls were with Gage's parents—she would pay for that later—and although she knew she wouldn't sleep tonight, at least there would be a few minutes respite during which she could shower and change and await the marital repercussions of her behavior.

Gage's flight had landed in Brussels a couple of hours earlier, and it was a matter of time before she heard from him. She'd been surprised, actually, that a response from him hadn't been waiting for her when she got her phone back from the evidence locker. Sometimes the switch to his international plan didn't go smoothly, though—once he even forgot to switch his SIM card until the next morning. Or so he'd said. She had texted both his domestic and international numbers in front of the arresting officer before turning in her phone: *I've been arrested. Big mistake, related to Parker. Please call a lawyer. I love you.*

And when they'd squeezed into Tom's truck after posting bail, she had tried again. *Hey. I'm out on bond. Please call. Huge misunderstanding but I think a lawyer would be useful tomorrow. Can you come home to help? Can we talk?*

So far, nothing.

Delia poured herself a large glass of wine and sank into the living room couch to wait. Was it possible he'd boarded the next flight home? It wasn't like him to be so impulsive, and the sensible thing would have been to make calls from Belgium tonight and fly back tomorrow morning. But if he were doing that, she'd have been able to reach him. It was almost eight in the morning in Brussels now.

Delia smiled in spite of herself. It was sweet, she had to admit, the idea that her sensible husband would be so worried about her that he hopped a plane right back home. She could see him now, towering over a petite flight attendant at the gate in Brussels, insisting in his pidgin French that they *must* get him on a flight. He'd pay. He'd offer to buy someone's seat. In coach, if necessary. *Poor man.* Perhaps she should go to bed now, because he'd text her when he was back in Atlanta and she'd need to go collect him from the airport.

But she was too wired to sleep, and she had this big glass of wine. And before she could give it any further thought, her phone buzzed with Gage's international number. The hope deflated from her chest.

"Are you all right?" Gage asked without preamble.

"I'm fine. I'm home now."

"What happened?"

She gave him the short version, about how the police were dragging in anyone with any connection to Parker, hoping to get clues about the Curringtons' missing money.

"They brought in lots of people?"

"Initially, yes. Just the four of us tonight."

"Doesn't that strike you as odd? That all these people were being interviewed over the last couple of days, but they only brought in four of you? Are you sure?"

"I'm pretty sure."

"God dammit," Gage said. Delia could hear the whooshing sound of a revolving door, followed by the street noises of a busy European sidewalk. "How is that possible?"

Delia had a few ideas, but she wasn't ready to share yet. "Did you call a lawyer?"

"I will. There was no point in calling anyone in the middle of the night, especially once you were out on bail. I need to know what we're dealing with."

That was sensible. Still, it would have been nice if he'd done it right away. Or at least called her to explain.

"Alright. This dude is a high-paid prostitute, and he blackmailed several and stole from at least one client before ditching town."

"It appears that way." She picked a stray piece of lint from the throw pillow.

"Did you have a sexual relationship with him?" Gage's tone was neutral. He might have been asking what she'd eaten for dinner.

She didn't answer right away, listening for clues to his feelings in the busy sounds of Brussels.

"Delia, did you pay this man for sex? Even if it was once, I need to know."

"Does it matter?" Her voice cracked a little.

"I think it does. If you participated in an illegal prostitution ring, that's going to impact how serious this is. I'll need to tell the whole story to whichever lawyer we get." A car beeped in the background: the high, thready sound of a European car horn. Gage let out a frustrated sigh. "Dammit, Delia. Why didn't you tell me this sooner?"

She hadn't told him anything, but he clearly took her silence to mean she'd slept with Parker. "I didn't want to hurt you," she heard herself say, looking for a vein of feeling. *Like you've hurt me.*

"It's not about me being hurt, Delia. It's about our family, my—our—reputation. I can't believe you would be so foolish. We've always agreed to be discreet, and this guy's been in the fucking news."

"You're worried about what people think?" Against all reason, she kept lobbing him these emotional softballs, hoping he would knock one out of the park by correcting her. Fighting with her. Something. Anything.

I'm not worried about what people think; I'm worried about us.

How could you sleep with another man? The jealousy I feel is opening my eyes to how hard this arrangement must have been on you.

I love you and I don't want anyone else to have you.

"It's not that simple," the real Gage was saying. "The Belgians are skittish enough about this deal without my wife being involved in some sort of scandal."

Her patience broke. "But they aren't put off by the fact that you're having a longstanding affair with one of your colleagues? That seems like a bit of a double standard."

"Casual infidelity is one thing; a prostitution ring is another."
Casual infidelity. He said it academically, unaware that he'd broken
her into a thousand pieces. "And I don't broadcast my relationship
with Alana. To them, or, I'll remind you, to *you*. I've respected your
wishes to keep things aboveboard at home, where we live with
our girls." He paused. "Obviously you haven't shown the same
courtesy to me."

And that was it. That was the closest Gage would come to being
angry about Parker. Still, she tried to bait him one last time. "I
didn't intend for things to happen this way with Parker," she said.
"It was just…more intense than I expected."

Gage laughed. He actually fucking *laughed* at her.

"What are you, some kind of dewy-eyed schoolgirl? Don't tell
me he convinced you that he loved you?"

"Of course not," Delia said. It was true, but Gage misunder-
stood the tremble in her voice.

"God, women are as stupid as men are about these things. It's
not *real*, Delia. I would have expected you of all people to understand."

"I thought I understood that *you* loved me. But I would think
you'd be a little more concerned and sympathetic. Maybe even
jealous or hurt, or having *some* feeling."

"Oh, I see. That's what this is about. It's like I'm back at the
goddamn eighth grade dance."

"That's not fair."

"You've gotten yourself arrested in a very public way, put everything I've worked for at risk. That means everything *we* have,
darling. For us, for the girls. And instead of being practical and
helping clean up your mess, you want me to carry on like some
sappy guy who is devastated that his wife allowed another man to
touch her? I thought we were above all that, weren't we?"

Delia didn't answer. They'd always said so. But she wasn't sure
they'd had the geography right.

"I thought we both believed in marriage being practical—it's
about respect and common goals and loyalty, right? Not all these
puritanical ideas about possessing each other and sentimentality."

"We did. I did." She took a healthy sip of wine. "I still think
most of that."

"Don't tell me you're picking this moment to try to change everything about our relationship? Because I didn't hit the roof that you chose to fulfill your physical needs with some other guy? You *want* me to be irrational? Hypocritical? Possessive? Because I find that confusing at this stage of the game."

"Of course not." Delia sighed. He was right. They had always had this agreement, and her need for him to prove his passion for her like some romantic movie was irrational and unfair. "Sorry. It's been a long day."

"Look, let's not fight." Gage's voice softened. "What's done is done. We're into damage control now. We need to protect the girls, and our assets, and the business."

A little thrill ran through her at the "we," and she longed to see Gage's face, to see that light in his eye when he was coming up with a plan for them to execute together. "Are you coming home, then? Can you get away?"

For a moment, she could only hear the street noise of Brussels. "Gage?"

"Sorry, just...I'm about to go into this meeting and I had to check something." The soft whoosh of the revolving doors, and the background noise transitioned from the hustle of the street to the reverberating echo of dress shoes on marble floors. "Look, D. I don't think I should come home. The best thing I can do is keep these guys distracted from any news that might reach them. Reassure them I'm a solid, stable guy...no matter what might be going on at home."

Ah. *Team Gage and Delia* was now *Team Gage and the Belgians.*

Or maybe it had always been *Team Gage.*

"You understand, right, darling?" There was the sound of an elevator bell, and then quiet. *He was going up to the office. Going about his day.* "I'll call Sid West as soon as it's morning there. He'll help you with the legal side. But whatever happens, if we let it sink my career, we're screwed." He paused. "It's not like you have a career we can fall back on."

"Right." She choked on the lump in her throat. "I understand. You're right, as always." She let him reassure her, let him feel that he'd been helpful and dutiful and that everything would be all right, so that he could focus on his meeting.

When he hung up, Delia held her glass of wine up to the light, studying it. Then she threw it as hard as she could against the stone hearth, where it exploded into shards of glass and acrid crimson.

40

CARRAS

"I CAN'T BELIEVE JESS WOULD DO something like this," Stuart said into the darkness.

"It wasn't just Jess, babe. It was all four of us." They were lying in bed together, side by side, not touching. "We all thought it would help our marriages. You know, spice things up. Keep it interesting."

"I get that. But I never thought when we moved here to be near them that Jess was capable of something like this. That she would pull you into something illegal."

Carras's hands balled into fists at her sides. "Stuart, I keep telling you. Jess did not talk me into this. In fact, I was on board before she was."

"I don't understand. You don't have to protect her. Tom is my best friend and I love Jess like a sister."

Carras sat up in the darkness. "I am not protecting her, and I wish you would stop protecting me."

Stuart sat up and flicked on the bedside lamp. "What do you mean?"

"You have to quit being so nice to me all the time."

He laughed, and this infuriated her. "See? Stop. I'm not being funny. You should be pissed at me right now. I lied to you. I got involved with something illegal to try to get your attention. And you will do anything except blame me."

"I don't understand. That's a bad thing? You want a husband who gets angry all the time and tries to control you?"

"Of course not. But I also don't want a husband who keeps me in a glass case, who thinks I'm perfect all the time. I can't live up to that, Stuart. No one could."

"I know you're not perfect. But you're wonderful, and you're the best thing that's ever happened to me. I never want you to question that."

Carras put a hand on his arm. "I don't question that. But you seem to be forgetting that you are also the best thing that's ever happened to me. Things need to be equal between us. We need to be able to call each other out when we're wrong. I need you to be strong enough to stand up to me, to hold me accountable. Otherwise I don't feel safe."

They both stared down at her ebony hand on his light, calf-skin-colored arm. Carras had read somewhere that babies love contrast, black and white, dark and light. Supposedly their little baby eyes could process contrast better than the range of colors in between. She and Stuart had contrast in their skin, but she wondered sometimes whether there was enough contrast in their relationship. Would Stuart be able to provide structure for her soft-ness, strength for her weakness, striking lines to balance her squig-gles and bumps? Or would he always blend himself into whatever shade he thought Carras wanted?

"So. You're upset right now because I flew home early from my presentation in Las Vegas and picked you up from jail, because you were arrested for solicitation with some guy you knew years ago. And the whole time you were hanging around with him, I never got suspicious. I never asked if you had a history with this dude from your old tennis days. And tonight I brought you home to our bed, no questions asked, and you're upset that I'm not angrier with you?"

Carras sighed. "I'm not upset. I wish *you* were more upset. That was the whole point of all of this."

"Oh, that was the whole point?" His voice dripped with sar-casm. "Thank you for explaining. I am relieved that there was a point to intentionally hurting me like this."

"I was not trying to hurt you, Stuart."

"No? Just wanted me to see that I'm not strong enough for you? Not man enough?"

"That's not what I—"

"I hate to break it to you, Carras. But I've known I wasn't good enough for you since the first day we met. Our whole relationship, I've been so in love with you, only half believing that someone like you could want someone like me. It makes me ecstatically happy—like ridiculously, embarrassingly happy—to wake up next to you every morning and realize you haven't figured out how out of my league you really are."

"That's the thing. I'm not out of your league. You are out of mine."

He laughed, short and humorless. "You want to be held accountable? Fine. I call bullshit. Bring one hundred people into this bedroom right now, have them take one look at you and one look at me, and if you can get a single one of those people to say we are evenly matched, I'll eat this fucking pillow." He lifted the pillow in demonstration. "So, yeah. I see you hanging around with a really attractive guy you knew years ago, a guy who plays tennis and has abs. And I choose—*choose*, Carras—to ignore what I'm seeing, what I'm afraid of, not because I don't care."

His eyes were red now, and tears brimmed over to splatter on the pillow. Carras reached up to wipe them away, but he leaned away from her, face contorting as he gathered himself. "Not because I don't care. But because I'm afraid if I saw what I thought I was seeing, it would confirm everything I've been telling myself since that first night at Comic-Con. That this," he gestured back and forth between them, "has been a delightful fiction. Bound to come to an end at some point. I guess maybe I figured the longer I kept you in that glass case, as you put it, the longer I could put off the inevitable."

Carras was crying with him now, big ugly tears. She had no idea he felt this way. And in trying to confront their problems, trying to accept what she saw as their reality, she'd made it worse.

She had started this conversation hoping to fight it out, to bare everything for each other and to make love again the way they used to, because they wanted to, because they couldn't get close enough to each other. She wanted Stuart to want her again, not just want to make babies with her. She wanted him to stop seeing her as fragile and weak, to feel his honest anger as a vote of confidence in her strength, their strength. Now she saw that it wasn't that simple.

"I love this face." She stroked his jawline lightly. "Someday our children will love your face, almost as much as I do."

"Someday." After a moment, he added, "But maybe not right now."

"You're right." Carras tried not to sound disappointed. "It's almost two in the morning."

"No. I mean, maybe we should stop trying so hard. I've been pushing you on this kid thing." He put his hand on top of hers and pressed it against his cheek. "I'm not stupid, Carras. I know you could have any life you wanted. I thought if we started a family right away, you'd...feel more rooted here. With me. And then we could be normal, together."

Carras couldn't help but laugh. "You thought pregnancy and children would make us normal?"

"Stupid, I know." He smiled. "Sorry if I've been treating it like a project. The first thing I thought when Tom texted me earlier was that I pushed you to this. I know things haven't been... The chemistry between us... Anyway. I think we need to step back for a while."

"Do you mean stop trying to have a baby? Or..." She forced herself to say the words. "Step back from us?"

"I don't know. Both, maybe? We need to reevaluate what we've been doing. Give ourselves a little space. I knew marriage was going to be work, but I can see now that I've been smothering you, and myself too. Maybe we need to let things happen more naturally." The words were sensible, but there was a sadness in his voice that broke her heart.

"Stuart, you're not giving up, are you? On us? On our family?"

He shook his head. "Couldn't, even if I wanted to. Like I said earlier, I'm crazy in love with you. But if this experience tells us anything, it's that me being in love isn't enough."

He reached for the lamp, and darkness flooded the room once again. He lay down with his back to her, but when Carras roped her arm through his and pressed herself against him, he didn't pull away.

"I'm in love with you, too, Stuart. You know that, right?"

It took a long time for him to answer, so long that Carras began to think he'd gone to sleep. It both startled and relieved her to hear the words "I do know that," spoken softly into the darkness.

41

MAIZY

A NDERS WAS OMINOUSLY QUIET ON the ride home from
the city jail. Maizy knew being the last one picked up didn't
mean anything. He'd been an hour and a half behind Tom and
Stuart. He had explained: something about the bank and getting
in touch with the right branch manager, someone who would not
"broadcast this little legal drama all over the fucking company."

She understood. But she still had a petulant, childish feeling of
hurt. Of being the last one picked up after school.

They drove in silence most of the way home. Maizy was exhausted; it was almost two a.m., and she had no idea what to say.
With all her planning, she had done nothing to prepare for a conversation with Anders on the way home from jail in the middle
of the night.

It had been far easier to focus on the positive side of her fantasies. Her favorite had involved a well-sexed Anders smacking
her on the ass in the kitchen in front of his whole family on their
next group vacation. She'd spent hours delighting in the shocked/
jealous expressions of her sisters-in-law. Sometimes she even took
the fantasy a step further, excusing herself from cooking with the
women to lead Anders to a bedroom. *In the middle of the day—can
you believe it? On the family vacation! With all of us in the next room!*
They'd be talking about it for years. Maybe for once, the other
Henriksson women would be asking for *her* secret, rather than
barraging her with advice.

As Anders pulled into their driveway, she noticed that there
were several other cars, and most of the downstairs lights were still

on. Not preparing for this contingency, Maizy realized, had been a huge mistake.

"What's going on?" She squinted to make out the cars in the darkness, and confirm the identities of their owners. "Why is your family here?"

"Because I have no idea how to handle this, Maizy. I don't know what's gotten into you lately, but we need support." Anders got out, closed the driver's door, and stood waiting for her.

She was so tired that she could barely get her feet under her, much less face an inquisition. She got out but did not come around the car. "Is this…? Some kind of intervention?"

Anders looked at his feet. "I don't know what to call it. But this is serious and you need help." He paused. "We need help."

There in her driveway, at two in the morning, something broke inside Maizy. A loadbearing wall holding up the structure of herself. Holding back something. "Are you fucking kidding me, Anders? Are you under the impression that I have some sort of drug problem?"

"I have to ask that you not curse at me. And that's the kind of thing I'm talking about. You've never been one for foul language. You've never been one to do these crazy things, associate yourself with this kind of people."

"I think a little foul language in your direction is called for," Maizy said. "It's two in the morning. I've been sitting in jail for the last several hours, waiting for my husband—who, by the way, was the only spouse among the four of us who was *in town all day* and still managed to be the last one there. You haven't wanted to know anything going on in my life for months, unless it impacted you. And now, on the worst day of my life, when I'm exhausted and scared and need to be held… You stage an intervention? Like I'm some kind of out-of-control teenager?"

"It's because we love you."

"You love me. At least I thought you did. Your family hates me. They're the last people I want to see right now."

"They don't hate you. You always say that, and it's not true. They want to help. You're freaking me out, Maizy. I didn't know what else to do."

Exasperated, Maizy stepped toward him. To her surprise, her

giant Norwegian husband, who towered over her, took a half-step backward. If she hadn't been so angry, she might have laughed. "If you're worried about me, why didn't you *talk* to me? How about, pay attention to me? How about, touch me like I'm your wife, not some pudgy roommate you happen to have children with?"

Anders looked aghast. It was the first time in twenty years of marriage she'd seen him speechless.

"I've got an idea, Anders. How about you come in from the bike trail on a Saturday, and fuck me on the kitchen floor, instead of trimming your stupid bushes, or putting in a new walkway between the stupid fire pit and the stupid grill?"

"You said you liked the fire pit."

"I love the fire pit, Anders. It's the best damn fire pit in the history of fire pits. It's beautiful. It should be on the front cover of a fucking fire pit magazine!" She was being mean now, and she knew it. But somehow, she couldn't stop.

"Why don't we ever have parties around that fire pit? Why isn't it a romantic spot for us, or even a place to make s'mores with the kids? The only time we use that thing is when your family is here." She gestured at the house, where she could see figures moving, opening curtains, silhouetted by her dining room lights. "Maybe we should use it now. You've got wood in the shed, right? Break out some beers. Maybe instead of talking about what's wrong with me and our marriage, you and your brothers can compare running schedules and protein shakes."

"You're being ridiculous."

"Right. Of course, this isn't the correct protocol for when your husband bails you out of jail after midnight, and greets you with his whole damn family. What's the etiquette here, Anders? Let's ask Marisol. I bet she can find an agenda online."

He'd been moving toward her, but he stopped, dropping his head and his arms at his side.

"Oh. My. God. She did, didn't she? Marisol printed out an agenda for tonight."

He didn't move.

Maizy had the weirdest sense of sudden clarity. It was as though the haze of tonight's time in jail, and the haze of the last several years, had dissipated like fog off the Chattahoochee River. She felt giddy, and dizzy, as anger and hope left her simultaneously.

"You were late coming to get me," she said without emotion. "Because you had to rally your family around you; had to figure out the plan with them first. Before you bailed me out. Before you even asked me for my side of things."

"I do want your side of things," he said. "That's what's been so confusing… It's not like you to do something like this. And to not tell me what's happening. That's why we figured, I figured, there must be something going on… Substance abuse or… Whatever it is, we'll handle it. I'm not very good at these things, but Marisol has a friend who's done AA for years…"

"Didn't it occur to you, even for a second, that maybe *I* might be the best resource for what's going on with me? I mean, if you had any reason to think I was doing drugs, if I were somehow endangering the children, I could maybe see… But I'm not doing drugs. I never have. I can't believe you would even think that."

Anders nodded. "You're right. Maybe I went about this the wrong way. But don't I get some kind of credit for the effort? I mean, what the hell am I supposed to do? You're like a different person lately."

She stretched out her palm.

The car keys dangled forgotten from his left hand, and it took a minute for him to realize what she was asking for. "Maizy, you can't be serious…."

"Hand me the keys, Anders." Her anger lent her voice more conviction than she felt. "Or I will make you exceedingly sorry."

"But… You got arrested…"

"Yes. I did. And the whole time I was in that jail, I was obsessing over how bad I felt that I've done this to you. What I could do to make it up to you." She snatched the keys from his tentative hand, and gestured with them at the extra cars in their driveway and on the street. "But this? This might be worse. At the very least, it's a tie."

She opened his door and slid in.

"Where are you going? It's two in the morning."

"I'm sure that there's some seedy motel open this time of night. That would suit me, don't you think? Maybe there will be a nice cocaine dealer on the corner out front."

Before he could answer, she had the car started and thrown in reverse. Her fantasies of shocking everyone on their next beach vacation—fantasies of mind-blowing sex with her tall, handsome husband—were swept away. She imagined instead their shocked faces—Marisol, Lars, her mother-in-law, the others—watching her from her own house. The fact that this fantasy was real, and that Anders would be dealing with them alone, gave her a guilty sense of gratification that lasted all the way to the parking lot of the Sugar Mills Hampton Inn.

42

DELIA

THE NEXT MORNING, SHE CLEANED up the mess. The glass shards were meticulously removed from her living room carpet, as though by a CSI team. By the time she finished, the wine stain was gone from the living room carpet. When Delia was able to talk about this later with some objectivity, it was going to be a perfect testimonial for her VikingHome instant stain solution. It was like magic in a bottle.

If only the solution for her marriage were so simple.

How could she tell the man who had plucked her out of the disastrous life she'd been leading in her early twenties—who had saved her and given her respectability and money and children—how could she tell him that she now needed more than he'd promised her? That the life she'd sworn to him (and herself) would be enough…wasn't?

Gage wasn't coming back to help her. He wouldn't hold her hand while she talked to Sid West or help her work through the impact her behavior would have on their lives. He was keeping his distance, letting her take care of it. Delia told herself it was the right thing to do. What she might have done if the situation were reversed. Except it was a lie. If Gage were in trouble, Delia would be on the first flight to wherever he was, hurdling over the other passengers at airport security if need be.

She thought of leaving sometimes, when he'd hurt her. When Alana's presence reared its ugly head in their lives, or—as was happening now—when Gage made it clear he would always choose practicality over passion. She had money set aside—more than he could've imagined—from the various product lines she'd been selling over the years. She could go if she needed to. But there were the girls to consider: Gage was a doting father; Lulu and Sadie needed him now more than ever as the teenage years descended upon them. The last thing they needed was for their parents to divorce just when their worlds got shaky and confusing.

Worse: Delia loved him. There was no hope for that.

Once she'd cleaned up the evidence of her tantrum, Delia flitted around the house, straightening things that were already straight and checking her phone every few minutes. Gage's mom had offered to keep the kids for as long as Delia needed. But she knew all too well there were strings attached to that offer. Barbed wire, more like. Besides, Sadie had an orthodontist appointment, so Delia picked them up early.

"What happened last night that we had to go to Grandma's all the sudden?" Sadie asked, typing away at her phone in the passenger seat.

"Just a last-minute meeting." Delia looked at Lulu in the rearview mirror. "Was it nice to see Grandma?"

Always truthful, Lu piped up. "She makes us dry out the bathtub with a towel when we're done using it. Because of mildew. And I even told her that it wasn't a bath night, that I only have to take a bath every other night. But she made me anyway. Her soap smells weird."

"I'm sorry, sweetheart. That's how Grandma is. But at least you're clean and you won't have to take another bath tonight."

Her youngest daughter was not to be pacified. "But *tonight* is a bath night. The whole calendar is going to be wrong now."

Not for the first time, Delia wondered whether she and Gage weren't messing their kids up a tiny bit, with their shared intensity and love of orderliness. Perhaps it made more sense to have a balance; maybe there should be at least one person in a marriage more laid-back, like Jess or Tom. Of course, with those two, things were constantly falling through the cracks and the house was always a mess. Maybe she and Jess could switch husbands and then everything would be perfect. Except that Tom's bad jokes and laissez-faire masculinity would drive her up the wall. She didn't want to be married to Tom; she just wanted Gage to have a Tom *side*.

"Mom," Sadie said with irritation. "You missed it."

"Missed what, baby?"

"Um, hello? The orthodontist? The whole reason you picked us up? You passed it." She said this as though Delia were the dumbest human being she had ever had the misfortune of meeting. The tone of voice was familiar these days, but it was still surreal sometimes: a person who literally lived inside you for nine months having so much contempt for your existence. If this was what the teenage years held, boarding school had a certain appeal.

"Sorry, honey. I was in my own little world." Delia tried to be cheerful, both to combat Sadie's foul attitude, and to amuse Lulu. As she did a U-turn at the next traffic light, Delia sang, "my own little world" to the tune of some cutesy princess show the girls had loved a few years ago.

Lulu loved this, of course, and began singing the show's theme at the top of her lungs. She loved singing, and in this case, it had the bonus attraction of annoying her older sister. "Look at me, look at you, there is nothing we can't do..."

"Lulu, stop! I *hate* that song."

As anyone other than Sadie would've been able to predict, this had the effect of making her younger sister louder. "In my heart, I'm still an ordinary girl..."

"Stop! That's a baby song!"

"But now I am the princess of my own little world..."

Delia was doing her best not to laugh as her younger daughter hammered it up in the backseat with over-the-top high notes and jazz hands. Sadie, however, went from being understandably annoyed to a full-blown meltdown—shrieking at her sister and crying—that Delia shushed Lulu and put her hand on Sadie's knee as they pulled into the orthodontist's parking lot. Sadie was sobbing by the time Delia got the SUV in park, so she threw her arms around her daughter and held her, making reassuring shushing noises the way she had when the girls were babies.

"I was just singing," Lulu said, half defensive, half concerned.

"Shhh..." Delia said. "I know, baby. You didn't do anything wrong. Sadie, what's going on?"

"Are you and Daddy getting a divorce?"

Delia's heart squeezed. "What? Of course not." She held Sadie back a little, to look at her face. It was puffy and red, her eyes wide and childlike. Heartbreakingly beautiful, this baby of hers on the verge of womanhood. "Where would you get an idea like that?"

"Something I overheard Grandma say."

Anger welled up so fast in Delia that she could feel its physical presence, burning in her chest. She kept her voice steady. "Grandma said that Daddy and I are getting a divorce? She said that to you?"

Sadie shook her head. "I overheard her talking on the phone. To one of her bridge friends, the mean ladies." She gave Delia a tiny smile. They'd shared their mutual assessment of Grandma's bridge friends before. "She said there was no telling where you were, where you'd run off to. She said she'd tried to tell Daddy— she called him Gage—that it was all a mistake, before y'all even got married. She said even though she was right about you, he wouldn't listen to her with the next one either."

Here, Sadie glanced at her sister in the backseat, apologetic to say this in front of Lulu. "She thinks you have a new boyfriend or something. That Parker guy? And, like, Daddy would need a new wife."

Not for the first time since she'd met her indomitable mother-in-law, Delia stuffed her anger and bile deep into her gut, knowing there was nothing to be gained by letting her children see her frustration. Or by crossing Elizabeth Cargill.

She put her hands on Sadie's trembling shoulders. Delia needed to be firm, make her children feel safe. Sentimentality could wait.

"Now, listen. I don't know what Grandma Cargill said, or why. You girls have been in this family long enough to know that Grandma and I don't always see eye to eye. I'm sorry that you had to hear all that. But if that's what she meant, then I am here to tell you that she is absolutely wrong." Delia willed herself to stay calm, to look both girls in the eye in turn. "Daddy and I have no intention of getting a divorce. We love and respect each other. And we both love you; we are both proud of you."

"Is it true?" Sadie sniffled. "What she said about that Parker guy? That he was your...boyfriend or something?"

"Absolutely not." She took a deep breath. Better to be as honest as she could. "Parker was my tennis coach, and my friend. Now he's gone away, and the police think he did something bad. I hope that's not true, but if it is, I will be sad that he made a bad choice. That's all."

Delia looked at Lulu, who was becoming tearful in the backseat as her sister recovered composure. "Come here." Lu unbuckled and leaned forward, and Delia managed to wrap them both in a tight hug despite the awkwardness of the center console. "I love you both so much. I would never intentionally do anything to hurt either of you. I hope you know that."

"Or Daddy either," Lulu sniffed into Delia's shoulder.

"Daddy either," Delia repeated, kissing their hair, which smelled like a mixture of old sunscreen and Elizabeth Cargill's expensive rose soap. And she saw with sudden clarity that it didn't matter whether Gage adored her as he once had, or whether he rushed home to help and comfort her. She wasn't prepared to go to war, to let her girls be the casualties. Not until she knew she could protect them. "Now, let's get inside. We're late."

In the orthodontist's waiting room, Delia pulled out her phone and searched for news. So far, nothing had been published about their arrest last night—the last installment from the local news simply reported that the police were speaking to acquaintances of Parker Yung as they investigated the theft. She hadn't heard from Belinda, but Sandy Patterson reported that the Curringtons had retreated to their mountain cabin near Dahlonega with the kids, to get away from the attention. Delia was sure Belinda would have preferred their beach house in the Florida Keys, but according to Sandy, the police had told them not to leave the state.

The most recent news related to the theft was from a local consumer finance writer, who warned readers about the dangers of using common words or phrases for financial passwords, the importance of changing them frequently, and never keeping them written down where someone could find them. Housekeepers, nannies, even visitors to your home could be potential thieves if you made it too easy for them. He went on to talk about router security, and how thieves might be able to use a combination of malware and a poorly secured Wi-Fi router to break into your home, without ever crossing the threshold...

Delia's eyes glazed over at the technical analysis of various router types and advice for each model. *No way was* this *how Parker got into Belinda's bank accounts.* She skimmed to the end of the article. *He was savvy in many ways, but she couldn't see him staked out with a bunch of super-spy computer equipment.*

Eyes drooping, she went to her inbox and scanned her email messages, scrolling through order confirmations from Viking-Home, Pure Indulgences, and Skin by Suzette. She hadn't done any parties this month, but the downline of consultants beneath her was doing well and reorders alone were going to bring in over a thousand dollars.

She skimmed through her own orders to see several regular customers, and a couple of new women she'd met at parties in the spring. There were a few address updates, including…an order from Belinda last week. She was having several items from Pure Indulgences and Skin by Suzette sent to her vacation home in the Keys. *Must be nice,* Delia thought. *Even after you've been robbed, you can still plan a nice vacation. And never mind about texting me back.* She sighed and kept scrolling. There were several new list signups from an email promotion she'd done with her VikingHome line, and Delia was more than halfway to earning her bonus beach cooler tote. It was a cute bag, gray with pink polka dots, and included free monogramming. Usually Delia watched those promotions like her lottery numbers were coming in, but today it felt pointless and silly.

She put the phone back in her purse, picked up an ancient *Glamour* magazine from the side table, and watched Lulu playing with a younger child at the dollhouse in the corner. As she flipped the worn pages, her exhausted brain skipped from scene to scene like a bad 1980s montage: Parker, on the bridge in San Antonio, waiting patiently and without judgment for her to tell the truth about her marriage. Stuart, running to take Carras in his arms as though she'd been in prison for years rather than hours. Tom, one evening when they'd all played cards, watching Jess rearrange her hand for the fiftieth time as though she were a goddess strumming a magic harp. Parker, taking Belinda's hand and kissing it on the patio at the café…

Delia sat up straight, the realization hitting her. Of course, Park-er couldn't have pulled off a cyber heist alone, and of course the way he blackmailed them hadn't been all his idea either. The police were right: he had an accomplice.

Belinda Hayes-Fucking-Currington.

43

MAIZY

MAIZY GOT HOME AT ALMOST noon. She'd requested late checkout, slept in for the first time in years, and taken a luxurious hot shower with her phone off. But she had to go home eventually.

Anders was in the kitchen when she came in, washing dishes in the frilly pink "Bakers Gonna Bake" apron he and the girls had given her last Christmas.

"I thought you might be at work." She set her purse on the counter.

He shook his head but didn't look at her, drying off a bowl and hanging the dish towel on the hook. "I called in sick. Someone had to run the household today."

She ignored the jab, watching him put the bowl away. It was elegantly shaped and perfect white, like all their dishes. Anders couldn't stand the busy, mismatched dishes Maizy had before they were married, so they'd registered for clean, modern neutrals. "Where are the girls?"

"I took them to Lars and Marisol's. She's taking them shopping and to a movie."

"Marisol? Are you *serious*?"

He raised his hands in a gesture of surrender. "Look, I know. But she *does* care about us and the girls. I knew we would need to talk…" He looked helpless. "I made her promise to let them have junk food at the theater."

Maizy had to smile. She let her hands drop to the sides.

"I know you're angry." Anders sighed. "I am sorry about last night. Bringing my family here, after you'd had a terrible day was…a miscalculation."

"A miscalculation?"

"Stupid. Insensitive. Clueless."

"You're getting warmer."

He inclined his head, a slow nod that strained the tendons in his neck. "I concede the point. But I meant what I said last night: you *have* been different lately. Maybe it was wrong to assume it might be drugs. It's just, you hear these stories about bored house-wives… And I didn't know how to approach you about it. I've never been able to relate to that addictive personality, you know?"

Unless you count fad diets, mountain biking, and working in the yard until it looks like the grounds of Kensington Gardens…

Maizy kept these uncharitable thoughts to herself. "To be fair, I guess you weren't *that* far off about the bored housewife thing. The truth is, I was trying to get your attention by paying a male prostitute to flirt with me. Not exactly healthy behavior."

"I still don't understand, Maizy. *Why*? Have I been such a ter-rible husband?"

His expression, so defeated and confused, pulled at her heart-strings. Maizy started to wonder whether she'd been imagining all of it. Whether she'd overreacted at every turn, let her insecurities get in the way of her husband's ill-expressed affection. "I think I was worried I've been a bad wife," she said, more comfortable taking responsibility than doling out blame. At least in the daylight. "Sometimes I feel like I'm not what you had in mind, and you'd be happier with someone like…Marisol."

Anders threw up his hands. "Can we not make this about Mari-sol, please? For the last time, I do not have feelings for my brother's wife. You have no reason to be jealous of her."

Maizy furrowed her brow. "Feelings? I didn't say anything about you having feelings for her…" *And there it was.* Clicking into place like all the parts of one of those complex locking systems they showed on spy movies and cartoons. He was always mentioning Marisol, always wanting to bring his brothers over to show off his latest landscaping project. Maizy had assumed it was to impress his brothers: another volley in the constant competition between the four boys that had been running their whole lives. But he was trying to impress *Marisol*.

And who could blame him? She was gorgeous and smart and healthy, way out of Anders's league. Also, madly in love with her husband Lars. Any idiot could see that. *Poor Anders.* Maizy didn't know whether to hate him or feel sorry for him.

She looked him squarely in the face. "For the past few years, you've done nothing but criticize what I'm cooking, what I'm eating, how I look, whether I exercise…"

"That's not fair. We have always agreed we wanted to be healthy."

"Healthy, yes. Perfect, Anders? No."

"I'm only trying to encourage you, Maizy. We all need someone to remind us to keep working toward our goals. To push us in the right direction."

"Maybe we do. Maybe I do." She shook her head and looked up at him. "But that shouldn't be *you*. The person who loves you shouldn't be the person who points out all the ways you can be improved on. If I decide to lose weight or get in shape or eat better, that's one thing. I would hope I have your support."

"Yes. You know I'm here for you. We could do it together."

She stopped him. "Sometimes you look at me like I'm unfinished as I am. Like you won't be totally in love with me, won't fully accept me, until I'm…" She paused, gathering her courage. "More like *her*."

"That's ridiculous. I just want to help you be healthy." He looked at the ceiling in exasperation. "And for the last time, there is nothing going on with me and Marisol."

"Oh, I know there isn't." Maizy almost laughed. "But you have to admit, you would be happier, and our marriage would be better, if I were thirty pounds lighter, and got excited about having a mountain bike seat squashed against my butt for half the weekend."

He stared at her, the silence speaking volumes. "I don't see how any of this is relevant. I'm not sure why I'm the one being villainized the morning after you got arrested for hiring a prostitute with my money."

"*Our* money."

"Fine. I still think we're off topic talking about dieting."

"You know what?" Maizy said. "You're right. Let's talk about the mistake I made with Parker."

"Thank you. I knew you would see reason—"

"My mistake was that I was trying to get the wrong person's attention. I did all this to prove to you that I was worthy of you, that I could be valuable and lovable and sexy. But in the end, it was the other way around. It's *my* opinion of me that matters. My happiness in our marriage and our family is as important as yours. And this isn't your fault for ignoring me or criticizing me or comparing me to your sister-in-law, who you're half in love with."

"I'm not—"

"It's *my* fault for letting you do those things. I've given you way too much control over how I see myself. How I feel every day. And it ends here."

Maizy took a deep breath, feeling the sudden rush of words that had been building up in her chest for years. "You will not criticize or coach me anymore, Anders. I'll create my own standards; I'll decide if I want to meet them. Your family will not dictate what we do on holidays and vacations. You and I will decide that together. And *if* we both decide we want to stay married, we will parent together and choose how to spend our weekends together."

"*If* we stay married? Wait, Maizy…"

"I am not going to sit home alone for another Saturday while you're out enjoying yourself on the bike trails or futzing around in the yard, do you understand? My days of being ignored are over, Anders."

He looked baffled. "I've never thought—"

"And you know what else?" she interrupted triumphantly as the realization occurred to her. "No more Lutefisk! Not at Christmas, not ever. I hate that stuff and I'm not eating another bite of it. I don't care if your mother spontaneously combusts from the shock."

Anders was looking a little like a fish himself now, staring at her open-mouthed. It felt good to set her own terms for once, to get the frustrations off her chest. Anders was right; she was a different person now. Whether this new Maizy could stay in a marriage to the man in front of her remained to be seen.

Her phone buzzed on the counter. A text from Delia to their group: *Come over ASAP. It's important.*

"That's Delia. I have to go." She picked up her phone and spun on her heel to leave.

"You're going to walk out now? In the middle of this?"

Maizy shrugged. "It seems important. She may have talked to Gage about getting us some legal advice."

"But you said, '*if* we stay married.'" Anders was floored. As though it had never once occurred to him that Maizy might want to leave—a conversation or a marriage.

"I'm just going up the street." She patted Anders's arm. "You'll survive."

She didn't wait for a response, but pulled from his grasp and walked out. Stepping onto the front stoop, Maizy realized for the first time in their marriage that she didn't know what would happen when she returned later. Would their marriage rebound from this crisis, stronger than ever? Or would she always see Anders's gaze on her and know he was comparing her to someone she was tired of trying to be?

Either way, for the first time in years, Maizy had choices.

44

MAIZY

"HI," MAIZY SAID TENTATIVELY, WHEN Delia answered the door. She was still exhilarated from her conversation with Anders, but wasn't sure where she stood with Delia. "Did you hear from Gage?"

"Gage?" Delia looked lost for a second. "Oh, yes. He's arranging for us to consult with an attorney. One sec, Maizy." She called up the stairs: "Girls! I recorded a movie for you on the DVR, but if you want to come down instead… We're talking about our menstrual cycles and healthy sexuality!"

At the groans from above, Delia smirked. "If I'd told them we were having a private conversation, they'd be listening at the top of the stairs the whole time. They've seen enough of my Pure Indulgences products to want to steer clear of this."

"Impressive." Maizy followed Delia through to the kitchen, where Jess and Carras were already at the table.

Delia handed Maizy a mug of coffee, cream only, just how she liked it. "I was saying Gage isn't coming home straight away, but put us in touch with a great criminal lawyer who's very discreet. If we're prosecuted, he can recommend someone for each of us. But I doubt that will happen."

Maizy glanced at the other two women when Delia said Gage wasn't coming home. Their expressions were neutral; she couldn't tell whether they thought it was as strange and sad as Maizy did.

"You don't think they'll prosecute us?" Jess asked. There were dark circles under her eyes.

Delia shook her head. "I'm pretty sure they know the four of us didn't actually do anything wrong. Besides, the solicitation charges are small-time compared to the grand larceny and serial prostitution. If they can get to Parker or his accomplice, they might let us go."

It sounded reasonable enough, but Maizy's hours in the holding cell at Sugar Mills Jail had given her a new appreciation for the risks of prosecution. "But so far no one's heard from Parker, right? Do they have any leads?" Maybe she'd missed something. "Do they even know if he's still in Cuba?"

Carras shook her head. "I have a news alert set for his name, and nothing new has come out." After a pause, she said, "I can show you guys how to do it."

"*Millennials*." Jess rolled her eyes.

"So, no sign of Parker or this supposed accomplice. What if they never find them?"

"Well, that's why I texted you guys. We're going to do it for them."

There was a moment of stunned silence, and Delia added, "Not Parker. He's long gone. But I suspect his partner in crime is still close by. We're going to make sure she's found."

"What are we, vigilantes now?" Jess said. "Because I have to be honest, Delia, I don't think I have it in me. If this has taught me anything, it's that subterfuge is not my thing."

"No subterfuge," Delia said. "We're going to make her confess."

"Her, who?"

"Belinda Hayes-Currington." Delia glowed with triumph. "She was helping him steal Orson's money so she and Parker could run away together."

"How do you know this?" Maizy was careful to keep her tone neutral.

"I don't have *direct* evidence," Delia said. "Not yet. But it hit me this morning: Belinda ordered some stuff from me a couple of weeks ago—sunscreen, beach bag, massage oil, personal lubricant, waterproof vibrator—"

Maizy coughed. She knew sex toys were one of Delia's product lines, but she hadn't quite adjusted to someone dropping "waterproof vibrator" into the conversation as though she were saying "whole grain cereal."

"And she had it all shipped to their vacation house in the Keys."

"So?" Jess said. "Maybe they were planning a vacation, and she didn't want to fly with all of it."

"Or maybe," Delia said, "she was planning to sneak away to Cuba with Parker."

Jess snorted. "What, like, on a boat?"

"Maybe. Or from the Miami airport. It would be faster from there; she could tell Orson she wanted a day or two at the beach house, and then slip out of the country before he'd even noticed."

"She wouldn't leave the kids, would she?" Maizy asked. When she'd stepped out of the house today after her argument with Anders, Agatha and Elise had been foremost in her mind.

Delia shrugged. "Maybe she was planning to take them with her. Or maybe she was just…over all of it."

Maizy considered how it felt to wake up in the hotel room this morning, alone and quiet and free from responsibility. She could understand the impulse to change your life drastically. But the fantasy would lose its appeal after a day or two. She would miss her kids too much. "I can't believe a mother could do that. She's always at the school, and her kids are so…perfect."

"May I remind you this woman set us all up to be blackmailed? And, I have a theory …" Delia tapped the table with her index finger. "The police told us Parker has done the blackmail thing before, right? But I think he kept it small—enough to line his pockets but not so much that his clients couldn't handle it without upending their lives."

"Like he upended ours," Jess said. "I wouldn't have been able to pay what he was asking, even if the police hadn't been involved. I would've had to tell Tom."

"Exactly. And none of us could set someone else up like that. I think that whole thing about clients recruiting other clients was a lie. The whole 'some people have years of free tennis lessons just on referrals' garbage. I know direct sales consultants who stretch the truth like that to seem more legitimate when they're trying to get their businesses running."

"Stretch the truth?" Jess said.

"Fine, they lie. I didn't say *I* have ever done it. Anyway, I think Parker needed to scale his business quickly—maybe because he and Belinda were planning to run away—and the monthly minimums, the group discounts, making us pull in other suckers... That was all Belinda."

"You think it was Belinda's idea to have us recruit other people?" Jess said.

Delia grinned. "Multilevel marketing is a female business model, and this is MLM at its finest."

Maizy gaped. "They had to know this wouldn't be sustainable... No way could you force an entire community of women into a pyramid scheme without someone reporting it."

"You'd be surprised." Delia smiled, when normally she would have bitten Maizy's head off. Maybe they *had* turned a corner. "But they didn't need it to be sustainable. Think about it: they were planning to move Orson's retirement money offshore, but they needed quick cash for the short-term, right? Plane tickets and expenses until they could get access to the real money."

"So that was where our money went?" Jess said, appalled.

"Yep. Belinda's rich, but the money is all Orson's. She had the same problem we all did with our husbands: she couldn't take big chunks out without Orson noticing."

Carras furrowed her brow. "Parker needed cash. And once he got enough..." She trailed off, staring at her lap.

Maizy didn't know Carras very well, but there was something going on with her.

"I should have realized it sooner," Delia said. "We all assumed Belinda recruited us because Parker was blackmailing her. Like that was his business model... But, why would he need to recruit like that? We'd all heard rumors about Parker before Belinda introduced us. People would be able to find him through word of mouth."

"Exhibit A." Maizy raised her hand. "I pushed my own stupid way in."

Delia patted her arm. "We were all stupid. He collected ten thousand dollars from us in a month, and managed to gather enough fake evidence to keep us quiet..."

"This is what he meant," Maizy said. "When I was talking to him that night... He said something about how he was going to miss talking to me. I didn't understand. But now it makes sense."

"I bet Orson found out the money was missing too soon." Jess bit her lip. "Maybe they were going to run away the night of the party, but Orson checked his bank accounts earlier than they'd planned, and called the police. Parker got away but Belinda was stuck."

"Exactly. At the pool party, Belinda was pouring drinks down Orson's throat. I remember noticing and thinking she must be trying to knock him flat so she could get some alone time with Parker. Clearly her plans were bigger than that."

"Belinda turned us in!" Jess slammed her palm on the table. "She gave the police the blackmail evidence against us to create a distraction."

Delia nodded. "That's why it was the four of us there last night. She knew it would keep the scrutiny off her, buy her some time."

"What do we do?" Carras said.

"As it happens," Delia preened, "I've already done it. I called Orson."

"You what?" All three of them stared.

Maizy felt admiration, and a prickle of irritation that Delia had made them sit through the whole Nancy Drew case summary before revealing that she'd already made herself the hero. The woman *loved* to be the center of attention.

But then Maizy thought of Gage, still in Belgium, with no plans to come home to support his wife after her arrest. And Delia had patted her arm a moment before, when Maizy put herself down. *Fine, let her have this moment in the sun.* "Gee, Delia," she said with exaggerated interest. "What on earth did you say to him?"

"Why, I never thought you'd ask, Maizy." Delia grinned at her. "I told him that Belinda wasn't returning my calls, which is true, and her cell service up there at the cabin must be horrible, which is *so* not true. Anyway, then I said I was going through my Pure Indulgences orders for the month, and that Belinda had ordered some stuff to be shipped to their house at the Keys, and innocently asked if he thought she would want it sent to the cabin instead. I may have accidentally listed everything she ordered."

"What if they had been planning a vacation down there?" Carras asked.

"That would make the question legit, right? No harm done."

Delia tapped the side of her nose. "But I had a hunch they weren't. And I *may* have mentioned something about wanting to come stay at their place sometime, because I've always wanted a picture in front of that big striped buoy that says '90 Miles to Cuba.'"

"Did you think he made the connection?" Maizy was enthralled in spite of herself.

"I also said something along the lines of, 'Oh no, how insensitive of me. Isn't Cuba where the police think that Parker guy went? I'm *so* sorry for all you're going through. He seemed like such a good, close friend to Belinda...' Just to make sure."

"You little sneak." Jess was watching Delia with bemused interest.

"Based on his reaction, I would say they had no immediate plans to go to the Keys this summer." Delia smiled like a preschooler who'd beat everyone at Candy Land. "My guess: Orson is asking his wife some pretty tough questions right now."

"Do you think Orson will turn in his own wife?" Maizy said. "Oh! Those poor kids."

She thought of the three coiffed, monogrammed Hayes-Currington children, who had never been very nice to her own girls and were pretty much insufferable. But still. They were children, and from the sounds of it, their mother could be publicly humiliated, and maybe going to jail.

"Can you imagine Belinda in jail?" Jess said. "Using that awful metal toilet?"

Carras groaned. "Don't remind me."

Delia's nose wrinkled. "She'll have to hold it for a couple of years. Maybe nine months, with good behavior."

"If anyone can do it," Jess laughed, "Belinda Hayes-Currington can."

45

CARRAS

CARRAS PUT HER KEY IN the front door, realizing (not for the first time) that she'd forgotten to lock it when she left. The drawback of being raised in hotels with her father was that she always expected doors to click locked as soon as she let them swing closed. It drove Stuart crazy.

She locked the door behind her, and stopped to catch her breath halfway up the stairs. The hill was steep between Delia's house and hers, and despite that it was less than a quarter of a mile away, it was a walk to be reckoned with. Still, a few months ago she wouldn't have even noticed, and today she was huffing and puffing like Rush Limbaugh on a treadmill. *That was a sign, wasn't it?*

The blushing was new, too—feeling immense heat on her face in otherwise normal situations. Not that everything was normal, or even close. On top of the insane situation this week, the other women were starting to give her scrutinizing looks. Delia in particular seemed to suspect something. Carras didn't like all the curious attention, the pressure to reveal something she didn't know for certain herself.

It was time for answers.

First, she let herself flop face-first onto their unmade bed, relishing the feel of the cool sheets against her flushed face and body. The drugstore bag was in the closet, tucked into an old tennis bag she'd been meaning to give to Goodwill. It had been radiating there—out of sight but always in her awareness—for the last several days, waiting for Carras to find her courage.

She tore open the familiar box—a two-pack of pregnancy tests she'd purchased with cash, on a separate order from their groceries. Not that Stuart would read a grocery receipt anyway, but she didn't want to take chances. They'd stopped taking the tests months ago, no matter when her period showed up or didn't. Carras didn't want to become inured to the heartbreak. And the worst thing she could do to her husband now—next to betrayal—was false hope.

Despite that she'd done this a hundred times, she stopped to read the directions, her body shifting with the sudden need to pee now that the toilet was in sight. Stalling, Carras knew, wouldn't change a thing. But she was already burdened with hope, and if this test was negative, it would all disappear.

Carras stared at the white stick, pink lid in her hand. Four weeks was well past the window of certainty she always made herself observe to avoid wasting pregnancy tests and money on self-doubt and recalculation. It had been almost four weeks since San Antonio, and she had made sure she and Stuart made love the next day. If she was pregnant, it could still be her husband's. She would cling to that possibility. She would build a life on it.

She knew from experience that watching the window while the single pink line appeared was the worst sort of torture. She'd spent hours of her life sitting on the floor of this very bathroom, watching for the ghost of a line—the second line parallel to the control, which would mean a positive result—which never appeared. Often, she stared so long at a test that she imagined she could see a line there, the same way if you stared at a wall long enough, it would appear to waver. Sometimes there was a false line—some remnant of the testing process or some errant hormone in her body, which would make her hopeful until she took a confirmation test the next day, or even until her delayed period would appear.

And yet she couldn't make herself set the test down and walk away. She sat on the turquoise shag rug in front of the toilet with her legs splayed out, the test resting on her thigh while her head leaned against the wall. She closed her eyes and forced her muscles to relax, as though by not putting physical energy into waiting, she could somehow spare herself the emotional investment, too.

It will be okay, one way or the other.

Everything happens for a reason. This was her father's voice. *What doesn't kill you makes you stronger. When God closes a door, He opens a window.*

How would he feel, she wondered, about his death being the door that was closing in her life? And could this child, could any child, open the window enough to replace him?

She opened her eyes.

At first, she was sure the second line was her imagination. In fact, for several minutes she told herself that it had to be, as though denial of what was in front of her face could stave off the disappointment if it turned out to be wrong. But there it was. Lighter than the control line, but clear nonetheless, the sign she'd been waiting for. A bright pink indication that life was about to change.

Right, wrong, or somewhere in between: there was no going back now.

46

JESS

A WEEK LATER, JESS FINISHED THE dishes slowly, letting Tom take his time putting the kids to bed without her interference. Also, she needed something to do with her hands. She made a small pot of decaf coffee, and spiked two mugs with Irish cream, setting both on the table as she heard his heavy stride on the stairs. She straightened her ponytail in the reflection of the kitchen window, where the last bits of dusk were fading to the sound of crickets and cicadas on this late summer night.

"Irish coffee in July?" Tom said behind her.

Jess shrugged. "In the mood, I guess. We have beer if you'd rather...?"

"It's fine." He sat down, staring at his phone, and took a sip.

"I heard from Delia while you were upstairs. Sounds like Orson and Belinda talked to the police. It's not clear yet if he's going to press charges against her, or if she'll help find Parker. But their marriage is obviously in trouble."

"Obviously."

"The good news for us is that Belinda admitted to the police that she and Parker set us up. Delia said she thinks Orson shamed her into it. She told them that as far as she knew, none of us had knowingly hired Parker for anything except tennis and help around the house..."

Tom snorted. "*Help* is a broad term, I guess."

"Anyway. Nothing's been decided, but the lawyer Gage and Delia hired is putting pressure on the district attorney to drop the charges against us. He said something about harassment and malicious prosecution if they move forward. It seems likely we're off the hook."

"That's a relief," Tom said, still scrolling through Twitter.

She could tell by the set of his jaw that he was listening, but didn't want to meet her eye.

"I worry the kids haven't had a true summer experience this year," she fished again. "With everything that's been going on."

"They're fine."

But it wasn't fine. They'd postponed their vacation to make up for her bail money. She knew the kids had picked up on some of what was going on, even if they didn't understand the implications. Jess had been flinging herself at them randomly: alternately smothering them with her need for them to be okay, and trying to give them freedom to enjoy the summer. It would've been easier if things had been okay between her and Tom, but they weren't, and the kids weren't stupid. They knew.

Not to mention, when Tom wanted to avoid a tough conflict with her, he always threw himself into work. Like now, for instance.

She sipped her coffee, ignoring the thin bead of sweat that accumulated on her top lip. He was right; it was too hot for this.

"We're going to have to talk eventually," she said.

"About what?"

She waited. When he looked up, Jess hit him with the only thing left in her arsenal: her "are-you-shitting-me-we've-been-together-forever-do-you-seriously-think-I'm-buying-that" look.

A smile flickered across his features. He put down the phone. "Fine. Let's talk."

"Okay…what do you want me to say?"

He picked up the phone again. "Oh, my bad. I thought you were ready to be an adult and take responsibility for the problem you created in our marriage. If you think I'm going to lead the conversation, I have better things to do."

Anger and shame forced out the question that had been on the tip of her tongue for weeks. "Is this going to end us?"

"What are you talking about?" He put down the phone.

"Are you going to divorce me over this? Because, Tomás, I can't see a way forward with you on your…fucking phone during the rare instances we are alone together. This is co-parenting, not mar-riage." She paused. "At least not a marriage I want to be a part of."

He stared at her for a long time. "You know this is my work…" It was a well-worn path, an argument they'd had on and off for years.

"It's not about the phone."

Tom kept his gaze locked on hers. "I know. But the phone is easier."

Her shoulders relaxed. "I know."

"Fourteen years of marriage, and that's the first time either of us has uttered the D-word."

"It's not what I want."

"But you said it."

"Because it's starting to feel like what *you* want." With those words, her resolve crumbled, and she sank into a chair. "I can't blame you, but I need to know. I can't exist in this netherworld forever."

"So, this is, what? An administrative conversation? You need to know whether to get a divorce lawyer? It's been a little over a week, and you need me to quit wallowing in my feelings about my wife's betrayal so you can get on with your life?"

"That's unfair. I don't think you're wallowing. You have every right to your feelings, and I can tell you again how sorry I am. We can go to counseling, I will answer questions…"

He put up a hand to stop her. "You're right."

The concession stopped her mid-plea. "What was that?"

"You're right. It's time we resolve this thing and put it behind us. I have thought about starting this conversation myself, a hun-dred times. I guess I'm always blocked. Maybe it's my stupid pride, that you would need some other guy…"

Jess started to object, but he put up a hand. "I know, I know. Nothing happened, it was about us, not him…blah, blah, blah. But that's the thing, Jess. I worry that you taking desperate measures is a sign that things are so far gone between us, maybe you don't want me back. Anymore. Whatever."

"But I do want *you*. That was the whole point…"

"That's what you keep saying. I believe that you believe that, Gardner. I really do." He pushed back from the table. "But maybe, on some unconscious level, this was your way of telling both of us that something is wrong with our marriage."

A sob knotted itself around her vocal cords and tears dripped onto the ratty white T-shirt she'd thrown on for doing dishes. "You don't mean that." She shook her head to push the idea away. "You don't think our marriage is in serious danger."

His face softened. "No. But I'm worried that you do. Which is why I've been avoiding this conversation. And just now, when you brought up divorce—" Tom's voice shattered on the word. Even though he didn't move from his chair, Jess could see the emotion he was fighting to contain in his clenched fists, in the veins that protruded from his neck and forearms with the effort of keeping still.

There was no other response. She went to him, put her arms around him, pulled his head into her chest as if she were comforting one of their children. "Oh, God. Tom. I'm sorry. I didn't mean... I was afraid that you wanted... I feel so ashamed."

He gripped her waist, not moving or speaking. If someone had looked in on them then, it might look like nothing more than casual affection. Only the force with which he held her showed Jess how terrified he was of losing her, how strong he'd been forcing himself to be. She ran her hands through his wiry hair, loving the outline of softer, redder skin where it had begun thinning in front and exposed new skin to the sun. She loved this man, loved the signs of his humanity, proof that they were growing old together. She would take his imperfections over someone else's perfect. Any day.

"Can we start this conversation over?" she said when she had gathered herself. "With the D-word off the table?"

He nodded, rubbing his face into her belly—childlike and familiar and sexy all at once. She felt overwhelmed with tenderness.

"I don't want to start over," he murmured. "I want to put it to rest. Forever."

She pulled his face up to meet hers. His cheeks were dry but his eyes were red and strained. "How do we do that? You tell me. Tom, I'll do anything."

He smiled, a fleeting thing. "I want to know...why. I mean, not why Parker or why this stupid scheme with Delia and whatever.

But why didn't you think you could talk to me about this? If you weren't happy with our sex life, why not tell me? I miss us, too." He pulled her onto his lap. "You may have forgotten this, but I'm a big fan of sex. Have been most of my life. And it's even better when you're involved."

She saw the pain beneath his joke and stroked his hair again before answering. "Well. To be fair, I did try." He opened his mouth to protest but she cut him off. "Not very well, and not hard enough. Obviously. I kept thinking that talking about it too much would make it worse. You know, you do everything for our family and you work so hard and of course you're exhausted when you get home from a trip. I didn't want to be the nagging wife who also demanded mind-blowing sex every night on top of it."

"Every night?" He smirked.

"You know what I mean. I didn't want you to think I was criticizing you by saying we weren't doing it enough, or that it wasn't… I don't know, as interesting as it used to be."

"Well, bringing in another dude to make me jealous certainly satisfies the interesting requirement."

"And you have to admit, Tom, even though I was totally, totally wrong about the whole thing with Parker—it was a huge mistake and I'd undo it if I could—you have to concede that it *did* work. The sex that night was…."

"Spectacular."

"Yes. Right? Wasn't it?"

"Until it almost derailed our lives."

"Well, yes." She sighed and tousled his hair. "Until then."

"Don't you think we could get to spectacular on our own? I mean, without all the weird mind games and illegal shit?"

"Maybe. I suppose I could have tried harder. There's a book I heard about that has all these suggestions for spicing things up. Maybe if I'd had more faith in us, we could have done something like that."

"Why can't we do something like that now? Or just, you know, do the stuff we used to do before the kids and everything. We were pretty hot back in the day. Remember the whipped cream and chocolate?"

Jess laughed. "Ugh. That was a sticky mess. And I never could get the carpet clean. My roommates and I lost our security deposit."

"Okay, but maybe, I don't know...there have to be other ways to shake things up." He pulled her around to face him, so that she was straddling him against the table.

"Look," he said. "I've been mad at you, and you deserved it."

"Now, *that's* sexy."

"But, I'm sorry for my part in this too. I've taken you for granted, taken us for granted. I know you always preferred for me to take the initiative with sex, and after the kids it was hard, and you're so hard to read sometimes, and yeah, I'm tired..."

"Wait. I don't always need you to take the initiative. You don't like it when *I* do."

"What? That's insane. What man doesn't want his wife to jump his bones?"

"You said it yourself. You said, 'I'm not into that whole dominatrix thing.'"

Tom was incredulous. "*When the hell* did I say that?"

"I don't know. Years ago, before we lived here."

"When, Jess? If you're going to put those ridiculous words in my mouth..."

She bit her lip, trying to remember. He had said it, she was sure. And she'd been disappointed, because they had only been married for a few years... "Oh! I remember. It was at our Glenridge apartment, when you were home for all of December and bored out of your mind."

"You mean when you made me watch all those movies? Including *Basic Instinct*?"

"Wait. Did I?"

"YES!" His frustration was giving way to triumph. "You said I needed a pop culture education, remember?"

It was coming back to her now. She put her hands over her face, cringing. "Oh, God. I said Sharon Stone was an underrated genius."

"Yes. You. Did." He patted her hip. "Don't feel bad about it. I said Barry Bonds and Sammy Sosa would be vindicated by history. We all make mistakes."

"So when you said that about women on top...?"

"Look. I don't remember saying it, but if I did, it was definitely icepick-freakout-related." He put a hand on her shoulder. "I'd love for you to take the initiative, okay? Is it too late to change our pattern?"

"Of course not," she said, more certain than she felt. "But you have to promise you won't make fun of me when I suggest new things. You have to be open to new experiences."

"How new are we talking?" He let his hand drift casually to her breast. "I'm getting to be an old man, you know. It's hard to teach us new tricks."

Jess rolled her eyes and kissed him, letting herself grind playfully against his lap. It was a jokey gesture at first, speaking the comic language they were both most comfortable with, but soon she felt herself relax into the kiss. Tom's body responded, and he grew hard beneath his worn cargo shorts. *Very* hard.

He wrapped his arms around her waist as they kissed, and she could sense that he was trying to reconnect with her in more than one way. The intensity of the embrace thrilled her. "You need me, too," she observed, as if it were new information. And in a way, they'd both forgotten it.

"Oh, God. Jess." He ran both hands up her back beneath her T-shirt and clutched her shoulders, pulling her harder against him, making her skin ripple with gooseflesh. "I am absolutely fucking hopeless without you." He said it without irony, without the requisite one-liner to make it funny and burst the bubble of emotional tension.

She realized with a deep, aching pleasure that she was the one person in the world with whom Tom could abandon his trademark sense of humor, and that for him, *that* was true intimacy.

For the first time in years, Jess was swept away by her feelings for her husband. She reached for his shirt and pulled it over his head, frantic to have nothing between them. These clothes were obstacles, this kitchen chair inadequate to the purpose. They enraged her, and she launched herself into his kiss with ferocity that felt as if it belonged to someone else.

"Should we..." he murmured into her mouth, "take this upstairs?"

She bit his lip and lifted herself from his lap, carefully moving his coffee cup before sliding onto the table. "No. Here. Now."

"Here?" He gave her a quizzical look, clearly thinking of the kids and the lights all being on and the fact that they'd never done it outside the bedroom since Mina was born.

In response, Jess peeled off her shirt and tossed it at him, and then—faster than the junior high locker room—removed her bra while his face was covered.

"Here," he agreed, looking down at her with a smile.

She pulled him toward her by the button of his shorts, kissing him with renewed enthusiasm. Her desire fueled itself: the insatiable need to have him closer to her made her delighted at her own sense of wantonness, which made her want more, more, more... More of this feeling. More of herself as a sexual being, alive and electric and fully present in her own skin. And more *Tom*.

He seemed overcome with the same positive feedback cycle, because his hesitation evaporated. Urgently kissing her neck and chin, he unbuttoned her shorts and slid a practiced hand beneath her panties, slipping a finger into her as deftly as he used to swing the bat at a juicy fastball floating over home plate.

"You need me, too," he said with husky gratification.

She slid to the edge of the table in agreement, pressing against his callused hand in sweet agony. She wanted him to stop. She wanted more. She didn't want him to stop.

There was something sweet and wonderful about the familiarity between them. Tom knew every inch of her, and even as she grabbed his forearm to take control—she wanted all of him, right this minute—he ignored her and continued at his work, stroking her with practiced expertise, kissing the spot on her earlobe that made her insane. And not a single ounce of nervous fumbling or hesitation.

Jess's orgasm surprised her with both its speed and intensity, rocking through her body and making her bite down on his shoulder in sweet, shuddering agony. Her thighs squeezed together on Tom's hips, her body wanting to curl into itself with tremulous pleasure, but he pushed back—held himself apart from her and tugged her shorts and underwear down. Soon his hand was on her again, this time pushing her legs apart. And then, he was inside her, firm and familiar and perfect. He pulled her hard against him again, fingers digging in to her outer thighs for purchase. She helped, bucking and thrusting against him, with her arms tight around his neck. He groaned and pushed her backward onto the table, shoving the salt and pepper shakers out of the way in the process.

Tom leaned over to kiss her breasts, one at a time, flicking her nipples with his tongue in a way he hadn't done since... *Oh, God. Who could remember?* He bit one nipple, giving her a devilish grin when she raised her head in surprise. She clenched her pelvic muscles as hard as she could in response, feeling her own strong body enveloping his with a control she'd never had before all those ridiculous Pure Indulgences Kegel exercises.

"Wow." He groaned. "That's new."

"I'm no Sharon Stone." She laughed. "But I know a trick or two."

He wanted to laugh with her, she could tell, but the feeling overpowered him, and his eyes rolled back as he lost himself to the pleasure. Within a few seconds, his thrusts sped up, pushing her farther onto the table and bringing Jess a new wave of her own heightened sensation. She arched her back to better push against him and threw back her hands, feeling the hard porcelain of her coffee mug behind her. It tipped, spilled, rolled and shattered on the floor behind her, at the exact moment her husband of fourteen years called out her name in love and agony and utter abandon.

They were still panting and lying collapsed, half-naked together on their kitchen table—surrounded by Irish coffee and salt granules—when they heard the footsteps on the stairs. Tom extracted himself and threw on his shorts and T-shirt to go head off whichever kid it was; Jess scrambled off the table, winding up with liquored coffee down one whole side. It soaked through her shirt as she frantically located her panties and shorts and shoved Tom's boxers into the nearest cabinet. She was buttoning her shorts when Mina marched in, sleepily gripping Tom's hand.

"See?" he told their daughter. "Mommy's right here, and she's fine."

"What's wrong, sweetie?" Jess said, not meeting Tom's eye.

"I heard a crashing sound. Like a robber breaking in," Mina said. "I'm scared to go to my room alone."

Jess strode to her daughter and hugged her. "Everything's fine, baby," she said. "Mommy dropped a coffee mug."

Mina pushed back, wrinkling her nose. "Did you drop it on yourself? Is that why your shirt is all messy? And your hair?"

Jess's hand shot up to her wrecked ponytail. She wondered whether this moment would stick in Mina's memory, so that one day she'd look back on it and realize exactly what was going on here, and be totally grossed out.

Tom snickered, then coughed to cover it. "Come on, scaredy-cat. I'll take you upstairs and put you back to bed."

He grinned at Jess as he turned toward the hallway and the stairs beyond. "Sorry to leave you with cleanup duty," he said. "I guess there are some things about our new normal that we can't change."

"I wouldn't change it," Jess said as she watched him retreat into the darkened hallway. "Not for the world."

EPILOGUE

DELIA

DELIA SHIFTED AT THE INSTITUTIONAL table, waiting. She'd followed the prison visitation guidelines to the letter, wearing jeans, close-toed shoes, and a simple navy T-shirt that didn't expose either chest or shoulders. She'd left her purse in the visitors' locker and now—as the website suggested—had only a Ziploc bag with $20 worth of quarters.

She didn't recognize Belinda at first: her normally-tanned skin was pale and callow above the khaki Department of Corrections jumpsuit. Dark-brown roots had taken over the top three inches of her blonde hair, which she had pulled into a messy knot. But Belinda smiled perfunctorily and made her way to the table.

"I guess khaki is the new orange?" Delia said, by way of greeting.

"Yeah." Belinda glanced down. "Funny."

"I brought you some change for the vending machines." Delia pushed the Ziploc toward her. "I wanted to bring you some Skin by Suzette, but that's a no-go with the facility."

Belinda didn't look at the change. "What do you want, Delia? Orson said you wanted to see me, but I have to be honest, I can't think why."

Delia wasn't sure of the answer herself. "I thought you could use some company. Besides Orson and the kids. You know, a female friend…"

"You know this is a women's prison, right? I have like a thousand girlfriends if I need a chat." Belinda made a show of looking around. "And since you were instrumental in putting me here, I don't appreciate you showing up to gloat."

"I'm not gloating," Delia said truthfully. "I am sorry that this happened to you. Even if you did try to throw me under the bus first."

A surprising half-smile flitted across Belinda's features.

"You've heard that there's still no trace of Parker?"

"So my attorney tells me. Honestly, I don't care anymore. My marriage is over, I'm a convicted felon, and my children have to visit me in a room that smells like Pine-Sol and Doritos." Belinda folded her arms. "I don't care what happens to that little shitbag."

Delia smiled. "Yes, you do. You loved him, Belinda."

To her surprise, Belinda didn't argue, just stared at the linoleum floor. "You know they have a dog training rescue in here? I'm thinking of applying for it. They teach you how to train dogs for people who need them. I could be good at that, I think." She gave Delia a grim smile. "I'm pretty good at manipulating behavior, right?"

Delia laughed. "I'll give you that. But I suspect even *you* got played by our favorite tennis pro." It was one reason Delia was here. The story had been rattling around in her head for weeks, and she wasn't sure why, but she had to confirm her suspicions. "You thought you were playing Orson, and playing us, but he turned the tables on you."

Belinda didn't have to answer. The hollow look in her eyes was affirmation enough.

"I realized it after your plea bargain. I was thinking about the night of the pool party. It was Maizy Henriksson who helped me put it together. I saw her with Parker that night, and she told us he seemed to be struggling with something big. It's not like him to feel guilty, but I think he was, because betraying you was the biggest scam he'd ever pulled."

Delia looked at Belinda, whose eyes were watery. She was on the right track. "Maizy and I were talking about your house, and the broken lamp, your underwear drawer. And it didn't make sense that you and Parker would stage a break-in if you'd already moved the retirement money. I mean, that wouldn't be a distraction *from* the theft, it would call attention *to* the theft. The first thing a guy like Orson would do when his house is robbed is check all his accounts, right?"

"The very first thing," Belinda agreed.

"You said in your plea hearing you moved the money *before* the party. First from Orson's retirement account to yours, then to the offshore account, where it disappeared." Delia tried not to sound like a television detective. She'd been far too interested in all this stuff lately, and the girls had been calling her Nancy Drew for weeks. "When I saw you at the party, you were trying to get Orson drunk."

"You saw…? Were you spying on me?"

Delia smiled. "I was looking for you, trying to figure out what was going on. At that point, I wasn't entirely convinced you would've knowingly set us up."

Belinda looked down again, sullen. "Sorry about that."

"You're doing your time," Delia said. "But obviously, the whole reason you wanted Orson good and hammered that night was so you and Parker could catch the flight to Miami together, then on to Cuba the next day. Your kids were with his parents, and with a nasty hangover he probably wouldn't have missed you until lunchtime."

"If then." Belinda snorted. "Orson has always been oblivious."

"But he didn't pass out when you got home, because your house had been ransacked. Pretty sobering, I guess. That must have been really awful for you, realizing that your lover had broken into your house to bring Orson's attention to the theft, and was long gone. He must have done it right after he talked to Maizy by the tennis courts, and by the time you got home, he was already at the airport."

A tear splattered on Belinda's khaki jumpsuit. "And? What is the point of all this now? Yes, I loved him; yes, he screwed me over. Does that make you happy? Everyone in Sugar Mills used to look up to me—hell, half of Atlanta looked up to me—and now I'm looking forward to a promising career cleaning up dog shit. You win, Delia."

Delia shook her head, put a hand on Belinda's arm.

"No touching, please," said a female officer walking past.

Delia pulled her hand away. "I'm not here to win, Belinda. I wanted to understand. And I wanted you to understand something, too."

"Oh, God." Belinda rolled her eyes. "This isn't a lecture, is it? You're not leading me to Jesus or anything, are you?"

Delia laughed and let herself lapse into her North Georgia accent. "Girl, your relationship with the Almighty is your own damn business." She leaned forward again, keeping her hands in her lap. "I want you to know that it isn't over for you. You don't have to always be the person you think you are right now, or even the person you were a year ago. You can re-create yourself, and be whoever you want."

Belinda raised a skeptical eyebrow.

"I know, because I've done it. More than once. The person you thought you were supposed to be doesn't have to be who you *are*." Delia gestured at the prison around them, where groups of husbands and children and parents were beginning to cluster up and move toward the door. "Maybe all this is an opportunity to be a new version of yourself. Someone you will actually like. Someone your kids will respect."

She knew how corny it sounded. She knew people had to figure this kind of thing out for themselves. But she had to try, and now she had.

"Visiting hours are up, ladies." The officer returned to their table.

Delia stood. "I'm not mad at you, Belinda. And honestly, it's okay if you're mad at me. But if you get out and you need a place to start, or someone to talk to…" She smiled. "Well. I'm pretty resourceful. And you know where to find me."

She followed the officer toward the exit, leaving the bag of quarters on the table. Maybe Belinda could stock up on Snickers or tampons or whatever they let you have in here. She didn't know anything about prison, and probably couldn't help Belinda much, but she made a note to binge-watch every season of *Orange is the New Black* in solidarity.

"Delia!" Belinda called out just as Delia was getting to the security line for the exit. "Thanks for coming." She grinned. "Tell the old neighborhood I said hello."

Delia returned the smile and waved. And even though the sun was going down and the evening air chilly, she drove all the way home with the windows down.

~THE END~

ACKNOWLEDGMENTS

MY PROFOUND THANKS GO, AS always, to my friends, family, and readers. To Sam Turetsky, Charlie Turetsky, and Jonah Turetsky: you are my whole damn world. I love you profoundly, fiercely, and deeper than words can express. (Thanks to Sam in particular for not taking this novel even a little bit personally.)

To my critique partners and on-call guacamole support system: Emily Carpenter, Kimberly Brock, Chris Negron, Becky Albertalli, and George Weinstein. Thank you for reading, supporting, listening to me vent, and understanding the twisted landscape of a writer's mind. You are my coworkers, and you make me feel saner than I probably should.

For the beta readers, sensitivity readers, cheerleaders, and subject matter experts who've made this book a little less crappy with each draft: Vernie Andrews, Jenna Denisar, Kristal Goelz, Christy Hall, Mary Ann Kavorous, Heather Pacin, Dara Shifrer, McRae Stephenson, and Brenda Turetsky. I offer you my heart, but you know you have it already.

Giant thanks to Tiffany Yates-Martin of FoxPrint Editorial for developmental editing and consultation, Kim Killion and Jennifer Jakes of the Killion Group for formatting and the gorgeous cover design, and Faith Williams of the Atwater Group for copyediting and general hand-holding.

Thank you to all the coffee-shop strangers who watched my stuff when I had to pee.

OF COURSE, my immense gratitude goes to the Distracted Readers group for all their love, support, and comic relief—and for spreading the word about this and other books. You guys light up my life!

ABOUT THE AUTHOR

M.J. (MANDA) PULLEN IS THE author of playful women's fiction and quirky romantic comedies. She has also worked as a non-profit fundraiser, corporate trainer, psychotherapist and mom of two young boys. Each of these jobs has eroded her sanity and contributed to her writing equally.

Manda loves cheap wine, expensive beer, and coffee at any price. She lives in Roswell, Georgia, with her husband, two young boys, and Zelda and Zora the Wonderpups.

WANT MORE M.J.?

Read on for a taste of

SUGAR RUSH

Book #2 of the Sugar Street Series...

COMING SOON:

SUGAR RUSH

Book 2 of the Sugar Street Series

JESS WAITED AT THE BAR, eyeing the door and checking her phone every few minutes. This was a bad idea.

"Blind date, huh?" The bartender, who was just a couple of years younger than Jess, looked sympathetic. She had streaky blonde hair pulled back under a baseball cap and strong tattooed arms that looked elegant and oddly graceful beneath her tank top.

"I guess you could say that."

"Been there, honey." The bartender lifted Jess's empty bourbon tumbler and rattled the ice as she wiped down the bar beneath it. "Get you another?"

Jess nodded. Then, thought better of it. "Can I have a Diet Coke instead?"

"You got kids, right? Me, too. It's so much harder dating at this age, don't you think?" The bartender gave her a knowing smile. "I'll give you one piece of advice: don't let them anywhere near your kids until you've been going strong for a good three months."

She paused, looking thoughtful as she sprayed Diet Coke into a fresh glass from a nozzle. "You know what? Scratch that. Based on my experience with the last guy I dated, I say don't let them meet your kids until the wedding."

Unconsciously, Jess fiddled with the soft spot on her left hand where her wedding ring had been. *This was a bad idea.* She should be home with the kids. School was starting back next week, and they'd barely had a summer, with all the drama in their lives. *It was too soon for this.*

"How long has it been?" the bartender asked. Jess stared. The woman shrugged. "It's fresh, right? Your divorce? I can tell. I have a knack for reading people. Comes with the territory."

Jess flushed. "Oh, we're not divorced... We, um..." She stared at her naked ring finger, awkward and embarrassed, on top of her existing apprehension.

"Buy you a drink?" A deep voice echoed in Jessica's ear, a strong hand on her back. "Sorry I'm late. If I'd known how incredibly gorgeous the woman was I'm meeting, I would've been at least half an hour early to prepare myself." He slid a twenty across the bar. "Corona Light with lime, please, and one of whatever the lady is drinking."

The bartender gave him a suspicious look, raising an eyebrow at Jess. "Another diet? Or bourbon?" Her eyes flicked up to the man as she mentioned the second option, making clear her opinion that this dude's charm had not earned any leeway with her.

"Bourbon, please." Jess gave the bartender a reassuring smile. Misguided though it was, she appreciated the female solidarity. As the woman walked away to the other end of the bar, Jess turned on her stool to face her date. "You're late. I was starting to reconsider this whole thing. Thinking maybe I should go home to my kids and my husband."

"Your husband doesn't deserve you." Tom ran his hands up her bare arm and leaned in close. He nipped playfully at her ear and spoke low. "No matter what he did wrong."

Jess pinched him just below the ribs, and Tom squirmed away as the bartender returned with their drinks.

"I'm assuming you don't need change, sir?"

"Um..." Tom seemed to consider this. He was a generous tipper, and with his job, he relied on service industry workers constantly, respected them. But he didn't like when people made assumptions. Tom wanted the opportunity to be generous. Jess watched him wilt under the icy gaze of the blonde in the baseball hat. "Nope. No change, thanks."

"She does not like me," he said, watching the bartender make her way to a pair of customers at the other end of the bar.

"She's just being protective," Jess said. "She thinks we're divorced. Well, she thinks I'm divorced and that you're my first blind date since. She's worried about you meeting my kids."

"You mean *our* kids. I met them the second each of them was born." He kissed Jess on the forehead, reaching behind her to grab his beer from the bar. "No going back now."

Jess picked up her own glass and sighed. "I'm thinking this was a bad idea. That we should go home to them. It's been a rough summer. Mina is being so sketchy these last couple weeks. And your mom will have no idea what to do if Dash throws up after dinner. She'll completely freak out."

"Don't you start wussing out on me, Gardner. This whole thing was your idea. My parents are in town. I paid for a hotel room and put on cologne already." He grinned, pulling her close with his hands on her hips. He smelled amazing; he was wearing the cologne she'd given him for Christmas years ago, and only put on for special occasions. "I'm pretty sure I vomited at least once during my childhood, and my mother managed to survive it. She'll be fine. The kids are fine. And we promised we wouldn't talk about them tonight."

"You're right," Jess conceded. "I'm sorry. I'm just a little nervous. They're both in such vulnerable places right now."

"I know, but they are fine. Kids are more resilient than we give them credit for." Tom pulled up the stool next to her and sat so that their knees overlapped between them, keeping a hand on the tight black cocktail dress Delia had helped Jess pick out for tonight. "And I thought the whole idea here was to make sure our kids' parents are happy. And by happy, I mean well-sexed. And by well-sexed, I mean where the hell did you get this dress? It's like you had it painted on."

Jess glanced down and began tugging self-consciously at the edges of the dress. It was outside her comfort zone by a long shot. There didn't seem to be nearly enough fabric at the top or the bottom. "I know, I'm sorry. Delia made me buy it."

"Leave it." Tom covered her hand with his, gently reversing her movements so that the bottom of the dress rode up her thighs another couple of inches. "It's perfect. You look amazing. No, you look smoking hot. I may even write Delia a thank-you note."

"I would say it's the least she could do," Jess said.

Tom rolled his eyes. "You're absolutely right. But this dress goes a long way to making things better." He ran an appreciative hand over her hip and up her side. "And as for what Delia owes me, that's yet another subject we aren't going to discuss tonight."

With his hand running along her dress, and his voice low and sultry in her ear, Jess had to admit she did feel sexy and free. She inhaled her husband's familiar scent, and let her hands run along his shoulders. "Is this a new shirt?" He was wearing a lavender Oxford she'd never seen, a perfectly starched collar in contrast to the T-shirts, polos, and athletic shorts that were his typical uniform when he was at home.

"Just bought it today. Do you like it?"

"I love you in purple," she said softly. "I'm always saying you don't wear it enough."

"I know," he said, his voice husky. "That may have factored in to my buying it."

She kissed him then, a sudden rush of affection and the bubbly warm feeling of bourbon overwhelming her. Tom's hands slid along her waist and behind her back, pulling her close, taking her in. The noise of the bar and the thumping of music faded into the background. Tom's mouth was hot and familiar on hers: the taste of beer and lime mingling with her bourbon, his rough stubble brushing against her face. *How long had it been since they had even kissed in public, much less made out like horny teenagers?* As if in answer, Tom pulled her closer and let a hand drift down her hip and thigh to the hem of her too-tight dress. As the other hand cradled her face, he kissed her deeply, and let his fingers roam in casual circles up the inside of her thighs. Jess heard herself whisper his name. Whether it was supposed to be a reprimand or a groan of pleasure, she couldn't be sure.

The bartender cleared her throat, breaking the spell. Jess let out a nervous apology. But she wasn't the least bit sorry. She couldn't imagine what the woman must be thinking, that a newly divorced mother of small children was making out in a bar with her first blind date, whom she'd known for ten minutes. To Jessica's surprise, the idea of the woman's disapproval just made her *more* turned on.

"So, shall we go ahead with our date as planned?" Tom removed the hand from under her dress and took her hand in his own. "I have a whole list of date questions prepared to ask you. I'm ready to get to know you again, from the very beginning, just like we talked about."

It *was* what they'd talked about. A few weeks ago, their marriage of fourteen years had been at its most precarious point. Jess had been feeling they'd lost the spark, and made the possibly understandable but still ill-advised choice to hire a male escort/tennis pro to make Tom jealous. It had worked (sort of), but it had also backfired in a multitude of ways. Tom did get jealous of Parker, the handsome and irritatingly seductive tennis pro, but only after Parker had used a staged picture of himself and Jess to try to blackmail her. Then Parker had stolen a couple of million dollars from another client's husband, and skipped town. The search for the missing money, and the missing tennis pro, had led to exposure and a humiliating evening spent in their affluent suburban small-town jail. When Tom found out the lengths Jess had gone to, trying to get his attention, he'd been devastated and understandably angry. Their marriage had come close to imploding on the spot. Now, Jess was on a mission to regain not only Tom's trust, but also the spark she'd been looking for in the first place.

This whole meeting-at-a-bar, role-playing thing was their first big step toward rekindling intimacy. And fine, she'd gotten the idea from a Reese Witherspoon movie. Did that make it less valid?

"I just thought we could, you know… It's stupid. Let's just go home."

"Absolutely not."

Jess sighed. "Okay, let's go to the hotel and order room service, then. I feel silly sitting here all dressed up and pretending we're strangers."

"Come on, Gardner. You suggested this for a reason." He pulled her off the stool and gestured to a small booth tucked into the corner of the bar. "Let's go have a real date. No talking about the kids, or bills, or anything normal and mundane."

"You're turning down room service?"

He rolled his eyes. "I have room service at least twice a week when I'm on the road. What I don't have is you in that dress." He leaned over to her. "Plus, I already slipped the bouncer twenty bucks to hold the booth."

Jess let him lead her to the booth, where Tom chivalrously gestured for her to sit first, then slid in next to her with both their drinks. To her surprise, he pulled out one of the little moleskin notebooks he used for reporting and flipped it open. "All right, let's start with where you were born."

She smacked him. "You know that already. Northside Hospital, Atlanta. And you were born at San Antonio Regional. That isn't the kind of first date questions I was talking about."

He gave her his playful sideways grin and ducked away from her. "All right, all right. I was just starting out slow, like I do in a real interview."

"Please don't tell me you ask every baseball player you interview where they were born."

"Hey! It can be interesting. Sometimes…" He scanned down the page. "Okay, how about this? What is your ultimate sexual fantasy?"

Jess nearly choked on her bourbon. "That's your idea of a first date question?"

"I don't get it." Tom shook his head. "The guys always respond well to that one on MLB Radio."

He was doing his usual Tom thing, making jokes to cover the discomfort of their situation. But he was trying. And maybe they needed to be uncomfortable for a while.

"Fine. Kidnapping."

"Excuse me?" The notebook tipped out of his hand and he fumbled to catch it, almost knocking over his beer bottle in the process. "Did you say *kidnapping*? Like, that's your fantasy?"

At his shock, a prickle of shame crept over her. Jess could feel her chest going red and splotchy, and although she desperately wanted to take it back, she forced herself to continue looking her husband in the eyes. "Yes. I know, it's weird, but I like that idea of being stolen away and tied up…" She trailed off. Out loud, it sounded *horrible*. The look on Tom's face didn't help.

"Like, kept in someone's basement on a urine-stained mattress? Like those poor women in Cleveland?"

"What? NO." She smacked him again. "Not like *real life* kidnapping. Like…I don't know, *Pirates of the Caribbean*. Being stolen away, held prisoner until my hero comes to rescue me." She rubbed his arm, feeling the muscles that—although not as prominent as they had been in his baseball days—were still respectably firm beneath the lavender Oxford. *He'd bought a new shirt for her.* The thought made her smile.

"Ah, so it's a *rescue* fantasy, not a kidnapping fantasy... Wait, don't tell me you're into all that Fifty Shades Red Room shit, because I don't think I'm man enough for that."

"No," she said. "That book is *awful.*"

"So awful it was on our nightstand for three months? And it got pretty worn out, if I remember correctly."

"It did not. I dropped it in the bathtub."

Tom laughed. "It's okay. I know I'm out of town a lot. You're entitled to...take care of you while I'm gone."

Jess coughed. Her masturbatory habits were not what she thought this conversation would be about. "Anyway, I'm not into that stuff at all, okay? Maybe the tying up part."

He raised an eyebrow.

"And possibly the occasional spanking..."

He slammed the notebook closed and stuck it back in his shirt pocket. "Well, I think we have all we need here." He stood, practically pulling her behind him out of the booth. "Great interview, babe. I mean date. The hotel is two blocks away. What do you think? Walk? Uber?"

She laughed. "Whichever is faster?"

"Amen to that." He squeezed her hand and dragged her out in to the warm Georgia evening.

COMING 2019!
To pre-order Sugar Rush, visit M.J.'s website at
www.mjpullen.com/books/**sugar-rush-2**/

You can also sign up to be notified about new book releases
here: www.mjpullen.com/newsletter/
(You may also choose to receive updates, free content, birthday greetings and/or blog post notifications)

Facebook: /mjpullenbooks
Twitter: @MJPullen
Instagram: mjpullenauthor

CPSIA information can be obtained
at www.ICGtesting.com
Printed in the USA
LVHW05s1503110918
589802LV00005B/934/P